Brazeal

D1083805

The 1904 Anthropology Days and Olympic Games

Critical Studies in the History of Anthropology

SERIES EDITORS

Regna Darnell

Stephen O. Murray

UNIVERSITY OF NEBRASKA PRESS

LINCOLN AND LONDON

The 1904
Anthropology Days
and Olympic Games

Sport, Race, and
American Imperialism

 EDITED BY SUSAN BROWNELL

Chapter 6, "'Leav[ing] the White[s] . . . Far Behind Them': The Girls from
Fort Shaw (Montana) Indian School, Basketball Champions of the 1904
World's Fair" by Linda Peavy and Ursula Smith, was first published under
the same title but in an abbreviated format in the *International Journal of Sport
History* 24, no. 6 (Summer 2007): 819–40, and appears here by permission
of the publisher, Taylor & Francis, Ltd. www.informaworld.com.

Library of Congress

Cataloging-in-Publication Data

The 1904 anthropology days and Olympic games :

sport, race, and American imperialism

/ edited by Susan Brownell.

p.   cm.

— (Critical studies in the history of anthropology)

Includes bibliographical

references and index.

ISBN 978-0-8032-1098-1

(cloth : alk. paper)

1. Sports—Anthropological aspects—United States.

2. Louisiana Purchase Exposition

(1904 : Saint Louis, Mo.)

3. Olympic Games

(3rd : 1904 : Saint Louis, Mo.)

4. Indians of North America

—Exhibitions.

5. Indians of North America

—Public opinion.

6. Ethnology

—United States.

7. United States

—Ethnic relations.

8. United States

—Race relations.

9. United States

—History.

10. Imperialism.

I. Brownell, Susan.

GV706.2A17 2008

796.0973—dc22

2008021832

Set in Quadraat by Bob Reitz.

Designed by R. W. Boeche.

I dedicate this book to my father,
Robert Brownell,
whose footsteps I followed in becoming a university professor.

Contents

Introduction

Bodies before Boas, Sport before the Laughter Left

1

Susan Brownell

1. A "Special Olympics"

Testing Racial Strength and Endurance

at the 1904 Louisiana Purchase Exposition

59

Nancy J. Parezo

2. The "Physical Value" of Races and Nations

Anthropology and Athletics at the Louisiana Purchase Exposition

127

Mark Dyreson

3. Pierre de Coubertin's Concepts of

Race, Nation, and Civilization

156

Otto J. Schantz

Illustrations

Photographs

Map

Tables

Figure

Acknowledgments

This book began as the "International Congress on the St. Louis Olympic Games and Anthropology Days: A Centennial Retrospective" at the Missouri History Museum in Forest Park, St. Louis, Missouri, on September 10–11, 2004. It was organized by Susan Brownell and co-hosted by the Department of Anthropology and the Center for International Studies of the University of Missouri–St. Louis and the Missouri Historical Society (MHS). The conference was in conjunction with an exhibition at the Missouri History Museum on "The 1904 World's Fair: Looking Back, Looking Forward" that featured a section on the 1904 Olympic Games. Funding for the conference was provided by a University of Missouri Research Board Award, supplemented by a fellowship from the Center for International Studies. Toby Shorts and Daniel Cohen were my student assistants and conference coordinators. Karl Lennartz, John Lucas, and John MacAloon made valuable contributions at the conference. The contributions of Suzuko Mousel Knott, Jon Marks, and Christine O'Bonsawin were solicited afterward. I am grateful for the generous support of the institutions involved.

The conference and book particularly benefited from the efforts of Nancy Parezo, who put me in touch with Linda Peavy and Ursula Smith, provided background expertise on anthropology at the St. Louis World's Fair, and generously offered to share her then-unpublished book manuscript (with Don Fowler) and other materials. At Linda Peavy's and Ursula Smith's invitation, the conference was attended by Barbara Winters, the granddaughter of Emma Sansaver, a member of the "world champion" Fort Shaw Indian School girls' basketball team. Barbara's attendance and testimony to her grandmother's fond memories of the fair interjected a counterbalance to the overwhelming conference themes of racism and imperialism. In October, 2006, Linda and Ursula invited me to act as a discussant for a roundtable on their work at the Western History Association annual meeting in St. Louis, which was attended by the descendants of another team member, Nettie Wirth: her granddaughter Wynona Mail Weber and her great-granddaughters Nicole and Stephanie. Barbara Winters was "virtually" present in the form of a videotape. Emma's and Nettie's granddaughters and great-granddaughters made us feel the palpable presence of history in the present and also reminded us that we had a responsibility to try to see the world through the eyes of the people we were writing about and not to simply repeat the objectifying gaze of the science that we were criticizing. This task is admirably accomplished in Linda's and Ursula's chapter in this book, in which their passion for the mission of telling the story of the "basket ball world's champions" of the fair shines through.

I feel privileged to have had the opportunity to collaborate with these outstanding scholars. I learned a lot from them and I would like to express my gratitude for their willingness to attempt a new analysis of old events.

The reviewers for the University of Nebraska Press, Regna Darnell, Stephen Murray, and Dan Fowler gave very helpful and thorough comments and the book benefited greatly from the time and effort they put into their reviews.

Series Editors' Introduction

REGNA DARNELL AND STEPHEN O. MURRAY

The Louisiana Purchase (Centennial) Exhibition in St. Louis in 1904 had far less influence on the concepts and institutions of anthropology than did the 1893 Columbian Tetracentenary Exhibition in Chicago. One might conclude that scrutiny of the "living exhibits" of various cultures and the displays of athletic prowess of various "Others" (of non-European descent) would be, therefore, of only antiquarian interest. But editor Susan Brownell and the sophisticated historians of sports and anthropology (coming to the project from a range of disciplines) contributing to this volume frame the very Americanness of the 1904 Olympics, with their strange and generally ethnocentric shows, in a larger, even global context that is often missing from purportedly critical histories of anthropology.

In 1904 St. Louis, the "tribal games" or Anthropology Days were juxtaposed awkwardly with the third modern Olympic Games. These were grounded in the certainty of Anglo-American racial superiority. The universalism of the ideals of neoclassic revival clashed with non-European entries to the Olympics as well as with the "primitive" anthropological living exhibits. In both cases, a "scientific racism" still familiar today emerges from attributing athletic performances to differences of "race." Brownell and her colleagues emphasize the intercultural spaces created by both Anthropology Days and the Olympics. The "sport, race, and American imperialism" of the volume's subtitle crossed both domains. Moreover, boundaries between the scientific and the popular imaginaries were very blurred with racial stereotypes prominent in pre-academic anthropology, as carried to St. Louis by WJ McGee (who preferred no periods or spaces between these initials), then president (the first one) of the American Anthropological Association.

The cultural construction of the ethnological gaze and its imperialist context played out in ambiguous and conflicting ways. If so-called savages excelled, as did the Blues—the Native American women's basketball team from Fort Shaw, Montana—the victory must be due to physical superiority compensating for the mental inferiority that came from "civilization." Less threatening to beliefs in Euro-American superiority were track events in which racial Others with no previous experience of the rules, such as how to stop at the end of foot races and how to attend to lines painted on the ground, were disqualified. The results of poor performance at unfamiliar tasks provided quantitative corroboration of mental as well as physical inferiority of non-whites, in general, and the particular peoples inveigled into participation. Since "primitive peoples" were believed to lack individual differentiation, those whose sense of racial superiority was bolstered by these Euro-American athletic "victories" did not see any reason why pitting the best athletes from Euro-American communities against persons from other human communities who happened to be in St. Louis was any obstacle to drawing conclusions about racial differences.

Historians of anthropology recall the impresario of the Anthropology Days, WJ McGee, as an advocate of outdated evolutionary racism, soon to be relegated to the junk pile of anthropological theory by Franz Boas. "World" fairs and big exhibitions of the late nineteenth and early twentieth centuries were exercises in nationalism. Visitors were offered public pedagogy valorizing the superiority of America and its frontier vision. Challenges to this self-congratulatory exceptionalism were inevitable with the European influx of the Olympics superimposed on the ethnographic living museum exhibit as object lesson for an American audience.

Introduction

Bodies before Boas, Sport before the Laughter Left

SUSAN BROWNELL

This volume reunites two strands of history that are usually treated separately: the histories of anthropology and the Olympic Games.[1] It does so by looking back to a time at the start of the twentieth century when the discipline of anthropology, the phenomenon of modern sport, and the performance genre of the modern Olympic Games were just starting to take a definite form. It was a time of "polymorphous performativity"[2] when the distinctions between "education" and "entertainment" were not as institutionalized as they are now—when the lines between museums, zoos, circuses, historical reenactments, sports, Wild West shows, Olympic Games, and world's fairs were not as clear as they are now. In the last decade or so, histories of the Olympic Games, world's fairs, museums, zoos, and circuses have come to constitute minor historical genres. However, this is an artificial separation that it is now possible to make in hindsight, after a century in which the divisions between them became institutionalized and culturally crystallized. It is only possible to understand these histories by examining their earlier shared history, as well as the forces that ultimately drove them apart. And by understanding the forces that drove them apart, we will arrive at a greater understanding of our contemporary times and the great cultural performances that define them. Why do Olympic Games now attract much greater global attention than world's fairs, when a century ago they were only a minor side event? What does this reversal tell us about the times in which we now live?

John MacAloon argues, "The modern social sciences and the Olympic Games were born of the same historical era; it is hardly surprising that their root problematics are identical. . . . Olympic history illuminates the origins of modern social science."[3] The discipline of anthropology and the Olympic Games both emerged out of a mash of theories and performance genres that were fermenting at the fin de siècle. This mash had been first stirred together in the mid-nineteenth century by the forces of exploration, colonization, imperialism, industrialization, and capitalism. The feature shared by anthropology and the modern Olympics was that they were ways of making sense out of the cross-cultural encounters between human beings that began to take place on an unprecedented scale. In the encounter between the West and "the Rest," sports were used as "intercultural spaces" or "contact zones."[4] The fascination with savages strengthened the identity of the West by defining "who we are not." It proceeded in tandem with a fascination with ancient Greece and Rome that defined "who we are" by constructing a history of "Western civilization." The modern Olympic Games emerged out of the neoclassical revival that began in the Renaissance and gained momentum from the French Revolution and the Greek war of independence; philhellenism provided the West with a shared ancestor, ancient Greece, which defined the West in opposition to its Others—the Orient and the exotic "savages."

One of the sources of the Olympic Movement[5] was what John MacAloon has called "popular ethnography," a "crosscultural voyeurism" that became accessible to the mass public for the first time in the late nineteenth century.[6] At the same time that "scientific" ethnology was being organized by intellectual elites, "popular ethnography" was being elaborated by nonintellectual elites as well as entrepreneurs from all walks of life, including the "savages" themselves who took advantage of the popular interest in them for their own profit. Philhellenism and anthropology were complementary poles of the same phenomenon: both Western civilization and its opposites were reflected in the popular ethnography of the times—for example, circuses and world's fairs typically included classical "living statues," chariot races,

2

and gladiator combat as well as displays of exotic animals and humans from Asia, Africa, and North America.

Toward an Interconnected History of Anthropology, Sport, and the Olympic Games

Through examining the unique association of the Olympic Games with an event called "Anthropology Days" at the Louisiana Purchase Exposition (LPE) in St. Louis in 1904, it is possible to look back at a moment in time before specialized performance genres had emerged out of the hodgepodge of popular ethnography. The Olympic Games are described in detail in the chapters by Nancy Parezo and Mark Dyreson. In brief, the official sports program during the fair was contested from May 14 to November 19. It was organized by the director of Physical Culture, James Sullivan, one of the founders of the Amateur Athletic Union (established in 1888), who was perhaps the most powerful figure in U.S. amateur sports at that time. Over nine thousand athletes competed in four hundred events ranging from high school interscholastic meets to national championships. Almost all of them were labeled "Olympian," while the "Olympic Games" that took place from August 29 to September 3 entailed only 80 competitions, with 687 entrants, of whom the vast majority were American. They were all men but for the six women who competed in archery. The International Olympic Committee (IOC) never generated an official report, so today historians debate which events constituted the "real" Olympic Games and which nations competed in them, an effort that matters for modern bureaucratic recordkeeping, but which anachronistically imposes today's Olympic structure on an event that did not conform to them.[7]

Parezo asserts that, contrary to what is stated by other historians, Anthropology Days was Sullivan's idea. WJ McGee, director of the LPE Anthropology Department and the publicity office of the exposition, had emphasized the athletic prowess of the Natives on display.[8] But James Sullivan believed in the superiority of Caucasians. He proposed a "Special Olympics" in which Natives would compete in a selection of sports, and their performances would be measured against the existing records (he controlled the keeping of American records because he was the editor of the national arbiter of records, *Spalding's Official Athletic Almanac*). McGee recruited the participants from the living villages at the fair and several foreign pavilions, the Philippine Reservation, the Indian School, and the ethnological concessions on The Pike and paid them to participate in trials. The top three placers were selected for the final, where they were not paid to participate because of Sullivan's requirement of amateurism—and so many Natives refused to participate, though the top three in the finals received prize money. Between the competitions, Natives staged dance competitions, sang, or performed dramatic enactments—and these were organized by the Natives themselves. The *Daily Official Program* and contemporaneous media state that these events were held on August 11–12, but McGee gave dates of August 12–13 in the final report of the Department of Anthropology filed on May 10, and Sullivan repeated these dates in *Spalding's Official Athletic Almanac for 1905*. Though these dates were apparently incorrect, they are the ones most frequently cited by later historians.

The accounts of the time show that the spectacle of white men trying to persuade Natives to engage in sports that they did not understand was regarded humorously by the spectators as well as many of the participants themselves. In his official report, Sullivan complained, "The Pigmies from Africa were full of mischief. They took nothing whatever seriously outside of their own shinny game and the tree climbing."[9] There was a conflict between the seriousness with which people like Sullivan and McGee regarded their games and the tricksterism of the indigenous peoples who refused to conform to "civilized" rules in sport, as well as in their lives on the fairground (described in Parezo's chapter). The performances by the Natives were far below the existing records and the Olympic performances, and Sullivan gloated over his ideological victory. Parezo recounts that McGee felt he needed to regain face, so he held another set of contests in September, preceded by training meets, and with prize money as remuneration.

4

The results of this "anthropological meet" have been lost and it is often overlooked by historians.

Already there was a tension surrounding the 1904 Olympic Games and Anthropology Days indicating trends to come: physical educators and anthropologists with serious professional aspirations for their fields sought to separate out scientific anthropology and Olympic sports from their popular ethnographic sources. Both sports (as pushed by Sullivan) and anthropology (as pushed by Franz Boas) were undergoing a process of professionalization that was intended to give greater social legitimacy to anthropologists and physical educators, and which also reflected the changing class structure in the United States as a whole (Sullivan was Irish and Boas Jewish, two groups that were both striving for legitimacy in the United States at this time). In the names of "science" and "education," they attempted to distance themselves from the popular entertainments that served new markets in the expanding global consumer economy. Ironically, as they strove to create professional, salaried niches for themselves as educators, serious anthropologists tried to distance themselves from profit-seeking "Show Indians," while serious physical educators tried to use the ideology of "amateurism" to distance themselves from professional athlete-entertainers. In other words, they sought to secure financial stability for themselves while denying it to Natives and working-class athletes who were not "pure" enough for their brand of science. The excesses in St. Louis helped to crystallize their thinking. This is the source of the historical importance of the 1904 World's Fair to both the history of anthropology and the Olympic Games.

The juxtaposition of civilized and savage was the key symbolic dichotomy at the fin-de-siècle expositions and was reflected in their organization of space, architecture, rhetoric, and multiple other symbolic expressions. But the juxtaposition of the civilized and the savage in Anthropology Days ultimately aroused the disgust of many of those involved. Pierre de Coubertin, the founder of the first modern Olympic Games in 1896, later wrote that "the only original feature offered by the program was a particularly embarrassing one," and called Anthropology Days "a mistake," "inhuman," and the Olympic Games "flawed."[10] Echoing a common sentiment among European historians, Pierre Boulongne summed up the significance of the 1904 St. Louis Olympic Games and Anthropology Days with a note of Old World condescension: "The St. Louis Olympic Games, the first to be held on the American continent, were a success in sporting terms and benefited from the crowds attending the World's Fair. Alas, their memory remains tainted by the 'anthropological days,' for all they were not part of the official program. But this was 1904 in the United States of America."[11]

There are a number of scattered articles on the Anthropology Days of the St. Louis World's Fair, but the topic has never been systematically treated in one place, and only Henning Eichberg has treated it with theoretical sophistication.[12] Anthropology Days expressed an ideology of evolution, civilization, and progress that was widely shared, and which underpinned all the international expositions from 1851 on. Why, then, has Anthropology Days been regarded so negatively? The contributors to this volume offer different answers to this question. Adopting Eichberg's position (this volume), I would like to suggest here that perhaps this stark juxtaposition in the bodily world of sports exposed tensions in the underlying cultural logic that were not so evident in the other realms. The "sportive body" that displays standardization is different from the "spectacular body" that displays strangeness. The seriousness of the Olympic Games, which embodied the essence of Western civilization, could not stand up to juxtaposition against the ridiculous spectacle of untrained and unmotivated Natives halfheartedly attempting to follow the rules of the sports of "civilized" men. Anthropology Days exposed the arbitrariness of Western sports and even Western civilization as a cultural construction. It raised the question of whether the Natives could ever be like civilized men—or worse, whether they even wanted to. This was an unmentionable question in those times when colonialist and imperialist aspirations still reigned. Anthropology Days embodied sport before the laughter had left.[13] The events in St. Louis hastened its departure.

Frames and Cultural Performances

Several of the authors in this collection utilize the idea of "ramified performance genres" developed by John MacAloon, who focuses attention on the interpretive "frames" that distinguish types of cultural performances.[14] The notion of a "frame" is elaborated by Erving Goffman: it refers to the basic elements that people use to organize experience by creating definitions of social events and their subjective involvement in them. A frame is the answer to the question, "What is it that's going on here?"[15] If, for example, someone asked this question while observing two scantily clad men running in a large circle, a fellow spectator might answer, "a sport," thus revealing one of the cultural frames in which such behavior could be understood. Depending on the cultural context, there would be definite behaviors, practices, and meanings that mark the event as a "sport." If the spectator were not familiar with these rules, she or he would be left just as confused as before. Indeed, this was part of the problem with the 1904 Anthropology Days, as will be seen: the uninitiated Native participants did not understand that they were engaging in "sports," certainly did not understand the basic rules of the game, and thus did not behave as expected. The same initiated spectator could also have answered to the confused observer, "the Olympic Games," thus revealing that multilayered levels of interpretation, or frames, can be attached to the same event; frames exist within frames. Goffman's concept of the frame is useful because it emphasizes the arbitrariness of the meanings that are assigned to a given "strip" of experience: they can be contested; change over time; are often defined by processes of social negotiation; they can even, in retrospect, be "wrong."

As attested to in the various chapters in this book, a sport contest could be framed as a living museum display, a freak show, tribute to an imperial power, a scientific experiment, a method of education and assimilation, an amusing game, a serious pursuit of records, a contest for national honor, and a host of other interpretations—often more than one at the same time.

An important contribution of this volume is to document the tremendous variety of interpretive parameters within which sports were framed, each shaped by a cultural logic that extended outward to broader worldviews. "Science"—scientific inquiry, research, and the worldview that is disseminated as the result of them—is one of the primary frameworks that people around the world now use, to greater or lesser degree, to organize large chunks of experience. But the scientific framework was not as systematized in 1904 as it is now, making it possible to see some of the cracks in its structure that still persist today in the realm of sports. These cracks are discussed by a number of the authors in this volume, particularly Jon Marks and Nancy Parezo. The afterword will return to this theme.

MacAloon proposes that frames of "spectacle," "festival," "ritual," and "game" embrace each other in a series of concentric frames, moving from the most inclusive (spectacle) to the most basic (game), and serve as the main interpretive frameworks for understanding the performance system of the Olympic Games as it became elaborated over time.[16]

In MacAloon's formulation, spectacles are characterized by grandeur bordering on excess and are primarily visual, watched by "spectators." Festivals are above all joyous. The Olympics have been characterized as a "festival of humanity" from their inception to today. Rituals invoke sacred forces and effect social and spiritual transformations. Games have fixed and public rules that separate them from everyday life, are "fun," and are rich in symbolism.[17]

MacAloon concentrates on the "metagenres" or "megagenres"[18] that have been meaningful to social scientists and sophisticated thinkers like Coubertin. His meta-analysis allows him to describe the Olympic Games as a neatly ordered system of nested frames, which reflected Coubertin's effort to create a "whole system" united by a single principle, which he sometimes called "eurhythmy."[19]

Olympic scholars have generally been content to stop at MacAloon's metalevel of analysis and as a result have failed to adequately fill in the abstractions.[20] The on-the-ground reality was that world's fairs and Olympic

Games were creative combinations of various performance types that did not encompass each other, but were thrown together in a hodgepodge that was never completely systematized. As will be seen below, the Olympic Games were by no means a unified "performance system" in 1904, but the events in St. Louis spurred their development in that direction.

Further, these labels had their own culturally specific meanings, which changed over time and varied across the nations of Europe and North America, which should not be confused with MacAloon's social-science abstractions. So, for example, in American circuses since the late eighteenth century, "spectacle" (or "spectacular") referred to the grand entry pageant that opened the show.[21] It was also used to describe events, of large or small scale, seen by the eyes that challenged comfortable categories: thus, a world's fair could be a spectacle, but so could Anthropology Days or, in Coubertin's famous formulation, the sight of women engaging in sport.[22] "Festival" and "ritual" were categories that were meaningful to Coubertin—as well as to sport organizers who sought to continue his legacy—because he was raised in a "culture of festivals" with origins in the French Revolution (Festkultur in Schantz's analysis), out of which the Olympic Games emerged, and was inspired by that tradition to try to create a secular religion, religio athletae, out of their revived form.[23] But despite Coubertin's effort and its legacy among Olympic organizers, it is not clear that the Olympic Games have ever been clearly recognized as a festival or a ritual by their popular audiences.

The important methodological conclusion from MacAloon's work is that paying attention to actual performances is a much-needed exercise because it was the performance quality of the genres considered here that gave them such a powerful popular impact. Scholars writing about world's fairs, museums, the Olympic Games, and so on, have tended to give priority to the intellectual histories that shaped them as institutions and have not analyzed them as events in ongoing social processes. For example, sport historians have failed to contextualize the Olympic Games within the vibrant milieu of nineteenth-century neoclassical reenactments in the West—such as classical

Greek theater, the "hippodramas" in circuses, and so on. There seems to be a general academic distaste for linking any performance with cultural or educational pretensions to lowbrow forms of entertainment such as circuses, world's fairs, vaudeville, or burlesque. Yet in their heyday circuses and world's fairs touched more people than any other popular cultural genres. In 1903, on the eve of the Louisiana Purchase Exposition, there were ninety-eight American circuses—more than at any time before or since, and the circus reached almost every American.[24] The exposition in St. Louis covered 1,272 acres, a greater area than any other world's fair before or since.[25] According to official attendance figures 19,694,855 people passed through the turn-stiles between April 30 and December 1, 1904, equaling 26 percent of the population of the states and territories (76,303,387 in 1900).[26] Circuses and world's fairs exerted a tremendous influence on the development of mass culture, and high-cultural forms like museums and classical Greek theater, and the intellectual disciplines that accompanied them, arguably were as much shaped by them as they shaped them.[27]

In the following sections of this introduction, I will outline the neoclassical revival and anthropological theory that gave meaning to and derived meaning from cultural performances at the fin de siècle. I will next summarize the performance types in existence at the turn of the century that formed the broader context for the 1904 St. Louis Olympic Games and Anthropology Days. I will conclude by making a few suggestions as to why the Olympic Games eclipsed the world's fairs in global attention by looking at the specific case of the Parade of Athletes, and will comment on what this tells us about the character of intercultural interactions in our times.

The Neoclassical Revival

Neoclassicism occupied a central role in the French Revolution as revolutionary thinkers took the pagan practices of ancient Greece as inspiration for the construction of new social forms to take the place of the rejected forms of medieval Christianity, associated with the toppled monarchy. They developed the concept of the "civil religion," in which worldly abstractions like reason, equality, liberty, and nature were raised to the level of the sacred and celebrated in art, architecture, monuments, and other civic symbols—and with newly invented festivals.[28]

The American Revolution, the presence of the Ottoman Empire to the east, and the explosion of pilgrimage and travel contributed to the emergence of a pan-European identity. Greece became a symbol of a common European past. Europe saw itself as the heir to Greek civilization. Western Europe's romantic fascination with ancient Greek culture created philhellenism, a radical wing of the Romantic Movement. Philhellenism soon became wrapped up in the Greek struggle for independence from the Ottoman Empire.

The Greek revolt against the Ottomans began in 1821. Hundreds of philhellenes fought in the war, from all parts of the West: Poland, Italy, the German principalities, France, North America, and more. In October 1827, the British fleet, supported by French and Russians, destroyed the Turkish-Egyptian fleet in the Battle of Navarino, a turning point in the war. The war ended in 1828 and an independent Greek state was established in 1832. Otto I was installed as king in 1833. He was the son of Ludwig I, the king of Bavaria, himself a philhellene, whose capital in Munich was a center of philhellenism.[29] Greece was in semi-colonial subjugation; the Great Powers (England, France, Bavaria, and Russia) determined the form of government of the new state. When Otto II was forced out of power in 1862, he was replaced by a Danish prince, renamed George I.

The significance of the philhellenic movement to the story being outlined here is that, as C. M. Woodhouse phrased it, "These were men who had for the time being renounced nationality. . . . Philhellenism was in a sense supra-nationalist, though a nation was what it helped to produce."[30] Philhellenism was an undercurrent of the major international expositions of the late-nineteenth and early twentieth centuries and a predecessor of the Olympic Movement. A transnational movement that served national causes, it was based on an ideal of shared humanity that often conflicted with the reality of nationalism and racism.

The first book on the history of the ancient Olympic Games was published in the Netherlands in 1732.[31] From the 1830s onward many books by German authors on ancient Olympia and the Olympic Games were published. English and Scottish poets had been passionately concerned with Greece since the mid-eighteenth century, and when the Parthenon Marbles were exhibited in London in 1807 and Greek art was seen by large numbers of people for the first time, it created a huge craze for "pure" Greek art.[32]

The modern circus was invented by Philip Astley in London in the 1770s, and the equestrian spectacles or "hippodramas" at Astley's Theatre featured Alexander, Hercules, and Roman gladiators. At the 1904 St. Louis World's Fair, the "Ancient Rome" concession on The Pike featured a hippodrome with races between twelve chariots pulled by forty-eight horses, an arena with broadsword combat between gladiators, and boxing contests between men whose fists were bound with the *cestus*, the Roman boxing glove.

Classical Greek drama was also revived, and athletic routines from the circus and sports were sometimes featured in plays.[33] The theatrical drama *Olympia* inaugurated the State Theater of Athens in 1838.[34] A vogue for the performance, in the original Greek, of classical Greek drama moved from Germany to Britain in the 1880s. In Germany, Greek tragedy was performed in Greek in 1845, in England at Oxford and Cambridge Universities in 1880 and 1882, and in the United States at Harvard University in 1881.[35] In 1875 full-scale excavations were carried out at Olympia by a German team headed by the eminent archaeologist Ernst Curtius and sponsored by King Friedrich Wilhelm IV. Germany held a particular fascination with Greece due to its own search for a national identity as a latecomer among the nation-states—Germany's unification as a nation-state is dated to 1871.

The neoclassical revival in the United States is reflected in the architecture of the buildings that housed the new central government, a style imitated in state capitols and city halls throughout the country—as well as in the buildings at the American expositions. The 1893 Chicago World's Fair was known as "the White City" because of its sea of gleaming faux marble facades. The influence

1. Neoclassical architecture in the Government Building at the Louisiana Purchase Exposition. From David R. Francis, *The Universal Exposition of 1904*, 91. Image from the Missouri Historical Society Digital Library, St. Louis.

of French neoclassicism in the United States is seen in that most emblematic symbol of American values, the Statue of Liberty, a neoclassical figure that was a gift from France. In the St. Louis World's Fair, the only permanent building—the Art Museum—and most of the temporary buildings featured neoclassical architecture, including the Government Building and the Indian School, the latter of which juxtaposed Native displays in the plaza in front of it against the symbolism of Western civilization in the background.

The concepts of "race" and "nation" used by political philosophers, which shaped the rise of European nation-states in the nineteenth century, derived from the Greek concepts of *genos* and *ethnos* as they had taken shape among Greek intellectuals under the Byzantine and Ottoman empires;[36] the latter word also became the key root word for defining what anthropologists study (ethnology, ethnography, ethnic groups). Posed against these words is *demos*, "the people of democracy," which Eichberg proposes to recapture for contemporary use in his chapter.

Pierre de Coubertin's Philhellenism and Racism

One of the important heirs to the French Republican and philhellenic traditions was Pierre de Coubertin, the French aristocrat who led the revival of
the modern Olympic Games. Coubertin visited ancient Olympia in 1894 and
famously asked, "Germany had brought to light what remained of Olympia;
why should not France succeed in rebuilding its splendors?"[37] Otto Schantz's
chapter in this book is the first extended attempt to relate the European intellectual milieu out of which Coubertin and the Olympic Games emerged to
Coubertin's ideas about race. Influenced by the International Congress of
Colonial Sociology held during the 1900 Paris Universal Exposition (Exposition Universelle), Coubertin's attitude during the years surrounding the St.
Louis Games echoed the "scientific" racial paradigm of the Third Republic. While Coubertin—like Sullivan and McGee—clearly arranged the races
along a hierarchy from inferior to superior, his racism was mitigated by
his Republican humanism, while the racism of his American counterpart,
James Sullivan, was much less restrained. They did not like each other, which
exacerbated the conflict between Europeans and Americans over Olympic
sport, described in Dyreson's chapter.[38] Another factor in their conflict was
the difference between a classically educated French aristocrat and an "uncul-
tured" lower-middle-class Irish entrepreneur. After World War I Coubertin
would become less racist and more committed to a faith in the universal
educability of humans.

The Emergence of American Anthropology

The head of the Department of Anthropology of the Louisiana Purchase Exhibition was WJ McGee, founding president of the newly established American
Anthropological Association (AAA). The founding of that organization in
1902 had involved a conflict between McGee, who had no formal education
after his irregular secondary school education, and Franz Boas, who had a
PhD in physics from Kiel University and considered that at that time only

about thirty other anthropologists in the United States could "lay claim to a fairly symmetrical training." McGee wanted the new national organization to include self-trained "amateurs"; Boas wanted it limited to professionals employed in anthropological work and with formal graduate training. McGee outmaneuvered Boas and the AAA was incorporated along the inclusive lines he desired, which favored him as its leader. McGee had been the ethnologist-in-charge of the Bureau of American Ethnology from 1893, which made him the most influential organizer of anthropology in the United States, until he was forced out in 1903 and took up the position of director of anthropology in St. Louis.[39] Afterward he became the first director of the St. Louis Public Museum until 1907.

Boas's career had been insecure; he had been chief assistant to Frederic Putnam at the 1893 World's Columbian Exposition in Chicago and, having nowhere to go, had agreed to stay on to organize the inherited materials into anthropology exhibits at the new Field Museum, but left after disagreements with its leaders.[40] By 1902 he had appointments at Columbia University and the American Museum of Natural History. In addition to their different organizational philosophies, Boas was critical of McGee's dogmatic cultural evolutionism. George Stocking argues that the real conflict here was more than an organizational one; a paradigmatic change was taking place in world science that was reflected in Boas's theoretical outlook, which during this period became that of American anthropology as a whole.[41] Curtis Hinsley concurs that McGee's downfall signified that the tradition of nineteenth-century American anthropology had reached its political and historical limits.[42]

Continuing the tradition begun in Paris in 1889, an International Congress of Art and Science was held in conjunction with the 1904 World's Fair. The designer of the congress, Hugo Münsterberg, aimed to show that American scholarship had come of age and that it was the equal of the German scholarship that had until recently dominated in the United States. He railed against "European prejudices" against the "utilitarian" nature of American scholarship, stating that some German newspapers had editorialized that the scientific congress would be a "scholarly Barnum circus." The Old World criticisms of the congress are interesting because, as discussed below, the same criticisms were leveled against the Olympic Games, with Coubertin complaining about "utilitarian America." Ultimately the congress was more international than the Olympic Games, probably because the former paid the way of the invited participants and gave them an honorarium, while the latter did not. Ninety-six foreign participants took part in the congress. The assertion that it constituted "the most noted assemblage of thinkers the world has ever seen" was not far from the truth, with the participants including Max Weber, Ferdinand Tönnies, Henri Poincaré, and many others.[43] The congress also brought together leading thinkers in physical education, helping to publicize it and consolidate it as a discipline.[44]

As Parezo and Marks argue in their chapters, the scientific congress marked a turning point in American anthropology from evolutionist physical anthropology to Boasian cultural anthropology. McGee died in 1912, while Franz Boas would define a new trajectory for the discipline in which cultural anthropology replaced physical anthropology as the central paradigm. However, taken together, the careers of both McGee and Boas reveal the contours of American anthropology at the turn of the century. At a time when they did not have stable employment, both of them found work at world's fairs and at the museums created afterward from the exposition collections. Museums occupied an uneasy intermediate space between science and popular ethnography; Boas considered their focus too materialistic and not theoretical enough.[45] In the decade after the 1904 exposition, under the influence of Boas, universities would eclipse museums as the principle sites for the practice of anthropology.[46] Marks's chapter outlines this process as it has played out over the last century.

The Intersection of Anthropology and Sports

The chapters in this volume show that, in the nineteenth century, sports played an increasingly important role in the encounter between the West and its Others. In her chapter Christine O'Bonsawin recounts that in 1860 Albert Edward, Prince of Wales, was the first British monarch to visit Canada and his visit was celebrated with cultural performances by indigenous peoples, including "Indian Games" in Montreal. The lacrosse matches included one match between two Indian teams, Algonquin and Iroquois, while another pitted the white men of the Montreal Shamrocks against the Iroquois. Kahnawá:ke Mohawk lacrosse tours in Europe, 1868–83, became a tool in Canadian government attempts to attract immigration. John Bale notes that in the early 1880s in Paris, the dances and wrestling matches of Native peoples were examined and measured by anthropologists. In Paris in 1893, a party of Dahomeans traveling to the 1893 Chicago World's Fair were invited to take part in a 100-kilometer steeplechase against French sports stars—and a Dahomean won. In 1907, the Duke of Mecklenburg measured and photographically documented Tutsi high jumping in Rwanda.

In 1879 the first Indian School in the United States, the Carlisle Indian School, was founded in Pennsylvania, with sports playing an important role in its efforts to assimilate American Indians. The Fort Shaw Indian School, whose girls' basketball team is described by Linda Peavy and Ursula Smith in this volume, was founded in 1892. In 1901 the sports festivities at the Pan-American Exposition in Buffalo, New York, were opened by a game between Carlisle and Cornell that pitted Natives against whites (Dyreson, this volume).

The combination of industrial expositions and sports was exported through imperialism. In 1898 the United States annexed the Philippines as the spoils of victory in the Spanish-American War; the first Manila Carnival was organized as a commercial fair in 1908 and by 1912 had become the national championships in a number of sports (Gems, this volume). St. Louis 1904 was China's first major international exposition after the inception of the Qing Dynasty's New Policies era; in 1910 the Nanyang Industrial Exposition in Nanjing was China's first attempt at an international exposition on Chinese soil, and held in conjunction was a sporting event organized by the YMCA that later came to be known as the first national athletic games.[47] In 1913 the first Far Eastern Championship Games were held in Manila, and their importance in East Asia grew so rapidly that the International Olympic Committee considered them a rival to the Olympic Games; they were known in Manila as an "Olympic kindergarten." In 1913, Pierre de Coubertin remembered Anthropology Days in St. Louis as the "beginnings of exotic athleticism," and a "precedent" for the Far Eastern Games, although the fact that Asians of "ancient and refined civilizations" had competed with near barbarians was "hardly flattering" and "a mistake."[48]

In these examples, it is possible to see the links between Native sports and some of the longstanding practices of empire: Native sports could be one of the acquisitions of imperial conquest displayed as tribute to honor the king; they could be means of assimilating natives to the culture of the imperial center. But these old imperial usages were being modified by forces emerging in the nineteenth century: imperial entertainment shaded into publicity stunts serving the needs of the capitalist economy (e.g., Mohawk lacrosse as tribute to the prince vs. advertisement for immigration); cultural assimilation . shaded into pseudoscientific studies of physical (racial) difference (Indian school physical education vs. Indian-white contests as measurements of superiority attracting large-paying audiences).

Anthropology and physical education intersected not just in practice, but also in their practitioners. Some of the key figures who straddled both realms mentioned in this book are: the Duke of Mecklenburg, an anthropologist and explorer who studied Tutsi high jumping in Rwanda and was later a member of the German national Olympic Committee (Bale, this volume); Luther Gulick, a leader in the application of anthropometry to physical education and a member of the American Olympic Committee; E. P. Thwing, president of the New York Academy of Anthropology and in the founding group of the American Association of Physical Education (1888), which embraced anthropometry; Franz Boas, legendary founder of the American school of cultural anthropology, member of the founding group of the AAA, and a member of the editorial board of the *American Physical Education Review* from 1898 to 1904. In the Physical Education section of the scientific congress in 1904, anthropologist Frederick Skiff spoke on the value of athletic exercises and WJ McGee on the influence of play in racial development. Skiff was a member of the Amateur Athletic Union and the American Olympic Committee (the American connections are discussed by Dyreson). These connections were not just coincidental; sports and anthropology were nodes in an interconnected network united by a shared ideology of civilizational progress. In Greece, for reasons described by Kitroeff in this volume, folklore dominated over physical anthropology; the founder of the discipline of folklore in Greece, Nikolaos G. Politis, was a member of the competitions committee of the 1896 Athens Olympic Games, architect of the renovation of the Panathenaic Stadium, and wrote two chapters in the official report.[49]

In both anthropology and physical education the dualistic interest in the physical body and in the effects of enculturation and training was reflected in the notion of the "natural" (as opposed to the implicitly "cultural") athlete. Both Marks and Bale discuss the history of this false dichotomy and its persistence to present times. Since "science" is one of the themes running throughout this volume, Marks's chapter is intended to alert the reader to the logical pitfalls with which the science of race and sport was and is fraught, reminding us, "Posing a question that cannot be answered rigorously, and then pretending that it can be, is pseudoscience. Except in rare cases, unfortunately, pseudoscience is only identifiable as such in retrospect." He observes that for over a hundred years now, racial "science" has perpetuated two key logical errors: the first is the failure of science to consider within-group variation while only paying attention to an erroneously conceived between-group variation; the second error is to analytically remove humans from their cultural context, thus failing to take into account their biocultural nature.

The common roots of evolutionary theory and physical education are also evident in the importance of the notion of physical "fitness" for each, albeit with different connotations.

The Human Zoo

It is not surprising that anthropologists were so interested in humankind as a physical being, since one root of anthropology extended into natural history. The observation of animals initially served as a model for the study of humans. Still today, natural history museums quite frequently include anthropological displays, a practice that has come under fire for equating Natives with animals. Likewise, at the turn of the century zoos and ethnological displays were not distinct genres. In 1904, the premier zoo in the world was Carl Hagenbeck's zoological park in Hamburg, Germany, established in 1874. When supply began to exceed demand in the 1870s and the animal trade became less lucrative, he accidentally discovered a "remedy" when a friend suggested that it would be "most picturesque" if he could import a family of Lapps along with some reindeer. He gave orders that the reindeer were to be accompanied by their masters. They took up abode behind his house and the "ethnographic exhibition" was a huge success. Having learned that "ethnographic exhibitions would prove lucrative," in 1877 he hired the Norwegian Adrian Jacobsen to go to Greenland "for the purpose of inducing a few Eskimos to accompany him back to Europe," which he did with the help of the Danish government.[50] With this action, Hagenbeck seems to have invented the practice of dispatching agents to remote regions to bring back exotic peoples for "public display and private profit."[51] By the late 1870s he organized one tour every year.[52] In 1884 he traveled about Europe with a "Cingalese" exhibition of sixty-seven persons with twenty-five elephants and assorted other animals. Feeling this would be difficult to top, he next turned his attention to animal training, which until that time utilized brutal methods. His experiment in "gentle" training was successful, and his trained lions first appeared in the Paris exposition of 1889, and an expanded show appeared in Chicago in 1893 and St. Louis in 1904.

The point of this summary of Hagenbeck's career is to illustrate that the global trade in exotic animals and humans went hand in hand; it was made possible by exploration and the opening up of Africa, it was driven by the profit motive, and it found its biggest audiences at world's fairs. It was not a big step to move from training animals to jump, to training humans to jump, although Hagenbeck himself does not seem to have attempted it. However, as will be illustrated below, attempts to use sports to "civilize" Natives were not far behind.

A second point is that Hagenbeck was part of a global network drawn together by the exotic trade and the great expositions. The importation of non-Westerners became big business; major circuses and amusement establishments had full-time agents who combed the globe for curiosities. The legal status of the "freaks" varied: some came under contract to their governments of origin with a specified period of service; in other cases they were "owned" by their exhibitors and remained indefinitely in the United States.[53] American Indians were typically persuaded to leave their jobs on the expectation that their income from tips from spectators for their performances would exceed their wages—thus the origins of the stereotype of the exhibitionist and profit-seeking "Show Indian." Geronimo, on the other hand, was brought to St. Louis as a prisoner of war under the constant surveillance of the U.S. government.

In Europe and the United States, the connections between showmen and anthropologists were close. Special presentations of the Natives drew press attention and large crowds to scientific sessions; scientific certification of the authenticity of the Natives increased their drawing power and profitability for the showmen. The leading German anthropologist Rudolf Virchow defended the practice of examining traveling troupes in published reports; Hagenbeck was an honorary member of the Berlin Society for Anthropology, Ethnology, and Prehistory that he founded.[54] In 1886, while he was preparing his *habilitation* (a higher degree after the PhD) at the Royal Ethnological Museum in Berlin, Franz Boas studied the language, legends, and music of a troupe of Bella Coola from Canada, and published several articles about them.[55] Perhaps this was his first encounter with the First Nation peoples of the Pacific Northwest who became his ethnographic specialty after his immigration to the United States the following year. At the Chicago World's Fair, the Kwakiutl (Kwakawaka'waka) whose presence was arranged by Boas performed a Hamatsa cannibal ritual that was banned in Canada at that time, which not only boosted their income by attracting audiences nearing ten thousand but also attracted the ire of Canadian officials toward Boas for selecting Canada's most "degraded" representatives.[56]

That the trade involved calculations of profit is indicated by McGee's complaint that the St. Louis exposition lost its Australian Blackfellow, this "most distinctive type of mankind not represented on the grounds" due to the intervention of the "narrow monetary margin" of the department. Nobly, McGee did not acquire any Eskimo for fear that the St. Louis summer would kill them, although he noted that the commercial venture on The Pike "assumed the risk, to the interest and benefit of many thousands of visitors."[57] McGee contracted the African adventurer Samuel Verner as a "special agent" and paid him $8,500 to acquire twelve pygmies of specified age and sex, four Red Africans, and two other ethnic types of his choosing.[58]

P. T. Barnum's Circuses

P. T. Barnum had established his "American Museum" in New York in 1841, a place in which a visitor could view exotic animals, aquariums, ethnological artifacts, historical artifacts, paintings and sculptures, waxworks, freak shows, and other curiosities; the visitor could also attend theatrical plays with an "educational" message.[59] "Museum" referred to what we now call a "sideshow," a word which became more common in the 1890s although some circuses used "museum" through the 1930s.[60] When the American Museum was burned in a fire, Barnum turned his efforts to realizing his idea of a "Congress of Nations," which he had had in mind at least since the 1840s. He conceived of it as "an assemblage of representatives of all the nations that could be reached by land or sea. I meant to secure a man and a woman, as perfect as could be procured, from every accessible people, civilized and barbarous, on the face of the globe."[61]

The year 1872 marked Barnum's first visit to the Hagenbecks in Hamburg, after which he became one of their chief customers.[62] In that year he founded a circus with a name that embodies "polymorphous performativity": "P. T. Barnum's Great Traveling Museum, Menagerie and World's Fair," which featured "Fiji cannibals, Modoc and Digger Indians, and representative types of Chinese, Japanese, Aztecs, and Eskimos." In 1873 Barnum purchased duplicates of the chariots, costumes, and props from the Congress of Monarchs in the circus of John and George Sanger in London—a grand parade of famous monarchs and emperors from around the world, which made some attempt to be historically accurate. In the following year he launched his second traveling show, the Great Roman Hippodrome, at the start of which he partly realized his vision: the show started with a parade sometimes called the Congress of Monarchs and sometimes the Congress of Nations, a pageant of thirteen of the "ancient and modern monarchs" of the "civilized nations" in chariots accompanied by attendants and national flags, with white performers reenacting famous figures such as Confucius, George Washington, and Queen Victoria, as well as rulers from Turkey, India, and China. Following the Congress of Nations were chariot races, horseback riding, and high-wire acrobatics by men and women.[63]

In 1884 Barnum launched his "Ethnological Congress" and for the first time brought in authentic human "specimens" from their native habitats, altogether (it was claimed) "100 uncivilized, superstitious and savage people"—never mind that among them were representatives of Egypt, India, and China, which had been among the "civilized nations" in the Congress of Nations. Newspaper ads proclaimed that it would be of "incalculable benefit to scientists, naturalists, and students."[64]

Barnum's shows featured parades of nations two decades before the intermediate 1906 Olympic Games in Athens, the first Olympic Games in which athletes paraded into the stadium behind national flags (see Kitroeff, this volume, and the discussion below). The development from a British Congress of Monarchs to an American Congress of Nations and Ethnological

Congress mirrored important political developments of the times. "Congress of Nations" was a central concept in world peace movements, dating at least to Immanuel Kant's 1797 call for a permanent Congress of Nations in *The Metaphysical Elements of Justice* (*Metaphysische Anfangsgründe der Rechtslehre*). He meant by it a general assembly for resolving national differences peacefully. The original German *Staatenkongress* might not have inspired Barnum's mental picture because of its reference to states rather than nations. The 1815 Vienna Congress had been the first large-scale effort to carry it out, but in Europe at that time nations were represented by monarchs. This was reflected in popular ethnography by the Congress of Monarchs in the Sangers's circus.

In 1831, William Ladd published "An Essay on a Congress of Nations" and the phrase became a key term in the New England peace movement. This reflected the American opposition to monarchy and the call for an international congress of national representatives.

In popular culture, the link between neoclassicism, the circus, and the quest for peace among nations was noted as early as 1857 in a verse on an advertising bill for a circus:

> Here are strange wonders! Olympia to Columbia yields,
> Exchanged, are modern acres for Elysian fields;
> Tents now take the precedent of ponderous Marble Halls,
> Thousands are encircled within its woven walls;
> The flags of every nation flutter in the breeze,
> A universal Brotherhood it thus at once decrees.[65]

A Universal Peace Congress was held at the Chicago World's Columbian Exposition in 1893. The formation of the League of Nations in 1919, spearheaded by U.S. president Woodrow Wilson, was one of the outcomes of the world peace movement. Barnum would have been familiar with the New England peace movement since he lived in Connecticut, was active in politics, and attended at least one peace meeting during the Civil War. He was well-read and described himself as a person who promoted low culture but who himself preferred a "higher grade of amusement."[66]

Barnum's 1874 Congress of Nations prefigured by thirty-six years the shift in international politics from the European-led Congress of Monarchs to the American-led League of Nations. However—also prefiguring the real political difficulties—Barnum was unable to realize his original inclusive idea and ended up representing only the "civilized nations" in his Congress of Nations. Ten years later his Ethnological Congress represented only the "uncivilized, superstitious, and savage people" and his "Congress" never brought civilized and savage peoples together.

Following Barnum's lead, a Congress of Nations seems to have become a standard feature of many American circuses in the following decades. The later Barnum and Bailey Circus also had parades with themes of nations and peace.

The above time frames raise the possibility that developments in popular ethnography preceded developments that occurred in the realm of official ideology and politics at a later date. This is not so unlikely if we realize that world's fairs, circuses, and other traveling displays were probably the major shaper of concepts about ethnic, racial, and national differences for the vast majority of the European and North American populace in the days before television and widespread higher education. In the ever-shrinking world, they offered an imaginary vision of ethnic and national diversity for the future.

Buffalo Bill's Wild West Show

In 1883 William F. Cody, or "Buffalo Bill," invented the Wild West show, building on the circus tradition. A combination of exotic animals and individuals demonstrating skills and reenacting historical fictions, the shows included riding, roping, shooting, historical reenactments (such as "Custer's Last Stand"), and dramatic narratives. They were lent a certain authenticity by the claim that the cowboys, army scouts, and—most importantly—American Indians in the shows had participated in the actual events. Between 1883 and 1916, his Wild West shows toured throughout Europe and the United States. In Kasson's assessment, the appeal of these shows was that they used a combination of romance, reality, and adventure to tell the "story of our country," contributing to the defining of American identity both in Europe and at home.[67]

Buffalo Bill took his shows to the world's fairs in Paris in 1889 and in Chicago in 1893. He added a "Congress of Rough Riders of the World," inspired by Barnum's congresses—it was also billed as "a Kindergarten of Anthropology" targeted to students "of human progress, of racial peculiarities, of national characteristics." In a dialectic between fact and fiction, in the Spanish-American War of 1898 Theodore Roosevelt superseded Buffalo Bill in celebrity with his storming of San Juan Hill with his Rough Riders.[68] Particularly after his election as U.S. president in 1904, Roosevelt would lead the formation of an American national identity intimately linked with sports, the "Sporting Republic." Roosevelt's celebrity was boosted by the addition in 1899 of the storming of the hill to Buffalo Bill's Wild West show, complete with "detachments from Roosevelt's Rough Riders." He also added "Strange People from our New Possessions" to the show, including the "finest representatives" of Puerto Ricans, Sandwich Islanders, and Filipinos. Celebrating the four hundredth anniversary of Christopher Columbus's first voyage to North America, it expressed America's claim to be the heir of Western civilization.[69] All of these themes would be repeated in the Philippine displays at the 1904 World's Fair, as described in Gems's chapter.

In St. Louis in 1904 the Mulhall and Cummins' Wild West Show on The Pike featured two hundred Indians in displays of riding, roping, historical reenactments, and other activities.

Dyreson's chapter describes how those responsible for the United States' assimilationist efforts among Indians opposed their work to Wild West shows, which they regarded as vulgar expressions hindering their high-minded efforts. Samuel McCowan, the assistant to the director of the anthropology exhibits at the 1904 fair—assigned to that position by Commissioner of Indian Affairs William A. Jones—complained to Director of Exhibits Frederick Skiff about the awarding of concession licenses to Wild West shows along The

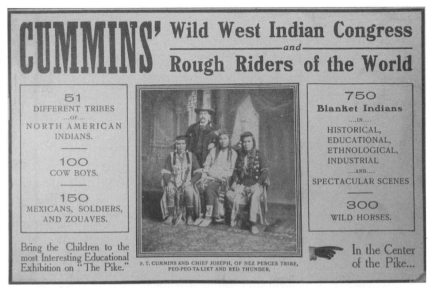

CUMMINS' **Wild West Indian Congress**
—and—
Rough Riders of the World

51 DIFFERENT TRIBES ....OF.... NORTH AMERICAN INDIANS.		750 **Blanket Indians** ....IN.... HISTORICAL, EDUCATIONAL, ETHNOLOGICAL, INDUSTRIAL ....AND.... SPECTACULAR SCENES
100 COW BOYS.		
150 MEXICANS, SOLDIERS, AND ZOUAVES.		300 WILD HORSES.

Bring the Children to the most Interesting Educational Exhibition on "The Pike."

F. T. CUMMINS AND CHIEF JOSEPH, OF NEZ PERCES TRIBE, PEO-PEO-TA-LIKT AND RED THUNDER.

In the Center of the Pike...

2. Advertisement for the Cummins' Wild West Show on The Pike. From the St. Louis Public Library Online Exhibit "Celebrating the Louisiana Purchase."

Pike. The Navajo and Zuni villages there, and the Hopi Cliff Dwellers, had but one purpose—to make money. He told Skiff that the government exhibit on the fairgrounds would be "large and realistic, strictly educational, and entirely free from barbarous features that do not now exist"—a reference to the ritual and historical reenactments typical of Indian Shows.[70]

World's Fairs, Anthropology, and the Olympic Games

In London, in 1851, the Great Exhibition of the Works of Industry of All Nations, housed in the magnificent structure known as the Crystal Palace, became the largest industrial exposition to that time, with thirty-four nations represented. The national exhibitions were arranged along a line of progress from the Tasmanian savage through the Eastern barbarian civilizations, across Europe to the pinnacle of progress, Great Britain.[71] The "savages" were little represented at the Great Exhibition, but they were featured with increasing prominence in subsequent international expositions. This went hand in hand with the rise of ethnology as the scientific framework for the study of savages. George Stocking began his book on *Victorian Anthropology* with a description of the Crystal Palace exhibition because it dramatically expressed a disjuncture in history between the ancient and the modern: the classic works of British sociocultural evolutionism, he argues, could be described as "an attempt to understand the cultural experience symbolized by the Crystal Palace."[72]

Over the centuries, sports had been one of the popular entertainments associated with European market fairs. Industrial expositions drew upon this tradition and sports were often associated with them, typically as a minor, peripheral activity. Unofficial amusement zones began to pop up outside of world's fairs beginning with the Paris Exposition of 1867. This was also the first world's fair that included sports, drawing on the tradition of the festivals of the French Revolution, which had included contests of different kinds.[73] The amusement zones grew in size and excess over the years; they were often regarded with official disapproval, but in fact they also spurred the development of the fairs, which were hard-pressed to compete with the more entertaining and less educational attractions outside their borders.

From 1851 to 1908, fourteen principal world's fairs (or universal expositions) were held in London (three times), Paris (three times), Vienna, New York, Philadelphia, Chicago, Buffalo, and St. Louis.[74] Although the 1896 Olympics were a stand-alone event, the next three Olympic Games were all held in conjunction with major international expositions: the 1900 Paris Exposition, the 1904 Louisiana Purchase Exposition in St. Louis, and the 1908 Franco-British Exposition in London. Between 1900 and 1908, there was only one major international exposition held in addition to these three, the 1901 Pan-American Exposition in Buffalo, New York—and that one included an attempt to hold its own version of the Olympic Games. James Sullivan, the commissioner of the Physical Education Department for the exposition, had declared that the IOC did not control the Olympic Games and that he would organize them in 1901, but he ultimately backed down.[75]

The second through fourth Olympic Games were auxiliary sideshows to expositions—and although Pierre de Coubertin and the IOC regarded this association as undesirable after the failures of the 1900 Olympic Games, they were unable to separate the Olympic Games held in Europe or North America from expositions until the 1912 Stockholm Olympics. The two Olympic Games held in Greece (1896 and the intermediate Olympics in 1906) were stand-alone events and were considered much more successful. As the decades progressed the Olympic Games slowly eclipsed the world's fairs in prestige and public attention. This raises two questions: Why were the third and fourth installments of the modern Olympic Games held in association with world's fairs despite the desire of their founder? And why was Greece able to mount successful stand-alone Olympic Games while the much wealthier nations of France, America, and Britain could not? The second question will be dealt with below.

The answer to the first question is that according to prevailing worldviews of that time, the association of the Olympic Games with world's fairs made more sense than it does to us now. First, they continued the traditional association of sports with market fairs. Second, they were both linked to an underlying cultural logic that gave them a natural affinity. Anthropological exhibits and the Olympic Games illustrated the beginning and end of the march of progress: Anthropological exhibits illustrated the evolutionary beginnings of civilization, and Olympic Games the superior physical achievements of civilized men. Third, world's fairs were clearly the premier international institution of the day and the Olympic Games, as Coubertin phrased it, their "humiliated vassal."

The 1904 Olympic Games were originally awarded to the city of Chicago but were transferred to St. Louis when the world's fair had to be delayed for a year (it was a celebration of the centennial of Lewis and Clark's 1803 expedition to explore the Louisiana Territory). The St. Louis organizers considered Chicago's Olympic Games a threat to the extensive program of athletic events they had planned for their fair. They threatened to use their superior financial resources and backing of the U.S. government to prevent Chicago from hosting the Games. Chicago backed down and the IOC reluctantly agreed.[76]

The 1908 Olympic Games were originally awarded to Rome, but when difficulties were encountered that were never made public, the IOC transferred them to London to be held in connection with the Franco-British Exposition. With the exception of the special situation in Greece, the Olympic Games were simply not strong enough to stand on their own financially. Coubertin stated that the 1904 and 1908 Olympic Games were held in conjunction with world's fairs "for budgetary reasons."[77]

The 1889 Paris Exposition

The Paris Exposition of 1889, which celebrated the centennial anniversary of the French Revolution, was a key moment for both anthropology and sports. The 1876 Centennial Exposition in Philadelphia had displayed Native Americans and other exotic peoples. But in 1889, Native peoples were included on a large scale for the first time, and in their recreated habitats, with 182 Asians and Africans imported to recreate whole villages in which ethnic people were displayed in their "natural" settings, engaging in Native handicrafts.[78] From this point on in the world's fairs, the display of people became a central feature in exhibitions and living humans took over center stage from ethnological artifacts.[79]

The 1889 Paris Exposition was also the first to aspire to include a scientific congress that would assemble the top minds in the world. The Congress of Physical Exercises was led by Pierre de Coubertin, who in the previous year had become secretary-general of the two newly formed national organizations for the promotion of physical education and sport. The congress included an extensive program of sports activities at different sites in the city, mainly contested by Parisian schoolboys, but including some international competitors from other parts of France and even Algeria. They included riding, fencing, track and field, Swedish gymnastics, swimming, tennis, and rowing.[80] "Scientific" physical education shaded into sports as cultural display: the exposition events included a demonstration of Scottish Highland Games as well as Buffalo Bill's Wild West Show (Eichberg, this volume). The success of the athletic and physical education program in 1889 encouraged Coubertin to support the holding of the second installment of the modern Olympic Games together with the 1900 Exposition Universelle in Paris. What initially seemed like a good idea, however, did not fulfill its potential. This will be discussed further below.

An elaborate reconstruction of the buildings and monuments of ancient Olympia was also on display in the Palais des Beaux-Arts in the exposition, where Coubertin would have seen them.[81] He also attended a speech on the Olympia excavations.[82]

The 1893 Chicago Exposition

The 1893 Chicago World's Columbian Exposition exerted the biggest influence on the 1904 St. Louis World's Fair for several reasons. It was the major exposition that immediately preceded it in the United States, Chicago was the closest major city to St. Louis, and many of the organizers of the Chicago Exposition also played a role in St. Louis. Frederic Ward Putnam, director of the Peabody Museum at Harvard, was the head of the Department of Ethnology and Archaeology, and Franz Boas his chief assistant. One of the more successful exhibits was that on games of the world organized by Stewart Culin, one of the founders of the AAA.

Putnam's vision of anthropological exhibits with educational value conflicted with that of Thomas Palmer, the president of the National Commission for the Fair, who was equally interested in the sheer entertainment value of the exhibits. He put Putnam in charge of both the fair's ethnographic sections and the exhibits in the amusement zone, the Midway Plaisance (inspired by the circus midways that had become common in the 1870s, themselves inspired by Barnum's American Museum). Putnam proved incompetent and Sol Bloom, the entrepreneur who had bought the rights to display the 1889 Paris Exposition's Algerian Village at future events, was engaged to install the exhibits on the midway.[83] He did not subscribe to cultural evolutionary theories and later recalled that placing Putnam in charge of the midway was "tantamount to making Albert Einstein manager of Barnum and Bailey's circus."[84]

The Midway Plaisance, a mile-long strip of carnivalesque attractions, included recreated "ethnological" villages. When halfway through its six-month run the fair's backers became concerned that it was not going to repay its debt, the publicity stunts used to attract spectators included boat races and swim meets between the inhabitants of the midway. Zulus, South American Indians, Dahomeans, and Turks competed against each other. The *Chicago Tribune* observed, "The races were notable for the lack of clothing worn by the contestants and the serious way in which they went at the task of winning five-dollar gold pieces."[85]

The idea of sports competitions for the resident Natives was not a new one in 1904, nor was the idea that they generated publicity.

The 1900 Paris Universal Exposition and Olympic Games

As MacAloon notes, in 1889 Coubertin could not foresee the incompatibility of world's fairs with Olympic Games and, "seduced by the exposition tradition," he allowed the 1900 Olympic Games to be associated with the Paris Exposition.[86] Frustrated with bureaucratic delays, he organized a private committee and planned to carry out the games apart from the exposition; however, the Paris Municipality counterattacked and cut the budget, Coubertin resigned, and a new chairperson emerged. Coubertin went along and salvaged as much of the Games as he could, but they were badly organized and peripheral to the fair. He concluded that never again should they "allow the Games to become dependent on or be taken over by a big fair where their philosophical value vanishes into thin air and their educational merit becomes nil."[87]

The 1904 Louisiana Purchase Exposition and Olympic Games

Some fourteen hundred Native peoples were on display inside the fairgrounds, and when added to the number in the concessions on The Pike, the amusement zone outside the fairgrounds proper, the total was around three thousand. The Olympic Games and Anthropology Days were only one of a myriad of contests and athletic displays that took place both inside the fairgrounds and on The Pike.

Every Sunday at Cummins' Wild West Show on The Pike, there were horse races, chicken pulls, lacrosse contests, archery, spear throwing, and tipi-raising competitions. The Indians waged bets with each other and the tourists. Patagonian "Red Giants" (the Tehuelches) competed against American cowboys. On The Pike, the Eskimo and Cliff Dwellers (Zuni and Moki) demonstrated their "native sports." The Boer War extravaganza included combat. There were Roman gladiators. A large building was built on The Pike for the Cuban game of jai-alai, but was closed by the police after three weeks because of gambling.[88]

Even the sports program organized by Sullivan included ethnic events such as lacrosse, "Irish Sports" in track and field, the Irish hurling championships, the Gaelic football championships, German Turner exhibitions and contests, and "Bohemian Gymnastics."[89]

As described by Gems, Parezo, and Dyreson, on the fairgrounds proper, one of the attractions of the Philippines display was the Natives engaging in their own "aquatic sports." The Indian School and the Department of Physical Culture sponsored Indian-only events in football, lacrosse, baseball, track, and boxing. At the Indian School there were daily demonstrations of fitness—a kindergarten class of Pima did calisthenics in the morning, and older students did athletics in the afternoon on the school parade grounds. On the official Olympic program in the intercollegiate division, the Indian schools of Carlisle and Haskell played each other in football—billed as the first-ever meeting of two Indian schools, they played to a standing-room crowd of over twelve thousand fans and each school received five thousand dollars for the event. Parezo notes that Natives competed in field sports for one hundred dollars in monetary prizes in front of the Indian School. There were intertribal archery or spear-throwing contests, running races for men and women, tug-of-war, lacrosse, and shinny games, bolo throwing from horseback, and even timed tipi-raising competitions for women.

Native American men shot arrows at nickels and quarters dropped by the spectators—if they hit it, they kept it. Since almost none of the Natives were given a wage, they earned their money through the tips and bets given by spectators during the events. Therefore these events were organized by the Natives themselves—a rather stark contrast with Anthropology Days and the formal competitions for "assimilated" Indians. As Parezo notes, these events were motivated by a combination of the visitors' need for novelty and the Natives' need for money.

In the era of rapidly expanding commercialism, sports were already well-established as a publicity tool in 1904. And Natives engaging in sports were also recognized as a particularly effective attention-getter. Peavy and Smith note that a major impetus for the encouragement of girls' basketball at the Fort Shaw Indian School was that Superintendent F. C. Campbell recognized its benefits as a public relations tool in publicizing the accomplishments of the school. O'Bonsawin notes the use of Mohawk lacrosse tours in Europe to promote immigration to Canada. Dyreson notes that in an 1899 publication McGee had dismissed the notion of savage athletic prowess as the product of the imaginations of travel writers trying to sell books, but five years later he was not above using the same stereotype to sell the exhibits of his financially strapped Anthropology Department. Parezo notes that James Sullivan used Anthropology Days to increase flagging interest in the Olympic Games, and that the LPE Corporation considered that sports provided inexpensive publicity.

More generally, McGee, the founding president of the American Anthropological Association, had a keen eye for marketing. At the end of the fair, he estimated attendance at the Anthropology Building at one and a half million, the Indian School above three million, and the "alien camps and groups" at over four million (a total of eight and a half million); he also estimated that the current press items and academic essays inspired by the anthropology exhibits formed a quarter to a third of all of the spontaneous publications of the fair. He was satisfied with the combination of entertainment and education that was achieved, concluding: "So the assemblage of human types was not only a source of attraction, but served serious ends."[90]

Hinsley asserts that the Columbian Exposition in 1893 had been the first of a series of shocks to Franz Boas's faith in public anthropology, the second being the Spanish-American War of 1898. By 1900 he had already become disillusioned with museum anthropology as an educational tool.[91] Although he did not have an official position, Boas was an advisor to McGee in 1904 and took part in the scientific congress. One might imagine that the St. Louis World's Fair strengthened these feelings. However, like the Olympic Games, anthropology was not well-established enough to stand on its own. It needed the financial resources provided by the mass entertainment market. That popular ethnography at this time outweighed the fledgling status of anthropology as a science is indicated by the contrast between the central role of anthropology at the fair and its minor role in the scientific congress. McGee was married to the daughter of Simon Newcomb, one of the leading men in American science, and the president of the scientific congress. Perhaps due to McGee's presence, anthropology achieved recognition as a discipline and was assigned a minor niche as Department 14, Anthropology, under Division C, Physical Science. Eight speakers presented.

The International Expositions and the Zappas Olympiads in Athens, 1858–89

Greeks surely participated in the global network of expositions and exotic trade described above, but the connection with the Olympic revival has yet to be established. The far-flung, well-connected, and wealthy Greek diaspora, which was particularly important in the global shipping industry, was all-important to the successes of the 1896 and 1906 Olympic Games.[92] There were large Greek communities in Chicago and St. Louis at the times of those world's fairs (see Kitroeff, this volume). For the 1893 fair, George Pangalos, a member of the Greek diaspora in Alexandria, Egypt, shipped 175 residents of Cairo, along with exotic animal and architectural features stripped from old buildings, to his concession on the Chicago midway.[93] He later published an essay boasting about it in the June 1897 issue of *The Cosmopolitan*. Since Alexandria, Cairo and Chicago were major centers of the Greek diaspora, the presence of a Greek entrepreneur in this trade is not surprising. In 1904 he reprised his "Streets of Cairo" concession on The Pike. It is thus not far-fetched to assume that the organizers of the first modern Olympic Games operated within the global networks already described.

This returns us to the question: Why was Greece able to mount successful stand-alone Olympic Games while the much wealthier nations of France, America, and Britain could not?

The peripheral status of the sports associated with major industrial exposi-tions was perhaps first contested in Athens when the first Zappas Olympiad was held in 1859 (discussed further in Kitroeff's chapter). The wealthy Greek merchant who funded the Olympiad, Evangelis Zappas, had intended to re-vive the ancient Olympic Games, but the Greek foreign minister who led the organization of the Olympiad, Alexander Rangkavis, favored an industrial and agricultural exposition of the kind that had already become common in Western Europe as a means of showcasing national economic achieve-ments. Rangkavis viewed athletic games as archaic practices unsuited to the modern era. The countervailing nationalist view was that Western Europe would not be much impressed by the primitive state of Greek industry, but that an authentic revival of the Olympic Games would bring glory to Greece. Rangkavis blocked the realization of Zappas's wishes, and the athletic events played only a minor role in contrast to the exposition, for which a great hall—the Zappeion—was newly erected. The exposition was the first time that Greeks from the entire Mediterranean—including areas still under Ot-toman control—had come together in such numbers, which strengthened a national consciousness.[94]

The next Olympiad was held in 1870 on a much larger scale. The ancient Panathenaic Stadium was excavated and restored for use in the athletic events. Between twenty and twenty-five thousand spectators filled the stadium on the final day to watch athletes from across the Greek-speaking world. Zappas Olympiads were held again in 1875 and 1888–89. Over time, the content of the rhetoric surrounding the games moved beyond the simple political goal of national unity to encompass the broader social goals of all-around education, the strengthening of body and spirit, reverence for the Muses, and finally ideas of world peace—the seeds of an emerging Olympic ideology.[95] The success of the sporting events led Rangkavis to claim in 1888, after the death of Zappas, that the idea of combining athletic competitions with intellectual contests and industrial exhibitions was his own.[96]

Historical and Cultural Reenactments
and the Olympic Revival in Athens, 1896

Historical reconstructions had become very popular in Europe in the Romantic period. Private and commercial masquerades (a British reinterpretation of Continental festivals), and carnival all flourished in Britain between the 1720s and 1790s; typical costumes imitated historical or ethnic figures, including neoclassical and Ottoman images.[97] These were no doubt one of the precursors of the Sangers' Congress of Monarchs. In the 1820s at England's Vauxhall Gardens there had been a two-hour reenactment of the Battle of Waterloo.[98] In the United States, an early example was a buffalo hunt staged by Barnum in 1843. In 1853, at a racecourse in New York, ten thousand spectators watched a medieval tourney, a deer hunt, a steeplechase, and Olympic Games.[99] Buffalo Bill's Wild West Shows, the Congress of Monarchs in Britain, and Barnum's Congress of Nations in the United States all continued the tradition of historical reenactments. The Boer War was re-fought daily on The Pike at the St. Louis World's Fair. As described, ritual reenactments and sports were the main ways in which the Natives entertained the spectators at the world's fairs.

The connection between reenactments and the revival of the modern Olympic Games has yet to be fully explored, but it was clearly important, particularly in Greece. Reenactments were probably no more common in Greece than elsewhere in the world, but a unique convergence occurred there. The neoclassical revival in the West converged with Greece's search for a national identity and the result was the form of the modern Olympic Games, which were initially conceived as a kind of historical reenactment. Kostas Georgiadis argues that classical theater and the Olympic Games were considered the most important classical institutions that should be revived to create a modern Greek national culture.[100]

The sports in the Zappas Olympiads were clearly more reenactment than sport. As Christina Koulouri notes, this reinvention of ancient games occurred *before* the modern physical education and sport movement had taken root in Greece. The language and rituals of the games were almost all inspired by ancient practices, even to the wearing of body stockings by the athletes to imitate ancient nudity. The concept of all-around education was linked to the ancient ideal of a "sound mind in a sound body."[101] The Zappas Games took place after the revival of classical Greek theater in Greece (1838) and Germany (1845) and immediately preceding the 1880s fad for classical Greek theater in England and America described above.

Enactments of classical Greek and Latin plays had been initiated as a humanistic pedagogical method on the Continent in the fifteenth century and spread to England, where they were popular in the sixteenth century until the Puritans closed theaters in the seventeenth century and forbade performances involving costumes and scenery; only school recitations continued. In the late eighteenth century the schools initiated the revival that became popular in the British universities at the end of the nineteenth century.[102] In the nineteenth century, there were multiple examples of imitations of the ancient Olympic Games employed as pedagogical tools. In one of his first published references to the Olympic Games in 1887, Coubertin stated that athletic games on the "Greek" model were a useful pedagogical tool for exciting schoolboys to emulate the "dust of Olympia," and were a more appealing method than the reenactment of historical events.[103] If at this early time Coubertin conceived of "Greek" sports as a simple historical reenactment used as a pedagogical tool, his conception later became more complex and grandiose.

The first international Olympic Games in Athens in 1896 continued this tradition. They were viewed as a historical reenactment by Europeans and North Americans as well as the Greeks themselves. This can be seen in the Greek attitude toward the discus, as contrasted with the American: The Greek athletes threw the discus as they believed the ancients had, judging from statues; the Americans experimented with the method that caused it to fly the farthest, and won.[104] In his announcement of the preliminary program of the Olympic Games in the 1904 *Spalding's Official Athletic Almanac*, James Sullivan described the modern Olympiads as "the reproduction of the famous games of ancient Greece."[105]

Moreover, the Athens 1896 Olympics included an initial proposal for cultural reenactments that is interesting for its similarity to American practices. In theory, Coubertin supported the expression of cultural diversity within the Olympic Games, stating in an 1895 *Bulletin of the* IOC, "It is in no wise to be desired that each Olympiad only repeats the same picture only in a different frame. The uniqueness of each People, in its own style, to organize a festival and carry out physical exercises—it is that which will give the modern Olympic Games their true character, and make them perhaps more splendid than their predecessors."[106] Thus, it was in keeping with Coubertin's thought and the already well-developed traditions of expositions that for the first modern Olympic Games in Athens, the reception committee proposed dozens of cultural performances, including music, classical and modern plays, and a torch race.

As described by Kitroeff (this volume), Greek intellectuals had limited engagement with the racist and evolutionary anthropological theories that would dominate at the 1904 St. Louis Olympics, but since the 1830s they had engaged intensely with German folklore because of the furor incited by the Bavarian folklorist Jakob Philipp Fallmereyer, who argued that modern Greeks were not descendants of ancient Greeks, but were of Slavic stock. Thus, Greeks were influenced by the German Romantic notions of the nation as *Volk* (described in the chapter by Suzuko Mousel Knott). At the 1896

Athens Games, folklore intersected with the Olympic Games in the person of Nikolaos G. Politis, who was the founder of the discipline of folklore in Greece.[107] Politis was a professor at the University of Athens and a member of the committee that oversaw the competitions at the Athens Olympics. Although he was not on the Commission for the Preparation of the Greek Athletes, which initially proposed to organize cultural reenactments, it does not seem unlikely that he might have had a hand in such a proposal.[108]

As described by Georgiadis, along with the reception committee this committee proposed to organize performances of folk dancing and of reenactments of the customs of "free" Greeks in Greece and "enslaved" Greeks in the Ottoman Empire, which would take place between the athletic contests or in the evenings.[109] The goal of the performances was to show to the spectators not only the glories of ancient Greece, but also the current conditions of Greeks from the far corners of the world. Six reenactments were proposed: three ethnic dances, a Vlach wedding with its traditional abduction of the bride, the "Fair Nitsa of Stenimakhos" procession of schoolchildren depicting the rape of a Greek maiden by Turkish Janissary troops, and a reenactment of the Olympic Games of Ortaköy in Asia Minor (an enactment of the ancient Olympic Games that had occurred regularly during the Ottoman period). However, it was feared that these plans would encounter the resistance of the dancers and in particular the women from the proposed cities and villages, who would refuse to appear in the stadium before a large crowd. Eventually the plans for twenty theatrical performances were dropped because of budget cuts. The reenactment of the ancient games in Ortaköy was dropped because it might be regarded as a parody. The only approved performances were a philharmonic orchestra performance to be accompanied by an especially composed hymn (the Olympic hymn by C. Palamas) at the opening, a torch relay, and a single show at the theater of Herod Atticus.

The initial plans are interesting because they echo the American practice in which Natives performed during the intermissions of sports events. As Parezo mentions in her chapter, during the breaks in 1904 Anthropology

Days, the Natives held dance competitions, sang, or performed dramatic reenactments. Peavy and Smith recount that the girls on the Fort Shaw Indian School girls' basketball team opened their competitions by playing the mandolin, reciting Longfellow's "Hiawatha" in buckskin dresses, and singing a chorus in Grecian gowns. It would have been in keeping with this tradition for Greece to display its ancient and modern culture during breaks in the sports. The fact that ultimately this was not done at the first Olympic Games is worthy of further analysis. Georgiadis's account suggests that the proposed performances were too controversial because of questions about gender impropriety, disrespect for the ancient past, and (based on his account—on this point one can only guess) inflammatory depictions of Greek oppression by the Ottomans. Greeks felt their past should be treated with respect, and the question of whether Olympic reenactments were a "parody" seems to have been often debated.[110]

In the United States, by contrast, there does not seem to have been such concern about expressing respect for the past, not even by Franz Boas who, as mentioned, seemed to support the Kwakiutl Hamatsa rituals in 1893 that the Canadian government found embarrassing. In the same time period, Buffalo Bill Cody was one of the most popular figures in the United States. The performances by the Fort Shaw Indian School girls described by Peavy and Smith could be seen as improper, disrespectful toward the ancient past (Indians in Grecian gowns?), and insensitive to the violent subjugation of American Indians. Why were they acceptable in America while the proposed performances, finally, were not acceptable in Greece? One key difference was that people like Boas or Superintendent F. C. Campbell were reconstructing the past of Others, a past that they believed to be dead or dying, and did not claim as their own. America was becoming an imperialist power and by that time Indians formed no real threat to that power, while Greece was relatively weaker and more vulnerable. As romanticized national history, the Wild West show represented a violent conquest of the savages by a "civilized" imperialist power, while the Olympic Games represented a peaceful coming together of rival peoples.[111]

Athens 1896 set a precedent in which explicit displays of cultural diversity were excluded from the sports fields of the modern Olympic Games. It was the first step in the move toward a world monoculture of sports, which was given further impetus by the events in St. Louis. But, as Eichberg warns us in his chapter, we should question such an apparently linear history. The ethnic people (*ethnos*) of self-determination and the people (*demos*) of democracy have a way of disappearing—and then reappearing again. Their reappearance is a response to the culture of recognition or nonrecognition—or in the case of Anthropology Days, as Mousel Knott argues, misrecognition—embodied in sporting events and their accompanying cultural performances.

The 1906 Parade of Athletes:
The Rise of Nations and Nationalism

I would like to take the notion of reenactments as a starting point to offer a hypothesis about the trajectory followed by the Olympic Games after the events in St. Louis. As described by Mousel Knott and Kitroeff in this volume, the symbolic representation of nations in the 1904 Olympics was fluid. Teams were composed of immigrants, native-born athletes, and athletes of ambiguous citizenship. Some athletes competed virtually as individuals. Felix Carbajal, a Cuban, traveled to St. Louis using money raised in exhibitions in Havana, but lost his money in a crap game in New Orleans, hitchhiked to St. Louis, and showed up at the marathon start wearing street clothes.[112] Len Tau and Jan Mashiani were part of the Boer War exhibition at the fair and also ran the marathon in street clothes.[113] Complicating this situation was the fact that the sports events lasted from May until November, ranging from high school interscholastic meets to national championships, and almost all of them were labeled "Olympian." In short, the St. Louis "Olympics" did not function as a neat symbolic package for nationalist displays.

Only two years later at the intermediate 1906 Olympic Games in Athens, the premier nationalist ritual of our times, the Parade of Athletes, was instituted, and it became a fixture from then onward.[114] From this point on, nationalist rituals in the Olympic Games would become increasingly elaborate.

In 1896 the opening ceremonies had reinforced the status of the Greek king. A reception of the royal family at the entrance of the stadium was followed by a procession of the family and dignitaries to the royal seats led by the king and queen.[115] After their entrance, the athletes from different nations lined up in double file, but their entrance seems to have been rather understated.[116] The band played the royal anthem, the crown prince made a speech addressing the king, the king proclaimed the Games open, and the band and choir performed the newly composed Olympic anthem. After the first day's sports events, the royal family departed. In the evening there was a torch procession through the streets of Athens. At the awards ceremonies, the flag of the winner was raised and the band "saluted" it by playing a song, which was not necessarily the national anthem of the country.[117]

At the 1900 Olympic Games, there were opening ceremonies for the exposition and not specifically for the Olympic Games.[118] In 1904 the opening ceremony for the sports program had taken place in May on the first day of the first sports event, the Olympic Interscholastic Meet. This was not part of the designated Olympic events, which were held from July 1 to November 23. Similar to the royal procession in Greece, the president of the LPE, David Francis, with the United States secretary of state, John Milton Hay, led a double line of silk-hatted officials and commissioners to their boxes in the grandstands. A band played "The Star-Spangled Banner." Francis, Hay, and Sullivan walked to the starting line, where Sullivan fired the gun that started the first heat of the 100-yard dash.[119] The Olympic Games were opened on July 1 by a walkabout in which Francis, Sullivan, Frederick Skiff, and a cortege walked among a double file of athletes followed by the judges and inspectors. At the end of the walk, a band of musicians signaled the athletes to start their warm-up exercises.[120]

As described by Georgiadis, the protocol was much more formal in Athens in 1906. The opening ceremony began with the formal entry of the royal

3. American team marching past the royal family on the opening day of the 1906 Athens Olympics. From J. Sullivan, ed., "The Olympic Games of 1906 at Athens," 50.

family with their foreign royal guests. After that, nine hundred athletes paraded into the stadium grouped into national teams led by the coach and the national flag, with the Greek team bringing up the rear. Crown Prince Constantine, president of the organizing committee, read a formal speech and then King George declared the Games open. Again the day's program ended with the exit of the royal family, and afterward there was a reception for the athletes in the Zappeion Hall. At the end of each contest, the national flags for the three top placers were raised on three different poles, a novel arrangement at the time. The awards were presented in a closing ceremony in which each medalist was announced by name, country, and sport, and the athlete walked up to the king, bowed, and received his medal—a reference to a similar practice in the ancient Olympic Games. Georgiadis further observes that in 1906 the awards were made by the king, who stood higher than the athletes; today, awards are made by IOC members, and the athletes stand on pedestals. Thus, the ceremonies chart an improvement in the symbolic status of the athletes.[121]

Coubertin later wrote that the Parade of Athletes had been one of the "wishes" expressed at the 1906 Consultative Conference on Art, Letters, and Sport in the Comédie Française in Paris, which had brought together

44

artists and sportsmen with the purpose of linking sport, art, and letters in Olympism.[122] However, the intermediate Olympic Games had opened on April 22, and the advisory conference on May 23–25. The conference record published in the *Revue Olympique* only suggested that the recent Athens ceremonies had been "painful" to watch because the athletes processed in their travel suits, and the majesty of the place should have required more respect and deference. The "wish" expressed was that they should wear their sport uniforms. A black and white photograph of the American team passing the royal family on opening day reveals that they were wearing suits and ties of varying shades of light and dark, and white berets. That these ceremonies were not entirely without Olympic precedent is indicated by their formation into the same double file reported for the Athens 1896 and St. Louis 1904 opening ceremonies.[123] Furthermore, the *Revue Olympique* recommended that the award ceremony should be modeled on the medieval ceremony in which the winner received a prize from a lady before whom he knelt.[124] Ancient Greece trumped the medieval ages, and this idea lost out to the classically inspired practice begun in 1906. Coubertin's claim for the Parade of Athletes, then, was apparently an example of his tendency to claim pride of place for himself as the creator of the Olympic Movement, which sometimes led him to underplay the contributions of the Greeks.

Karl Lennartz notes that historians have not been able to discover why the Parade of Athletes was introduced in 1906 and hypothesizes that it might have been a result of the fact that this was the first Olympics in which only accredited national Olympic committees could send athletes.[125] But, as has been previously noted, Parades of Nations behind flags had become common in popular culture at least since Barnum's Congress of Nations in 1874, and they were associated with an ideology of world peace. Although we take such parades for granted now, it is possible to imagine that a century ago the image of representatives of all the nations of the world parading together peacefully was novel and exciting—perhaps almost miraculous. Thus in 1869 Barnum wrote of his Congress of Nations idea, "Even now, I can conceive of no exhibition which would be more interesting and which would appeal more generally to all classes of patrons."[126] His original idea of procuring a perfect male and female specimen evokes the biblical legend of Noah's ark. Could the double file formation in St. Louis in 1904 and in Athens in 1896 and 1906 be related to this? It was not a huge leap to turn a procession of Olympic athletes into a Parade of Nations—it required only a people with a particular interest in national identity and world peace, combined with neoclassical revival.

Georgiadis argues that the Athens ceremonies had two purposes: to unite Greeks around the royal family, and to display links between ancient and modern traditions that were meaningful both to Greek national identity and to Westerners enculturated into neoclassicism and philhellenism.[127] Processions had been a common feature in ancient Greece, with the Panathenaic procession of particular importance. At their height, the ancient Olympic Games had begun with a procession from Elis to Olympia of the judges (hellanodikai) followed by other officials, next the athletes and their trainers, and then the horses and chariots with their owners, jockeys, and charioteers.

If we examine this sequence from 1896 onward, we can see that in the Greek Games that bracketed St. Louis, displays of royalty and references to the classical past played an important role; these were important components of nationalism not just for Greece but for all European nation-states. In St. Louis, on the other hand, not only were there no royalty to be acknowledged, but there was not even a head of state present, with the highest government official being the secretary of state. From that perspective, the American Games were more about sports and less about national politics. This was also reflected in the messiness of the representation of nations by the athletes.

The 1908 London Olympic Games were the first Olympic Games in the quadrennial cycle in which the Parade of Athletes by nation took place. They paraded around the stadium in groups by country in alphabetical order and lined up before the rostrum where the royal family was seated, the king declared the Games open, and the British national anthem was played. As it played, all the national flags were lowered as a sign of respect. But a major difference was that the head of state was, for the first time, invited to open the Games by the president of the IOC—Pierre de Coubertin—who would do this again in 1912, 1920, and 1924, followed thenceforth by his successors.[128] At the awards ceremony, the queen awarded gold medals, and the national anthems of the winners and the British anthem were played.[129] In sum, in 1908, the nations and the athletes that represented them were in several ways symbolically subordinated to the monarch as well as to the nation of Britain. But in one important way, they were all subordinated to the IOC.

By 1912, amidst the tensions that would lead to World War I, the Olympics had become important enough that governments began to be interested in interfering in them. The groupings in the parade of nations and the flags to be raised in case of victory were a source of conflict. The IOC became involved in arbitrating which peoples could be symbolically represented as "nations" when the Austrian Empire protested against the presence of an independent delegation from Bohemia, and Russia lodged a similar protest about Finland. Coubertin observed, "The Olympic Games are becoming an affair of State. Royal families were becoming involved and governments, too."[130]

For What Did Athens 1906 Save the Olympic Games?

The promotional blurb on the back cover of a book about the 1906 Athens Olympic Games, by the premier Olympic historian Karl Lennartz, states that the 1906 Olympic Games "saved the Olympic Movement after the organizational problems in 1900 in Paris and in 1904 in St. Louis."[131] The notion that Athens 1906 "saved the Olympics" is the common storyline in Olympic history (see Dyreson and Kitroeff in this volume). But *from* what did Athens 1906 save the Games, and *for* what?

I argue that Athens 1906 saved the Games *for modern nationalism*. The brand of nationalism embodied in the Games was the kind that was to dominate in Western Europe from 1906 until World War II, which was also dominant in the International Olympic Committee and the Olympic Movement. It was a kind of nationalism that over the next decades organized the world into an increasingly rigid system of nation-states with their own monarchs, flags, anthems, and other symbols, with claims to be the pinnacle of a civilizational progress that traced its roots to ancient Greece. It differed from the kind of nationalism taking shape in America, which was reflected in the conflicts between the Americans and Europeans surrounding the 1904 Games. As Dyreson notes in his chapter, the St. Louis Games crystallized a long-term conflict in the Olympic Movement between American and European notions of what purposes Olympic sport should serve. He concludes, "Efforts to Americanize the Olympics, and resistance to those efforts, would shape the movement for the rest of the twentieth century." Building on Dyreson, Kitroeff argues that the Greeks "felt empowered to 'Hellenize' the 1906 Games in the wake of the so-called American Games."

That Coubertin felt Athens 1906 had saved the Games from a shift too far away from neoclassicism was indicated in his statement in 1909 regarding Anthropology Days: "Nowhere else but in America would anyone have dared to put such a thing in the program of an Olympiad. But for the Americans, all is permitted." He also stated that he had wanted Rome to host the next Olympic Games "because there alone, after its excursion to utilitarian America, would Olympism be able to don the sumptuous toga, woven with skill and much thought, in which I had wanted to clothe it from the beginning." He said that "transferring the Games to St. Louis had been a misfortune" with regard to his goal of including the arts in the Olympic Games, and was one reason that he summoned the advisory conference in May of 1906 to "reestablish" the link between art and sport, which he later mistakenly credited with inventing the Parade of Athletes.[132]

In the next three decades, the power of monarchs would wane while that of elected heads of state and dictators would wax, but the neoclassical symbolism would continue to expand. This process culminated in the 1936 "Hitler" Olympics in Berlin, the first to include a torch relay. Their neoclassical symbolism was documented by Leni Riefenstahl's classic documentary, *Olympia*.

MacAloon says that the history of the Olympic Games from 1900 to 1936 is a "story of the simultaneous differentiation, elaboration, and lamination of the performative genres of game, rite, festival and spectacle . . . the development of this new 'ramified performance system' accounts more than anything else for the fantastic global interest in the Olympics and its emergence, over all rivals, as the dramatic celebration of world-historical process."[133] Between St. Louis 1904 and Athens 1906, the ceremonies, rites, and symbols of the Olympic Games were systematized and more strongly unified around a central theme. The IOC took away from St. Louis the lesson that the "mutual respect" between nations was better represented through monocultural, global sports. From 1904 on the Olympic Games would distance themselves from indigenous sports, "cultural" divisions of the world's peoples would not be recognized, the only legitimate global units would be nation-states, and festive laughter would be replaced by ritual seriousness—whether for better or worse now needs to be reassessed.

From What Did Athens 1906 Save the Olympic Games?

But *from what* did Athens 1906 save the Games? As has been argued in this introduction, and as will be argued throughout the rest of the volume, the 1904 Olympic Games, despite all their messiness—and even despite an inclusiveness that we might find admirable today—took place within an emerging ideological system that had coherence. It was imperialist and it was racist in a most vituperative way, because it enlisted "science" in its service in an unprecedented manner. What the Greeks gave to the Olympic Movement in 1906 was a way of dividing the peoples of the world into units defined by their songs, their flags, their history, their customs—their *culture*—not their *race*. In the realm of academics, this was the difference between the folklore that reigned in Greece and the evolutionist physical anthropology that reigned in the United States. With respect to popular ethnography, this was the difference between a people who used the ancient Olympic Games to reenact their national history versus a people who used the Wild West show. As elaborated in the chapter by O'Bonsawin, the contrast between the United

States and its northern neighbor, Canada, is instructive. Despite the fact that U.S. and Canadian Indian policies proceeded alongside each other, there were evident differences in the treatment of Native sports. Canadian Indians were excluded from the 1904 fair exhibits—except for the five Northwest Coast Indians preferred by the Americans for their fearsome rituals—and did not participate in Anthropology Days but did take part in the Olympic lacrosse game. Nearly a century later, this difference was seen in the creation of the Arctic Winter Games in 1970 and the North American Indigenous Games (NAIG) in 1990 as an expression of ethnic self-determination through sport in Canada, with no such equivalent in the United States—where the mascot controversy (discussed in the afterword) has typed sports as a realm for negative stereotyping rather than ethnic self-determination.

Since the 1870s, the international expositions had been organized around themes. Peace, brotherly love, and understanding among nations were the most common themes—even while "displays of military technology, imperial conquest, and abject racism" were erected on the sites themselves.[134] Although Zappas in Greece, William Penny Brookes in England, and many others had conceived of reenacting Olympic Games to promote *national* unity, it was Coubertin who had the inspiration of reviving the ancient Olympic Games as an *international* event for promoting peace between nations. He was thus the one to hit upon the idea of combining in the medium of sport the lofty aspirations and educational goals of the world's fairs with popular ethnography and the neoclassical revival. The Olympic Games provided a symbolic model that was needed in the era that would soon lead to two world wars and the worst atrocities against humanity that science could commit. The Wild West show provided a model that had run its historical course and could no longer be sustained—and in any case, it was not a shared history claimed by half of the globe. Fortunately, after 1904, American anthropologists almost immediately began to turn away from the racist physical anthropology embodied in McGee and toward the cultural anthropology embodied in Boas.

As MacAloon has noted: "There is a remarkable structural relationship between the sociocultural contexts of the ancient and modern Olympics. In the nineteenth and twentieth centuries, the nation-state arose as the dominant and segmentary form of social and political organization, and with it came the modern Olympic Games as one, though the most notable, cultural expression of 'pan-human' (rather than 'pan-Greek') identity."[135]

What is significant about the events in St. Louis in 1904 is that this was a time of "polymorphous performativity," of experimentation with different kinds of "intercultural zones" or "contact zones." Some of these performance genres, such as Wild West shows, cultural reenactments, ethnological displays of living people, and freak shows, have largely been left in the dustbin of history. Others, such as zoos, circuses, amusement parks, classical Greek theater, and historical reenactments, continue in somewhat different form. World's fairs, in a modified form, are still important global events, but are not the important purveyors of novel intercultural experiences that they once were. They have been eclipsed by the Olympic Games, which have been growing in size and significance for over a century. The urge to "scientifically" measure the intercultural contact that occurred in these zones may have produced some bizarre (by today's standards) science in St. Louis, but the urge itself did not disappear and in some ways accounts for the replacement in popularity of the world's fairs—which prioritized visual experience—by the Olympic Games—which produce "records" as a seemingly objective quantification of national difference.[136] This will be discussed further in the afterword.

It is important to take note of what, in retrospect, might have been the most important contribution of the St. Louis Olympic Games and Anthropology Days to the Olympic Movement. As has been shown, the organization of cultural performances in 1904 was ultimately driven by the profit motive and an emerging consumer economy. Boas's retreat to the universities was in part an effort to save anthropology from the forces of the market. American organizers recognized the commercial potential of sport and used it as a publicity tool.

If Greece saved the Olympic Games from American racism and imperialism, it was ultimately unable to save them from American capitalism. In 1904

4. Advertisement for Spalding athletic goods featuring a Louisiana Purchase Exposition award diploma. From J. Sullivan, ed., "The Olympic Games of 1906 at Athens."

this was also the wave of the future. The pattern was repeated again in 2004, when the Olympic Games went "home" to Athens after their hypercommercialized foray to utilitarian Atlanta in 1996. A century later, Greece and the United States still represented two poles in the global order: Old World culture versus New World utilitarianism.

Notes

Henning Eichberg, Kostas Georgiadis, and Allen Guttmann gave useful comments on this introduction. Jon Marks originally suggested "Bodies before Boas" as a title for the book.

1. John MacAloon's foundational work pulled together the scholarship that existed in 1981; this introduction continues some of the lines of inquiry opened by his work and also cites some of the work that has appeared in the last two decades, when there has been a rapid increase of relevant scholarship. MacAloon, *This Great Symbol*.

2. Kasson, *Buffalo Bill's Wild West*, 43.

3. MacAloon, *This Great Symbol*, 268.

4. MacAloon, "Humanism as Political Necessity?" 234; Pratt, *Imperial Eyes*, 26. See John Bale's discussion in this volume.

5. Coubertin conceived of the Olympic Movement as an educational and world peace movement, and the term is today the official term used by the International Olympic Committee to label the world system of Olympic sports. I use it here in that sense, without making a judgment as to whether it constitutes a "movement" in the social science sense.

6. MacAloon, *This Great Symbol*, 44–47, 134–36, 217–21, 236–41, 262–69.

7. The effort taken as most definitive is that by Olympic chronicler Bill Mallon, who applied his own standards to the "highly unusual" 1904 Games to establish which events were "truly of Olympic caliber." See the afterword in this book. Mallon, *1904 Olympic Games*, ix.

8. William J McGee preferred the name WJ McGee (without periods or spaces after the initials).

9. J. Sullivan, "Anthropology Days at the Stadium," 257.

10. Coubertin, *Olympism*, 409, 695, 407, and 742. Coubertin also mentioned in 1932 that there were some people who "conveniently malign and denigrate [the St. Louis 1904 Olympics] in retrospect, to suit the ambitions of certain individuals" (p. 518). I have not been able to ascertain to what this refers.

11. Boulongne, "Presidencies," 125.

12. Carlson, "Giant Patagonians and Hairy Ainu," 19–26; Eichberg, "Forward Race and the Laughter of Pygmies," 115–31; Gøksyr (misspelling of Goksøyr), "'One certainly expected a great deal more from the savages,'" 197–306; Stanaland, "Pre-Olympic 'Anthropology Days.'"

13. See Eichberg, "Forward Race and the Laughter of Pygmies," and Eichberg's chapter in this volume for a discussion of the subversive nature of laughter to the ritual seriousness of modern sports.

14. MacAloon, "Olympic Games and the Theory of Spectacle," 241–80.

15. Goffman, *Frame Analysis*, 10–11, 8.

16. MacAloon, "Olympic Games and the Theory of Spectacle," 257–59.

17. MacAloon, "Olympic Games and the Theory of Spectacle," 240–58; *This Great Symbol*, 271.

18. MacAloon, "Olympic Games and the Theory of Spectacle," 250.

19. Coubertin, *Olympism*, 451–52.

20. Two exceptions are Karl Lennartz and Otto Schantz, whose articles tracing the influence of the Munich Oktoberfest and the festivals of the French Revolution, respectively, on Olympic festivities are examples of the kind of concrete histories that are needed to fill in background on the "festival" frame as it was adapted to the modern Olympic Games. Lennartz, "Munich October Festival," 264–87; Schantz, "Französische Festkultur," 64–85.

21. Davis, Circus Age, 286n30. Apparently unaware of its use as a label for the circus entry parade, MacAloon argues that "spectacle" did not become a nominative performance category until later in the twentieth century, but does not document that shift. He also argues that it was not until long after 1904 that the excesses of the world's fairs came to inspire doubt and skepticism as they sought to successively outdo each other as spectacles inspiring awe and wonder in their audiences. MacAloon, This Great Symbol, 271; "Olympic Games and the Theory of Spectacle," 240–48. I would suggest the opposite: "spectacle" was morally suspect long before 1904 because of its association with the morally suspect circus, and the nominative performance category of the circus spectacle shaped its later abstract application to other morally suspect events.

22. In 1935, Coubertin wrote, "Personally, I do not approve of women's participation in public competitions, which does not mean that they should not engage in a great many sports, merely that they should not become the focus of a spectacle." Olympism, 583.

23. Coubertin, Olympism, 580.

24. Davis, Circus Age, 229, 13.

25. Benedict, Anthropology of World's Fairs, 21.

26. WJ McGee, "Anthropology at the Louisiana Purchase Exposition," 826; Twelfth Census of the United States, 1900, xviii.

27. The lack of attention to performance genres is a general problem not limited to sport historians. Hall and Macintosh argue that the history of classical scholarship should be more closely tied to performance history, but has not been because of disciplinary boundaries and a dismissive attitude toward popular culture. Hall and Macintosh, Greek Tragedy and the British Theatre, xv, xx, 268, 371, 388–90. Helen Stoddart observes that the circus played an extensive role in the consolidation of Orientalism in the late eighteenth and early nineteenth centuries but this is rarely mentioned by scholars. Stoddart, Rings of Desire, 102. I would like to acknowledge here my intellectual debt to Victor and Edith Turner. Participation in their famous ritual reenactments as a student in 1982–83 initiated my lifelong interest in reenactments, and their processual (i.e., event- oriented rather than structure- oriented) view of society, with its emphasis on performances, underlies the conceptual orientation of this chapter.

28. Schantz, "Französische Festkultur," 65–74.

29. Georgiadis, Olympic Revival, 19.

30. Woodhouse, Philhellenes, 165.

31. Antonides and Antonides, Olympia.

32. Bernal, Black Athena, 290.

33. Croft-Cookes and Cotes, *Circus*, 7; Hall and Macintosh, *Greek Tragedy and the British Theatre*, 388–89, 371.

34. Georgiadis, "Olympic Ceremonies," 81.

35. Hall and McIntosh, *Greek Tragedy and the British Theatre*, 431–32; Easterling, "Early Years of the Cambridge Greek Play," 28.

36. Augustinos, *Consciousness and History*, 12.

37. Coubertin, *Olympic Idea*, 1.

38. The conflict is described in J. Lucas, "Early Olympic Antagonists," 258–72.

39. Stocking, "Franz Boas," 12, 8; Darnell, *And Along Came Boas*.

40. Hinsley, *Savages and Scientists*, 250–51; Conn, *Museums and American Intellectual Life*, 81–82.

41. Stocking, "Franz Boas," 9, 14.

42. Hinsley, *Savages and Scientists*, 256.

43. Coats, "American Scholarship Comes of Age," 412, 411, 415 n. 53.

44. J. Lucas, "Great Gathering of Sport Scientists," 6–12.

45. Hinsley, *Savages and Scientists*, 251; Parezo and Fowler, *Anthropology Goes to the Fair*.

46. Conn, *Museums and American Intellectual Life*, 102.

47. Fernsebner, *Material Modernities*, 34, 64; Morris, *Marrow of the Nation*, 19–21.

48. Coubertin, *Olympism*, 496, 695.

49. Chapters by Nikolaos G. Politis in Polites, Lambros et al., *Olympic Games*.

50. Hagenbeck, *Beasts and Men*, 18–20.

51. Hinsley, "World as Marketplace," 345.

52. Hagenbeck, *Beasts and Men*, 20.

53. Bogdan, *Freak Show*, 56.

54. Poignant, *Professional Savages*, 115 18.

55. Cole, *Captured Heritage*, 71–72.

56. Hinsley, "World as Marketplace," 350; Raibmon, "Theatres of Contact," 182–84; O'Bonsawin, this volume.

57. WJ McGee, "Anthropology at the Louisiana Purchase Exposition," 822–23.

58. Bradford and Blume, *Ota*, 97.

59. B. Adams, *E Pluribus Barnum*, 75–163.

60. Bogdan, *Freak Show*, 44.

61. Barnum, *Struggles and Triumphs*, 170.

62. Hagenbeck, *Beasts and Men*, 11.

63. B. Adams, *E Pluribus Barnum*, 167, 173.

64. B. Adams, *E Pluribus Barnum*, 175–80.

65. Stoddart, *Rings of Desire*, 40.

66. Barnum, *Struggles and Triumphs*, 115.

67. Kasson, *Buffalo Bill's Wild West*, 421, 65.

68. B. Adams, *E Pluribus Barnum*, 194, 25.

69. Kasson, Buffalo Bill's Wild West, 251–53, 97.

70. Moses, Wild West Shows, 156. Lest it be thought that only lowbrow showmen engaged in spurious reenactments, recall that Boas was accused of the same thing by Canadian officials with respect to the Kwiakiutl at the 1893 World's Fair.

71. Kasson, Buffalo Bill's Wild West, 3–5.

72. Stocking, Victorian Anthropology, 6.

73. Schantz, "Französische Festkultur," 69. Coubertin also recalled the 1867 exposition as his earliest memory of public life. Coubertin, Olympism, 752.

74. Benedict, Anthropology of World's Fairs, 31.

75. Dyreson, Making the American Team, 74. The Pan-American Exposition was also notable because President McKinley was shot while opening the exposition and later died.

76. Mallon, 1904 Olympic Games, 7.

77. Coubertin, Olympism, 394.

78. MacAloon, This Great Symbol, 135.

79. Greenhalgh, Ephemeral Vistas, 85–87, 82.

80. Boulongne, "Presidencies," 30.

81. MacAloon, This Great Symbol, 138.

82. Boulongne, "Presidencies," 35.

83. Larson, Devil in the White City, 133. Bloom's first application for a concession in Chicago was rejected, so he sought the aid of Mike De Young, publisher of the San Francisco Chronicle and one of the commissioners of the fair, who not only got him his concession but also an appointment as overseer of concessions on the midway (p. 136). De Young decided that San Francisco should have its own exposition and spearheaded an exposition in Golden Gate Park that opened in January 1894. Profits from the exposition were used to build the De Young Museum (www.thinker.org/deyoung/about/subpage. asp?subpagekey=79). Avery Brundage, the only American president of the IOC (1952–72), had one of the greatest collections of East Asian art in the United States, which he donated to the De Young Museum starting in 1959, housed in a specially built wing until the Asian Art Museum became independent in 1969. It was the first museum in the United States devoted exclusively to the arts of Asia (Web page of the Asian Art Museum, www.asianart. org/history.htm, accessed November 2006).

84. Hinsley, "World as Marketplace," 348.

85. Larson, Devil in the White City, 311.

86. MacAloon, This Great Symbol, 138.

87. Coubertin, Olympism, 394.

88. Jerry Berger, "Q&A," St. Louis Post-Dispatch, March 10, 1996. This building was converted to an ice rink, the Winter Garden, in 1916 and became a center of St. Louis high society as well as of the sports of figure and speed skating. See Brownell, "Figure Skating in St. Louis," 81–86.

89. Mallon, 1904 Olympic Games, 14–15, 31.

90. WJ McGee, "Anthropology at the Louisiana Purchase Exposition," 826.

91. Hinsley, "World as Marketplace," 363.

92. See the overview in Brownell, "View from Greece," which draws on Georgiadis, *Olympic Revival*, and Kitroeff, *Wrestling with the Ancients*.

93. Larson, *Devil in the White City*, 207–8.

94. Georgiadis, *Olympic Revival*, 36; Young, *Modern Olympics*, 15, 18.

95. Georgiadis, *Die ideengeschichtliche Grundlage*, 70–79.

96. Georgiadis, *Olympic Revival*, 77.

97. Castle, *Masquerade and Civilization*.

98. Kasson, *Buffalo Bill's Wild West*, 66.

99. Boulongne, "Presidencies," 36.

100. Georgiadis, "Olympic Ceremonies," 81.

101. Koulouri, "Athleticism and Antiquity," 144.

102. Hall and Macintosh, *Greek Tragedy and the British Theatre*, 243–46.

103. MacAloon, *This Great Symbol*, 81.

104. Mandell, *First Modern Olympics*, 118–19, 126–27.

105. J. Sullivan, "Universal Exposition," 184.

106. Georgiadis, *Die ideengeschichtliche Grundlage*, 226.

107. Herzfeld, *Ours Once More*, 97–122.

108. This is only my conjecture based on the work of Herzfeld and Georgiadis, neither of whom could contribute any further information about Politis's involvement in the 1896 Olympics when I personally contacted them. E-mail from Michael Herzfeld, April 2004; e-mail from Kostas Georgiadis February 6, 2007.

109. Georgiadis, *Die ideengeschichtliche Grundlage*, 201–2; *Olympic Revival*, 115–16; "Olympic Ceremonies," 83–84.

110. Georgiadis states that the organizers were particularly careful to show respect for their ancient traditions because they had had some negative experiences in the Zappas Olympic Games. E-mail, February 6, 2007.

111. Thanks to Christina Koulouri for suggesting American imperial power and Greek political weakness as an explanation.

112. Mallon, *1904 Olympic Games*, 13.

113. C. P. Lucas, *Olympic Games 1904*, 17. Lucas named them "Lentauw" and "Yamasani," but recent research revealed their names to be Len Tau and Jan Mashiani. They were not Zulu, but were likely Tswana. Van der Merwe, "Africa's first encounter with the Olympic Games," 29–34.

114. John MacAloon makes the argument for the crucial importance of the ceremonies to the Olympic Games and the place of national symbolism in them in "Olympic Ceremonies," 29–43.

115. Georgiadis, "Olympic Ceremonies," 85.

116. Llinés, "History of Olympic Ceremonies," 65.

117. Georgiadis, "Olympic Ceremonies," 85, 90.

118. Llinés, "History of Olympic Ceremonies," 65.

119. Mallon, 1904 Olympic Games, 11.

120. Llinés, "History of Olympic Ceremonies," 65.

121. Georgiadis, "Olympic Ceremonies," 87–89.

122. Coubertin, Olympism, 424, 451, 545. Coubertin also exaggerated the number of athletes in the opening parade as fifteen hundred (p. 424).

123. Lennartz, "2nd International Olympic Games," 288–348.

124. "Choreography," 89. Thanks to Anne-Sophie Blank for translating it for me. Coubertin's summary is from Une Campagne de vingt-et-un [A Twenty-One-Year Campaign] (1909) and is found in Olympism, 615.

125. Lennartz, "Parade of Nations," 551–52.

126. Barnum, Struggles and Triumphs, 170.

127. Georgiadis, "Olympic Ceremonies," 89.

128. MacAloon, This Great Symbol, 214.

129. Llinés, "History of Olympic Ceremonies," 66.

130. Coubertin, Olympism, 463.

131. Lennartz and Teutenberg, Die Olympischen Spiele, back cover.

132. Coubertin, Olympism, 620, 408.

133. MacAloon, This Great Symbol, 271.

134. Greenhalgh, Ephemeral Vistas, 17.

135. MacAloon, This Great Symbol, 142.

136. Thanks to Allen Guttmann for this insight. He comments, "Of course, there were efforts at the fairs to quantify and compare the achievements of different peoples, but the kinds of quantification and comparison were orders of magnitude less than what modern sports allow" (e-mail communication, January 23, 2007).

Chapter 1. A "Special Olympics"

Testing Racial Strength and Endurance at the
1904 Louisiana Purchase Exposition

NANCY J. PAREZO

*A spectacle indeed extraordinary and rare in
the records of human experience.*

President Francis,
The Universal Exposition of 1904

The date: August 11–12, 1904. The place: St Louis, Missouri. The venue: The
Louisiana Purchase Exposition (LPE). The special event: Anthropology Days.
Basilio, a Negrito from the Philippines, has just won a heat of the pole climbing
competition and been awarded an American flag. Basilio was one of almost
three thousand indigenous men and women from all over the world who
came to St. Louis to serve as demonstrators, educators, research subjects,
and entertainers. Many agreed to participate in athletic competitions and
demonstrations of physical ability during the fair's eight-month tenure. On
this hot, humid day in August, over a hundred men performed in the Special
Olympics' contests of spear and baseball throwing, shot put, running, broad
jumping, weight lifting, pole climbing, and tugs-of-war before a crowd of
approximately ten thousand.

The "Special Olympics"—or Anthropology Days—is a little-known chapter in the history of anthropology and its relations with indigenous peoples

who constituted the field's subject matter in the early twentieth century. It constitutes an example of how cultural and physical anthropology were combined by the first president of the American Anthropological Association and head of the LPE Anthropology Department, William J McGee, in order to present to the American public examples of the "many long chapters of human evolution" that he had assembled to represent the world's races and cultural types at the St. Louis World's Fair and to demonstrate that his department was producing invaluable new empirical knowledge during the exposition.[1] The LPE's Special Olympics is also an instance of how James E. Sullivan, head of the Department of Physical Culture and a major proponent of physical education, was determined to demonstrate that American athletes were the best in the world, superior to all other races and cultures. In this paper I relate the story of how this Special Olympics was conceptualized and quickly became a comedy in bad science through the use of a badly flawed anthropometry methodology to prove central premises of social Darwinian and unilinear evolutionary paradigms. In addition, I demonstrate how the results of these athletic events were transformed into so-called scientific conclusions about the superiority or inferiority of different groups of peoples that were transmitted to the press and accepted by countless Americans, reinforcing their preconceptions. In short, I theorize about both the dynamics and structures that led to Anthropology Days being conducted using a rigged protocol ensuring that "primitives" failed and Caucasians were "scientifically proven" to be the superior race.

In order to understand these unique anthropological and physical culture events, they must be contextualized into the world of early-twentieth-century anthropology, physical culture, and international expositions. Like other international fairs of this period, the LPE was designed to be a universal mecca for the display and dissemination of knowledge about the peoples of the world, their origins, and technological accomplishments.[2] This information was intended to serve as both the "before advancement" picture and as the foil for technological, industrial, and social changes lauded as progress, the hallmark of the early twentieth century. These fairs were also tools by which imperialist countries and the business class justified and essentially celebrated capitalism, imperialism, forced assimilation, and the subjugation and dispossession of indigenous peoples worldwide and the exploitation of their natural and cultural resources.

Anthropology was a new discipline during the exposition period, attempting to claim its place in the academy and a professional status. To accomplish this, anthropology had to prove to the general public that it had specialized and esoteric knowledge that was useful and necessary. One place it did this was at international expositions, using a special brand of anthropology that I call "exposition anthropology." Exposition anthropology is intimately connected with museum anthropology and involves a basic concern with categorizing and disseminating anthropological concepts and principles so that they are understood by the general public, who will hopefully see that the discipline is a practical science on the same level as chemistry, physics, biology, and medicine. Static and interactive anthropology exhibits at the international expositions held between 1851 and 1915 were deliberately designed to educate viewers about cultural differences and the universality of human biological and social progress, both central tenets of early unilinear evolutionary anthropology. In the process, exposition anthropologists used Native peoples to justify the new science of anthropology as well as visualize the superiority of its conceptual framework, theories, methodologies, and techniques. Simultaneously, those professionals who were trying to position anthropology as the discipline to understand the world's colonized peoples inadvertently (and sometimes purposely) provided rationales for how Western European and American societies conceptualized and treated Native and colonized peoples. In St. Louis, WJ McGee saw the LPE as the place to prove once and for all that anthropology was the most important science ever conceptualized, the umbrella under which all other sciences naturally fell. Anthropology Days was intentionally designed to show that anthropology held the key to understanding Native peoples and their place in the modern world, as well as to provide a critical understanding for how race affected all arenas of life, including athletic ability.

Native Peoples at the St. Louis Fair

The 1904 Exposition in St. Louis, held to commemorate the United States' purchase of the Louisiana Territory from France, covered over twelve hundred acres. Twice the size of the 1893 World's Columbian Exposition in Chicago, it was the largest fair ever attempted and one of the most complex. It had five major objectives: (1) to promote the city of St. Louis and demonstrate its sophistication; (2) to make money for stockholders and bring economic development to the Midwest; (3) to demonstrate the superiority of American democracy, capitalism, and culture; (4) to celebrate industrial, social, commercial, and technological progress; and (5) to predict the future and see education as a cornerstone in future progress. Designed as the "University of the Future," the fair cost almost twenty million dollars and attracted over nineteen million visitors who learned about the technology, imperialism, and development that had become enshrined in Western ideologies of "progress." The LPE was designed to provide a summary or compilation of all existing knowledge at the turn of the century and thus help visitors find purpose in a rapidly changing world. The fair, wrote William F. Slocum, president of Colorado College, in *Harper's Weekly*, gave visitors "new standards, new means of comparison, new insights into the condition of life in the world."[3]

The LPE contained numerous implicit and explicit comparisons of American society and its civilized way of life with the world's "primitive" Native populations and their cultures — both prior to and under colonizing regimes. Organizers presented new insights, new information, and new standards through the use of adjectives in label copy, the placement of objects, the location of strange peoples on the midway (The Pike), and the use of synthetic exhibits that documented the universal technological development of fire, the knife, and other tools.[4] The primary mechanism of comparison, however, relied on what Professor Frederic W. Putnam, the head of the 1893

Columbian Exposition's Anthropology Department, called "life and movement" exhibits: actual Native demonstrators living in appropriate habitations on the fair grounds, practicing authentic, preindustrial, indigenous customs for the education and edification of visitors.[5]

These living exhibits could be found in many parts of the fairgrounds, for it was anthropology "which not only bound together the Louisiana Purchase Exposition as a whole, but gave [the Fair] its broadest, highest and grandest significance."[6] Anthropologist Albert Jenks arranged an ethnological display for the U.S. War Department: a village of over twelve hundred Filipino natives—Igorots, Negritos, Bagobos, Bontocs, Tinguians, Moros, and Visayans—as representatives of the lands recently annexed by the United States. Native artists demonstrated pottery, basketry, and textile productions in state and foreign pavilions. The New Mexico Territorial Pavilion hosted Lena Geronimo, the famous Chiricahua Apache leader's daughter, while the Alaska Territorial Pavilion presented a Haida musical group and totem pole carving demonstrators. The Pike had Japanese, Burmese, Moroccan, Syrian, Turkish, and Egyptian Natives performing in "Fair Japan," the "Mysterious Asian-Indian," "Streets of Cairo," "Bazaars of Stamboul," and the "Moorish Palace." Zulu ("Kaffirs") built a village and reenacted scenes from the Boer War while Puebloans from San Juan and San Ildefonso performed commercialized versions of Hopi snake dances in Tobin's four-story Cliff Dwelling concession. In "A Trip to the North Pole" and at "Crane's Esquimaux Village" tourists saw Inuit families, who were attending their third world's fair, reenact marriage ceremonies, pretend to be on a seal hunting expedition, and stage a fight between hunters and polar bears. Every afternoon over two hundred American Indians from forty tribes performed in Cummins' Wild West Show and Indian Congress.[7]

A large concentration of Native participants came to St. Louis under the auspices of the LPE Corporation–sponsored Anthropology Department. Section N (ethnology, archaeology, history, and anthropometry) constituted the official statements about Native peoples and evolution, financed by the LPE

Corporation (a for-profit stockholding corporation), supplemented by appropriations from the federal government.[8] Designed as a Congress of Races and a narrative of human "progress," Natives were conceptualized, organized, and administered by WJ McGee, a prominent geologist, anthropologist, and theoretical evolutionist.[9] McGee wanted the Anthropology Department to summarize and visualize "the science of man" using an evolutionary model that combined biologically based "race-types" with "culture-grades" or "culture-stages." Anthropology's ultimate goal, according to McGee, was "to trace the course of human progress and classify individuals and peoples in terms of that progress, and thus to learn as much as may be possible of the origin and destiny of Man."[10]

To accomplish this ambitious undertaking, McGee argued, anthropological scientists must undertake to study *anthropogeny*, the science of human phylogeny—a comparative, taxonomic, and essentially tautological pursuit in which humanity was divided into families, stocks, and races as a framing mechanism to systematically study each race's social and cultural traits through time. The anthropologist as scientist, McGee further claimed, investigated the development of manual dexterity among different races to see how the progressively more refined hand accompanied the development of thought, physical appearance, gesture, and ability to produce tools. The results of these correlations were summarized in a universalizing, hierarchical paradigm characterized by what the different races produced, industrially or socially, or what people did "as human creatures rather than what they merely are as animal beings."[11] McGee thus saw anthropogeny as an advance over strictly biological conceptions of anthropometry as it had been pursued during the nineteenth century. Culture was as critical as biology in understanding evolutionary development. However, because individual culture histories were irrelevant in his theory, different contemporary groups could serve as archetypes or examples of humanity's supposed biocultural development.

Whether speaking in terms of "race-types" or "culture-grades," McGee tried to pigeonhole all of humanity into a universal hierarchical matrix of physical-cultural development, which closely followed Lewis Henry Morgan's evolutionary paradigm of savagery, barbarism, and civilization. McGee inevitably used the Caucasian or white "race-type" as his example of man's highest enlightenment. Because the St. Louis Exposition itself was a manifestation of the products of America's progressive "culture-grade" (i.e., "enlightened civilization"), McGee organized the Ethnology Section as an implicit comparison to the industrial and technological displays—electricity, mechanical engineering—that proclaimed America as the most technologically and intellectually advanced culture in the world. He invited different groups to St. Louis to show Americans how far they, as individual visitors and as a society on the verge of ascending even higher, had come along humanity's evolutionary trajectory.

Native peoples were also selected to serve as examples of exotic and distant pasts, racial types, physical developments, primal social organizations, makers of strange tools, and cultural anomalies. McGee was an ambitious but economical man and wanted to get the most for the corporation's money, or so he argued to the LPE Corporation Board when he asked for funds to stage well-publicized expeditions to bring groups to St. Louis. (McGee had originally asked for one million dollars but was only appropriated forty thousand.) Each Native culture expressed special scientific and racial features, according to McGee, that would be so interesting to scientists that they would race to St. Louis to study them. The Ainus, for example, were desired because McGee felt the group was composed of two subtypes divided on sex lines: the men showed their tree-climbing ancestry through "their small stature, their centripetal (or bodyward) movements, their use of the feet as manual adjuncts, their elongated arms and incurved hands, and their facility in climbing."[12] As a contrast to the small Ainu, McGee felt it was critical to include the Patagonian "giants" (the Tehuelches), whom he held to be heroic in stature. The Cocopas were selected because McGee considered them an anomaly: extremely tall men and short women. The Dakota Sioux were to serve as examples of tallness, powerful body build, and agility, while the Pueblos would represent short stature. Some groups (for example, the Mbuti Pygmies and Negritos) were chosen to represent the world's "least known ethnic types," groups thought to be the "least removed from the sub-human or quadrumane form."[13] McGee sought others whom he considered were developmentally closer to the mentality of the highest human forms, had extraordinary creativity, or were members of races that should be studied systematically by trained scientists before they disappeared in the face of Western imperialism's onslaught.

McGee's scheme was brought to life in a forty-acre outdoor village of in-digenous peoples from seventy-five societies, arranged around an artificial lagoon called Arrowhead Lake. In specially sited compounds, Native men, women, and children resided in "traditional" habitations, which each group built using culturally and environmentally correct materials shipped from their homelands. Here, individuals demonstrated culturally appropriate industries, games, and ceremonies, produced aesthetic products for sale, spoke their native languages, and endured fairgoers. McGee and his staff tried to ensure that taints from American civilization (such as gifts of Western-style cloth-ing from visitors) did not mar the illusion of primitive purity, exoticism, and timelessness. Mirroring the compound layout of the Philippine Reservation across the lake, the Anthropology Colony and Indian Village encampments were arranged so that visitors would first meet the most "primitive" group, the African Pygmies (Mbuti). As they walked up a small hill, visitors saw examples of races sited in McGee's biocultural evolutionary model, until they reached the government's assimilationist Model Indian School on the summit. The contrast continued inside the school: "In order to illustrate the development in the arts," McGee told one reporter, he and Superintendent Samuel Mc-Cowan (the Indian Service agent in charge of the school) had designed the exhibits to "display family groups living in the Stone Age, others just at the beginning of metal working, others engaged in primitive pottery-making and basket-weaving, and so on through to civilization."[14]

Special public programs, designed to both educate and entertain,

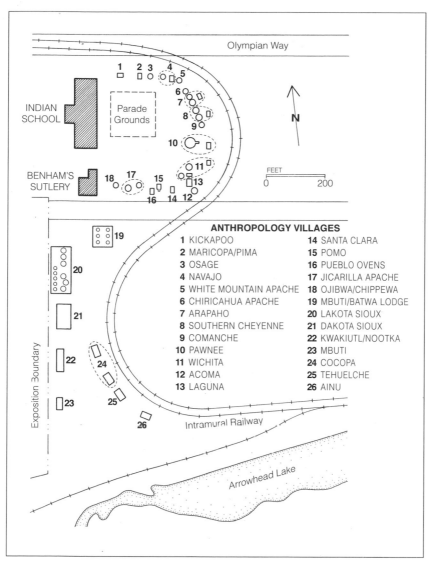

Olympian Way

INDIAN SCHOOL

Parade Grounds

N

BENHAM'S SUTLERY

FEET
0   200

1 KICKAPOO
2 MARICOPA/PIMA
3 OSAGE
4 NAVAJO
5 WHITE MOUNTAIN APACHE
6 CHIRICAHUA APACHE
7 ARAPAHO
8 SOUTHERN CHEYENNE
9 COMANCHE
10 PAWNEE
11 WICHITA
12 ACOMA
13 LAGUNA

ANTHROPOLOGY VILLAGES

14 SANTA CLARA
15 POMO
16 PUEBLO OVENS
17 JICARILLA APACHE
18 OJIBWA/CHIPPEWA
19 MBUTI/BATWA LODGE
20 LAKOTA SIOUX
21 DAKOTA SIOUX
22 KWAKIUTL/NOOTKA
23 MBUTI
24 COCOPA
25 TEHUELCHE
26 AINU

Exposition Boundary

Intramural Railway

Arrowhead Lake

Map 1. Ground plan of the ethnological exhibits and Indian School, with the Mbutis in the bottom slot, #23, and the Model Indian School at the top. Map by Charles Sternberg. Originally published in Parezo and Fowler, *Anthropology Goes to the Fair*, fig. 5.1. Courtesy of Nancy J. Parezo and Don D. Fowler.

67

supplemented the village displays. There were lectures by anthropologists, congresses of scientists, meetings of educated Indians, band concerts by Indian students, dance exhibitions, dramatic presentations, and parades. Some of the most popular special events were athletic contests and demonstrations of physical skills in which Natives competed for prize money. On June 2, for example, there was a special program of field sports held in front of the Indian School in which over one hundred dollars was distributed to indigenous participants: Yellow Hair, head of the Dakota delegation, won a two-dollar first prize and Cherry, a Cocopa, a one-dollar second prize in the archery contest. There were also almost weekly intertribal archery or spear-throwing contests, running races for men and women, tug-of-war competitions, lacrosse games, and timed tipi-raising contests for women. These events were one way Native demonstrators earned money while in St. Louis for, with only a few exceptions, none was given a wage.[15]

Daily there were informal displays of athletic prowess — shinny contests between the Arapahos and Pawnees or exhibitions of bolo throwing from horseback by the Tehuelches, organized by the Natives themselves rather than exposition officials. Visitors' demands for novelty and demonstrators' need to earn money sparked many of these impromptu events. Marksmanship was an area where Native American men excelled as well as had a well-earned reputation, which was unfortunately commented on stereotypically in newspapers. Nickels and quarters provided by visitors became archery targets. Whoever hit the coins, tossed at a distance of about twenty to twenty-five feet, kept them. In other cases, boys from different tribes competed for the visitors' coins; generally a Cocopa youth won these impromptu intertribal competitions. In the name of "authenticity," McGee did not allow marksmanship competitions using firearms, even though most Indian participants were more used to shooting with rifles than bows and arrows by 1900. Every Sunday afternoon impromptu horse races and chicken pulls, lacrosse contests as well as archery, spear hurling, and tipi-raising contests occurred at Cummins' Wild West Show. Indians waged with each other and tourists over the outcome of these popular events (an activity which both McGee and McCowan frowned upon). More formal competitions were also held just for Indians in football, baseball, track, lacrosse, and boxing sponsored by the Indian School and the Department of Physical Culture. On November 26, the Carlisle and Haskell boarding schools played each other for the NCAA football championship in what was billed as the first "Olympic College Football" tournament. Carlisle, under the direction of legendary coach Glen S. "Pop" Warner, won 38 to 4.[16]

Demonstrations of physical fitness were also highlights of the Indian School's official daily programs. Educators held that compulsory physical training was morally uplifting. The Indian Service's Uniform Course of Study stated that "[i]n order to get the best out of life, it is necessary to look into the physical condition of pupils and give them the training that will counteract the influences of unfortunate heredity and strengthen the physique, in order that they may be able to bear the strain that competition in business and earning a living will impose."[17] Every morning the Pima (O'odham) kindergarten class from the Gila River Reservation in Arizona performed callisthenic exercises in the auditorium; every afternoon older students from dozens of tribes performed marching drills or held athletic competitions on the school's parade ground. These were not remunerated events since they were considered part of the required curriculum, but they were extremely popular and students were often discreetly given tips. Of special interest to visitors was the girls' basketball team from Fort Shaw, which performed several times a week in competitions, exhibitions of skills, and practice drills.[18] They always attracted large crowds wherever they played.

Athletic competitions and displays of physical dexterity were entertaining and drew the crowds that justified the Anthropology Department's expenses, but McGee hoped they would be sites where new scientific knowledge could be generated. In many ways, the Anthropology Villages, the Philippine Reservation, The Pike, and the Indian School constituted a research laboratory, and events were designed to reinforce anthropology's assertion that its professional knowledge was based on rigorous scientific research. McGee claimed that since the exposition comprised a more complete assembly of the world's peoples than had ever before been brought together, it was proper and desirable that "this assembling of races and peoples will be utilized in systematic studies of both the physical and mental characteristics of mankind."[19] As a result, an active research agenda was planned to be an integral part of the Anthropology Department.

The sections of anthropometry and psychometry, located in the basement of the anthropology building (Cupples Hall on the campus of Washington University), were established as an interactive exhibit to compare the physical and mental characteristics of individual races, including visitors, using the popular instruments to measure biodiversity. The goal was basically evolutionary: to create "records of the types of mankind assembled on the Exposition grounds . . . —i.e., such impressions as those of the passing throng are so tabulated and arranged as to afford a means of tracing with scientific accuracy the physical as well as the intellectual development of mankind."[20] In addition to having a memorable experience and helping advance scientific knowledge, visitors would better understand how pure and applied science operated. Euro-American participants would also gain new understandings from their service as research subjects; they would see how individuals functioned as organisms and how their physiologies, minds, and anatomies (critical human attributes and features of McGee's anthropogenic theory) had advanced over other races. Scientifically obtained information would help visitors ultimately understand the value of anthropogeny as well as their place in the course of human development.

Ashley Montague has defined anthropometry as "the technique of expressing quantitatively the form of the body. . . . It consists primarily in the measurement of dimensions of the body."[21] The science of anthropometry or biometric ethnology—the attempt to statistically discern racial and individual differences in body proportions, body shape, or form and to discern why these differences occur—was well established and highly popular in

1900. It was used to try to identify criminals, women who would make good wives, good athletes, and potential artists or geniuses. It was highly influential in the development of racial taxonomies and a cornerstone in evolutionary models in several fields (criminology, psychology, sociology, anatomy, physiology, and anthropology). It required pattern recognition, the quest to make observations quantitatively meaningful and rigorously consistent, and the belief that races existed and that the physical differences between races were discrete and meaningful.

By 1900 there were detractors who were questioning the central premises of anthropometry: whether "races" were psychologically, socially, or culturally commensurable and how this commensurability, or lack thereof, could be demonstrated scientifically without statistical error. The real issues, of course, had to do with apologies for, and campaigns against, slavery, the subjugation of colonized populations (including Native Americans), the internal sociopolitical structures of the recently freed colonies of Spain—and whether indigenous races were ready for self-government—and internal issues of social class, cast in racialist terms in France, Germany, Great Britain and the United States.[22]

Wanting to pursue impeccable science, McGee was concerned with the quality of previous anthropometric research, which used faulty research designs and reached spurious conclusions. He strove to ensure that past methodological errors would not be duplicated. The department's comparisons between Natives and Euro-American visitors (i.e., "primitives" and "advanced men") would be valid, he argued, because all the individuals tested would involve "average" representatives of their groups, thereby making a consistent comparison. He held that the numbers to be tested would be large, lending reliability to the conclusions reached and avoiding small-sample-size errors.[23] While these were admirable goals, McGee was wrong in his contentions with respect to the tests conducted under the guise of the "Special Olympics."

Psychologist Robert S. Woodworth, an assistant professor at Columbia

University, and his graduate student, Frank G. Bruner, were hired to organize and run the section on the recommendation of Dr. Aleš Hrdlička, curator of physical anthropology at the Smithsonian Institution, Dr. James McKeen Cattell, head of the Department of Psychology at Columbia University, and Dr. Franz Boas, who had organized a similar laboratory at the 1893 Chicago World's Columbian Exposition. Since 1896 Boas had taught a course in statistics applied to anthropometry (a general introduction to variation) as well as physical anthropology (including morphology) at Columbia University.[24] For commensurability and a more controlled comparison, McGee requested that Woodworth and Bruner use the same measures Professor W. H. R. Rivers of Cambridge University, England, was using on Torres Strait Natives as well as those they chose to develop for themselves. Woodworth was interested in motor control, physiology, mind-body relationships, and the development of quantitative experiments. He spent several weeks testing and measuring immigrants in New York City to ensure that the procedures would work. Such pilot studies were key to this type of experimentation to ensure properly consistent measurements.[25]

Beginning on May 16, Woodworth and Bruner entertained crowds of visitors, usually between one thousand and three thousand per day, taking measurements on stature and weight, rates of respiration and pulse, memory, feet shape, color blindness, the acuteness of senses, and reaction times on willing volunteers. Quickly they accumulated data on over two hundred middle-class white adults that they used as a baseline for comparisons with other races and ethnic groups. Subjects were given a copy of the results as a souvenir of the experience. Over twenty-five thousand visitors watched the experiments weekly in June.[26]

In late June Woodworth and Bruner began to systematically measure Native demonstrators starting with those who were directly associated with the Department of Anthropology: American Indians (e.g., Maricopas, O'odhams, Lakotas), Ainus, Mbuti Pygmies, Batateles, Bakubas, Batwas, Badingas, Cocopas, Kwakiutl-Nootkas, and Tehuelches, followed by the Indian School students. In order to assure measurement consistency and eliminate researcher subjectivity or observational bias, each subject was measured twice on each test and Aleš Hrdlička later replicated a sample. The first two groups, the Cocopas and the Kwakiutl, were completed by July 20. The results were given to the press who reported: "[A]after a series of mysterious experiments it was found that the Cocopa exceeds in strength and the Alaskan in intelligence."[27] In all, they tested almost nine hundred Natives, although work with some groups was slow and in a few cases nonexistent. Few Cheyennes or Chippewas agreed to submit to the tests. Meanwhile, Charles Carpenter of the Field Museum photographed Natives standing still and in movement to record body shape—what I call anthropological mug shots.

Some of these tests involved fairly simple, standard physical measurements. For example, to measure height the subject stood on the floor barefoot with heels placed together. A Tiermann vertical measuring rod was placed behind him with the rod touching the heels, calves, buttocks, shoulders, and backs of the head. To measure height while sitting, the subject sat in a straight-backed chair with the buttocks and back pushed against the base of the upright rod. Chest measurements were a bit more complicated: To measure chest breadth a Narragansett shoulder caliper was used to record the distance between the nipples during the extremes of gentle inhaling and exhaling, then the two numbers were averaged to form a mean. Chest depth was measured the same way with the calipers placed on the front and back of the chest. Other tests included vision, hearing, muscular strength, speed, and accuracy.

Many of these physical and anatomical measurements were proxies for mental ability. For example, color recognition (color blindness and the ability to recognize and name colors or shades) was considered a critical sign of mental progress. For example, Woodworth wanted to answer the question of whether dark-skinned peoples or "primitive" races were especially different from whites or "advanced" races in their recognition of the color blue. He ultimately concluded that there was no difference in color recognition based on race, thereby refuting a commonly held assumption of his day. McGee held that these comparisons of "primitive and advanced" people were the exhibition's most substantial contribution to humanity. "It was in this branch of the Department," McGee said, "that the original or investigative work of the Exposition culminated and the conduct of the work was a constant source of interest and attraction to visitors while its results form a substantial contribution to knowledge."[28] How lasting it was is questionable, however. Most were never published, although Bruner used the auditory data for his dissertation and Woodworth used one of his conclusions about race in his vice-presidential address for the American Association for the Advancement of Science in 1909.[29]

One area in which McGee hoped anthropometric experiments might be used to generate "scientific" laws was comparisons of Native men to Caucasian male athletes trained in Western-style competitions. Woodworth, however, was skeptical because this required one to assume that the athletes were representative of all Caucasians and that the small number of Natives could stand for a racial population. Hoping that he was addressing Galton's problem, McGee held that comparisons between Natives and Euro-American athletes (i.e., "primitives" and "advanced men") were valid because all individuals tested would involve "average" representatives of their groups, thereby making a valid comparison (i.e. comparing apples to apples, not apples to oranges).[30] For James E. Sullivan, the head of the Department of Physical Culture, who had a vested interest in insuring that trained Caucasian Americans won athletic contests, such tests were very important. In fact, the athletic tests were his idea, not McGee's, as has been assumed in the sports science, anthropology, and popular literature.

The Department of Physical Culture and the Olympics

Athletic events were serious business and major features of the LPE, not only for the Anthropology Department. The LPEC Board thought that athletic events would be inexpensive attractions and generate free publicity.[31] The human body was on display as much as the human mind and both were measured for evidence of advancement. Sport was also seen as a way to advance the American republic and meld immigrant peoples into a single body politic. As historian Mark Dyreson has insightfully noted, "Many Americans came to see sport as a powerful reform instrument that could revitalize their rapidly modernizing nation. Intellectuals espoused ideas that mixed sport into the struggles between classes, races, ethnic groups, and genders."[32] Physical fitness was seen as a prime mechanism to improve the moral and mental condition of Euro-Americans as they entered the twentieth century. A trim body and good endurance were the enemies of illness and laziness; athletic competitions celebrated the healthy human body and "the national culture of strenuous living."[33] The development of the human body was also an important component of Social Darwinian theories and schemes of cultural progress reflected in public opinion and policies. If progress meant obtaining better health through a fit body, LPE organizers wanted to demonstrate that Americans were the fittest people in the world. By extending this logic, they claimed that Americans were the most progressive people, naturally selected and poised for future greatness (i.e., "survival of the fittest"). It was almost inevitable that ideas about primitive peoples, assimilation, the value of modern education, and progress would be expressed through a Department of Physical Culture.

An important and popular division of the St. Louis Exposition was the Physical Culture Department, under James E. Sullivan's direction. Sullivan was a former athlete, who had won many trophies for running, and was a professional sports writer, editor, and publisher. A self-taught Irish immigrant, he had worked his way up the social ladder, been instrumental in the development of the formal organization of American sports since the 1880s, was a founder of the Amateur Athletic Union, and had served as president of the Pastime Athletic Club in New York City and vice president of the National Association of Amateur Athletics of America. He was, apparently, extremely ambitious, powerful, arrogant, influential, and a superb self-promoter and meticulous organizer. By 1900, from his position as the editor of the official *Athletic Almanac* and chair of the records committee, he virtually controlled all championship competitions and their records. LPE publicists stated, probably without exaggeration, that Sullivan had "managed more athletic meetings than any other man in America."[34] He was the nation's "acknowledged authority on athletics and the preferred referee at nearly all the important athletic meets in this country."[35] He was in a position to implement programs to make his vision of an America as home to healthy bodies and minds a reality. Sullivan also had considerable experience organizing athletic competitions at international expositions, having worked in the U.S. pavilion and been a delegate to the second Olympics held in conjunction with the 1900 Paris Exposition and served as the director of athletics at the 1901 Pan-American Exposition in Buffalo, New York.[36] Sullivan wanted Americans to be healthy and the world to know that American methods of scientific training produced the best athletes in the world.

One purpose of Sullivan's Physical Culture Department was to exploit scientific physical training and demonstrate the progress Americans had made in attaining better health through sport. To reveal that there was a rational, scientific basis to his assertions, Sullivan convened a committee of like-minded scholars, reformers, and activists who developed a wealth of exhibits (photographs, charts, diagrams, catalogues, circulars, text books, and programs) that told the story of how man as an athlete could be trained.[37] He also obtained the newest gymnastic and anthropometric equipment and established laboratories to measure athletic ability and visitors' physical fitness. Located behind the physical culture building, next to the Anthropology Department on Washington University's campus, was a new gymnasium, a model schoolroom, and a model playground. There was also a large stadium for track and field events that could seat ten thousand with enough space for equestrian polo, football, and baseball competitions as well as a one-third-mile track.

The physical training section revolved around an elaborate demonstration program using American, German, and Swedish techniques, with a special section on military training. Authorities spoke on physical training and the human body as part of a World's Olympics Lecture Course that carried college credit. Topics included the history of physical training, psychological and social aspects of physical training, dancing for schools, physiology of exercise, theory and practice of school games, the influence of "manly" sports on people, and adaptation of physical exercise to the conditions of modern life. Several men lectured on anthropological topics: Paul C. Philips, of Amherst College, spoke on "Anthropometric Methods"; G. Stanley Hall, president of Clark University and an eminent psychologist, discussed "Health as Related to Civilization"; Luther H. Gulick, a Brooklyn physician and director of New York City's public school educational program, theorized about "Athletics and Social Evolution"; and McGee presented his evolutionary ideas in a lecture entitled, "The Influence of Play in Racial Development, with Special Reference to Muscular Movement." Each lecturer gave popular as well as scholarly talks. In July and August the department hosted a series of physical training and educational conventions, including those of university and public-school physical educators. Several scientists conducted experiments on visitors and athletes.[38]

To the general public, however, the department's main raison d'être was to hold professional and amateur athletic competitions. Sullivan strove to have all known sports represented. Over ninety-five hundred athletes competed in four hundred separate events between May 14 and November 19: secondary school and college meets, competitions for seniors and handicapped individuals, an amateur baseball tournament, the world fencing championship, a golf tournament, lacrosse, bicycling, and lawn tennis contests, and college football games. There were also Gaelic football, quoits, skittles, lawn tennis, and equestrian polo. The most popular events were the gymnastic exhibitions, which drew hundreds of participants and tens of thousands of spectators; the least popular was roque (croquet played on a hard surface), with only three participants, and a mere hundred spectators. But while these events were important, the quest to glorify the fit male body was ultimately accomplished by "holding the greatest athletic tournament known to history and the most extended exposition of the science of physical culture that has ever been made" — the Olympics.[39]

The official Olympic Games lasted one week, from August 29 to September 3. Events were open to amateur athletes who could pay the two-dollar general entrance fee and fifty cents per event. The program had been expanded from the previous Olympics in Athens and Paris. In addition to the official events (running, jumping, weightlifting, steeplechase, pole vaults, wrestling, swimming, shot put, hurdles, gymnastics, and the marathon race) there were myriad demonstrations (boxing, dumbbells, and basketball). There was an international tug-of-war won by the Milwaukee Amateur Club team, and one official demonstration event for women, archery. To be designated an Olympic event, the contest had to be open only to amateurs and include foreign participants. Despite these restrictions Sullivan referred to almost every athletic competition held at the fair as an Olympic event, creating a great deal of confusion. Many of his "Olympic" competitions were never officially approved, although he did convince the International Olympic Committee IOC to designate eighty competitions as official Olympic contests. Several events simultaneously served as U.S. championships.

Over four thousand individual entrants, whom exposition officials modestly declared were the "greatest athletes in the world," participated. Of the 687 competitors in the official Olympic events, 525 were American and 41 Canadians; most European countries and individual foreign athletic clubs did not send delegations. France pretended the games did not exist and Russia, Japan, and Great Britain declined because they were at war. Most foreign athletes paid their own way, and some countries refused to allow their citizens to participate in "barbaric" sports. As one participant remembered, "The Olympics didn't amount to much then. They were only a little tiny part of the big show in St. Louis. There was not much of international flavor to the Games. It was largely a meet between American athletic clubs. I ran for the Milwaukee A. C. and I never gave any real thought to the idea that I was representing the United States of America."[40]

5. George Poage, representing the Milwaukee Athletic Club, wins the bronze medal in the 200-meter hurdles. Poage became the first black person to win an Olympic medal when he won the bronze in the earlier 400-meter hurdles. He also led the final of the 400 meters until fading in the stretch. From Bennitt and Stockbridge, eds., *History of the Louisiana Purchase Exposition*, 567.

While it was a decidedly North American, Caucasian, and male affair—basically a rivalry between Eastern and Western athletic clubs according to the press—there were memorable moments from the standpoint of racial participation. Black and Native American men officially competed for the first time in Olympic competitions. Two "Zulu" men, members of the Boer War Spectacular concession, Len Tau ("Lentauw") and Jan Mashiani ("Yamasani") ran in the marathon. Both had been dispatch runners for the Boer leaders during the Boer War. They did well—Len Tau finished ninth, running barefoot, and Jan Mashiani twelfth—after a series of incidents including being chased well off the course by two dogs early in the race. George Poage of Milwaukee won a bronze medal in the 400-meter hurdles, the first black to win an individual Olympic medal. The first American Indian, Frank Pierce (whose tribal affiliation is not recorded but was Comanche), worked for the Wild West show and is pictured in *Spalding's Official Athletic Almanac* wearing number nine in the marathon, a first unfortunately not listed in any Olympic history.[41]

The IOC basically washed their hands of the entire affair. Pierre de Coubertin refused to attend, feeling politics had tainted the entire affair. The Olympics, he predicted, would be a financial disaster, little more than an exposition sideshow. This left Sullivan with a free hand to organize the events and create novel events — such as what he termed a "Special Olympics" — and use the games for research projects.[42]

Sullivan had a less-publicized agenda for the Department of Physical Culture. Like McGee, he hoped the LPE would be the site for the generation of new knowledge, hopefully insights that supported his theories on physical training, as well as the locale where he could further generate the societal authority needed to promote his new professional field. The early twentieth century was a period of experimentation in sports science, just as it was in anthropology. Researchers sought to learn how biological traits and physical morphology could be influenced by physical education. They were beginning to ask: What makes a successful athlete? Was it physiology and natural endowments, biomechanical features, or skills traits? How did sports differ? What is an ideal body shape for a particular sport? How did physical fitness and optimizing training influence performance? Was race a factor? From simple studies that correlated weight, height, age, or somatotypes to performance, to more complex multivariate correlations with evolutionary implications, scholars involved in sports tried to find answers to these elusive questions that are still being addressed today.[43]

Sullivan's scientific experiments had two purposes: to identify which types of training and which drugs and stimulants would enhance performance. All athletes were apparently asked to undergo anthropometric testing and extensive records were apparently taken on performance, although I have not located them to date. To test his more radical ideas Sullivan and several personal trainers chose the marathon, the most grueling race of the competition, assuming that the results could be extended to less strenuous races. The marathon thus serves as an excellent (and infamous) example of Sullivan's combination of flawed science and dubious comparisons that contextualize

6. Start of the 1904 Olympic Marathon. Frank Pierce, a Comanche representing the New York Pastime Athletic Club, wears number nine. From Bennitt and Stockbridge, eds., *History of the Louisiana Purchase Exposition*, 565.

the "Special Olympics." Sullivan's ideas to test indigenous athletes pale in comparison to those conducted on Caucasian athletes.

The marathon was run on a hot, humid August day, beginning in mid-afternoon. Thirty-two men began and fourteen finished the grueling 24.85-mile course in oppressive ninety-degree heat and humidity over dusty, uneven, hilly roads. Sullivan provided only one official water-stop to minimize fluid intake to test how far purposeful dehydration could be taken, a common practice as well as research question at the time. The marathon was a test of the athletes' wills because of the track conditions.[44] At the start of the race a dozen men on horseback raced over the course to clear it of spectators, raising a cloud of dust. Next came a dozen official automobiles traveling in front of the runners while personal trainers, physicians, nurses, and scientists rode in cars, essentially surrounding each runner. There were actually more cars producing noxious fumes on the course than runners and one man almost died of asphyxiation. According to one reporter, "The roads were so lined with vehicles that the runners had to constantly dodge the horses and wagons. So dense were the dust clouds on the road that frequently the runners could not be seen by the automobiles following them."[45] William Garcia was rushed to the hospital halfway through the race with severe cramps; he had ingested so much dust that it had ripped his stomach lining. Luckily emergency surgery saved his life. The streets and roads were also busy with cross-town traffic, delivery wagons, railroad trains, trolley cars, and men walking their dogs. Reports make it sound as if the race should have been classified as a steeplechase.

Research subject Thomas Hicks ran a good race, leading for the first fifteen miles. When he showed signs of collapse his personal trainer, Hugh McGarth, gave him "assistance" that almost killed him. Like Sullivan, McGarth believed that drinking water hindered performance. He denied Hicks water but at milepost seventeen gave him a grain of strychnine sulfate and an egg white. At mile twenty, he gave Hicks another dose of strychnine sulfate, two egg whites, and a sip of French brandy. McGarth administered a shot of brandy and two egg whites when Hicks entered the stadium after three and a half hours of running. Denied water, except for being sponged in hot water heated by a car radiator, the dehydrated Hicks lost eight pounds. He was so weak and dazed that he had to be held up by two men to cross the finish line. Exhausted, he wandered around the stadium in a stupor; he was rushed off to bed without receiving his trophy. Sullivan wisely concluded that strychnine sulfate did not enhance performance, but was not ready to admit that dehydration could be a significant factor in the slow performance.[46]

The marathon was the last and most controversial scientific experiment undertaken by the Department of Physical Culture. Sullivan saw the athletic competitions as an excellent venue to test theories about fitness and the benefit of physical training. Most experiments listed in Sullivan's reports appear to be fairly harmless (i.e., not life-threatening) and involved measuring athletic endurance under different conditions or evaluating the equipment effectiveness or training techniques through descriptive performance records and semistandardized observations. As dubious as the marathon, however, but for different reasons, was the series of bizarre experiments called the Special Olympics or Anthropology Days.

Are Natives Really Natural Athletes?

This brings us to two critical questions: Why test Native peoples' athletic abilities? And how did those three thousand Native demonstrators fit into

Sullivan's research, social, and political agenda? As John Bale discusses in his chapter, the idea of the natural athlete and his association with primitive man had a long association in European thought. Sullivan absolutely believed that Caucasians were the best natural as well as the best-trained athletes in the world. Whites (especially those of Northern European heritage) were the superior race and America, because of its racial heritage, was a peerless culture, which would only progress further if it adopted his programs. But since the days of exploration there had been accounts of remarkable physical abilities of indigenous peoples. Sullivan had noticed what he called "numerous disturbing statements" made by the press about the speed, stamina, and strength of the Native peoples participating in the exposition. One newspaper report stated that the Cocopas were superb swimmers, while another held that Patagonian "horsemen of the plains are . . . nearer living Centaurs than any other riders on the earth."[47] Sullivan wanted to know if the heralded presumptions of Indians' "marvelous endurance" as long-distance runners, the stamina of black South Africans, the Filipinos' remarkable climbing and diving feats, the agility and muscular strength of the "giant Patagonians," and the natural all-around physical abilities of "savage" peoples—as asserted in McGee's and the exposition's extensive publicity—were true.[48] If they were valid and could be proven, these public assertions, read by all fairgoers, could undermine Sullivan's entire philosophy and social agenda as well as make the purpose of his department suspect.

Sullivan called these assertions "startling rumors" in letters and his final LPEC departmental report and he thought they should be scientifically tested.[49] What better place than the LPE—where an extensive array of scientific experiments was already underway as part of "the exposition university" and where McGee claimed he had gathered all the races of the world—to put these "rumors" to rest once and for all? The proposed direct correlation between race and athletic ability could be tested without the contestants even realizing that they were being studied, thereby guaranteeing that the investigations were not unintentionally "biased." Sullivan suggested a "Special Olympics"—a term he coined to distinguish these contests from the real Olympics — to accompany and promote the regular Olympic competition. The event would be held in the track stadium in July or August so that "many physical directors and gentlemen interested in scientific work could be present and benefit by the demonstrations."[50] In addition, Sullivan saw the proposed research competition as a way to counter the flagging interest in the real Olympic Games (i.e., sell more tickets). To Sullivan, a Special Olympics for Native peoples would ensure good publicity for the real events.

Sullivan wrote to McGee and suggested a jointly sponsored event. He told McGee that the assertion to be tested was that "primitive" people had extraordinary physical abilities because they led lives that demanded a high level of physical performance.[51] McGee liked the idea that environment affected physical development because it fit into his evolutionary theories, but he hoped to prove that "lower races" had natural abilities that, through assimilation, could be improved. McGee and Woodworth had been searching for more efficient ways to test several hypotheses about the comparative strength and endurance of different races. Sampling had become an issue because they had trouble obtaining permission from many Native peoples, like the Ojibwes and Osages, who refused to be measured for the anthropometry and psychometry tests. Most Moros, Visayans, and Cocopas also refused to be photographed. Except for two individuals, the Negritos refused to climb trees in their bare feet simply to see how long it would take or to measure the shape of their feet before they were given shoes when winter weather came. Several experiments had bogged down, partly because the researchers were undertaking too many at once, and Woodworth informed McGee that he did not think he could finish by November, potentially negating all their hard work. He suggested that some anthropometry experiments be redesigned. Instead of continuing with the unrealistic full suite of tests, McGee and Woodworth decided to concentrate on strength, speed, and stamina using Sullivan's proposed special competitions.[52]

McGee readily agreed to the proposition and Sullivan named the event

"Anthropology Days" in honor of McGee, who, Sullivan later recalled, "[u]sed his influence toward making the days the brilliant success which they terminated in."[53] McGee began to search for participants. He informed his special agents that the object of the contests would be "to obtain for the first time what may be called interracial athletic records."[54] Scientific "evidence" would be used to test "common beliefs" about naturally athletic "primitive" man. McGee's letter to Dr. W. P. Wilson, chair of the Philippine Exposition Board, is fairly typical of his numerous requests for assistance.

> Doctor J. E. Sullivan, Chief of Physical Culture, suggests a general Anthropology Day in his stadium July 8 for athletic contests open to the world, barring Americans and Europeans, with the understanding that the events will be determined by the customs of the respective peoples participating, and the further understanding that so many winners in these events as may desire may participate in finals open to all the world on the day following; professionals to be barred on both days. . . . I think Doctor Sullivan's plan an excellent one, and hope that you, Mr. McCowan, and the leading concessionaires on The Pike will cooperate. I am proposing to cooperate through my alien peoples from outside the United States; yet the program cannot be made a success without your support and that of Mr. McCowan and the entry of our Filipinos and Indians.[55]

McGee never directly asked any Native man if he wanted to participate; he worked exclusively through agents. While expedient from a hierarchical and organizational standpoint, it was not very courteous when viewed from Native standards of etiquette. McGee assumed that if the Caucasian in charge of a group told Native men to participate, they would. He was wrong.

Arranging for participants in this way was actually laborious and ineffective as well as discourteous. It yielded meager results. On June 28, McGee wrote again to Wilson.

> You may recall a letter from me, written at the instance of Doctor J. E. Sullivan some weeks ago, asking your pleasure as to participating in a general

*athletic competition among non-Caucasian peoples in the Stadium. . . . On
that writing your plans were not sufficiently mature to permit a decision
as to whether you would participate. My feeling is that if you decide to
participate the feature will be a success; but that if your decision is negative
it would hardly be worth while for the rest of us to proceed. Since the time
for arranging the program approaches I should be glad to have you advise
me informally of your pleasure, when the matter may come up formally
in the department and elsewhere.*[56]

When Wilson agreed to the proposed athletic events, McGee informed the
world in the *World's Fair Bulletin*. The test competitions had changed from those
proposed in his initial correspondence. Gone were Native-chosen sports. Now
the contests were modeled on Olympic protocols and theoretically designed
as tests of strength and endurance. Taken together, they would measure "the
relative physical value of the different races of people," as a proxy for the
department's anthropometry experiments. "Pretests" would be conducted
during July in various locales under the guise of tree-climbing exhibitions,
archery contests, and running races. The goal, McGee assured his readers,
was to "cover the widest possible range in physical development as well as
in ethnic affinity."[57] And they did. Woodworth and an assistant, whom I have
been unable to identify, kept records on body measurements and performance
at every possible event to see if any variable could be correlated directly with
race.[58] Sullivan had corresponding measurements taken of "typical" Euro-
American athletes preparing for the Olympic Games or participating in other
athletic contexts, probably without their knowledge as to the real goal of the
research, in order, again, not to bias the results.

Ascertaining how many Native people actually competed in trials and the
actual events is difficult because no complete participant lists have survived
and no LPEC reports record any numerical figures. There are some incom-
plete lists, however. Native demonstrators working for the Anthropology
Department, several foreign pavilions, the Philippine Reservation, the Indian

86

School, and The Pike concessions participated in the trials and the top three contestants were asked to participate in the Anthropology Days competition, whose results would be recorded as the *official* comparisons to white athletes. But many Natives, including a fair number of the American Indians, who had participated in the trials now refused to be in the "real" event because they were not to be paid, as they had been for other athletic competitions and entertainment events, including the trials. Others refused because they did not understand what was expected of them. To help convince more Natives to participate and simultaneously demonstrate the superiority of American sports, Natives were "allowed" to watch Olympic trials not held in the stadium. They saw American Caucasian athletes jump, race, lift weights, and swim. McGee hoped Natives would gain an idea of what would be expected of them. Unfortunately no one explained any contest rules, nor were Natives given a chance to practice. After watching the swimming trials, everyone except the Samal Moros refused to even consider a proposed swimming race. Aquatic events became highly unlikely.

Anthropology Days

Flyers around the fairgrounds billed Anthropology Days as the first world's athletic competition in which Native peoples were the exclusive participants. As a result of the persuasive abilities of McGee and his agents, the Native men listed in tables 1 and 2, and unnamed others, assembled at the stadium on the morning of August 11 for the trial heats of the Anthropology Days.[59] Other Natives staged dance competitions, sang, or performed dramatic reenactments between the races. McGee stated in his final report to the LPEC that most of the Native peoples participated freely but this statement is highly suspect. He obviously convinced some foreign Natives under his direct supervision but not many of the American Indians and certainly only a small percentage of the Filipinos. He never provided exact figures or stated how these men were convinced to become unpaid athletes and unknowing research subjects. Nor did he report that several Indian groups, most noticeably the Arapahos

Table 1. Partial list of Native participants in Anthropology Days

Group	Participant
African Mbuti/Pygmies	Shamba, Prince Latuna, Lumbango, Kondola, Malengu, Lumo, Ota Benga
African Bantu	Bomashubba, Latuna, Lumbango, Shamba
Ainu	Kutoroze, Goro, Osawa, Sangea
Cherokee	George Rye
Chippewa	Poitre
Cocopa	Artukero, Chingan Sacup, Skik, Chief Pablo Colorado, Cherry, Chizi, Nethab, Ilpuk
Crow	Black White-bear
Filipinos	Somdud, Mande Cochero (Samal Moro); Samindud, Timon, Lanao (Moro); Lanale, Teman, Samdude (Lanal Moro); Basilio, Sayas (Negrito); Basilio (Igorot)
Lakota and Dakota Sioux	William Dietz, George Mentz, Simon Max, Mr. Warrior
Pawnee	Frank Moore, Tom Moore, and unnamed man
Pueblos: Santa Clara	Simon, Aniseto Suaz, Vincenta Suaz, Simon Marks
River Rock Lakota	DePoe
Syrians	J. Hana, Yousouf Hana, Maroof Zaytoun
Tehuelche	Bonifacio, Casimiro, Colojo, Sinshek, Guechico
Tswana	Len Tau

and Wichitas, had recently left or that several special agents had previously informed him that many people refused because they would not be paid or given prize money or tips. As amateur events, Sullivan had insisted that monetary remuneration not be given in order to adhere to Olympic guidelines. For those Natives who considered the Special Olympics simply another athletic performance, not being given money or some form of reciprocity for their time and effort meant that they would not consider participating.

None of the native participants had had any experience in Olympic-style field sports, nor did many understand what was expected of them. Nor apparently did most of the "officials" and "referees." McGee assigned Stephen C. Simms, assistant curator of anthropology at Chicago's Field Columbian Museum of Natural History, to organize, decide on appropriate events, oversee, and run the program with only a week's warning. Simms actually arrived from Chicago two days before the event and found the conditions in the Indian

Village and Anthropology Villages in disarray because of the poor sanitation conditions. Anthropology Days, on top of everything else, made Simms so upset that he threatened to go back to Chicago.[60]

Not having been involved in the trials or the research planning, Simms looked over the list of scheduled events and began to eliminate those he felt were ludicrous. He removed swimming because he felt that many people (Native and non-Native) did not know how to swim, even before he learned that only the Samal Moros had agreed to participate. Simms also felt that competitive swimming, like tennis and water polo, required special training, which the Native participants did not have, so any comparison to Caucasians would be spurious. He thought the same was true for tennis and most forms of weightlifting. (Sullivan, however, insisted there be at least one strength test.) Relay races should not be included because Sullivan insisted most events had to be based solely on individual performance measures. (The only exception was the tug-of-war, a team sport.) Simms concurred but for different reasons.[61]

Sullivan, however, insisted on the running relay races. He considered running to be the ideal competitive sport. Everyone runs and everyone could run by himself in individual events. Sullivan also felt that running was a particularly important event given the representations of Indians as fleet-footed. Simms agreed because he thought there was a good chance that all Natives knew how to run; it was a universal human activity. Five of the Special Olympic events, and those with the largest number of heats, were individual foot races.

Dr. Luther H. Gulick served as referee. Gulick (1865–1918), the son of a Protestant missionary to Japan, was the nation's foremost authority on physical education and children's play.[62] He believed that organized physical education had the same "uplifting" relation to the body as religious education did to the soul and that proper training in team sports would help young men control their emotions. Dr. Martin Delaney of St. Louis University, demonstrated the basics once before the start of each event and explained the procedures,

Table 2. Anthropology Days results for August 12

Competition[a]	Participants and Placement			
Event	Winner (Time)	Second	Third	Fourth
Running: 100-yard	George Mentz, Sioux (11⁴/₅s)	Artukero, Cocopa (13s)	Bonifacio, Tehuelche (13³/₅s)	Shamba, Mbuti (14³/₅s)
Running: 100-meter	George Mentz, Sioux (11s)	Samdude, Lanal	Frank Moore, Pawnee	
Running: 440-yard	George Rye, Cherokee (63s)	Yousouf Hana, Syrian (1m,6s)	Artukero, Cocopa (1m, 6s)	Kondola, African (1m, 10s)
Running: 120-yard hurdles	George Mentz, Sioux	Tom Moore, Pawnee	Poitre, Chippewa	Samdude, Lanal Moro
Running: one mile	Black White-bear, Crow (5m, 38s)	Yousouf Hana, Syrian	Len Tau, Tswana	
Running broad jump	George Mentz, Sioux (17ft)	Frank Moore, Pawnee (15ft, 6in)	Poitre, Chippewa (15ft, 3in)	Mande Cochero, Samal (15ft)
Shot Put	William Dietz, Rosebud Sioux (33ft, 10in)	Poitre, Chippewa (33ft, 10in)	Black White-bear, Crow (32ft, 10in)	Casimiro, Tehuelche (30ft, 5in)
Baseball Throw: distance	Poitre, Chippewa (266ft)	W. Dietz, Sioux (260ft)	De Poe, River Rock (251ft)	George Mentz, Sioux (239ft)

Event				
Baseball Throw: accuracy	Chief Guechico, Tehuelche	Tom Moore, Pawnee		
Weight Throwing	George Mentz, Sioux (15ft, 11in)	Black White-bear, Crow (15ft, 9in)	DePoe, Rock River Lakota (14ft, 6in)	Frank Moore, Pawnee (14ft, 6in)
Running High Jump	George Mentz, Sioux (47ft, 7in)	Black White-bear, Pawnee	Poitre, Chippewa	
Archery	Skik, Cocopa	Sangea, Ainu	Shamba, Mbuti	
Tug-of-war	Tehuelche	Asians		
Pole Climbing: 50 feet	Basilio, Igorot (20s)	Bornashubba, African (39s)	Sayas, Negrito (42s)	Timon, Moro (52s)
Bola Throwing	Colojo, Tehuelche	Borifacio, Tehuelche	Casimiro, Tehuelche	
Javelin	Teman, Lanal	Shamba, Mbuti	Kutoroze, Ainu	

[a]The heats in the 100-yard run and the order of their finish were (1) Africans: Shamba, Prince Latuna, Lumbango; (2) Moros: Somdud, Samal tribe; (3) Patagonians: Bonifacio, Casimiro, Colojo; (4) Syrians: Yousouf Hana, Maroof Zaytoun; (5) Cocopas: Artukero, Chingan Sacup, Skik; (6) Indians: George Mentz, Frank Moore, unnamed Pawnee.

[Table reproduces names and tribes as they appeared in original sources.]

scoring, and rules in English. Unfortunately, this was done without interpreters. Simms later told McGee that many participants wanted to rerun heats once they understood the rules; for others, the goals of the competitions and what was expected of them remained elusive. Gulick did not allow reruns because it would have "violated" the research design, that is, the established rules for track meets, and invalidated the racial comparisons. Since the white athletes had only one chance to perform, so should Natives. In addition, the stadium was booked for only two days. There was no time.[63]

After each event had been "explained," heats were held in which members of each "race" competed amongst themselves to determine the fastest African, Indian, Filipino, or Asian, with an "other race" category thrown in for good measure. Winners were then asked to compete against each other in the finals on the second day to determine the fastest "primitive." It was this winning time that Sullivan intended to compare to the Olympic winners' performances. At 1:00 p.m., Tehuelches, Indians, Cocopas, Moros, Negritos, Ainus, Mbutis, and "Zulus" ran six separate heats in the 100-yard dash. Sullivan noted in his final report that while everyone knew how to run, none of the men had ever tried sprint racing before. "With eight or ten men on the mark it was a pretty hard thing to explain to them to run when the pistol was fired. In running their heats, when coming to the finish tape, instead of breasting it or running through it, many would stop [to wait for friends] and others run under it."[64] Cooperation was more important than "victory." Anyone who disregarded any rule was eliminated until it was discovered there would not be enough participants for the second day. Apparently to Sullivan, such behavior meant not following his rules, which from his standpoint was not permissible and a sign of mental weakness not to be encouraged. Sullivan never understood that waiting for friends was a sign of graciousness and a symbol of respect in many cultures.

There were six heats in the 100-yard dash and the order of their finishes was: (1) Africans: Shamba, Prince Latuna, Lumbango; (2) Moros: Somdud; (3) Tehuelches: Bonifacio, Casimiro, Colojo; (4) Syrians: Yousouf Hana, Maroof

Zaytoun; (5) Cocopas: Artukero, Chingan Sacup, Skik; (6) Indians: George Mentz, Frank Moore, and an unnamed Pawnee. Those with the fastest time who had crossed the finish lines by themselves were invited back to compete against each other on August 12. Other running races were conducted the same way. The 40-yard run, 400-yard run, and the 120-yard hurdles each had four heats: Indians, Africans, Filipinos, and "others."

There were also field event trials on August 11: 16-pound shot put, 15-meter tree climbing, running high jump, running broad jump, and throwing "stones" for accuracy and distance. A 220-yard loaded run in which each man carried 25 percent of his weight in a bag was the last event, by which time the participants were apparently so tired that only a few ran. Unlike the Olympic events, Natives participated in multiple events on the same day; it was more analogous to participating in a decathlon with all the events held on a single day. Simms decided there were not enough participants to warrant a final in many events by the late afternoon. Heats for relay races were held but the results were so poor, because no one quite knew what to do with the baton, that the finals were also scratched. Following these elimination heats, athletic demonstrations were staged; the Mbutis (Pygmies) played shinny—a game they had learned from the Indians, Mohawks from Canada played Senecas from New York State in a lacrosse game, and Indian students from the Haskell and Chilocco Indian Schools scrimmaged at football.[65]

The finals were held on August 12, beginning with foot races and hurdles, followed by jumping and throwing events and a new set of athletic demonstrations (blow guns, fighting methods, and bola throwing). They closed with a dance contest, somewhat like a modern powwow, and a mud fight. Runners did "better" this time and no one waited before crossing the finish line. In the 100-yard dash, the fastest time was turned in by George Mentz, Sioux, at 11 4/5 seconds. Second was Artukero, a Cocopa youth with a time of 13 seconds, followed in third place by Bonifacio, Tehuelche, with a time of 13 3/5 seconds, and Shamba, Mbuti, in 14¾ seconds. The 440-yard-run final was won by George Rye, a Cherokee who worked at the Oklahoma

Territorial exhibit, with a time of 63 seconds, followed by Yousouf Hana, a Syrian who worked on The Pike in the Moorish Palace, Artukero, a Cocopa demonstrator, and Kondola, a Batatele interpreter for the Mbutis. Other finals held on August 12 were the 16-pound shot putting, 15-meter tree climbing, 56-pound weight throwing, running high jump, running broad jump, throwing for accuracy, throwing for distance using a baseball, archery, and javelin hurling for accuracy.[66]

Natives also competed in sports they chose. These demonstration events included a range of activities McGee felt illustrated manual dexterity and physical fitness and in which the Natives had lots of experience. Skik, a young Cocopa boy, shot nickels and dimes at distances set by the audience. Sullivan noted in his final report that there was "the most marvelous performance at pole climbing ever witnessed in this country given by an Igorot [Basilio], who climbed a pole about fifty feet in height in twenty seconds." Sullivan noted that all the tree-climbing times were praiseworthy, the only instance of his enthusiastically praising Native performances. All Native participants beat the American pole-climbing record holder, S. E. Raynor, by ten seconds (a fact that Sullivan conveniently never included in his official publications). "This performance showed conclusively," Sullivan argued, "the marvelous agility, strength of limb, and great endurance of this particular Igorot, and it is doubtful if we have any trained athlete in America who could duplicate that performance with years of training."[67] Sullivan, unfortunately, did not generalize from this individual performance to other events as he did for all of his dyadic racial comparisons in which the Natives were slower than American athletes. Nor did he generalize to a racial population or social level when a "savage" beat a "civilized" individual. He felt this was an anomaly—the exception that proved the rule.

There are unfortunately no records that provide direct, unequivocal, indications of how the Native athletes felt about Anthropology Days, and of course we can no longer ask them, but there are indications that some events were more interesting to them than others. According to Sullivan, the distance baseball-throwing competition—a new event for the second day of competition—had many enthusiastic contestants, more than any other competition, because many Native men were anxious to see what throwing a baseball was like. "There seemed to be a weird fascination about the ball that appealed to them. No less than two dozen took part in throwing the baseball."[68] Sullivan, however, was not impressed with the results since only three men were able to hit a telegraph pole at a distance of twenty-five feet on their first throw. He concluded that "primitives" had poor upper-arm strength and eyesight, implicitly comparing Native results to American baseball pitchers. Chief Guechico of the Tehuelches won this competition and was given an American flag, donated by the Filipino commissioners, rather than a gold medal and cup such as winners in the regular Olympics received.

While throwing a baseball was an entertaining novelty, almost no one agreed to participate in the 56-pound weight-throwing competition, an idea that many men must have thought was asinine, given the previous day's suggested weight competition. Three Tehuelches agreed, and the best hurled the weight ten feet, six inches; three Ainu men threw from three to seven feet. All refused second attempts when offered the opportunity to improve their performances. Simms reported that all the Indians thought the event was silly and not worth the effort. Sullivan refused to consider this a valid reason to explain what he considered feeble performances and concluded that "it can probably be said, without fear of contradiction, that never before in the history of sport in the world were such poor performances recorded for weight throwing."[69]

Sullivan was similarly disappointed in the javelin-throwing competition, and from this he generalized about racialized physical development. He assumed (incorrectly) that javelins could be thrown in the same manner as a spear and therefore Native peoples would excel in the contest since they were all "naturally" hunters. To him a javelin was simply an enlarged spear. While over twenty-four men participated in the competition, and each made three attempts, only three hit a post at a twenty-five-foot distance. Based on this performance, Sullivan concluded that "savages" had poor upper-body strength, never questioning that practice is required to effectively use any tool. In addition to tree climbing, Sullivan was guardedly impressed with the performances of the large men (although he thought they lacked speed) in the tug-of-war competition and bolo demonstrations. He concluded that though some muscle groups were well developed in these Native participants, they had no balance.[70]

If Sullivan was disappointed with the Special Olympics, by the end of the two days Simms was thoroughly embarrassed by the competition and said that no conclusions could be drawn from any test nor any overarching racial dyadic comparison made. He told McGee and anthropologist George Dorsey (his boss at the Field Museum) that the whole thing was a farce and that, at best, all that was being tested was how modern training could make one run faster and throw farther. The performances had nothing to do with race or evolution. He felt that the Anthropology Department, particularly McGee, had misused the Natives and should have known better. If they ever held the events again, and he hoped they would not, the Native contestants needed to practice as much as the Caucasian athletes and have events explained to them in their Native languages. He advised McGee and Woodworth not to use the data they had collected because it was hopelessly flawed.[71]

Sullivan's Assessment of the Special Olympics

It is telling that the detailed report and assessment of the Anthropology Days competitions are described in Department of Physical Culture reports, rather than McGee's Anthropology Department reports. In fact, McGee basically ignored them, providing only basic information, possibly heeding Simms's recommendation to downplay the program. Sullivan ignored Simms and used selective parts of the data to "prove" his theories of Caucasian and American superiority. His conclusions were clearly designed to support his evolutionist and reformist suppositions—that enlightened Americans were the best athletes in the world, that unorganized and uncontrolled sport was

inferior, and that team sports and training would solve social ills and promote political socialization into an American model in a rapidly changing
world. To Sullivan the Anthropology Days results proved that his opinions
about sports as a medium for shaping the moral and cognitive development
of young people were correct but that Native peoples were intellectually,
socially, cognitively, and morally inferior by nature. They were not as good
prospects for assimilation as European immigrants.

Sullivan began his report by stating that he was disappointed with the
results of every event. While he noted that the public liked the Mbutis' mud
fight, which he thought was "one of their favorite pastimes," he disparaged
individual participants' and Native peoples' capabilities in manual dexterity, coordination, and physical fitness. When speaking of the winner of the
100-yard dash, Sullivan marginalized his time by declaring it was one "which
almost any winner of a school boy event would eclipse at will." He was equally
dismissive of others, at one point saying insultingly that a twelve-year-old girl
could have beaten the Native winner. His statements about the equation of
evolutionary primitiveness with childishness were most evident in his evaluation of the Mbutis whom he considered the most primitive group. He saw in
their performances the ultimate proof to refute the theory of environmental
influence on "primitive" man's natural abilities. "Now the African Pygmy
leads an outdoor life, hunts, runs, swims, jumps, and uses the bow and arrow
and spear, and if anything, his life might be termed a natural athletic one,
but nevertheless, we find that it takes him 13 3/5 seconds to run one hundred
yards. Arthur Duffey, or any of our American champion sprinters could easily
have given the African Pygmy forty yards and still beat them."[72]

Extrapolating from the dubious records, Sullivan concluded that primitive
peoples were not intelligent enough to participate in team sports—which
were a key component of his agenda. Following G. Stanley Hall's evolutionary psychological theories, both Sullivan and Gulick held that moral lessons
and physical skills were learned through team sports. The ability to be a team
player was a prerequisite necessary for any citizen's successful adaptation to

modern society.[73] By extension, the ability to participate in team sports was a marker of an ethnic group's (immigrant European or indigenous) ability to assimilate to enlightened civilization. When discussing the Cocopa and Mbuti shinny games, Sullivan spoke with scorn and asserted they demonstrated primitive people's archaic organizational skills and incapacity for cooperation: "The uninteresting exhibition showed conclusively the lack of necessary brain to make the team and its work a success, for they absolutely gave no assistance to each other, and so far as teamwork was concerned, it was a case of purely individual attempts on the part of the players."[74] Of course, Sullivan never learned the rules for shinny but simply assumed it was European soccer run amok.

Not surprisingly, Sullivan found most of his preconceptions reinforced. For example, like others of his era he had developed ideas about the athletic capacities of large men—they would have upper-body strength and there was a direct correlation between size and speed. He assumed that men as large as the Tehuelches would be slow and probably slower than American men who had more advanced musculature, but he was still surprised at how slow they were. He described the participants' speed as "very poor running for even an ordinary man in a healthy condition." Sullivan was disappointed with their performance in general, suggesting that he no longer believed the extensive LPEC publicity hype or McGee's romanticist lauding of the Tehuelches' physical abilities and exoticism. He was even more disillusioned about their supposedly giant-size strength. When describing the shot-put contest he stated:

> It was in this particular competition that everyone naturally supposed the Patagonians would excel, on account of their size, strength, and remarkable performances credited to them in strength contests, but nevertheless, the best performance of the Patagonians was 30ft. 5 in. This, for putting the 16lb. shot is such a ridiculously poor performance that it astonished all who witnessed it. It is 18ft. 2 in. behind the American record, many

feet behind the interscholastic record, and it is doubtful if there is a high school championship that is not won with a better performance. This was one of the disappointing features of the day's sport.[75]

Sullivan did, however, admit that in the tug-of-war competition, the large and strong Tehuelches showed remarkable ability. He offered an explanation for these supposedly contradictory performances by referring to the training of specific muscle groups. "At bolo and perhaps at pulling, hauling, and dragging, they must have developed muscles that are useful and strong, but the muscles for shot putting and throwing the weights had certainly been neglected."[76] Note the negative spin he put on this interpretation by using the word *neglect*. It was the indigenous peoples' fault that their cultures did not have the proper strength competition. Sullivan was equally good at facilely explaining away results when Indians did well, saying that the best were obviously "Americanized," that is, had received proper physical training in Indian Service schools, the molders of needed assimilation.

Sullivan also concluded that "savages" had little coordination. "The jumping of the Pygmies, the Ainu, and some of the Indians were really ridiculous," he said of the running broad jump. Making another comparison to an outstanding Euro-American athlete he declared that, "Ray Ewry jumped further in the standing jump than any of them could go in a running broad jump. The broad jumping, like other sports the savages took part in, proves conclusively that the savage is not the natural athlete we have been led to believe."[77]

In a few cases, Sullivan concluded that several assumptions about race-specific differences in primitive group performance had been proven and his preconceptions reinforced. He had predicted that the "Kaffirs" (i.e., Zulus and Bantus) and Indians would show great speed in the longer distance-running events because of their long legs. These events were won by American Indians, but with what Sullivan considered slow times and poor forms when compared to Caucasian athletes. The third-place finalist in the one-mile race, Lehouw (Zulu), showed a fine form, Sullivan conceded, but no speed.

In fact, according to Sullivan, each Native's "best performance was so ridiculously poor that it astonished all who witnessed it." Similarly, Sullivan was disappointed that the best performance in the running broad jump was "made by an Americanized Sioux Indian [George Mentz] . . . [but] was not equal to Ray Ewry's standing broad-jump record." Sullivan conveniently overlooked the fact that Ewry had been practicing for years, knew the rules, and had developed techniques to maximize his performance. Most Natives were actually disqualified for "jumping violations" and not given second chances. Finally, Sullivan complained that the best the Tehuelches could do in the shot put was only ten and a half feet and that "John Flanagan's score exceeded the combined throws of three Patagonians."[78] Sullivan never considered that he should be comparing Ewry's or Flanagan's first attempts to that of the Natives.

Like other individuals who are absolutely convinced of their views, Sullivan had convenient counterarguments with which to dismiss any evidence that drew into question his preconceptions about Caucasian superiority. Rationalizing away unexpected results (i.e., when the "wrong" race or tribe won a contest) was prevalent in his assessments of the Special Olympics. To Sullivan these unexpected results were always due to a sampling problem—unequal representation of the different races—but this did not stop him from generalizing competition results to all members of a supposed culture-grade (or race) for use in broader hierarchical comparisons, especially to white Americans. Sullivan's conclusions about the results of the archery competition are a case in point. There should have been stiff competition in all the archery contests, he argued, and a Plains Indian should have won. "We have been led to believe that the Igorot, the Africans, the Pygmies, the Cocopa, and the Ainu, who have been living for years with the bow and arrow, and with whom shooting with the arrow is an everyday occurrence, would exhibit the most marvelous target shooting that had ever been witnessed."[79] This was not the case, however. Only two individuals hit the center of a target at a distance of forty-two yards; others fell short or struck the bottom of the

7. American Indian archery contest. From Bennitt and Stockbridge, eds., *History of the Louisiana Purchase Exposition*, 573.

target area. As expected the winner was an Indian, but unexpectedly it was a slender Cocopa youth rather than a vigorous Plains warrior. Sullivan could not accept the fact that he had fallen prey to a stereotype.

Sullivan explained away his conundrums using arguments about age (as a confounding variable) and representativeness. By definition, since all Indians *should* be excellent archers, those in St. Louis were obviously old, gray-haired, and no longer strong. Thus, they found it impossible to hit the target. Eventually, he grudgingly admitted to another possibility that had been voiced by one of his colleagues: "Dr. Simms claimed they [the Indians] did most of their shooting from horseback at moving objects."[80] Therefore, they were not accustomed to target shooting while standing still. Sullivan dismissed this explanation, holding that if one could shoot while in motion one could shoot standing still. He did not care enough about the possibility to propose another contest to test the refined hypothesis, as Simms had suggested.

In concluding his report, Sullivan stated that he and other (unidentified) scientists and physical education directors found "the only disappointing feature of the season" to be Anthropology Days. He was equally disappointed in anthropology as a science and thought that the discipline had been hoodwinking people for years with "statements made by those who should know about the innate abilities of Native peoples." Anthropology, McGee, and primitive peoples could be dismissed because the performances were so bad. "Of course, none expected that the Patagonians would be John Flanagans or the Indians Arthur Duffeys or Alexander Grants, but we certainly expected a great deal more from the savages who competed in the Anthropology Days than events proved. The Anthropology Days were only successful in that they were destructive of the common belief that the greatest natural athletes were to be found among the uncivilized tribes in various parts of the world."[81] To Sullivan and Gulick the results of the scientific experiment demonstrated that adult "savages" had abilities that were the equivalent of civilized children, a common idea of Social Darwinism, which viewed advanced society as a complex organism. Without supervision they expressed unhindered "anarchy." Team sports required obedience to the game's rules and attitudes of obedience, loyalty, willingness to sacrifice glory to a common cause, and the glorification of victory.[82] Adult "primitives" had not racially developed the group consciousness and cooperation that was a cornerstone of team sports. Like Gulick, Sullivan no longer thought there was hope for their evolutionary advancement or assimilation. He concluded that Native peoples were destined to disappear or remain wards of the state.

The Native participants, of course, did not realize that they were disappointing anyone. Nor did they know that their performances were being used to reach conclusions about the athletic abilities of all "primitive" peoples or that their supposed location in an evolutionary hierarchy would be reaffirmed by the rigged competition, faulty logic, or Sullivan's overgeneralizations. From Simms's correspondence, it appears that the Native men saw no purpose in the events, but thought the races were harmless fun or sometimes ridiculous.[83]

As noted above, McGee, Woodworth, and Sullivan had planned to conduct special anthropometric and psychometric tests on Euro-American athletes as they participated in the regular Olympics. The idea was to establish norms of physical fitness for this special group of Caucasians and see how they compared to those of average visitors and Natives. Unfortunately, Sullivan was so dismayed with the Native results that he became lukewarm about continuing the research project; there was no longer any need to continue the experiment, he told McGee, since the results were so obvious as to simply reinforce what everyone already knew—trained Americans made the best natural athletes. He would continue his own anthropometric tests on out-standing athletes but without further racial comparisons. As a consequence the planned tests of visitors' athletic ability in running, jumping, climbing, or shooting were never undertaken. There were thus no real "scientific" data on which to base racial comparisons, although this did not stop Sullivan from drawing sweeping conclusions.[84]

The grand comparison of "racial" athletic abilities was a fiasco as far as Sullivan was concerned but McGee and Woodworth were not ready to give up, nor could they. They had to recoup the money spent on the anthropometry labs and save face—the reputation of anthropology was now an issue for McGee because of disparaging letters that he heard Sullivan had written to Director Skiff, LPEC President Francis, and the LPEC board, apparently in an attempt to distance himself from what he considered a public relations humiliation. McGee decided to take Simms's advice and try again, this time letting the Natives practice and explaining the events in native languages through their interpreters.[85]

The September Races

For McGee, the real disappointments of Anthropology Days were that he had not been able to educate more people, including Sullivan, about the scientific value of anthropology and that he had not filled his departmental coffers. McGee had counted on ticket sales to help finance the event and also help pay for his department's large grocery bills. He was also disappointed with the meager advance LPEC publicity for the Anthropology Days competition and the resulting poor attendance. He decided to organize a second competition in September to "give the audience a chance to see the pick of the primitive tribes contesting in modern and native games of strength, endurance, and agility."[86] If their Special Olympics proved to Sullivan that the "savages" were hopeless and that "primitive" man lacked any natural athletic abilities, to McGee the August performances simply meant that the participants had not understood the events. They needed to be educated and to practice, just as American athletes did. McGee suggested to Sullivan that if they could find a professional trainer for a short time and practice they could restage the event after the regular Olympic Games. He predicted that then the Natives would be as proficient as many Americans and a valid comparison could be made.[87]

Sullivan was not convinced and refused to approve the expenditures McGee suggested or plan for additional competitions. Again he stated that there was simply no need: "The exhibitions given on these particular days do not speak well for them. The whole meeting proves conclusively that the savage has been a very much overrated man from an athletic point of view."[88] Deciding to continue, McGee convened an "Emergency Exploitation Committee" to organize the event and generate publicity. He attempted to raise prize money since he knew that the Native demonstrators expected financial remuneration for their efforts. Albert Jenks donated another set of American flags for the winners of each event, stating that they would show Natives the power of the United States and instill patriotism.

Groups began to practice under Simms's direction but without the desired professional trainer. Several "training meets" were held; on August 22, there was a special Filipino Field Day of track-and-field events. The groups competed against each other, ethnic group by ethnic group, using the same model devised for the Special Olympics. Jenks and McGee eventually talked Skiff into loaning them money for winning performances: two dollars for first place, one dollar for second, fifty cents each for third and fourth place. McGee also gave every entrant twenty-five cents for participating in an event from his contingency fund.[89]

The September event was relatively successful, attracting an audience of about thirty thousand according to McGee, of whom almost three thousand paid ten to twenty-five cents to sit on bleachers erected in front of the Indian School.[90] He called the event an anthropological meet, because Sullivan would not permit him to use the words "Special Olympics" or "Anthropology Days." As a reporter remarked, "The meeting was a grand success from every point of view, and served as a good example of what the brown men are capable of doing with training."[91] Simms and his assistants kept records of participants and their times. Unfortunately, these have not been located so I cannot identify the participants or compare their results to the August meet to determine whether training had produced improvements. (Hopefully, someone will locate them some day.) McGee did say in a special report to Skiff when he repaid the loan that the results were better, but since he provided no records we cannot assess his statement.[92] President Francis attended and noted in his final report on the exposition that it was the results of these races rather than the August Anthropology Days that had the greatest scientific value, probably parroting McGee's attempt at damage control. Francis also stated that the anthropological meet was much more colorful and visually interesting than the Olympic Games because the participants wore their full Native attire.[93]

McGee's Assessment of Anthropology Days and the September Meet

The "scientific" outcome of the comparative sets of tests for McGee was almost a preordained conclusion, even if he was ambivalent about them. Interestingly, while McGee kept several hundred newspaper articles on indigenous participation or the Anthropology Department in his personal scrapbooks, there are none on Anthropology Days.[94] After assessing the results from the September races, McGee concluded, based on these competitions but not the Anthropology Days results, that

> [o]n the whole [the results] are in harmony with the view of the course of human development by which the plans of the Department were shaped; making every allowance for the lack of training on the part of the primitives, the tests nevertheless established in quantitative measure the inferiority of primitive peoples, in physical faculty if not in intellectual grasp, and especially in that coordination of mind and body which seems to mark the outcome of human development and measure the attainment of human excellence.[95]

The games in fact demonstrated nothing of the sort, but McGee had too much at stake to acknowledge this publicly — although his report actually does just that. McGee alerted readers to several important caveats, as well as actual flaws, in the research design. He concluded that: (1) the comparisons were one-sided since American athletes did not have to compete in Native events, like tree climbing and bolo throwing; (2) results differed "significantly" from August to September; (3) important anomalies had to be explained not simply shoved aside; (4) there were sampling problems; and, (5) the Natives were simply not interested. People do not put time and effort into things they find boring or culturally meaningless.[96]

What Anthropology Days and the September Meet ultimately hinted at was that the competitions were culturally meaningful but consequential in different ways to organizers, viewers, and participants, that practice did affect performance, and that people who had been sedentary for five months would not perform well in a series of athletic events that had never been explained to them and were not part of their cultural or performative repertoire. There were no valid measures of "natural ability" being tested. The games really demonstrated that most Natives were simply not interested in "Olympic" athletic events (except for the marathon and tug-of-war) or performing for visitors' amusement without compensation.

At best Anthropology Days, the September Meet, and all the other athletic competitions were performative events during which Native demonstrators had a good time and poked fun at the entire undertaking. They were not rigorous scientific tests. Certainly the competitions were not something that Native participants (or the press) regarded with the solemnity with which Sullivan imbued his "sacred" Olympic Games. McGee noted that some participants, especially the Mbutis, thought it was fun to satirically mimic the events, pantomiming the athletes and referees, disrupting the proceedings, and choosing to conduct the "races" their way. According to Sullivan and also recounted in many newspapers, the Mbutis were mischievous and took nothing seriously except for their own cultural activities or those they particularly enjoyed.

"With the Pygmies it is only fair to state that they entered into the spirit of the competitions for fun, and only became interested in the pole climbing and their mud fight. For the other sports, they seemed to think that they were brought there to do certain things, and they did them, which may account for their poor performances. They tried to run, but did not persevere. Many of them did not perhaps know that they were expected to do their best."[97] Sullivan did think that the Mbutis showed great dexterity in ducking, throwing, and running, and through their mud fight (which reminded him of his children's snowball fights) "redeemed themselves for their lack of interest in other sports."[98] The cultural bias of Sullivan's expectations is obvious. He could not understand such an attitude and could only conceive of the Mbutis' behavior as childish, that is, that "primitive" peoples naturally behaved like children because their minds were undeveloped—a common assumption of popularly held unilinear evolutionary models, which lack a sense of humor and satire. To do otherwise would have undermined one of the central premises on which Sullivan's athletic agenda was built.[99]

Rather than measure natural ability, the performances of Native participants clearly demonstrated cultural preferences and cultural knowledge. The sports events illustrated that Native peoples could not be bothered with silly games, especially when they were not fully explained, when they saw no purpose in the effort, or when no financial incentive or reciprocity was provided. The athletic events also demonstrated that cultural training, cultural perspectives, and practice affected performance. Even Sullivan conceded that the races were unknown to the participants but never understood that cultural interpretations mattered. To McGee cultural understanding was important, a variable not to be dismissed, but it was not as important as biocultural evolution.

The flaws of the athletic competitions as the basis for racial comparisons of physical value, and the ethnocentric notions underlying any competitions or test measurements whereby different "cultures" or "races" are compared, are glaringly obvious today. They clearly demonstrated the kind of problems also faced by measurements of "IQ": as a field experiment Anthropology Days abounded in Type I and Type II errors, sampling problems and selection bias, nonrandom comparisons of apples and oranges, sample-size issues, scaling problems, the inclusion of outliers in measuring central tendencies, the elimination of contradictory evidence, and an "exception proves the rule" reasoning. There were also ethnocentric, racist, stereotypic, and often prejudicial assumptions and categorization problems, instrumentality issues, and logical and interpretive flaws. The statistical naiveté and the failure to use appropriate control groups meant the tests had no predictive value. Basically everything was intentionally or unintentionally arranged to assure that civilization and whiteness won the race, that assumptions and hoped-for conclusions would dominate in the end. In short, the research design's internal validity was low and the results had no predictive power. Anthropology Days was bad science, if it could even be called science at all. It was pseudoscience used to justify a desired position. McGee came close to dismissing the athletic anthropometry tests as such. In his reports he walked around the issue, but in the end could not bring himself to reject the flawed experiment, because it would have brought his whole assessment of anthropometry and anthropogeny into question and made his position at the fair and in anthropology even more marginal than it was.[100]

Like many who held to evolutionary theories, both McGee and Sullivan had counterarguments for any incident that drew their central assumptions and paradigm into question, but they used different arguments. Sullivan dismissed any suggestion that the games were unfair contests or led to invalid comparisons. "Of course the argument may be made that these savages have not been taught the art of shot putting. Quite true, but one would think that the life these men have led should enable them to easily have put this shot many feet further."[101] McGee felt that Sullivan was too harsh in his condemnation and dismissal of the importance of culture. Referring to his expertise as an anthropologist and evolutionist—a rationale to provide himself with more knowledge and therefore more authority than had Sullivan — he offered several alternative explanations for the differing racial performances:

> Anthropologists will necessarily make allowances for the low records of the primitives on various accounts, including: (1) the fact that they were absent from habitat and worked under unaccustomed conditions (an important factor since primitive peoples are much more dependent on immediate surroundings as well as general environment than are advanced peoples); (2) the fact that most of the primitives were not even in habitual training and were leading indolent and enervating lives; (3) the almost total absence of incentive and esprit de corps, such as arise in native contests on native soil, and such as white athletes (and Americanized Indians in large measure) designedly develop; and (4) the fact that nearly all the primitives were average individuals whose records should be compared not with those of athletic experts or specialists but with those of average whites in order to show useful results. [102]

To further support his argument that familiarity and practice were critical, McGee argued that the Native performers had been embarrassed by the venue site and rendered hesitant or uncertain by the unusual surroundings of the stadium. If they had been on the playing field before, had witnessed any of the regular Olympic competitions held there, or become familiarized with the competitions' goals, their performance would have improved. In addition he noted that their ignorance of English and Gulick's and Simms's inability to communicate in any Native tongue led to unsatisfactory interpretation of instructions. Contestants did not know what they were to do. Of course they had shown themselves at their worst in the stadium, he concluded. In retrospect, McGee believed the contest had been designed for them to fail. They should not have been staged as they had been. Natives should have trained before being asked to perform. The tests were bad science.

McGee argued that much better performance records would have been seen had contestants not only practiced but been coached and given a cash award to reward their endeavors and extra efforts. To support this contention, McGee again noted that American Indian youth often set up their own archery contests and were superb when they arranged the contests themselves and on their own terms, that is, when they set up their targets at about half the distance fixed by Dr. Gulick. At this range they were extremely accurate because they were used to it, just as the American archers were used to their distances. McGee also noted that they should have used other Native measures of success, not only those imposed on them by Sullivan. For example, they could have measured accuracy not by distance but by how many shots had to be taken to hit a very small object—copper pennies and nickels furnished by visitors and set in a bank of earth. Unfortunately McGee then undermined his argument as far as Sullivan was concerned by noting that, "anywhere from five to fifty shafts were usually shot before the coin was struck, yet it was exceedingly rare for the contestants to fail of striking the coin within a few minutes."[103]

To further support his argument that familiarity and practice were critical, McGee noted that the Tehuelches gave vastly better performances in Cummins' Wild West Show's roping contests after participating for several weeks with the new style of lasso. Here, even though they used unaccustomed Western saddles, rode horses they had not trained, and were "handicapped" by Humane Society restrictions, the Tehuelches had good records in competitions against champion Caucasian cowboys from Texas, Oklahoma, Colorado, and Montana. These roping contests measured "strength, alertness, and general physical and mental coordination (albeit with an element of chance) probably in a higher degree than any of the differentiated tests of professional athletics."[104]

McGee concluded that Natives were not worse physically than the more "advanced races"; they simply needed to be trained in Caucasian sports. The next time similar tests were conducted—as McGee assumed they would be because all good scientific experiments had to be replicated to eliminate confounding variables—the organizers and referees needed to use interpreters so that instructions could be satisfactorily conveyed. Competitors needed to know what they were to do, and to understand the contests' goals and rules and what was expected of them. He also thought that American athletes should be judged performing in Native sports using Native rules with the same amount of practice given to the Natives. Then there would be a real test and primitive races' natural athletic abilities would be evident. The LPE's Special Olympics did not change McGee's mind. Like Sullivan, he still believed what he had believed before the start of the fair.

Beyond Anthropology Days

By the turn of the twentieth century, world's fairs were established universal meccas for the explicit display and dissemination of Euro-American and European-based knowledge about the Native peoples, their material and technological accomplishments. The fairs also served as tools for the imperialist countries that staged them to justify and essentially celebrate the subjugation and dispossession of indigenous peoples worldwide. Anthropologists in their displays and programming of special events helped to convey this message even while they were trying to subvert misconceptions and stereotypes about Native peoples and introduce the concept of culture and cultural development. Their justifications were partially based on anthropometric data thought to speak to physical and mental capabilities of various races. Unfortunately, these data were flawed from the start, based on racist assumptions, and collected and interpreted using a plethora of methodological errors from the standpoint of a scientific experiment in a semi-laboratory setting. The "data" obtained during the Anthropology Days competitions constitute an excellent example of the shaky ground on which these evolutionary assertions were based. Unfortunately they served their purpose, if not for anthropology, then for other messages displayed at the fair. For what better way to support the status quo than to stage an essentially rigged athletic competition labeled as a "scientific" study?

The athletic competitions at the Louisiana Purchase Exposition demonstrated that fair personnel were not measuring natural or racial ability, they were using pseudoscience to "prove" their stereotyped preconceptions and evolutionary assumptions, which Sullivan, McGee, and others believed to be true: Caucasians, especially Americans, were the most enlightened and advanced society. They were also the fittest because they had natural physical, mental, and moral abilities that were enhanced by following proper training and control. Here was the future, a vision that did not include degeneration from a naturally superior "primitive" man. As Robert Rydell and several other scholars have noted, Social Darwinism and racism ruled the day in both St. Louis and America in 1904—with just a hint of cultural relativity standing in the wings as well as an awareness of the ridiculousness of the whole undertaking.

The St. Louis Post-Dispatch, on July 17, 1904, labeled McGee "The Overlord of the Savage World" since he had brought so many exotic peoples to the Midwest town, and also because his department reaffirmed notions of racial superiority while simultaneously challenging many popular stereotypes. Unlike Sullivan who dismissed all non-Caucasian races, McGee presented a powerful image of Native peoples and their dissimilarities to Euro-American society as well as a vision of a hopeful future for them, that is, the possibility for Native people's "progress." But in the end, McGee, newspaper reporters, Sullivan, and probably visitors all concluded that Native peoples were not as good athletes as white Euro-Americans. (Of course, no one asked the Native participants their opinions.) As McGee noted in his final report, "Still, after making all possible allowances, the lesson of the Anthropology Days at the Stadium remains very much as read by Chief Sullivan: Despite fair proficiency in the few lines specialized by each group, primitive men are far inferior to modern Caucasians in both physical and mental development."[105]

The irony of this conclusion could be found in the Indian School at the top of the hill with a remarkable group of athletes whom Sullivan and McGee conveniently ignored. The Fort Shaw boarding school's women's basketball team, as Peavy and Smith will recount in their chapter, played many Euro-

American school teams and amateur clubs. On July 1 they beat the Illinois girls, sponsored by the State of Illinois pavilion, and on July 3, the Missouri state champions. In fact, the seven women defeated every team they played. Schools around St. Louis began requesting the team to travel to their communities for competitions. On July 29 they played the O'Fallon High School team and won 14 to 3. "It was a warmly contested game, and while the Indian girls worked to some disadvantage on very uneven ground and without the back-stops to which they are accustomed, they were however, the favorites of the crowds, and won an easy victory," reported the *Indian School Journal*. "Two enthusiastic St. Louis basketball girls accompanied the Indian girls' team to Bellville. They 'backed' the Indian girls throughout the game. 'Why,' they said, 'They can't be beaten. They haven't a poor player on the team.'"[106] On August 25 the girls won the silver and gold cup for women's basketball at the fair, competing in the general competition, a fact conveniently omitted from *Spalding's Athletic Almanac*. Athletic ability had nothing to do with race, but powerful record· keepers did not want to admit this—nor would they in the future.

Similar tests comparing Native demonstrators with Olympic athletes were never held again, especially not at future Olympics. Anthropology Days became synonymous with Coney Island and sideshows. IOC president Pierre de Coubertin noted in his memoirs that in no other place but America would anyone have dared place a "Special Olympics" on the Olympic program. He wrote an assessment of the St. Louis Olympics in general and Anthropology Days in particular, even though he had not attended:

> So the St. Louis Games were completely lacking in attraction. Personally, I had no wish to attend them. I harboured great resentment against the town for the disillusionment caused by my first sight of the junction of the Missouri and the Mississippi rivers. After reading [James] Fenimore Cooper, what had I not been led to expect of the setting where these rivers with their strange resounding names actually met! But there was no beauty, no

*originality. I had a sort of presentiment that the Olympiad would match
the mediocrity of the town. As far as originality was concerned, the only
original feature offered by the programme was a particularly embarrassing one. I mean the "Anthropological Days," whose events were reserved
for Negroes, Indians, Filipinos, and Ainus, with the Turks and Syrians
thrown in for good measure! That was twenty-six years ago! As for that
outrageous charade, it will of course lose its appeal when black men, red
men and yellow men learn to run, jump, and throw and leave the white
man far behind them. Then we will have progress.*[107]

It was this sentiment that led de Coubertin to found the African Games in
the 1920s and 1930s.[108]

Anthropology Days became infamous in the literature on sports and apparently Olympic history, with scholars working from the scathing assessments
of both Sullivan and de Coubertin. My admittedly random search for references to it found the use of the words "colonialist," "insulting," "bizarre,"
"infamous," "disreputable," "embarrassing," "farce," "foolish," "shameful,"
"vulgar," and phrases such as "a final insult to the games," and a "parody
of the regular Olympic competition," "a spectacle of curiosity," "will long
live in infamy as the most ridiculous event at any Olympics."[109] Anthropology Days also became a symbolic scapegoat, the epitome of "bad taste" and
folly, and one reason why St. Louis has come to be considered a low point
in the history of organized sport. The approach taken by anthropology was
to pretend it never happened until recently.[110]

Even during periods when they were on the wane in biological anthropology,
anthropometric measures have continued to be an important part of sports
science because of the keen interest in body composition, fat, musculature,
and shape and the requirements of different sports in terms of physical efficiency, in short, the quest to answer the longstanding question: What makes
a successful athlete?[111] Researchers are still interested in the roles of heredity,
physiology, and biomechanics and how these can be combined with skill,

motivation, and training to enhance performance. Anatomists, physiologists, kinesiologists, biologists, nutritionists, sports doctors, and sports scientists have used standardized body measurements and sophisticated statistical models to understand aerobic capacity, the effects of cold, heat stress, and nutrition, and to correlate body shape with potential for muscular development or running ability. They have used biometrics to develop equipment and to understand how the body moves and reacts in water during aquatic sports, when diving, or riding on a bicycle. Sports medicine and anatomy have relied heavily on these studies for help in reconstructive surgery and to treat sport injuries, applications that have spread to the rest of medicine and helped trauma victims.[112] Educators use the indices to both define physical fitness and conceptualize surrogate measures. Exercise science relies on anthropometry to help develop the types of measurements, critical observations, and evaluative skills needed by physical education teachers, exercise specialists, coaches, occupational and physical therapists, and even sports psychologists to help athletes develop beyond the population norm for body types and shapes.[113]

How research populations are conceptualized for these studies has changed significantly since 1904. Elite athletes tend to be compared to elite athletes, not simply trained Caucasian athletes to untrained members of all other races or the general white population. More attention is paid to the relative spread of values within research populations, not only to differences between populations. Standard deviations are now part of the record as well as statistical means, and the idea of overlap zones has developed to enable more realistic comparisons of idealized somatotypes in different sports.

Anthropometric tests like those used in Anthropology Days were not seen again for a long time at Olympic Games, unlike the keeping of detailed records of performance, which are a foundation of sports science. Biological anthropologists went either into the field (i.e., in a foreign venue) or stayed in the university laboratory and were less often seen on the athletic field. This does not mean that anthropology was not interested in human bodies, evolution, motor control, sport potential, and race or that psychology was not interested in motivation and the mind-body continuum. As Mark Dyreson has noted, Carleton Coon at Harvard University was still searching for a race gene in the 1950s, as are proponents of sociobiology and evolutionary psychology today. Anthropologists remained interested in physical performance and motor control, but most now feel that the relationship between size and performance, while well documented, is weak due to a large number of confounding factors. The goal now is to understand these influences—including culture, microenvironment, nutrition, health, training, and activity level—by means of more sophisticated statistical techniques, such as multivariate analysis.[114] Recognition of the need for multivariate models as well as models that focus on populations was beginning to be articulated in 1904 in McGee's and Simms's assessment of Anthropology Days, but since the analyses were never published, they never had an influence on the field and its methodologies. Equally important for the dearth of anthropological science on the playing field is that anthropometry and cultural anthropology were beginning to split in 1905, in part due to Franz Boas's assessment of the unilinear evolutionary paradigm contained in his friend's—McGee's—anthropogeny model, the uncritical methodology, poor scholarship, and overgeneralization of Anthropology Day results, and the excesses and rhetoric of the fair.[115]

Physical anthropology continued to study the morphological characteristics of human beings at work and at play, especially the relationship between the structure and function of different parts of the body. There were a few studies that utilized the Olympic setting and its athletes to report on body structure—age, height, and weight—as well as somatotyping and other standardized measurements: Kohlraush studied athletes in 1928, mainly from Europe, with Japan, Indian, Mexico, and Chile representing the rest of the world. He concluded that there were differences in body dimensions when correlated by sport and that these were related to the stature of people by country of origin. Cureton studied American swimmers and track-and-field champions to estimate fat and somatotype ratings. Correnti and Zauli measured forty-five characteristics, including cephalic length, diameters, and skin folds, on men from thirty-eight countries, using a racial matrix of Negroids, Mestizos, Mongoloids, and Caucasoids. They compared the results to those of physical-education students from Rome. Similarly Tanner looked at somatotype distributions of athletes using discriminant function analyses and found that Caucasoid and Negroid athletes differed on selected variables when sport was controlled. Even more research was undertaken in Tokyo in 1964 dealing with size, age, morphology, and performance but as was common before, only men were measured.[116]

The largest and most organized research project to compare race (i.e., genetic populations) occurred in Mexico City in 1968 when biological anthropologists, physiologists, sports medicine experts, and sports scientists joined forces to conduct a series of experiments under the auspices of the first and second International Seminar for the Study of the Athletes of the Nineteenth Olympic Games. An international team, led by Alfonso de Garay, a Mexican geneticist, Louise Levine, an American biologist, and J. E. Lindsay Carter, an American sports scientist, developed an extensive protocol to understand the genetic and anthropological characteristics of the biology of athletes to "benefit all humanity by providing a better understanding of human excellence and diversity."[117] Their primary assumption was that athletes constitute a heterogeneous population composed of individuals with genetic preadaptations that make them capable of outstanding sports performances when trained. Their research population consisted of 1,265 athletes from 92 countries (30 percent of the total population of athletes) with a control group of 370 Mexican nonathletes. The subprojects were sociological (to look at the possible roles of parents and siblings in the development of an athlete's career, especially birth order), genetic (DNA, blood groups and proteins, taste sensitivity to PTC, and finger and palm prints), and anthropological (comprehensive anthropometric measurements of outstanding athletes to delineate the physique of body types for several sports and determine how important body components overlap in different sport specialties). Their finding was that Olympic champions do not possess the extreme body types that had been projected based on earlier work but that race did have implications for excellence. The authors' hope was that the information they provided would "find application in physical education programs, early identification and selection of potential athletic types, and perhaps most important, a deeper and more significant understanding of the nature of human diversity."[118] Again, the problem is that athletes do not represent a normal population; they are an outlier group in any population.

Of course, race as a variable has not gone away but is now talked about under different guises. It is intimately tied with anthropometrical research. As John Hoberman has noted in his book *Darwin's Athletes*, the origins of physical anthropology can be seen in early scientific speculation about the physical capabilities and potentials of non-Western peoples. Anthropology Days epitomizes the nineteenth-century ethnological goal of understanding the human organism as a whole. This agenda included making observations about strength, endurance, and what came to be called athletic skills and their mental corollaries. Anthropometry grew into an established methodology in sync with the development of scientific racism. There was always an element of competition in all these analyses to determine which was the "best race." Anthropology Days was a typical scientific experiment in this regard, "proving" that Caucasians were destined to win the race. It had all the flaws of nineteenth-century anthropometric and psychometric work as well as the newest measuring equipment. Like the fair itself with its impressive pavilions, gigantic in scope but meant to be pulled down by March, 1905, Anthropology Days' inclusive scientific protocol to settle long-standing questions reinforced what was popularly held to be true rather than produced new knowledge.

Notes

Francis, *Universal Exposition of 1904*, 530.

1. WJ McGee, "Strange Races of Man," 5185.
2. There is a large literature on international expositions. For basic information on

the history of world's fairs and issues of race and exoticism see Benedict, *Anthropology of World's Fairs*; Greenhalgh, *Ephemeral Vistas*; Rydell, *All the World's a Fair*; Rydell and Gwinn, *Fair Representations*.

3. Rydell, *All the World's a Fair*, 15; see also Findling and Pelle, *Historical Dictionary*.

4. Parezo and Fowler, *Anthropology Goes to the Fair*.

5. See F. W. Putnam's letter to Lehmann, reprinted in "Realistic Exhibits of Race, Life, and Movement for the World's Fair," 5. From the original Putnam Papers, Harvard University.

6. Hanson, *Official History of the St. Louis World's Fair*, 78.

7. Parezo, "Exposition within the Exposition," 30–39; Walker, "The Pike," 615–20; Francis, *Universal Exposition of 1904*, 531.

"Kaffir" is a derogative term used to refer to a number of cultures living in South Africa. They are actually Khosas and were not recruited for the concession. The blacks were most likely Tswanas from the Western Transvaal, South Africa. Van der Merwe, "Africa's First Encounter with the Olympic Games," 29.

8. WJ McGee, "Department N — Anthropology." The Department of the Interior used its funds to build a model Indian School and finance the participation of adult Indians from the Louisiana Purchase region and the Southwest.

9. McGee was a self-taught naturalist, meteorologist, botanist, and geologist whom John Wesley Powell brought into anthropology. He was a noted land surveyor and topographer who had also studied law and excavated mounds in Iowa. He held several patents on farm implements and had worked as a farmer and blacksmith. After his death, his sister described him as fastidious, methodical, hardworking, very ambitious, systematic, painstaking, a good organizer, extremely loyal, eccentric, proud to a fault, and an individual with a commanding presence. E. McGee, *Life of WJ McGee*. McGee had considerable fair experience; he had worked on Smithsonian exhibits at the Atlanta, Nashville, Omaha, and Buffalo expositions.

10. WJ McGee, "Report of the Department of Anthropology to Frederick J. V. Skiff," 4. (Hereafter referred to as WJ McGee, "1905 Report.") See Parezo and Fowler, *Anthropology Goes to the Fair*, for a history of McGee's life, theoretical ideas, and grandiose plans for the Anthropology Department.

11. WJ McGee, "1905 Report," 7

12. WJ McGee, "1905 Report," 19.

13. Francis, "Novel Athletic Contest," 527.

14. Untitled article, *St. Louis Sunday Republic* (September 6, 1903), no page. McGee Papers, box 32, Library of Congress.

15. "Indian Exhibit Formally Opens: Progress Which Red Man Made under Government Supervision Displayed in Many Ways," *St. Louis Republic*, June 22, 1904. McGee Papers, box 32, Library of Congress.

Most Native demonstrators were not given wages for participating in the exposition but were expected to produce their own income from the sale of art or tips after performances. The fair corporation only paid transportation and per diem.

16. "Field Sports and Winner," *Indian School Journal* 4, no. 9 (June 2, 1904): 4; WJ McGee, "1905 Report," 106. See also Parezo and Troutman, "The 'Shy' Cocopa Go to the Fair," 3–43; Troutman and Parezo, "'Overlord of the Savage World,'" 17–34.

17. Reel, *Uniform Course of Study*. There is a growing literature on Indians, boarding schools, and sports. See Oxendine, *American Indian Sports Heritage*.

18. "Exhibit News Notes," *Indian School Journal* 4, no. 26 (June 22, 1904): 1; "Indian Exercises Good," *Indian School Journal* 4, no. 45 (July 19, 1904): 1; Peavy and Smith, "World's Champions," 2–25.

19. WJ McGee, "Anthropology," 8.

20. WJ McGee, "1905 Report," 2; originally printed in "To Measure Men of All Nations," *St. Louis Republic*, May 1, 1904.

21. Montague, *Handbook of Anthropometry*, 3.

22. See Shipman, *Evolution of Racism*; Gould, *Ever Since Darwin* and *Mismeasure of Man*. Craniometry and anthropometry were major scholarly methods in the nineteenth-century attempt to metrically, hence "scientifically," define race. The entire attempt was futile; craniology indicated nothing of biological significance. The irony is that this critique had already begun long before the fair but McGee refused to acknowledge the problem. The techniques using more refined statistical models are still widely used in psychology, sports science, biological anthropology, and by designers.

23. WJ McGee, "1905 Report," 191.

24. "Recent Progress in American Anthropology," 466–67.

25. Hrdlička, *Proposed Plan*; Robert S. Woodworth, "Final Report of the Anthropometry and Psychology Section to William J McGee," contained in McGee, "1905 Report"; Woodworth, "Racial Differences in Mental Traits," 171–86.

26. Woodworth, "Final Report," 1905.

27. "Exhibit News Notes," *Indian School Journal* 4 no. 26 (June 22, 1904): 1; Woodworth, "History of Psychology," 373.

28. WJ McGee, "1905 Report," 22–23.

29. Woodworth, "Racial Differences in Mental Traits," 171–86; Woodworth, "History of Psychology," 359–80.

30. WJ McGee, "1905 Report," 191.

31. Findling and Pelle, *Historical Dictionary*, 20.

32. Dyreson, *Making the American Team*, 3; See also, Carnes and Griffen, *Meanings for Manhood*; Dyreson, "Playing Fields of Progress," 4–23.

33. Rydell, *All the World's a Fair*, 155.

34. Louisiana Purchase Exposition Corporation—Departmental Reports, Publicity, and Catalogues, *Physical Culture*, 57; Information on Sullivan is from John MacAloon, conference discussion, September 11, 2004; Findling and Pelle, *Historical Dictionary*.

35. Findling and Pelle, Historical Dictionary, 18.

36. WJ McGee, "1905 Report," 191; Findling and Pelle, Historical Dictionary.

37. Others in this volume discuss the irony of this, since Sullivan was decidedly anti-academic.

38. J. Sullivan, "Physical Training Programme," 185–86; J. Sullivan, "Physical Culture," 58; J. Sullivan, "Report of the Department of Physical Culture"; Louisiana Purchase Exposition Corporation—Official Daily Program, "Field Day for Primitive Peoples," 2; Bennitt and Stockbridge, History of the Louisiana Purchase Exposition, 565.

39. Bennitt and Stockbridge, History of the Louisiana Purchase Exposition, 565; J. Sullivan, "Report of the Department of Physical Culture," 58.

40. Johnson, All That Glitters, 120; Findling and Pelle, Historical Dictionary, 22; United States Olympic Committee, Athens to Atlanta, 37.

41. Becht, "George Poage"; J. Sullivan, "Physical Training Programme," 186. Van der Merwe's research revealed that the two so-called Zulus were probably Tswanas, and their names were probably Len Tau and Jan Mashiani. Len Tau was also the same Lehouw who placed in the one-mile run in Anthropology Days. According to newspapers he would have done better if he had not kept looking back and lost enough of his lead for a Syrian and Indian to pass him (van der Merwe, "Africa's First Encounter," 31).

42. United States Olympic Committee, Athens to Atlanta, 37; Dyreson, Making the American Team; Sullivan, letter to McGee, June 10, 1904, McGee Papers, box 17, Library of Congress. It is evident from Coubertin's memoirs that he intensely disliked Sullivan and did not want him associated with the IOC. The kindest thing he had to say about Sullivan was that he was a man often "carried away by enthusiasm." Coubertin, Olympic Memoirs, 41. See also Loland, "Pierre de Coubertin's Ideology," 26–45.

The fight to have the Olympics held in St. Louis is a fascinating example of politics and sports; see Dyreson, Making the American Team, for an insightful analysis.

43. For typical contemporary examples, see de Garay, Levine, and Carter, Genetic and Anthropological Studies; Holly et al., "Triathlete Characterization," 123–27; Khosla and McBroom, "Age, Height, and Weight of Female Olympic Finalists," 96–99; Parnell, Behavior and Physique.

44. According to John MacAloon (personal communication), it was a common practice to withhold water during marathons until the 1980s so that this variable should not be considered part of a scientific experiment at this time. However, Sullivan specifically mentions this test. Since attire and food were not variables under consideration, they were allowed. Participants found sustenance along the route and its consumption was not regulated. For example, Felix Carvajal of Cuba stopped to eat green apples (or peaches) and developed severe stomach cramps. He lay down until the cramps passed, resumed the race, and came in fourth. Carvajal, who had funded his own passage from Cuba and hitchhiked to St. Louis, ran in street shoes and long trousers and occasionally stopped to talk to fans.

45. Johnson, *All That Glitters*, 123.

46. Researchers today still look at the effects of dehydration on athletes. See Sawka et al., "Hypohydration and Exercise," 1147–53; Claremont et al., "Heat Tolerance," 239–43.

47. "Famous Giants at the Fair," *St. Louis Post-Dispatch*, April 24, 1904; "Patagonian Giants to Have Rivals," *St. Louis Post-Dispatch*, April 24, 1904.

48. J. Sullivan, "Anthropology Days," 249–66.

49. J. Sullivan to McGee, June 10, 1904; Sullivan, "Report of the Department of Physical Culture."

50. J. Sullivan, "Anthropology Days at the Stadium," p. 250; J. Sullivan to McGee June 10, 1904; see also, Rydell, *All the World's a Fair*, 166.

51. J. Sullivan, "Physical Culture"; J. Sullivan to McGee, June 10, 1904.

52. WJ McGee to James Sullivan, June 13, 1904f; P. Hoffman, "A Study of the Feet of Barefooted Peoples"; see also Parezo and Fowler, *Anthropology Goes to the Fair*, for a longer discussion of the anthropometry laboratory.

53. J. Sullivan, "Anthropology Days," 249. Both men called the proposed event the "Special Olympics" in their correspondence, but it was referred to as Anthropology Days in official publications. Both men also referred to themselves as "doctor." McGee had been awarded an honorary doctorate from an Iowa College the year before. It is not known where Sullivan picked up the honorific title.

54. WJ McGee to Samuel M. McCowan, June 13, 1904e.

55. WJ McGee to William P. Wilson, June 13, 1904g.

56. WJ McGee to W. P. Wilson, June 28, 1904g.

57. McGee, "Anthropology," 8–9.

58. Woodworth, Field notes; Woodworth, Monthly reports to McGee.

59. McGee, "1905 Report," 89. I have been unable to compile a complete list of events. The information in these tables is from McGee's Papers, LPE Corporation and Department of Anthropology records, Department of Physical Culture Records, Sullivan's records, and *Spalding's Almanac* for 1904 and 1905. For photographs of these events and snide comments about the participants' performances using prejudiced standards see Bennitt and Stockbridge, *History of the Louisiana Purchase Exposition*; and Breitbart, *A World on Display*. Apparently some concessionaires, like Tobin, refused to allow Native staff to be absent for two days because they were needed for performances. Concessionaires considered the games a financial burden for which they would not be compensated.

60. Stephen C. Simms to George Dorsey, August 11, 1904a; Parezo and Fowler, *Anthropology Goes to the Fair*.

Simms came to St. Louis to serve as manager of the Indian Village, much against his will. Simms hated the LPE but Frederick Skiff, director of the Field Museum and head of the LPE Exhibits Division, suggested he either change his mind or look for a new job. See Parezo and Fowler, *Anthropology Goes to the Fair*, for a fuller discussion of the problems managing the Native encampments.

61. Simms to George Dorsey, August 18, 1904a.

62. Cavallo, *Muscles and Morals*, 33; Dorgan, *Luther Halsey Gulick*, 1–5. Gulick had a long association with the Young Men's Christian Association physical education programs. He was interested in shifting the emphasis away from "Germanic" gymnastics and individual exercise toward a program of physical discipline that stressed the "social" aspects of recreation, that is, team sports as professed in G. Stanley Hall's theories. Gulick's student at Springfield College, James Naismith, is credited with inventing the quintessential team sport, basketball. Gulick also believed that physical education was critical for Americanizing European immigrants as an antidote to what he felt were America's urban social problems.

63. Sullivan confessed in his final report that it had been a mistake to not schedule an extra day and arrange for interpreters from each group to explain to the Native participants what was expected of them.

64. J. Sullivan, "Anthropology Days," 253.

65. Louisiana Purchase Exposition Corporation — Official Daily Program, "Field Day for Primitive Peoples."

66. Louisiana Purchase Exposition Corporation — Official Daily Program, "Field Day for Primitive Peoples," 5.

67. J. Sullivan, "Anthropology Days," 250, 258, 263. There were two men named Basilio at the fair, one Negrito and one Igorot. Most sources state that the Negrito man won the pole-climbing competition for which he was given an American flag.

68. J. Sullivan, "Anthropology Days," 256.

69. J. Sullivan, "Anthropology Days," 255, 258, 259.

70. The literature on javelin contests demonstrates that minor changes in equipment aerodynamic design alter performance. Critical is the center of mass and where the weight is in the shaft. When the weighting of a javelin was changed, the previous world record holders performed poorly. Bartlett and Best, "Biomechanics of Javelin Throwing," 1–38. For an analysis of tugging games see Eichberg, "Three Dimensions of Pull and Tug," 51–73.

71. Simms to George Dorsey, August 15, 1904; Simms to WJ McGee, August 14, 1904b; Simms, letter and report, to WJ McGee, August 16, 1904b; Simms, letter and report, to WJ McGee, August 17, 1904b.

72. J. Sullivan, "Anthropology Days," 253–54.

73. Cavallo, *Muscles and Morals*, 34.

74. J. Sullivan, "Anthropology Days," 259. One could speculate from this that Sullivan had never seen British rugby.

75. J. Sullivan, "Anthropology Days," 255.

76. J. Sullivan, "Anthropology Days," 259.

77. J. Sullivan, "Anthropology Days," 257.

78. J. Sullivan, "Anthropology Days," 273, 256–58, 263. "Lehouw" was the same Len

Tau who placed ninth in the marathon. Van der Merwe, "Africa's First Encounter," 31.

79. J. Sullivan, "Anthropology Days," 259.

80. J. Sullivan, "Anthropology Days," 259.

81. J. Sullivan, "Anthropology Days," 260, 251–52.

82. Gulick, "Some Psychical Aspects of Muscular Exercise," 793–805; Gulick, "Psychological, Pedagogical and Religious Aspects of Group Games," 135–51; Gulick, *Morals and Morale*.

83. Simms, letter and report, to WJ McGee, August 16, 1904b; Simms, letter and report, to WJ McGee, August 17, 1904b.

84. J. Sullivan to WJ McGee, August 20, 1904b.

85. WJ McGee to George Dorsey, August 20, 1904d.

86. WJ McGee to J. Sullivan, August 18, 1904f.

87. WJ McGee to J. Sullivan, August 18, 1904f.

88. J. Sullivan to WJ McGee, August 20, 1904b.

89. WJ McGee, Fiscal records.

90. McGee tried to have the event held on the exposition's main plaza, which had a high volume of traffic and good seating space, but had to settle for the Indian School's parade grounds.

91. "Moros Win Championship of Philippine Natives on Track," St. Louis *Globe-Democrat*, September 16, 1904, Louisiana Purchase Exposition Corporation records, Missouri Historical Society.

92. William J McGee, monthly report to Skiff, September 1904, Louisiana Purchase Exposition records, Missouri Historical Society.

93. Francis, "Novel Athletic Contest," 50. One can speculate that Sullivan would not have been happy with this remark, feeling that it marginalized the athleticism of the Olympics. Francis clearly understood the festival aspect of later Olympics, which have been described by John MacAloon, "Olympic Games and the Theory of Spectacle"; MacAloon, "Anthropology at the Olympic Games," 9–27; Handelman, *Models and Mirrors*; Roche, *Mega-Events and Modernity*; and MacCanell, "Staged Authenticity," 589–603.

94. See Dyreson, this volume, for a list of the extensive press coverage of the event.

95. WJ McGee, "1905 Report," 99–100.

96. WJ McGee, "1905 Report," 100.

97. J. Sullivan, "Anthropology Days," 257; "Pygmies Outdo Savage Athletes," St. Louis *Post-Dispatch*, August 14, 1904; Henning Eichberg, this volume, has an in-depth analysis of humor and comic inversion.

98. J. Sullivan, "Anthropology Days," 260.

99. For an extended analysis of these issues see also Henning Eichberg, this volume, and "Forward Race," 115–31.

100. See Dyreson, this volume, and Parezo and Fowler, *Anthropology Goes to the Fair*, for extended analyses of these issues.

101. J. Sullivan, "Anthropology Days," 257.

102. WJ McGee, "1905 Report," 190.

103. WJ McGee, "1905 Report," 190–91.

104. WJ McGee, "1905 Report," 191.

105. WJ McGee, "1905 Report," 191.

106. "A Trip to Bellville and Exhibit News Notes," *Indian School Journal* 4, no. 54 (1904): 1.

107. Coubertin, *Olympic Memoirs*, 43.

108. Karl Lennartz, personal communication at conference, 2004.

109. Eichberg, "Forward Race"; Greenberg, *Guinness Book*, 18; Johnson, *All That Glitters*, 124; Findling and Pelle, *Historical Dictionary*, 22.

110. Findling and Pelle, *Historical Dictionary*, 18; Stanaland, "Pre-Olympic 'Anthropology Days,'" 101–6; Toohey and Veal, *Olympic Games*; Croney, *Anthropometry for Designers*.

111. Anthropometry or biometrics has continued to be part of biological anthropology since the field is still interested in human variation. Today it is used in forensic anthropology, bioarchaeology, osteology, nutritional analysis, and health studies. It has also been used to measure human adaptability, for growth and development studies, environmental correlations, to help uncover population migrations, and to establish kinship relationships as well as the origins of the species. Anthropometry measurements are also used by engineers, physiologists, and designers (from cockpits in airplanes to work cubicles), in occupational safety and health (ergometrics), and to analyze anatomical movement (the placement of pedals or the steering wheel in automobiles). Norton and Olds, *Anthropometrica*.

112. This includes me. In 2006 I was the victim of an auto crash caused by a drunk driver and suffered multiple broken bones. I have been helped by excellent surgeons, doctors, and physical therapists who have benefited from sports medicine.

113. Baumgartner and Jackson, *Measurement for Evaluation*; Norton and Olds, *Anthropometrica*.

114. Norgan, "Anthropometry and Physical Performance," 141–59; Malina, "Anthropometry, Strength, and Motor Fitness," 160–77.

115. Boas, "History of Anthropology," 23–35. For this article Boas was asked specifically to comment on European anthropology and how it had and could affect American anthropology. Boas continued to teach a course in anthropometry and statistical methods at Columbia University after this but his ethnographic work shifted toward cultural historicism and increasingly developed critiques of evolutionary comparative methods. Because of Anthropology Days' notoriety, significant press coverage, novelty, association with an Olympic venue, and Sullivan's feelings of humiliation—as well as the fact that it reaffirmed popular notions of racial superiority that Boas was beginning to fight—and McGee's increasing marginality, it was not an experiment that could be easily hidden in academic obscurity. It had effects, but these affects have just not been remembered (see Parezo and Fowler, *Anthropology Goes to the Fair*).

116. Kohlraush, "Zuzammenhange von Korperform und Leistung," 187–204; Cureton, *Physical Fitness of Champion Athletes*; Correnti and Zauli, *Olimpionici 1960*; Tanner, *Physique of the Olympic Athlete*; Hirata, "Physique and Age of Tokyo Olympic Champions," 207–22; Jokl, *Medical Sociology*; Tittel, "Zur Biotypologie," 172.

117. De Garay, Levine, and Carter, *Genetic and Anthropological Studies*, xv. The study was funded by the Olympic Committee and included in the Cultural Program. There has been significant work in cultural anthropology on the Olympics, including by many scholars in this volume. Here I am specifically speaking of anthropometric research. Unfortunately the authors do not list which of the scholars on their team worked on the anthropological portion of the study.

118. De Garay, Levine, and Carter, *Genetic and Anthropological Studies*, xvi.

Chapter 2. The "Physical Value" of Races and Nations

Anthropology and Athletics at the Louisiana Purchase Exposition

MARK DYRESON

In his preview of the anthropology exhibits at the Louisiana Purchase Exposition, chief architect WJ McGee contended that his division provided "connecting links" for the great diversity of exhibits that made up the St. Louis World's Fair. McGee especially stressed the close connections of the Department of Anthropology to the Department of Physical Culture, where the third Olympic Games of the modern revival were to be held. The anthropologist noted that just to the west of his anthropology enclave "will stretch the extensive grounds allotted to the Department of Athletics, in which under a distinct and capable management, the more attractive and strenuous activities of mankind will be effectively displayed."[1]

In another section of his preliminary report McGee returned to the connections between anthropology and athletics. He predicted that the St. Louis Exposition would "comprise a more complete assembly of the peoples of the world than has ever before been brought together." McGee and his colleagues planned to use this collection of varieties of the human species to launch the most exhaustive anthropometric comparison of human types ever conducted. The Department of Anthropology had constructed an anthropometry laboratory which would use the latest equipment and techniques to measure human variations. In addition to "customary" measures such as height, weight, head shape, arm-spread, skin color, and head shape, the anthropologists announced that they also planned to calibrate physical abilities such as "strength" and "endurance." Those particular calculations, according to McGee, guaranteed that the study would reveal, "so far as measurements may—the relative physical value of the different races of people."[2]

In his preview McGee revealed that his anthropologists would measure not just the "savages" they typically surveyed but also the athletes gathered in St. Louis for the Olympic Games. "In these determinations it is designed to utilize not merely the primitive folk assembled in the department, but representatives of foreign nations and any alien peoples participating in the exhibits on The Pike; and through the courteous co-operation of Mr. J. E. Sullivan, Chief of the Department of Physical Culture, corresponding measurements will be made of typical athletes participating in the Olympic Games and other athletic contests, in order that comparative records may cover the widest possible range in physical development as well as in ethnic affinity," McGee contended.[3]

McGee's plan to make scientific measurements of races and nations in St. Louis fit precisely into the history of *fin-de-siècle* American designs at both world's fairs and Olympic Games. American experiences at the thriving international exposition movement of the late nineteenth and early twentieth centuries centered on the manufacture of national identities and the analysis of racial and ethnic typologies.[4] The world's fair movement gave birth to the Olympic Movement. Indeed, two of the first three Olympic Games, at Paris in 1900 and at St. Louis in 1904, found homes in international expositions.[5]

Since the 1896 revival of the Olympic Games in Athens, the United States had used the athletic contests to measure national strength and prowess. Americans had from the beginning of the modern games interpreted U.S. victories in Olympic contests as evidence of the cultural and social superiority of their nation. American measurements of national prowess invariably considered ethnic affinities. Generally, the multiethnic character of American Olympic teams was perceived as one of the nation's great strengths in international competition, although the racial dynamics of those squads and the larger national society produced a variety of interpretations. The first Olympic

Games on American soil would provide new opportunities for assessing the physical value of their nation against foreign rivals.[6]

The desires of both McGee and Sullivan to measure human prowess in order to make "scientific judgments" about the "physical value" of races and nations would eventually metamorphose into one of the most controversial episodes in the history of sport. On August 11 and 12, 1904, the Department of Anthropology and the Department of Physical Culture at the St. Louis Fair staged a series of Olympic contests known as "Anthropology Days," or the "Tribal Games" as the St. Louis press dubbed them.[7] These sporting competitions pitting "primitive" groups against one another in both "civilized" and "savage" games have generally been regarded as a bizarre aberration that highlighted a pattern of American excesses in the production of the 1904 Olympic Games. The founder of the modern Olympic Games and the president of the International Olympic Committee (IOC), Baron Pierre de Coubertin, dismissed Anthropology Days as a typical example of the vulgarity that infected every aspect of the first American Olympic Games.[8]

Olympic historians, following Coubertin's lead, have consistently assessed Anthropology Days, in particular, and the St. Louis Olympic Games, in general, as the nadir of modern Olympian spectacles. Ever after, the St. Louis Games have been regarded as the Olympics that almost killed the modern Olympic Movement. The conventional wisdom that the St. Louis Olympics was the worst ever staged obscures the real significance of the 1904 Games. In many ways the St. Louis Games set the template for the future. They helped to resolve certain difficulties that had cropped up early in the Olympic revival. After St. Louis, for instance, it became clear that the Olympics needed to escape the orbits of world's fairs lest they be obscured by the older and more gigantic spectacles. The St. Louis Games also served to crystallize certain long-term conflicts within the Olympic Movement. After St. Louis, for instance, it became clear that American notions of what purposes Olympic sport should serve differed quite dramatically from that of the European nations that made up the core of the IOC's leadership. Efforts to Americanize the Olympics, and resistance to those efforts, would shape the movement for the rest of the twentieth century.[9]

The Americanization of the St. Louis Games proved too much for the European power brokers in the IOC. Foreign athletes and officials stayed away from St. Louis in droves. The European press dismissed the 1904 Games as an exercise in American parochialism. Baron de Coubertin himself avoided St. Louis and condemned what he perceived as the vulgar extremism of the American Olympic show. Indeed, the general European impression of the St. Louis Olympics was so poor that many predicted that the Games would collapse after just three modern Olympiads.[10] Pressured by Greek patriots who contended that the Games should find a permanent home in the land of their ancient origin, and by factions within the IOC that wanted to return the Olympics to Athens for at least one more celebration, Baron Pierre de Coubertin acquiesced to a special Olympic meet at Athens in 1906 — a move that broke the supposedly inviolate quadrennial cycle. These intercalary games in Athens rekindled European enthusiasm for the Olympic endeavor.[11] In fact, in the turn-of-the-century American context, neither Anthropology Days nor the rest of the St. Louis Olympian spectacle were particularly peculiar. Anthropology Days was a part of the longstanding effort by the United States to Americanize the Olympic Movement. From 1896 forward, Americans have sought to define the Olympic Games around American cultural mores. The United States has tried to push American sports — from baseball, basketball, and American football to snowboarding, mountain biking, and beach volleyball — to the center of the Olympic program. The American media and public have interpreted Olympic results as indicative of the health and well-being of their national culture. American storytellers have historically used the Olympic Games in discourses about the problems and promises of their own national society. Americans have regularly used the Olympic Games to ponder the meanings of concepts such as "physical value" and racial and national difference.

When the Olympic Games came to St. Louis in 1904 they underwent a thorough Americanization. The U.S. organizers stripped control of the enterprise from Baron Pierre de Coubertin and the IOC and created an Olympian athletic carnival that suited American tastes. They selected a site at the Louisiana Purchase Exposition that fit the needs and desires of American boosters rather than the wishes and criteria of the IOC. They added American flourishes to the program, including baseball, basketball, and American football contests. They promoted the 1904 Olympics as an all-American festival. They used the Olympic Games to advertise American exceptionalism and to justify American expansionism. They linked the Olympic Games to American ideas about sport as a tool for fixing modern problems. They connected the Olympic Games to American efforts to assimilate immigrants and indigenous peoples.[12] They "imagined Olympians," to borrow John Bale's insightful concept, from the border regions of their burgeoning empire.[13]

The Olympic Games have consistently inspired the anthropological imaginations of modern societies as the perfect site for reading "body cultures."[14] At the Louisiana Purchase Exposition, the new discipline of anthropometry provided the initial linkage between academic anthropology and athletics. In fact, the so-called science of anthropometry provided a strong connection in the United States between the emerging fields of anthropology and physical culture. Anthropometry supported the foundation for what would eventually come to be known as physical anthropology in the developing new study of humankind.[15] Anthropometry was also one of the principal fields embraced by the newly organized American Association of Physical Education (established in 1885), a group that included an anthropologist among its founders.[16] The new journal of this physical culture society, the *American Physical Education Review*, frequently published anthropometry studies. Franz Boas, one of the guiding lights of early twentieth-century American anthropology, served on the editorial board of the physical education periodical for several years.[17]

At the St. Louis World's Fair the connections between the anthropologists and the new scientists who studied human movement were particularly apparent. Both the Department of Physical Culture and the Department of Anthropology championed the exposition's displays of anthropometric equipment and promoted anthropometric studies. One of the many "official" reports on the fair described the extensive preparation made by the experts: "In another section, devoted to anthropometry, or measurement of heights, weights, and systematic examination of men, there are charts, statistics, appliances, and instruments in great number, while contests are held daily, in court or field, in bowls, tennis, skittles, quoits, golf, basket-ball, croquet, polo, baseball, football, cricket, lacrosse, and a variety of track athletics, that preach the gospel of muscle, constitution, courage and good health."[18]

The scientific tests of "body cultures" at the St. Louis fair were designed not only by McGee and his anthropological staff but by the eminent physiologist Luther Halsey Gulick from the Department of Physical Culture.[19] When the Department of Physical Culture produced a "World's Olympic Lecture Course" by luminaries in the field, they included speeches by two prominent anthropologists. The director of Chicago's Field Museum of Natural History and the organizer of all the exhibits for the Louisiana Purchase Exposition, Frederick J. V. Skiff, presented a talk on "The General Advantage of Athletic Exercises to the Individual." The former president of the American Association of Anthropology, none other than WJ McGee himself, lectured on "The Influence of Play in Racial Development with Special Reference to Muscular Movement."[20] Several physicians in the same series delivered lectures on anthropometry, including Paul C. Phillips of Amherst College, on "Anthropometric Methods," and R. Tait McKenzie of McGill University, on "Artistic Anatomy in Relation to Physical Training."[21]

Skiff and McGee had other connections to the athletic section of the St. Louis Exposition. Skiff, along with sporting goods magnate A. G. Spalding, had been one of the two "Chicago men" who played instrumental roles in relocating the 1904 Olympics from Chicago, which won the original bidding war, to St. Louis. In addition, Skiff served as a high-ranking official in the Amateur Athletic Union (AAU), the most powerful organization in American sport in that era and the agency that ultimately ran the St. Louis Games.[22] Skiff later became a member of the American Olympic Committee (AOC).[23]

McGee's connection to sport was less obvious than was that of his colleague and former supervisor Skiff. McGee did not join Skiff in the AAU, the AOC, or in any other sporting organization. McGee did, however, participate in leadership roles in a considerable number of scientific societies. Born in rural Iowa in 1853, the self-educated McGee was a transitional figure in the history of American anthropology. Though he never earned a formal university degree, McGee played a key role in the development of the new disciplines of geology and anthropology. He began his career as a surveyor of geological features and archeological sites in his home state of Iowa. His work caught the attention of John Wesley Powell. In 1883 Powell hired McGee for the U.S. Geological Survey. A decade later McGee transferred to Powell's Bureau of American Ethnology (BAE). McGee took the position as lead ethnologist in the federal agency from Powell in 1894. McGee was a key player in a variety of social-science endeavors, serving as a president of the National Geographic Society and a vice president for the American Association for the Advancement of Science. With Franz Boas he expanded the *American Anthropologist* into a national journal and served as the first president (1902–4) of the American Anthropological Association.[24]

McGee began his relationship with the Louisiana Purchase Exposition when he took charge of designing the federal Bureau of American Ethnology's program for the fair. Offered the opportunity to head all of the anthropology exhibits at the St. Louis Exposition, he resigned from the BAE in 1903 and relocated to St. Louis.[25] His motives in resigning were complex. Angered that he had been passed over for leadership of the bureau after his mentor Powell had passed away, McGee's resignation was part of a major power struggle at the Smithsonian.[26] After leaving Washington McGee made it clear that he hoped to turn his fair exhibits into a permanent repository that would sponsor his endeavors, as Frederick Skiff had done in transforming the anthropology division of the 1893 Columbian Exposition in Chicago into the renowned Field Museum. McGee's projected post-exposition "St. Louis Public Museum" would never materialize.[27]

McGee was an ambitious polymath who lacked the formal credentials increasingly necessary for a career in science. Indeed, the title of "Dr." that preceded his name on many of his publications was an honorary award from Iowa's Cornell College. McGee was not a prominent theorist who advanced anthropology with dazzling new scientific insights. Instead, he was a career civil servant who was a key figure in the field as American anthropology moved from its government-sponsored roots to its new academic home in universities.[28] Trained by Powell in the arts of Washington gamesmanship, McGee was a shrewd promoter who understood that linking his esoteric new social science to the modern mania for sport could help raise anthropology's public profile. His political instincts led him to understand the athletic competitions at the Louisiana Purchase Exposition, and in particular to the Olympic Games, as fertile territory to generate popular interest in the Department of Anthropology. Indeed, his preview of anthropological exhibits stressed the connections between his area and the Department of Physical Culture.

Neither McGee nor his mentor Powell wrote extensively about sport. Still, they each believed that athletic performances were important characteristics in human culture. "Athletic sports are universal alike in tribal and national society," contended Powell in an essay contrasting "pleasurable" activities in primitive and modern societies.[29] In McGee's most extensive foray into sporting topics before the 1904 St. Louis Games, he argued forcefully that modern people of European descent were superior athletes when compared to ancient Greeks or to contemporary Asians, Africans, or indigenous groups. In fact, McGee dismissed the notion of "savage" athletic prodigies as the overheated imaginings of travel writers who wanted to sell books. He asserted that "those who know the races realize that the average white man is stronger of limb, fleeter of foot, clearer of eye, and far more enduring of body under stress of labor or hardship than the average yellow or red or black—despite the special proficiency along a few narrow lines sometimes displayed by the lower type and drawn large in travelers' tales."[30]

In promoting modern white men as the "race" with a greater "physical value" than even the Greek champions of antiquity, McGee anticipated later American commentaries on the St. Louis Olympic Games as indicative of the superiority of the United States to all other cultures — historical and contemporary. Such claims fit neatly into the evolutionary schemes McGee and most of his contemporaries in anthropology embraced.[31]

Curiously, McGee would make quite different claims about primitive athletic prowess in the months leading up to the "savage Olympics." Motives other than a change of conviction in the scientific superiority of European peoples account for the shift in his position. In St. Louis McGee had something to sell, not a romantic travelogue, but his exhibits at the Department of Anthropology. In addition, as one of his contemporary colleagues and rivals noted, McGee "had a personal fondness for the unusual."[32] That strain, combined with his expertise in selling exotic cultures to the American public in order to generate public enthusiasm for anthropology, explains why McGee played the role of promoter of "savage" strenuosity as superior to civilized athleticism at the St. Louis carnival. Obedient to Phineas T. Barnum's infamous American dictum that the only bad publicity was no publicity, McGee understood that his dream of making his anthropology exhibits into a permanent St. Louis institution required constant marketing. Attaching anthropology to the mania for modern sport at the first Olympic Games ever held on American soil seemed a stroke of genius. In spite of his earlier assertions that "primitives" were no match for modern athletes, McGee set out to market the very curiosity about "alien races" that he shared with much of the American public through events that measured the "vigor" of a variety of human cultures. He clearly framed his intentions in one of his many reports on his designs for the St. Louis Fair.

> A study of the world's peoples and nations reveals the interesting fact that,
> within limits not fully understood, the vigor of peoples is measured by

135

*complexity of blood no less than by extent of knowledge of culture. Herein
lies reason enough for the study of race-types; and here, too, may well lie
the basis of that innate and intuitive curiosity which renders alien races so
attractive to all mankind. It is the object of the Section of Ethnology at once
to gratify instinctive curiosity and to satisfy the more serious impulses of
students by bringing together a more complete assemblage of the world's
peoples than has hitherto been seen.*[33]

Significantly, McGee had employed sport to popularize anthropology
before his infamous St. Louis demonstrations. As the head of the Bureau
of American Ethnology, McGee invited Stewart Culin to publish the ency-
clopedic *Games of the North American Indians*. Culin, whose mammoth study
of indigenous North American sports had begun as an exhibit at the 1893
Columbian Exposition in Chicago, thanked McGee for his support in the
monograph's preface.[34] The portraits and artifacts illustrating the strenuous life of American aborigines exhibited first at the Columbian Exposition
became one of the most popular attractions at Chicago's Field Museum, a
development that did not go unnoticed by the shrewd McGee.[35] A keen eye
for entrepreneurial opportunity combined with his taste for the unusual led
McGee to promote anthropology through sport.

McGee had other connections to the new American cult of the strenuous
life. His career in Powell's corps of federally sponsored explorers made him
one of a select group of Americans heralded for their strength and endurance in the grand adventures that marked the conquest of the nation's final
geographic frontiers. In an era in which the fear of effeminate overcivilization
consumed much of the nation's middle and upper classes, Powell's men
were clearly not mollycoddles spoiled by modern luxuries.[36] They were cast
as hypermasculine American heroes, revered as much for their endurance
of wilderness hardship as for their scientific discoveries. Powell and his scientific soldiers created the "Indiana Jones" mystique that still occasionally
clings to anthropologists.[37]

Powell's and McGee's views on government Indian policy also betrayed their faith in the common American belief that sports could solve social problems. While they hardly embraced Native Americans as equals, the experts at the Bureau of American Ethnology did argue that military pacification and removal strategies had utterly failed. The BAE romanticized Native Americans as noble, if inferior, "savages" whom the civilized had a responsibility to raise up the evolutionary ladder. Powell and the bureau advocated rounding up the American West's remaining tribes and placing them on reservations. These reservations would serve as civilizing academies. A key feature in the assimilation process was the creation of Indian schools to train a new leadership class for the acculturation process. Powell and his lieutenants, McGee included, promoted their policy as a panacea for the nation's Indian troubles.[38] The advocates of acculturation assigned sport a key role in the civilizing process, especially at Indian schools. Indeed, the growing reputation of Carlisle Indian School's football teams and Haskell Institute's track- and-field squads convinced many that modern sport was quickly civilizing Native American tribes.[39]

The Louisiana Purchase Exposition provided McGee with a great opportunity to publicize the governmental science of assimilation. Following Lewis Henry Morgan's taxonomy, McGee and his colleagues designed the exhibits at the Louisiana Purchase Exposition to illustrate the evolution of humans from "savagery" to "barbarism" to "civilization."[40] They cleverly placed the Model Indian School between the "realistic" huts of the most "savage" human exhibits and the green fields of the modern athletic complex on the evolutionary scale. The roster at the school included tribes the general public knew as great warriors: Sioux, Arapahos, Cheyennes, Apaches, Navajos, Kickapoos. These tribes had only recently been vanquished in the conquest of the great western frontier that Thomas Jefferson had wrangled away from France in the Louisiana Purchase. Some of the most famous figures of the recently concluded Indian wars of the American West were featured at the fair, including Quanah Parker of the Kiowa and Geronimo of the Chiricahua Apache.[41]

8. American Indian tug-of-war in Native dress. From Bennitt and Stockbridge, eds., *History of the Louisiana Purchase Exposition*, 573.

McGee made certain that the former warriors and their peoples were exhibited as safely on the path to modernity in St. Louis, especially in their sporting habits. For the grand opening of the Model Indian School on the first day of June, 1904, organizers staged an elaborate pageant that included an extensive program of athletic contests. Athletes from the Indian School's various tribes competed in 100-meter dashes for boys and girls, a thirty-minute go-as-you-please foot race for men, an intertribal tug-of-war, various archery contests, a javelin throw, a demonstration of Native American shinny (a stickball game that resembled field hockey), and a variety of traditional field sports. Indian School athletes received monetary prizes for their victories in the various events. The Arapahos, once a Plains tribe known for their fierce warriors, won the tribal tug-of-war and a small cash prize while resplendent in full ceremonial regalia.[42]

The athletic contests continued while the Indian School remained in operation. Physical education programs comprised a key element of the Indian School's curriculum. The school's children played regularly at the model playground. McGee contended that one of the surest signs of "savages made, by American methods, into civilized workers" in his department were these daily gymnastic exercises the children performed at the school. Older students held daily athletic competitions. Adults from the various anthropology exhibits also frequented the model gymnasium at the exposition.[43]

The playground, the school, and the gymnasium represented the power of modern physical culture to transform "savages" into citizens of the American public. In placing sport in a key position in his anthropological showcases, McGee was inspired by previous exhibitions of "savage" athleticism. The Louisiana Purchase Exposition was not the first world's fair to showcase "savage" athletic prowess. McGee had seen the exhibits of "savage" sporting talent through artifacts at the 1893 Columbian Exposition. Live demonstrations of Native American athletic ability had also been exhibited at the 1901 Buffalo Pan-American Exposition. The Buffalo fair featured an extensive sporting program designed by James Edward Sullivan, who also served as the architect of the St. Louis Exposition's sporting extravaganza. An intercollegiate baseball game between Cornell University and the Carlisle Indian School opened the Pan-American sports carnival. Cornell and Carlisle also battled on the gridiron at Buffalo during the autumn of 1901.[44] Frank Pierce, a Seneca from Irving, New York, gained a great deal of notoriety for his distance-running feats at the Pan-American Fair.[45] In an exposition that featured a major "Indian Congress" and many Native American exhibits, these demonstrations of American Indian athleticism were significant portents for the Louisiana Purchase Exposition.[46]

The exhibitions of Indians at fairs proved a popular but controversial practice. The Buffalo Pan-American Exposition's depictions of Native Americans in Wild West shows and among the midway amusements created considerable controversy among government officials about the approach that St. Louis should take in displaying Indians. After Congress appropriated forty thousand dollars for "an exhibit of Indian customs and games" in St. Louis, the commissioner of Indian Affairs in the U.S. Department of the Interior, W. A. Jones, announced opposition to the plan. Jones angrily denounced popular Indian shows. He claimed that those presentations did not focus on the success of government acculturation policies but irresponsibly sensationalized Aboriginal peoples for public consumption. Jones complained that no one cared much about "the educational progress of the red man" or what "has been done by Uncle Sam to civilize and educate the Indian." Spectators, he grumbled, just "want to see foot races, fire dances, Indian games, etc., and they do not care to look at him [the Indian] unless he is wrapped in blankets and decked out in feathers." Besides, Jones groused, the easy money that Native Americans made from their athletic and dancing displays and for their pictures and autographs at the Buffalo exposition and at other fairs had made the Indians difficult to control when they returned to their reservations. "No living person loves admiration more than the Indian, and it ruins him to let him pose for a few months, receiving money from the crowd for his photograph and being made a lion by white people," Jones contended in his paternalistic defense of his wards against exploitation by the owners of Wild West shows and midway Indian burlesques.[47]

McGee and the Bureau of American Ethnology promised that they would neither exploit nor sensationalize the Native Americans housed in the Department of Anthropology. But the anthropologists admitted that they would focus on showing Indian sports, games, and amusements. They understood, in spite of Jones's carping, that "foot races" drew public throngs to their "scientific" displays.[48] In order to capitalize on public tastes they designed their exhibits in part around the "muscular excellence" of the peoples they displayed in their human zoo.[49]

In St. Louis the leadership of the Department of Anthropology built on Buffalo's innovations. In their blueprint for the exposition the anthropologists stressed that they planned to illustrate all aspects of "primitive" life, including "games."[50] The anthropologists looked for every opportunity to connect their exhibits with the Olympic Games. For instance, an early preview of the St. Louis Olympics hailed the inclusion of archery at the 1904 Games and marveled at the skill of American "savages" with bows and arrows. The author noted that American Indians had already shown their proficiency in the sport at the "Custer massacre" and other battles in the long history of North American Indian wars.[51]

In order to capitalize on the public fascination with Native prowess the anthropologists staged a day of "Indian games" highlighted by an archery contest. Three Cocopas from Arizona, a tribe that later played a central role in Anthropology Days, and a Sioux took top honors.[52] Although McGee promised that his display of the "so-called wild peoples" would not become the same sort of "sideshow attraction" that human zoos had offered at earlier world's fairs, his collection of Patagonian "giants" competed regularly and "creditably" against American cowboys in the riding and roping contests at Cummins' Wild West Show on the fair's midway.[53]

Demonstrations of "primitive" athletic prowess appeared in many other venues besides the Department of Anthropology. At the enormous Philippine exhibit fair officials displayed the most recent indigenous peoples who had fallen under the American empire. A colony of twelve hundred Filipinos selected from every major ethnic group and tribe in the Islands were displayed in "authentic" settings along the shores of Arrowhead Lake at the heart of the fairgrounds. They performed regular demonstrations of "their aquatic sports" in the shallow waters of the lake.[54]

The Louisiana Purchase Exposition's main entertainment venue, The Pike, also housed Native athletes. Cummins' Wild West Show claimed that "savages" from fifty-one different North American tribes participated in its daily pageants. The principles in the production, "champion lady rider of the world" Lucille Mulhall and Colonel Frederick T. Cummins, "one of the few white men who have been adopted by Indians as a chief," led the Indians through riding, roping, shooting, and Bowie knife demonstrations. The tribes showcased their "savage" abilities by engaging in a raid on an Overland stagecoach and recreating "hostile attacks on settler's cabins." The climax of the show featured "a thrilling battle to the death between the dreaded Sioux and their allies and their implacable foes the Blackfeet and their allies."[55]

Elsewhere along The Pike a group of "Esquimaux" (Eskimo) in a "polar landscape" thrilled fairgoers with displays of "marriage ceremonies," "burial rites," and, especially, "native sports." A combat between the Esquimaux and a polar bear brought down the curtain on the Arctic show. Nearby dwelt the fair's "Cliff Dwellers" from the "stone age," including Zunis and Mokis

(Hopi) from the American Southwest. Pike promoters proudly boasted that while Chicago's 1893 Fair housed cliff dwellings displayed on fake bluffs, the St. Louis version of the show included "real Indians" who "have never been shown in any Wild West display or in any Exposition." The Cliff Dwellers regularly displayed Native sports, games, and rituals, including a wildly popular "snake dance."[56]

The "Indian games," the Wild West rodeos, and the other demonstrations of Aboriginal athleticism culminated in Anthropology Days. Under the guise of science, McGee's Department of Anthropology crafted an "experiment" that they knew would generate enormous interest in their section of the fair. Capitalizing on the upcoming fascination with the late August opening of the main events of the fair's staging of the 1904 Olympic Games, McGee and Simms circulated rumors that the "savages" in their displays were the world's greatest athletes. McGee and Simms contended that their uncivilized charges were better runners, jumpers, and throwers than even the sterling field of Olympians who would soon be assembled in St. Louis. They based their contentions on the then common notion in Morganian evolutionary schemes that those groups lower on the scale of human development needed greater physical prowess in order to survive than the more advanced brain workers of civilized cultures.[57]

The experts in the Department of Physical Culture, particularly director Sullivan and physiologist Luther Halsey Gulick, disputed the anthropologists' contentions that the fair's savages were better athletes than their own Olympians. To put their assertions to the test the Department of Anthropology and the Department of Physical Culture designed a series of athletic competitions for the denizens of the human zoo. Clever St. Louis journalists immediately dubbed these contests the "Tribal Games." Newspaper previews played up the fable of the natural athlete, printing rumors that in practice sessions the uncivilized performers had threatened numerous civilized world records.[58]

The local press reported that the savages had threatened more than records. During a promotional event for the Tribal Games an African Pygmy

9. Negritos from the Philippines take part in the archery contest. From the St. Louis Public Library Online Exhibit "Celebrating the Louisiana Purchase."

practicing running broad jumps took offense to the gaggle of photographers gathered to document his efforts and menaced the St. Louis paparazzi with a spear. The anthropology staff was forced to intervene in order to prevent more picture-taking—or bloodshed.[59] Staged on August 11 and 12, the Tribal Games, or Anthropology Days as the scientists dubbed the contests, put the various theories about the development of human athletic skill to a very public test. Spectators who turned out for the contests witnessed a spectacle that according to the St. Louis Star presented "more real fun, if not bona-fide sport," than any other event at the Louisiana Purchase Exposition.[60]

Clad in "native costumes" and divided into teams by a strange amalgam of ethnic affinity and alleged level of Morganian evolutionary development, the Aboriginal athletes competed in a variety of modern track-and-field events and some supposedly "native" sports.[61] Cash prizes of three dollars for firsts or seconds and one dollar for thirds went to those who placed well in the events.[62]

The team of Americanized Indians from the Model Indian School won the "Tribal Games" handily. They scored, by the media's count, 34 points. A squad from the Philippines comprised of Moros, Negritos, and other Filipino ethnics, finished second with 16.5 points. With 10 points the "giant" Patagonians from South America (the Tehuelches) came in third. The Cocopa team from Arizona finished fourth with 5 points. The Syrians finished fifth with just 1 point. The African Pygmies did not score.[63]

Some of the press complained that the Indian School tribes should not have been allowed to compete since their familiarity with modern sports seemed to give them a great advantage. Indeed, they won all of the modern track- and-field events. None of the performances, however, not even those by the Americanized Indians, greatly impressed the observers of Anthropology Days. The running times and jumping and throwing distances turned in by the Aboriginal athletes could not even match those made by civilized children. Even the so-called Native Games staged at Anthropology Days did not impress most witnesses. James Sullivan dismissed the shinny game and the archery contests as pathetic athletic efforts. Only a "mud fight" between Pygmy factions and a pole climb by some of the Filipinos impressed the leader of the Olympic contests in St. Louis.[64]

Sullivan and his colleagues at the Department of Physical Culture clearly thought they had won the argument about whether the world's best athletes grew from civilized or savage cultures. Sullivan insisted that the Tribal Games "were most successful and interesting, and ones that scientific men will refer to for many years in to come." The contests "taught a great lesson," Sullivan contended. "Lecturers and authors will in the future please omit all reference to the natural athletic ability of the savage, unless they can substantiate their alleged feats." The myth of the natural athlete, Sullivan cheered, had perished in Anthropology Days. Civilized peoples dominated the globe in physical and in all other ways, he declared, a conclusion most fairgoers generally shared.[65]

A disappointed McGee tried to explain the poor performances of his primitive specimens. McGee argued that a lack of familiarity with the sports contested had caused the athletic failures of the savages. He insisted that a few weeks with a professional athletic trainer would make his Natives as proficient as many of the civilized Olympians who would contest in St. Louis at the end of August. Still, while McGee held onto his hypothesis that "primitive peoples" were experts in certain Native athletic pastimes, he finally admitted that in "all around development no primitive people can rank in the same class with the Missouri boy."[66]

In spite of the apparent scientific confirmation that Anthropology Days supplied regarding the specious nature of theories about primitive physical genius, the conjectures refused to die. Indeed, the performance a fortnight later at the "regular" Olympics of two "Kaffirs," South African Tswanas who were at the fair as part of the British reenactment of Boer War battles, and who had also participated in the original Anthropology Days, foreshadowed a future in which non-Western body cultures would increasingly dominate Olympian distance running. The African marathoners belonged to perhaps the most popular attraction at the exposition. One observer described the Boer War extravaganza as a "triumph of genius." The "wild antics of the Zulu" were a key feature of the mock combat. The realism of the reenactment astounded viewers. "By comparison, the exhibitions of the Roman Gladiators were tame, and the modern shows of the Wild West pale into commonplace," contended one witness.[67] The two African runners finished quite respectably, ninth and twelfth out of twenty-nine starters, in the 1904 Olympic marathon.[68]

Heartened by the marathon McGee, in spite of the athletic and public relations disaster of Anthropology Days and the apparently overwhelming negative evidence the Tribal Games generated regarding the athleticism of "savages," did not give up his quest. The anthropologist demanded another test of the theory of the natural athlete. Sullivan adamantly refused to participate with McGee in a second installment of the Tribal Games. McGee pushed ahead without the support of the Department of Physical Culture. In September of 1904, after the conclusion of the "civilized" Olympic Games and with about a month of training for the "savages," the Department of Anthropology put on a sequel to the Tribal Games. McGee could not find any more cash for prizes but did secure some American flags to give to winners.[69]

Approximately thirty thousand spectators turned out for the second Anthropology Days—a marked improvement over the August installment of the spectacle. The month of practice improved performances considerably. A St. Louis Globe-Democrat correspondent noted that "the meeting was a grand success from every point of view, and served as a good example of what the brown men are capable of doing with training."[70] While the Aboriginal athletes might have improved their performances under "civilized" tutelage, their feats certainly did not live up to the earlier hyperbolic claims by some of the anthropologists that the tribal performers would threaten Olympic and world records. Indeed, the lack of detail about the exact nature of the performances in the local or national press indicates that their improvement was hardly sufficient to rekindle faith in the myth of the natural athlete that enamored so many of the experts and so much of the public before the original Anthropology Days in August.

If McGee's second version of Anthropology Days failed to renew public interest in Aboriginal prowess, several other events at the fair did serve that purpose. In spite of the fact that even McGee admitted that the "savages" had failed to live up to their advanced billing as great athletes, the American public continued to "imagine" that sporting prodigies might be discovered among North America's indigenous peoples. Two sporting events associated with the model Indian School sparked new ruminations about "Indianness" and assimilation, nature and civilization. Recovering quickly from their fracas over savage prowess at the Tribal Games, Sullivan's crew and McGee's scientists teamed up to stage a major intercollegiate football game as part of the Olympic program. The gridiron tilt featured the first ever meeting between Indian school powers Carlisle and Haskell. The schools received five thousand dollars for playing the game. A standing-room-only crowd of more than twelve thousand fans watched the Carlisle Indians trounce the Haskell

Indians 38 to 4 on Saturday, November 26 — two days after the celebration of Thanksgiving and the romantic Indian lore that holiday evoked.[71]

The second incident began with much less fanfare. In mid-June a group of girls from the Fort Shaw Indian Boarding School in Montana arrived at the Louisiana Purchase Exposition.[72] They were members of Fort Shaw's interscholastic basketball team, a squad that dominated women's competition in their home state. Settling into the model school, they played intrasquad games twice a week. Their talent impressed the St. Louis press. Reporters speculated that their native agility had been honed by the civilizing processes at Fort Shaw to produce their flair for the American sport invented just thirteen years earlier at the YMCA institute in Springfield, Massachusetts.[73]

As their basketball demonstrations drew ever larger numbers of spectators, the Fort Shaw cagers were invited to take on high school teams from Missouri and Illinois. They handled all challengers easily. Fort Shaw's dominance irritated local basketball promoters. They schemed to defeat the Indian girls, putting together a powerful squad of alumni from St. Louis Central High School, the area's dominant team. A three-game series for the title of champion of the 1904 World's Fair would settle the issue. Fans flocked to the contests. The press covered the series extensively. Fort Shaw swept the first two games and won the title. They proudly took their world's fair championship trophy back to Montana.[74] Their triumph over "civilized" girls made an enormous impression in St. Louis. "We have learned to be humble before the achievements of other peoples whom we have fancied we long ago left behind in the march of progress," admitted one St. Louis correspondent of the impact of Fort Shaw's victory over the hometown squad.[75]

The ambivalent embrace of Fort Shaw's girls' basketball team highlighted the complexities of early twentieth-century American attitudes about racial and national identities. In that era, the term *race* referred both to ethnic groups and to larger social aggregations such as nations. Americans regularly debated the relative characteristics of Irish, Arapaho, and Jewish "races." At the same time they contemplated the power of an American "race" competing for global prestige against the "races" of Great Britain, Germany, Japan, and a host of other nations.[76]

If Anthropology Days focused on the narrow categories of ethnic kinship in comparing the "physical value" of races, Fort Shaw's girls opened windows on the burgeoning turn-of-the-century notion that the United States was a nation comprised of many races welded by sport into a world-dominating power. The regular Olympic Games at the Louisiana Purchase Exposition, contested in between the two installments of Anthropology Days, cemented this particular American interpretation of the nation's international sporting prowess. Although most of the rest of the world's athletes stayed away from the St. Louis Olympics, the American press celebrated the overwhelming U.S. triumph in the medal count as proof that the nation's heterogeneity made it superior to other societies, especially those of "old" Europe. Remarking on an American team that drew athletes from every social class and a great variety of ethnic groups, including the first African American to medal in an Olympic event, James Sullivan, himself the son of Irish immigrants, explained the exceptional vigor of U.S. athletes as the product of a social system that provided opportunities regardless of class standing or ethnic affinity.[77]

Of course, such hyperbole did not match the realities of a turn-of-the-century United States in which class and ethnic affinities mattered a great deal. Still, in 1904 at St. Louis the American Olympic team was invested with the power to represent the nation's ideals and aspirations. By the next Olympic Games the American team's self-proclaimed "melting pot" reputation would expand to include at least the Indian-schooled representatives of the nation's original inhabitants, as they graduated from Anthropology Days to places on the regular squad. In 1908 the press would celebrate an American team comprised of "Anglo Saxon, Teuton, Slav, Celt, Black Ethiopian, and Red Indian."[78]

In the next few years, press coverage of Native American Olympians such as Jim Thorpe, Louis Tewanima, and Duke Kahanamoku once again raised questions about the "physical value" of the nation's conquered groups to international demonstrations of American prowess.[79] Indeed, the practice of "imagining Olympians" among indigenous peoples was not just a U.S. but a North American pastime. Canadians hoped that Onondaga distance runner Tom Longboat would win national glory at the 1908 Olympic Games.[80] In the 1920s the endurance running feats of the Tarahumara tribe from the Chihuahua inspired Mexicans to dream of Olympic gold. Mexican sporting promoters pushed the IOC to add a 100-kilometer ultra-distance race to the Olympic program to highlight Tarahumara prowess.[81] The talents of the Tarahumara foot runners and the accomplishments of another "exotic," the Algerian Abdel Baghinel El Ouafi who won the 1928 Olympic marathon, led sporting enthusiasts in the United States to demand a scouring of the reservations of the American Southwest for Olympic distance-running potential among the Hopis, Zunis, and other tribes.[82]

Long after the Baron de Coubertin dismissed the "savage Olympics" with the contention that "in no place but America would one have dared to place such events on the program,"[83] speculations about the abilities of "primitive" versus "civilized" athletes and efforts to read racial and genetic differences as the determining factor in performances remain embedded in modern Olympic analyses. Indeed, one could argue that Anthropology Days at the St. Louis Games marked the beginning of a long tradition in the United States of using the Olympics to read the "body cultures" of the American nation and of the rest of the world's peoples.

Ultimately, the less than stellar performances at Anthropology Days did not extinguish the conjectures that Olympic champions might arise from the vanquished tribes of the original peoples of North America. The contemplation of racial and national difference remains a central feature of Olympic sport in the twenty-first century. Rather than discrediting scientific and popular measurements of the "physical value" of human populations, Anthropology Days embedded that practice in modern discourse.

Notes

1. WJ McGee, "Anthropology," 4–8; WJ McGee, "Anthropology," in *The Division of Exhibits* (n.p.: n.d.), 45, in World's Fairs microfilm collection, Smithsonian Institution Libraries, Washington DC.

2. WJ McGee, "Department N—Anthropology," 88. McGee, "Anthropology," (1904a):4–8; McGee, "Anthropology," (n.d.):45.

3. WJ McGee, "Department N—Anthropology," 88. McGee, "Anthropology," (1904a):4–8; McGee, "Anthropology," (n.d.):45.

4. Rydell, *All the World's a Fair*; Rydell, *World of Fairs*.

5. MacAloon, "Olympic Games and the Theory of Spectacle," 241–80; MacAloon, *This Great Symbol*; Roche, *Mega-Events and Modernity*.

6. Dyreson, *Making the American Team*, 73–97; Dyreson, "Playing Fields of Progress," 4–23.

7. For histories of Anthropology Days and the St. Louis Olympics see Carlson, "Giant Patagonians and Hairy Ainu," 19–26; Dyreson, *Making the American Team*, 73–97; Dyreson, "Playing Fields of Progress," 4–23.

8. Coubertin declared that "in no place but America would one have dared to place such events on a program, but to Americans everything is permissible, their youthful exuberance calling certainly for the indulgence of the Ancient Greek ancestors, if, by chance, they found themselves among the amused spectators." Coubertin, *Une Campagne de 21 Ans*, 161, as quoted in Guttmann, *Games Must Go On*, 20.

9. Dyreson, "'To Construct a Better and More Peaceful World.'"

10. Most scholars of the modern Games rank St. Louis at the bottom of Olympian spectacles. Popular accounts generally rank them, with the 1900 Paris Games that also attached themselves to a world's fair, as "fiascoes" and state that the 1906 Athens Games saved the Olympic Movement. Johnson, *All That Glitters*, 127. Academic tomes take a similar tone. "Historians consider the third Olympic Games, held in St. Louis, to have been the worst in the history of the Olympic movement," opines C. Robert Barnett in the opening line of his chapter on the St. Louis games. Barnett, "St. Louis, 1904," 33. Most scholarly accounts concur with Barnett and declare the St. Louis Games the nadir of the modern Olympic series. J. Lucas, "American Involvement in the Athens Olympic Games," 217–28; J. Lucas, *Modern Olympic Games*, 67–80; Mallon, *1904 Olympic Games*, 1–14; Mallon, *1906 Olympic Games*, 1–5; Guttmann, *Olympics*, 27; Senn, *Power, Politics, and the Olympic Games*, 26.

11. Kitroeff, *Wrestling with the Ancients*, 53–76.

12. Dyreson, *Making the American Team*, 73–97; Dyreson, "Playing Fields of Progress," 4–23.

13. Bale, *Imagined Olympians*.

14. I use the term "body culture" as Susan Brownell does, in *Training the Body for China*,

to refer to the systematic organization of ideas, symbols, and meanings through human corporeality. See also Eichberg, *Body Cultures*.

15. Patterson, *Social History of Anthropology*; Baker, *From Savage to Negro*; Eriksen and Nielsen, *History of Anthropology*.

16. The anthropologist was E. P. Thwing, president of the New York Academy of Anthropology. Park, "*Research Quarterly* and Its Antecedents," 1.

17. Boas served on the board of the *American Physical Education Review* from 1898 to 1904.

18. Buel, *Louisiana and the Fair*, 1458.

19. J. Sullivan, "Review of Olympic Games of 1904," 249.

20. Francis, *Universal Exposition of 1904*, 542–43; Bennitt and Stockbridge, *History of the Louisiana Purchase Exposition*, 567–68.

21. Abstracts of the lectures by Phillips and MacKenzie can be found in the *Olympic Games Programme*, 20–21.

22. A. G. Spalding to J. F. W. Skiff, October 9, 1902, Executive Committee Minutes; Sullivan, "Review of Olympic Games of 1904," 157; Hoch, "Olympic Games," 10–15.

23. Dyreson, *Making the American Team*, 128–30.

24. Hodge, "WJ McGee," 683–87; Darnell, "WJ McGee," 1–4.

25. W. Holmes, "Introduction."

26. "Row at Smithsonian?" *New York Commercial Advertiser*, August 14, 1903; "McGee, Ethnologist, Resigns from the Bureau," *Washington Times*, August 14, 1903; "Prof. McGee Resigns," *Washington Post*, August 14, 1903; "Prof. McGee Resigns," *Boston Record*, August 14, 1903; "Gives Up His Place," *Washington Star*, August 14, 1903; "Professor McGee's Resignation," *New York Tribune*, August 15, 1903; "Prof. McGee Resigns," *New York Times*, August 15, 1903; "Ethnologist McGee to Go to St. Louis," *Baltimore Herald*, August 17, 1903; "Professor McGee Resigns," *Boston Transcript*, August 14, 1903; "Professor WJ McGee Severs His Connection With Bureau of American Ethnology," *St. Louis Globe-Democrat*, August 14, 1903; in the Louisiana Purchase Exposition Scrapbooks, vol. 49, Louisiana Purchase Exposition Collection, Missouri Historical Society. Curtis Hinsley's chapter, "The Rise and Fall of William John McGee, 1893–1903," chronicles McGee's tumultuous tenure in the Bureau of Ethnology. Hinsley, *Savages and Scientists*, 261–81.

27. Hodge, "WJ McGee," 683–87; Darnell, "WJ McGee," 1–4.

28. Hodge, "WJ McGee," 683–87; Darnell, "WJ McGee," 1–4.

29. Powell, "Esthetology," 12.

30. WJ McGee, "The Trend of Human Progress," 413. In fact, McGee asserted that Europeans were superior to other groups in all human endeavors. "It is a matter of common observation that the white man can do more and better than the yellow, the yellow man can do more and better than the red or black; and the record of handiwork in the archeology of the world tells that faculty has grown steadily from age to age," he wrote, embracing the scientific racism so typical of his era.

31. Lynch, "Greek Olympic Games," 714–25.

32. Hodge, "WJ McGee," 685.

33. WJ McGee, "Introduction," ii.

34. Culin, "Games of the North American Indians."

35. Nash and Feinman, *Curators, Collections, and Contexts.*

36. Mrozek, *Sport and American Mentality*; Bederman, *Manliness and Civilization.*

37. Hinsley, *Savages and Scientists*; Stocking, *Romantic Motives.*

38. Worster, *River Running West*; Hinsley, *Savages and Scientists.*

39. Bloom, *To Show What an Indian Can Do*; D. Adams, *Education for Extinction*; Oxendine, *American Indian Sports Heritage.*

40. Morgan, *Ancient Society.*

41. WJ McGee, "Introduction," x; See also, "Native Dwellings at the St. Louis Exposition," 217–18; "Racial Exhibit at the St. Louis Fair," 412–14.

42. Parezo and Fowler, *Anthropology Goes to the Fair.*

43. WJ McGee, "Strange Races of Men"; LPEC—World's Fair Bulletin, "Model Playground," 12–13; LPEC—World's Fair Bulletin, Photograph of "Children of All Nations at the Model Playground," 21; LPEC—World's Fair Bulletin, " Thanksgiving Feast," 22.

44. J. Sullivan, "Athletics in the Stadium," 501–8; "Athletics at Indian School," *New York Times*, January 19, 1901; "Sports at Buffalo Meet," *New York Times*, February 25, 1901; "Pan-American Sports," *New York Times*, March 21, 1901; "In the Football World," *New York Times*, October 19, 1901. Cornell beat Carlisle 6 to 5 in baseball and 17 to 0 in football. "Cornell, 6; Carlisle, 5," *New York Times*, June 9, 1901; "Cornell 17; Carlisle, 0," *New York Times*, October 20, 1901.

45. Pierce won the five-mile race at the AAU Junior National Championships and the three-mile race at the Metropolitan (New York City) AAU Championships that were moved to Buffalo in 1901. He finished second in the five-mile run at the AAU Senior National Championships. "New York Athletes Win," *New York Times*, June 15, 1901; "Good Sport at Buffalo," *New York Times*, June 16, 1901; "Exciting Finishes in Buffalo Games," *New York Times*, July 28 1901. Parezo (this volume) notes that he is pictured in a photo of the 1904 marathon start.

46. "Col. Roosevelt in the Midway," *New York Times*, May 24, 1901; "Sunday Shows Prohibited," *New York Times*, July 29, 1901; Minnie J. Reynolds, "Exposition as an Educator," *New York Times Sunday Magazine*, October 6, 1901.

47. "No Wild West Show," *Winona (Minnesota) Republican*, October 31, 1902; "Indians at World's Fair," *St. Louis Globe-Democrat*, October 30, 1902; "The Indians at St. Louis," *Boston Transcript*, October 31, 1902; "Indian Exhibit at St. Louis," *New York Post-Telegram*, October 31, 1902; "Indian Exhibit at St. Louis," *New York Evening-Post*, October 31, 1902; "Indians for World's Fair," *Elmira (New York) Star*, November 15, 1902; "Indians at the World's Fair," *Albany (Oregon) Herald*, November 16, 1902; in Louisiana Purchase Exposition Scrapbooks, vol. 128, Louisiana Purchase Exposition Collection, Missouri Historical Society.

48. "Many Races to Be Brought Together," *Philadelphia North American*, March 13, 1903;

"Many Races to Be Brought Together," *Ansonia (Connecticut) Sentinel*, March 31, 1903; in the Louisiana Purchase Exposition Scrapbooks, vol. 49, Louisiana Purchase Exposition Collection, Missouri Historical Society.

49. "To Exhibit Man at the St. Louis Fair," *New York Times*, November 1, 1903; "Pigmy [sic] Men and Giants," *New Orleans States*, November 4, 1903; "Patagonia's Big Chief," *Atlantic City (New Jersey) Press*, October 8, 1903; "Tribe of Giants May Be Seen at the Fair," *St. Louis Republic*, October 7, 1903; "Indian Giants for Fair," *Chicago Daily News*, October 7, 1903; "Group of Giants for World's Fair," *New York Telegram*, October 7, 1903; "Patagonians for the Fair," *Boston Evening Transcript*, October 7, 1903; in the Louisiana Purchase Exposition Scrapbooks, vol. 49, Louisiana Purchase Exposition Collection, Missouri Historical Society.

50. Buel, *Louisiana and the Fair*, vol. 4.

51. Casselman, "Old and Novel Sport of Archery," 631.

52. Only four Indians managed bull's eyes in the contest, three Cocopas and a Sioux. WJ McGee, "Strange Races of Men," 5187.

53. Buel, *Louisiana and the Fair*, 4:1414; WJ McGee, "Introduction," v.

54. Secretary of the Committee on Ceremonies, *Military Camp and Special Days and Events*, 9; program in Louisiana Purchase Exposition Collection, Missouri Historical Society.

55. MacMechen, "A Ten Million Dollar Pike and Its Attractions," 5–36; MacMechen, "The Ten Million Dollar Pike," 2–32; in Louisiana Purchase Exposition Collection, Missouri Historical Society.

56. MacMechen, "A Ten Million Dollar Pike and Its Attractions," 5–36; MacMechen, "The Ten Million Dollar Pike," 2–32; in Louisiana Purchase Exposition Collection, Missouri Historical Society.

57. Dyreson, *Making the American Team*, 73–97; Dyreson, "Playing Fields of Progress," 4–23.

58. J. Sullivan, *Spalding's Athletic Almanac for 1905*, 249; "Moros to Win Tribal Games," *St. Louis Globe-Democrat*, August 11, 1904; "Moro Athlete Approaches World's Jumping Record," *St. Louis Globe-Democrat*, August 11, 1904.

59. "Indians Show Excellent Form in Intertribal Athletic Meet," *St. Louis Globe-Democrat*, August 12, 1904.

60. "Indians First; Filipinos Second; Patagonians Third," *St. Louis Star*, August 13, 1904.

61. LPEC—World's Fair Bulletin, "Novel Athletic Contest," 50; J. Sullivan, *Spalding's Athletic Almanac for 1905*, 249–57; Bennitt and Stockbridge, *History of the Louisiana Purchase Exposition*, 567–73; "Indians First; Filipinos Second; Patagonians Third" 4; "Pygmies in Mud Fight," *St. Louis Republic*, August 13, 1904; "Barbarians Meet in Athletic Games," *St. Louis Post-Dispatch*, August 13, 1904; "American Indians Capture Anthropology Athletic Meet," *St. Louis Globe-Democrat*, August 13, 1904; "At the Intertribal Games in the World's Fair Stadium," *St. Louis Star*, August 14, 1904; "Pygmies Outdo Savage Athletes," *St. Louis Post-Dispatch*, August 14, 1904.

62. LPEC — World's Fair Bulletin, "Novel Athletic Contest," 50.

63. LPEC — World's Fair Bulletin, "Novel Athletic Contest," 50; J. Sullivan, *Spalding's Athletic Almanac for 1905*, 249–57; Bennitt and Stockbridge, *History of the Louisiana Purchase Exposition*, 567–73; "Indians First; Filipinos Second; Patagonians Third"; "Pygmies in Mud Fight"; "Barbarians Meet in Athletic Games"; "American Indians Capture Anthropology Athletic Meet"; "At the Intertribal Games in the World's Fair Stadium"; "Pygmies Outdo Savage Athletes."

64. LPEC — World's Fair Bulletin, "Novel Athletic Contest," 50; J. Sullivan, *Spalding's Athletic Almanac for 1905*, 249–57; Bennitt and Stockbridge, *History of the Louisiana Purchase Exposition*, 567–73; "Indians First; Filipinos Second; Patagonians Third"; "Pygmies in Mud Fight"; "Barbarians Meet in Athletic Games"; "American Indians Capture Anthropology Athletic Meet"; "At the Intertribal Games in the World's Fair Stadium"; "Pygmies Outdo Savage Athletes."

65. LPEC — World's Fair Bulletin, "Novel Athletic Contest," 50; J. Sullivan, *Spalding's Athletic Almanac for 1905*, 253–57.

66. LPEC — World's Fair Bulletin, "Novel Athletic Contest," 50.

67. Filcher, "South African Boer War," 47.

68. Only fourteen runners finished the race. "How the Great Marathon Was Run and Won," *St. Louis Star*, August 31, 1904.

69. Parezo and Fowler, *Anthropology Goes to the Fair*.

70. Louisiana Purchase Exposition Scrapbooks, Missouri Historical Society, as cited in Parezo and Fowler, *Anthropology Goes to the Fair*.

71. "Football at St. Louis," *New York Commercial-Advertiser*, October 6, 1903; "Football Series at World's Fair," *New York News-Telegram*, October 7, 1903; "Football at Fair," *Denver News*, October 9, 1903; "Football Series at World's Fair," *Louisville Courier-Journal*, October 9, 1903; "College Games at the St. Louis World's Fair," *New York American*, October 11, 1903; "Football Among Olympic Games, *Shreveport Journal*, October 13, 1903, Louisiana Purchase Exposition Scrapbooks, vol. 31, Missouri Historical Society. See also, J. Sullivan, *Spalding's Official Athletic Almanac for 1904*, 184–85; J. Sullivan, "Review of the Olympic Games of 1904," 157–63; Francis, *Universal Exposition of 1904*, 536–42; "Football by Indians at the World's Fair," *New York Times*, November 27, 1904; Parezo and Fowler, *Anthropology Goes to the Fair*.

72. Fort Shaw also supposedly sent a boys' football team to the fair, although no evidence of their engaging in a football scrimmages exists. "Fort Shaw Football Team Will Go to St. Louis During the World's Fair," *Great Falls (Montana) Leader*, September 28, 1903, Louisiana Purchase Exposition Scrapbooks, vol. 31, Missouri Historical Society.

73. Peavy and Smith, "World Champions," 40–78.

74. Peavy and Smith, "World Champions," 40–78.

75. William Reedy, "The End of the Fair," *The Mirror*, December 1, 1904, as cited in Peavy and Smith, "World Champions," 65.

76. Banton, *Racial Theories*; Bowler, *Evolution*; Degler, *In Search of Human Nature*; Gossett, *Race*; Gould, *Mismeasure of Man*; Hannaford, *Race*; Jacobsen, *Whiteness of a Different Color*.

77. Dyreson, *Making the American Team*, 73–126; Dyreson, "Playing Fields of Progress," 4–23.

78. "Olympic Games," 636.

79. Nendel, "New Hawaiian Monarchy," 32–52; Wheeler, *Jim Thorpe*; Dyreson, *Making the American Team*, 127–207.

80. Kidd, *Tom Longboat*.

81. Dyreson, "Foot Runners Conquer Mexico and Texas."

82. "El Ouafi's Marathon," *New York Times*, August 7, 1928; "Indian Runners in Long Races," *New York Times*, July 14, 1929; John Kieran, "Sports of the Times," *New York Times*, October 21, 1929. On the racial dialogues surrounding El Ouafi's surprise victory see Dyreson, "American Ideas About Race and Olympic Races."

83. Coubertin, as quoted in Guttmann, *Games Must Go On*, 20.

Chapter 3. Pierre de Coubertin's Concepts of Race, Nation, and Civilization

OTTO J. SCHANTZ

Born in Paris in 1863, Baron Pierre de Coubertin, French pedagogue, historian, journalist, and sports leader, wanted his name to be associated with a great educational reform in France that would prepare young men for the challenges of the twentieth century. His reform was aimed at the classical triad of intellectual, moral, and physical education. Influenced by the English and the North American school systems, he considered vigorous sport to be an important educational tool and tried to promote it as such, first in France and later throughout the "civilized" world. In 1894 he founded the International Olympic Committee (IOC) and in the following years developed an ideological basis for the modern Olympic Movement. For this ideology—a syncretism that draws on ancient Greek philosophy, the Enlightenment, French humanism and festival culture, as well as British "muscular Christianity"—he coined the neologism *Olympism*. After having been president of the International Olympic Committee since 1896 he withdrew in 1925 in order to devote the rest of his life to the education of the working class. He was disillusioned by the Olympic Movement as it became increasingly governed by technocrats who did not care about the original ideals and significance of the movement. In 1937, when he passed away in Geneva, he was impoverished, having spent his entire fortune on promoting the Olympic ideals and his educational reforms.

Pierre de Coubertin did not attend the third Olympic Games of 1904 in St.

10. Pierre de Coubertin. From J. Sullivan, ed., "The Olympic Games of 1906 at Athens," 16.

Louis, even though he was at that time president of the International Olympic Committee and despite the fact that in March 1904 he had declared his intention to be present at the closing ceremony of the Games in November.[1] The reasons why he did not visit his beloved America are not clear.[2] Was it really his lasting bad impression of St. Louis, which he had visited as a tourist, as he pretended in his Olympic memoirs? Or was it a protest against the so-called Anthropology Days, as some researchers in Olympic studies suggest?[3] In any case, his critique of these Games was rather harsh, especially his comments on the Anthropology Days.

> The St. Louis Games did feature some original approaches. The "star attraction," so to speak, was incontestably what the Americans called, in their picturesque language, the "anthropological day," a day that lasted forty-eight hours, in fact. In the course of these singular athletic meets, competitions were held in the Stadium pitting the Sioux against Patagonians, the

11. Turk throwing the "javelin." The javelin was not contested in the 1904 Olympic Games. It made its first appearance in the 1906 intermediate Olympic Games in Athens, in which there was no American contestant because "it was an event that our athletes knew absolutely nothing about" (J. Sullivan, *The Olympic Games of 1906*, 91). Although the implement thrown in Anthropology Days was called a "javelin," it had a spear tip, unlike the smoothly tapered implement thrown in 1906, which resembled today's javelin. From J. Sullivan, ed., *Spalding's Official Athletic Almanac for 1905: Special Olympic Number, Containing the Official Report of the Olympic Games of 1904*, 264. From the LA84 Foundation Digital Archive.

Cocopa of Mexico and the Moro of the Philippines, the Ainu of Japan, the Pygmies of Africa, the Syrians, and the Turks—the latter [not] flattered, no doubt, at being included in such company.[4] All these men competed in the usual civilized contests, foot races, rope climbing, shot put and javelin throwing, jumping, and archery. Nowhere else but in America would anyone have dared to put such a thing in the program of an Olympiad. But for the Americans, all is permitted. Their youthful enthusiasm certainly enjoyed the indulgence of the shades of the great Greek ancestors, if, by chance, they happened to be wandering by at that moment among the amused throng.[5]

More than twenty years later, in his *Olympic Memoirs*, first published in the journal *L'Equipe* between December 1931 and March 1932, Coubertin gives us the following personal perspective on the Anthropology Days during the 1904 Games:

So the St. Louis Games were completely lacking in attraction. Personally, I had no wish to attend them. . . . I had a sort of presentiment that the Olympiad would match the mediocrity of the town. As far as originality was concerned, the only original feature offered by the program was a particularly embarrassing one. I mean the "Anthropological Days," whose events were reserved for Negroes, Indians, Filipinos, and Asians, with the Turks and Syrians thrown in for good measure! That was twenty-six years ago! Now tell me that the word [world] has not advanced since then and that no progress has been made in sporting spirit.[6]

In 1913, in another article entitled "An Olympiad in the Far East," Coubertin gave a somewhat different perspective on the Anthropology Days. In this article Coubertin proposed that it was the Asians, and not the Turks or Syrians, who were not flattered by the presence of the other "barbarian" participants.

We are now in possession of curious accounts of the beginnings of exotic athleticism. In truth, these are not really its beginnings. The festivities *recently held in the capital of the Philippines did have a precedent. During the competitions of the Third Olympiad, held in St. Louis in 1904, one or more days were reserved for performances by Asians. The Americans clearly see themselves as athletic preceptors in the Far East. The day-long festivities in St. Louis were hardly flattering for the people in that part of the world. These descendants of such ancient and refined civilizations were called on to compare with representatives of peoples scarcely refined out of their original barbarianism. This was a mistake.[7]*

These comments can be interpreted and have been interpreted in different ways. The French historian and journalist Françoise Hache thinks that Coubertin's comments on the Anthropology Days showed that he was amused rather than shocked.[8] Allen Guttmann, however, states that "although polite, Coubertin was clearly not amused.[9] For the critical French group of authors hiding their identities by signing "Quel corps?" Coubertin's statements concerning the St. Louis Anthropology Days are without a doubt an expression of racism.[10]

At first glance one could argue that Coubertin was offended by the fact that separate competitions were organized for "exotic people" during a festival that claimed to bring together athletes from all over the world. But if we take a closer look we see that he established a ranking of the different ethnic groups and expressed his disapproval of the fact that people from "refined civilizations" were obliged to compete with people from almost "barbarian" origins, with the latter including Native Americans and Pygmies from Africa. He clearly associates cultural difference with inferiority. It seems clear that these statements about the Anthropology Days are expressions of Coubertin's racist attitude, demonstrating that he practiced a "culture-coded form" of racism by ranking people according to their different cultural origins.[11]

Coubertin's writings and ideas provoke a large range of critique: some consider him a great humanist, others a proto-fascist and racist.[12] Many of Coubertin's critics are either hagiographers or bashing detractors.[13] In the following, I will analyze Coubertin's concept of race in order to better understand the anthropological foundations of his Olympism in general and his comments concerning the 1904 Anthropology Days in particular. I will examine to what degree Coubertin's views on race reflected the *Zeitgeist* in France and Western Europe, and to what degree his views were different from the American view that formed the rationale for Anthropology Days.

It would be easy to select from the huge written work of Coubertin just those quotations that more or less corroborate or contradict the hypothesis that Coubertin was a racist.[14] In order to avoid such a selective and biased perception, I have tried to incorporate all of the work published between 1888 and 1937 in my analysis. When they are accessible, I have also included unpublished manuscripts.

Race and Racism

Before contextualizing and analyzing Coubertin's concept of "race" and questioning his possible "racism," we must examine the definitions and assumptions of these terms. This is a dangerous endeavor, as the boundaries of these terms are ambiguous and fuzzy. Jeffrey Sammons warns: "Race is at best a confusing, if not worthless term, and, at worst, a dangerous one."[15] Today biologists generally agree that race is not a scientifically meaningful concept for classifying human beings.[16] From a social-science perspective race is a socially constructed and thus historically contingent concept.[17] But even within the same time period and the same social context the notion of race can take on different meanings.[18] As the use of this term was quite common during Coubertin's lifetime, and its meaning broad and indistinct, we have to be aware of this polysemy when analyzing his writings.

In a larger sense, which could incorporate a broad spectrum of social and historical contexts, race could be defined as "a social construction predicated upon the recognition of difference and signifying the simultaneous distinguishing and positioning of groups vis-à-vis one another."[19]

It is even more difficult to define *racism* or the different kinds of racism.

While considering race as a construction dependent on historical and social settings, we have likewise to find a common denominator to define racism, otherwise it would be difficult to avoid a totally relative position. A viable way to approach this problem is the "ideal typical definition" of Neil MacMaster "that restricts racism to those belief systems which categorized individuals in a deterministic way, whether expressed through biology or culture, such that they were incapable of moving from one social position to another."[20] The advantage of this definition is that, despite its minimal assumptions, it includes the element of culture. As Thomas C. Holt notices, "defining racism in the terms of the old idea of biological inferiority, for example, leaves unaddressed a lot of patently racist practices in contemporary life."[21] In some discourses that replace (in the form of a camouflage) the term *race* by the ideologically less charged terms of culture or ethnicity, we notice a kind of "racism without races."[22]

In the *Encyclopaedia Britannica* we can find the following definitions, which in general have the benefit of widespread acceptance: "Racism also called racialism [is] any action, practice, or belief that reflects the racial worldview—the ideology that humans are divided into separate and exclusive biological entities called 'races,' that there is a causal link between inherited physical traits and traits of personality, intellect, morality, and other cultural behavioral features, and that some races are innately superior to others."[23] In the popular mind, race is in general linked to physical differences among peoples like skin color, and such features as dark skin color have been seen as markers of low status.

Race and Racism in Nineteenth-century France

It is not the aim of this contribution to retrace the history of racism, but in order to understand Coubertin's conception of race we have to situate him in the *Zeitgeist*, the paradigm of his time. Heterogenic forms of racism, like anti-Semitism or hatred of black people, can be found in different cultures at least as early as medieval times.[24] It wasn't until the nineteenth century, however, that a more general and racist theory that included these different earlier forms was born in Europe. It was a more- or-less homogenized ideology claiming scientific evidence for the existence of distinct human races of differing values.

Heinz-Georg Marten distinguishes three different types of racial theories in nineteenth-century Europe: (1) a cultural-historical theory, which is based on an a priori inequality concerning political and cultural potential; (2) Social Darwinism, which focuses on the selection process; and (3) syncretistic theories, which combine the first two.[25]

Even though Coubertin often used the term *race* to categorize human groups, it would be anachronistic to consider him to be a racist based only on his use of this term. In nineteenth-century Europe, and even at the beginning of the twentieth century, race was a very fluid notion. Not only did the different disciplines use it in different senses, but even within the disciplines the definitions could fluctuate. Alfred Fouillé, one of the influential philosophers of the Third French Republic, complained that anthropologists had neglected the study of peoples' behavior and claimed that philosophers should do research on the psychology of the different races.[26] Fouillé defined race as "a group of individuals possessing certain hereditary traits."[27] Hippolyte Taine, a thinker who had much influence on Coubertin, gave a similar definition of race as inherent and hereditary traits that "varied between people."[28] The idea of race gained a strong historical connotation and was used as a synonym for "people" or "nation." It was employed, for example, to distinguish the Irish from the English.[29]

Coubertin's Political Position

In Coubertin's writings the semantic distinctions among "race," "nation," and "people" are not very clear. He often talks about the French, the German, or the Irish "race."[30] Coubertin even used this term to distinguish well-prepared and trained athletes from the man on the street. He considered that respect for his principles of Olympism would create a "race of sportsmen," a *race sportive*.[31] Such use of this term recalls the old signification of race in its sense of distinguished class or noble lineage, and as such it joins the "aristocracy of muscle," another expression that Coubertin often used to distinguish "true" sportsmen from ordinary people.[32]

In the nineteenth century in France, ethnocentrism, nationalism, and racism were not exclusively but were still closely linked to the conservative and rather rightwing political position. It is evident that Coubertin had a close relationship to this political milieu through his aristocratic origins and his education, at least until the end of the First World War. Most of his teachers and maîtres penseurs were conservatives.[33] He considered himself a rallié, somebody who joined the Republicans after having been a monarchist. But even among the Republicans, "racial thought" was common at the end of the nineteenth century in France. According to Carole Reynaud Paligot, a "racial paradigm" constructed by scientists, which was largely vulgarized in popular literature and accepted by a great majority of French society, characterized the French Republic from 1860 to 1930.[34] There were exceptions to the Republican principle of equality: There were "brothers and subjects" who were equal but not exactly equal.[35] Some Republicans, like Alexis de Tocqueville or Jules Ferry, tried to argue that human rights should not be applied systematically to all races, and that such an application should depend on the circumstances.[36] It is highly unlikely that this racial paradigm of the Third French Republic was without influence on Coubertin.

"Rebronzer la France" (that is, return its former strength, stability, and splendor to France) had been the motto and driving force for Coubertin's political statements and educational engagement from the age of twenty until the time of the Great War.[37] He was a fervent partisan of French national energy, a zealous patriot, but he was against all kinds of extremism. He called himself an "independent."[38] Except for his active involvement in 1898 as a candidate for the local elections in Le Havre, he always presented himself as an independent, refusing any adherence to any political party.[39] He was antisocialist but also against reactionary monarchists and was a strong enemy of Charles Maurras, the founder of the "Action Française."[40]

"The wonder about Coubertin," John J. MacAloon writes, "is not that he shared certain concerns with France's most notable reactionaries, but that he managed to escape the ideological excesses to which they led. It was his internationalism that saved him."[41]

Even though he focused his early efforts on a reform of the French educational system, Coubertin was already internationally minded, and tried to find models for his reform outside of his home country. Very early he encouraged international meetings in the field of sports. When in 1888 Pascal Grousset, one of his rivals in the field of sports education, proposed to celebrate a national Olympic Games, he provoked a stark reaction from Coubertin, who condemned the nationalist and militarist orientations of Grousset's educational ideas.[42] For Coubertin internationalism was one of the essential characteristics of sport. As early as 1891 he called for internationalization of the sports movement.[43]

Coubertin and Social Darwinism

Coubertin was convinced that utilitarianism was the mainstream philosophy of the early twentieth century. Education and physical training had to be a contribution to the struggle of life in order to be valued. He regarded his "utilitarian gymnastics," which he had developed around 1902, as such a contribution.[44] The American president Theodore Roosevelt, with whom he had an intense epistolary exchange, was a kind of role model for the modern man, physically and intellectually well trained for the struggle for survival of the fittest. Coubertin wanted to prepare the individual for this struggle of life. Education and training should provide a "strong individual culture."[45] However, contrary to the isolating form of individualism described by Alexis de Toqueville, he did not consider this individual culture a final objective but a means to strengthen society.[46] The improvement of the citizen was in the long term an improvement of the community: *Civium vires hodie cras civitatis vis.*[47] Like Theodore Roosevelt, under whose auspices the 1904 St. Louis Games took place, he was convinced that "a healthy state can exist only when men and women who make it up lead clean, vigorous, healthy lives."[48]

In Great Britain of the 1880s and 1890s, as well as in France, although with a short delay, the influence of Social Darwinism changed its form. The struggle of survival of the fittest began to be seen less on the level of individuals than on the level of a competition between nations. The question was raised "of whether individual 'races' were not better subjects for inquiry than a myriad of individuals, and whether 'advanced races' could control their destinies by governmental, social, or perhaps even genetic organization."[49]

Coubertin regarded loyal and legitimate international competition, the "healthy international emulation" in sports, industry, science, and culture—and if necessary in war—as a playing field or battlefield for nations to strengthen their national body, their race.[50] Colonialism was for him part of this universal competition between the great civilized nations, and Coubertin was eager to see France take part in this competition and keep pace with the great leading nations.[51]

Race and Nation, or the Nation as Organism

According to Hobsbawm, it was only in the late nineteenth century that racial and linguistic homogeneity became a determinant discriminator between nations.[52] The terms *race* and *nation* were used interchangeably. The nation was regarded as a group of biologically different persons, distinct by "essential characteristics in germ-plasm or 'blood.'"[53]

The term *race* was not just used as a synonym for *nation* but signified its racialization, which produced a new representation: the nation became a biological organism.[54] This organicism was typical of the traditional French right. In his voluminous work on the origins of France, Hippolyte Taine depicts the "Grand Nation" like a medical doctor would describe a deathly ill person.[55] The "biopolitical" paradigm was dominant in the nineteenth century.[56] Like Taine, Coubertin searched for medication for a degenerate society. However, the nation as biological organism should not be compared to the life cycle of a human being, his birth, youth, golden age, and finally decline and the death, as was common in the nineteenth century. Coubertin was convinced, as was Frédéric Le Play, that the youth of a people could be indefinitely preserved by its "own efforts and by the respect of healthy social traditions."[57] Parts of the essential remedies were physical education and sports.

Coubertin had a rather Lamarckian view of evolution; he was a defender of eugenics and was convinced that future generations would profit from the physical fitness and healthy life styles of today's generation.[58] Coubertin argued that if people neglected this important role of physical activities, it would "probably damage their health, but for sure that of future generations."[59] At least before the First World War, he thought that inherited traits could be acquired. Even though "heredity can not be replaced; it can decline or it can be slowly acquired."[60]

As a participant in the art competition of the 1912 Olympic Games he praised the eugenic functions of sports in his "Ode to Sport": "O Sport, you are Fecundity! You tend by straight and noble paths towards a more perfect race, blasting the seeds of sickness and righting the flaws which threaten its needful soundness. And you quicken within the athlete the wish to see growing about him brisk and sturdy sons to follow him in the arena and in their turn bear off joyous laurels."[61]

According to Christian Geulen, Social Darwinist concepts and the racialization of the nation did not—as one could imagine in the context of a mounting nationalism in Europe—contribute to the radicalization of nationalism in the sense of reinforcing the national conscience or strengthening national communities.[62] The racial discourse transcended political borders and led to a new conception of the nation as a biopolitical program.

Coubertin's concept of a national community was inspired by Ernest Renan. In his famous speech, "Qu'est-ce qu'une nation?" (What is a nation?), which he gave on March 11, 1882, at the Sorbonne University in Paris, Renan developed his vision of a nation élective (elective nation). This concept of nation is based on an "everyday plebiscite," a voluntary adherence combined with a strong sentiment of collective memory.[63] He thought that race was characterized by its plasticity; that it was shaped and reshaped in history.[64] Nation is for him a "spiritual principal"; it is independent of external characteristics like race or language. With respect to these aspects, Renan's concept is quite different from the romantic visions of Johann Gottfried Herder and Johann Gottlieb Fichte, who defend a nationalism based on race and language (note the discussion by Mousel Knott, chapter 7, in this volume). Renan's concept of nation, which is pragmatic and inspired by the ideas of the Enlightenment and the utilitarianism of John Stuart Mill, is still predominant today in French policy. Even though Coubertin regarded the national character as an expression of "race, milieu, and moment," according to Taine, he stuck more or less to Renan's concept of nation.[65]

On the one hand he recognized the possibility that different "races" or nations could compose one nation-state like, for example, the Walloons and Flemish in Belgium; on the other hand he supported the struggle for independence of nations that were part of imperial states like Hungary. In 1911, with the help of Jiři Guth-Jarkovski, founding IOC member from Bohemia, Coubertin introduced this concept of nation to the IOC.[66] For Coubertin a nation was not "necessarily an independent state"; he defended a "sport Geography which may sometimes differ from the political Geography."[67] This sport geography based on the elective concept of nation would cause never-ending discussions and trouble. Even though the term *nation* has been replaced by *country*, the discussions continued until 1997 when Rule 3 of the Olympic Charter defined the term *country* "as an independent state recognized by the international community."[68]

Ever since their beginning, the modern Olympic Games have been related to strong national feelings (see Kitroeff's chapter in this volume). Charles Maurras, the founder of the nationalist organization Action Française, who attended the first Olympic Games in Athens as a journalist, wrote that "instead of smothering nationalisms all this false cosmopolitanism [of the Games] inflamed them."[69] According to Point 4 of the decisions taken in 1894 by the founding congress of the International Committee for the Olympic

Games (later the International Olympic Committee), "no country should be represented at the Olympic Games by anyone but its own nationals."[70] Coubertin claimed that they should be "citizens by birth" or "have been duly naturalized."[71] "Residency, even lifetime residency" was not enough for him and his elective concept of nation, as "one must be able to draw inspiration from the flag under whose colors one is doing battle."[72]

The strongest symbol for national representation was and still is the Parade of Nations during the opening ceremonies. Such parades took place for the first time during the 1906 Intermediate Games in Athens and two years later at the 1908 Olympic Games in London.[73] Before, it was almost impossible to organize such parades, as the necessary organizational structures like the national Olympic committees or similar national organizations had been almost nonexistent. In any case, there were no opening ceremonies during the 1900 Paris and 1904 St. Louis Games, as they were drowned in the exhibitions. Coubertin welcomed the Parade of Nations and considered it to meet the requirements of the IOC art conference which took place in the same year as the intermediate Games.[74] Coubertin believed that the competition between nations, not the competition between races, improved humankind. But this competition for the betterment of humanity should respect nations. This respect was "the base of [his] conception of the modern time. It was the very first article of [his] credo."[75]

Coubertin and the Racial Problem in the United States

The first time Coubertin raised the racial issue was in his early writings when he described his travel experiences in North America. During his comparative educational studies in the United States in 1889 he witnessed racial segregation in the South and called it "shameful distinctions."[76] Traveling on the train during his visit to Florida, he was shocked by the humiliating treatment of a clean and well-dressed African American lady who was asked by the conductor to leave the seats reserved for white people. He explained the condition of the African Americans as a result of slavery, which "causes them to still be submissive to their former masters" and considered that "it would take time to bring back the sense of equality to the former and the latter."[77]

Hopefully the new generation would change this situation. He was astonished by the potential of the African American students in school who "learn marvelously and show that they are talented."[78] He was sure that they would soon catch up with their white comrades. In these early writings Coubertin showed empathy and sympathy for the African Americans. The distinctions he made were based on social class and not on "race." He preferred well-educated, middle-class African Americans to some white lower-class people. He found that these students were "sympathetic, more sympathetic than these dirty and drunken beings who [were] sitting sometimes next to [him] in the American trains."[79]

In 1903 his attitudes toward the African American had undergone a radical change. "Despite the progress made by the less advanced of the two races," he considered that the differences between white and black were still "shocking."[80] In his opinion neither the expatriation of African Americans to Liberia, as some suggested, nor "absorption" by mixing both groups were viable answers to resolve the racial problems in the United States. The first solution would not be realistic, he argued, as these people were born in the United States and would come back sooner or later anyway. The second solution is from his point of view too risky. Who could guarantee that "the qualities of the superior race would overcome the faults of the inferior race?"[81] He thinks that "as you neither can get rid of the negroes nor absorb them, there is no other solution than to tolerate them."[82]

In his fear of mixing "inferior" and "superior" races, Coubertin joins the ideology of Arthur de Gobineau, a French novelist who published with his *Essai sur l'inégalité des races humaines* (An Essay on the Inequality of Human Races) one of the most influential racialist theories in the nineteenth century. In a more literary than scientific way, Gobineau tried to explain the "degeneration" of empires as a result of the interbreeding of distinct races.[83] When talking about electoral manipulation by the white population who wanted to stop any access of African Americans to political power, he thinks that it is understandable that "the whites who think—rightly—to be much superior compared to the black, do not want to be governed by them."[84]

Race and Colonialism

Le grave est que "L'Europe" est moralement, spirituellement indéfendable.

Aimé Césaire,
Discours sur le colonialisme, 8

We can find probably the most evidence and the most seminal texts concerning Coubertin's attitude toward the racial issue in his writings on colonialism. He was a fervent advocate of colonialism. In one of his unpublished memoirs he wrote: "From the first day on I was a fanatic colonialist, a fact which provoked the indignation of my friends from the monarchist party."[85] He celebrated French colonialism and the French Republic, which was able "to write in forty years the most admirable story of colonialism."[86] He was a close friend of the famous Maréchal Louis Hubert Lyautey, a convinced royalist and pious catholic with progressive social ideas.[87] Lyautey tried in Morocco to realize a French protectorate with "a human face," according to Daniel Rivet.[88] Influenced by his professor, Paul Leroy-Beaulieu, and the colonial ideas of Jules Ferry, Coubertin believed that colonial activities reflected the grandeur and the power of a nation. He was an ardent defender of French colonialism, which to him was part of the effort to rebuild a strong and splendid France after the disaster of 1870–71 according to his motto, "Rebronzer la France."

There are many factors that could explain colonialism and many theories have been developed to do so, but we will limit our focus to Coubertin's perspective.[89] One function of imperialism was, according to Hannah Arendt, that of healing the inner wounds of a nation, which was after 1870 certainly an important reason for the great French colonial adventure abroad.[90] It contributed to building up the self-esteem of the French nation; it was a therapy for the French, especially for the French bourgeoisie, who were traumatized by the loss of Alsace and Lorraine. But at the same time colonialism was a great enterprise of civilization: colonialism as the "mission of civilization" (*mission civilisatrice*). According to John L. O'Sullivan, the idea of Manifest Destiny in the United States, Rudyard Kipling's "White Man's Burden" in the United Kingdom, and in France the *mission civilisatrice* all served as a leitmotif and god-given or natural call to imperialism.

The French mission of civilization was a mixture of Christian missionary vocation and the legacy of the Great French Revolution, which aimed to bring enlightenment and well-being to the whole world.[91] On the background of this lofty ideal, the brutal and inhuman colonial reality became compatible with the Republican principles of equality, liberty, and fraternity. Thanks to the French maternal assistance and caring, and severity if necessary, the inferior colonial subject would, ultimately, join enlightened humanity and attain the status of a French *citoyen* (citizen). This is the humanitarian justification of French colonialism, but in reality the Republic generated a two-faced and ambiguous discourse. The metropolitan policy claiming and trying to realize the Republican ideals was quite different from the colonial policy, which was characterized by domination of the indigenous subjects, consolidation of differences, and racial hierarchies.

During the second half of the nineteenth century a strong colonial culture emerged in France. Media, literature, and expositions constructed the right to colonize.[92] In Europe as in the United States, the display of "savages," which later became "indigenous" as part of the colonial empire, served to legitimize the civilizing mission by showing who was civilized and who had to be civilized.[93] From 1878 onward different "indigenous villages" and "foreign streets" were presented in all of the expositions and it was in 1889 during the Universal Exposition in Paris that a "negro village" (*village nègre*) was displayed in Europe for the first time.[94] There is no doubt that Coubertin was aware of this display, as he was involved in the organization of the 1889 Exhibition as the kingpin of the Congress of Physical Exercises held during this event.

During the 1900 Universal Exposition, which hosted the second Olympic Games, the place assigned to colonies was more important than ever. The organizers' objective was to persuade spectators of the necessity and the usefulness of colonial activities by a "politics of exhibiting."[95] The colonial section was a huge propaganda show, justifying and documenting the civilizing mission. While displayed objects and documents highlighted the benefits of colonial activities, indigenous art work, regarded as hideous, fortified the sentiment of the superiority of the civilizers. Unlike in 1889, there were no direct exhibitions of indigenous peoples or "indigenous villages" as Alfred Picard, the director of the exhibition, judged those displays to be "used and outdated."[96]

From the point of view of the Olympic Movement the 1900 Olympic Games was a "mediocre affaire."[97] Coubertin, who wanted to organize splendid Games in the cultural capital of the world — his hometown, Paris — was disappointed by the way these Games were ultimately diluted in the exhibition. Almost the same happened to the 1904 St. Louis Games. Coubertin imagined that in Paris "the crowds would have the competitions and the festivities of the Exhibition, while we [the IOC] would organize Games for the elite — the elite among athletes, who would be few in number but composed of the greatest champions of the world; the elite among spectators, men and women in society, diplomats, professors, generals, and members of the Institute."[98] Neither in Paris nor in St. Louis would Coubertin's wishes come true. The Paris as well as most of the St. Louis competitions lacked high standards. In addition, the participation of "uncivilized" tribes, which were not even at the level of sporting apprenticeship, in the St. Louis Games must have been a great affront to Coubertin's elitist and selective conception of the Games.

At the end of the nineteenth century, two different discourses can be distinguished among the French Republicans. There were those who believed in the equality of human races and considered indigenous people to be "educable" and able to reach — in the long term — the same level of civilization as the French *citoyens*. But in accordance with the growing racist discourse of contemporary science, many Republicans—like Jules Ferry—were convinced that racial differences were unchangeable. In their opinion other "races" could "be ameliorated" by long-term education, but would never reach the level of their French "model."[99]

Until the First World War, Coubertin's position varied between both Republican attitudes. In his travel notes on his experiences in the United States he expresses his belief in the potential of black Americans to catch up with white Americans. In various reviews after 1900 he published pro-colonialist arguments, which are clearly racist as he draws attention to the innate and definitive inferiority of some races, while at the same time he published declarations that considered racial differences and hierarchies to be ephemeral.

One of his harshest racist statements can be found in his 1902 *Chronique de France*, where he refers to the results of the 1900 Congress of Colonial Sociology. He states that this congress has definitely eradicated "the theories about the equality of races and of absolute progress, which had been disseminated by the Revolution and which have been guilty of so many errors and faults."[100] In the same year, he published another racist statement in which it is clear that he regarded a group of African people as innately and definitely inferior. While describing the Natives of South Africa, he argues that "these blacks are mediocre workers."[101] According to Coubertin there is no hope for great change, as "you can ameliorate them as you can improve the soil, but only in a restricted proportion; you will reduce the idleness of the former and the infertility of the latter, but you will never make them disappear."[102] Whereas in other publications he seems to believe in the educability and potential of indigenous peoples to attain European cultural standards, here he clearly points out a definitive racial gap. At the same time he reproduces here the common colonial discourse that identified certain racially constructed categories of people as naturally working class with more or less efficient productivity.[103]

One year before, in the 1901 *American Monthly Review of Reviews*, he establishes a hierarchy between the colonizing and the colonized races, but he considers that education could raise the latter to the standards of the former:

Another theory, that of equal rights for all human races, leads to a policy contrary to any colonial progress. Without including even the most lenient form of serfdom, not to mention slavery, the superior race is justified in refusing to extend several privileges of civilized life to the lower one. A fair treatment, justice to all, and special protection to the natives against the possible cruelties and encroachments of their rulers are enough, in many cases. Of course, it is the duty of the latter to try to raise the lower race to their own standard; but such educational work is very slow, and to hasten it is simply to injure it and, at the same time, to hinder colonization and weary those who are busy at it.[104]

One year later, inspired by a piece of theater by François de Curel, and drawing on the conclusions of the Congress of Colonial Sociology, he argues in favor of a progressive Europeanization of the "retarded peoples" in the colonies: "The great lesson from the experience and the conclusions of the last Congress of Colonial Sociology, organized at the occasion of the Universal Exposition, shows that we have to leave to the retarded peoples as much as possible of what they have acquired, and to bring to them only what seems to be really necessary for their progressive Europeanization."[105]

Those who "consider that this Europeanization is illegitimate, that their religions are equal to ours, that they are different but not inferior" lack realism and just preach "lovely sophisms."[106] But this Europeanization will be a long process as "heredity cannot be replaced; it can be lost or it can be slowly acquired. You can try to educate the barbarian, instruct him intensely, remove him, take him out of the country, [but] he cannot become similar to you; huge gaps will separate him from you."[107] Coubertin believed that it had been proven scientifically that Europeanization is possible, but only in the long term. This knowledge, he claims, has the advantage that it "will largely enlighten the effort of colonization without discouraging it."[108] He had a paternalistic attitude toward the colonies: "The colonies are like children: it is relatively easy to make them, but it is difficult to provide them with a good education."[109] Coubertin's position concurred with "the 'civilizing mission' of imperial ideology, which encouraged colonial powers to take up with the 'white man's burden' and raise up the condition of the inferior races who were idealized as childlike and malleable."[110] Further evidence of Coubertin's paternalistic attitude toward colonized peoples can be noted in his declaration of the Far Eastern Games as a "kindergarten of Olympism."[111]

The Role of Sports in the Civilizing Mission

For Coubertin educational reform in France was a necessary pillar for successful colonialism.[112] In the new educational system, adapted to the demands of the imperial twentieth century, sports had an important role to play to prepare the colonizers for the strenuous efforts abroad.[113] Coubertin considered it "an eminent factor of the colonial enterprise at such a point that colonizing without sporting preparation constitutes a dangerous imprudence."[114]

After the First World War, physical activities were no longer simply an auxiliary instrument for military, hygienic, or social purposes, but became an integral part of French colonial politics.[115] Sports were an efficient instrument in preparing the colonizers for their mission; at the same time sport was part of the superior civilization and as such it should be transmitted to the Natives. Coubertin was convinced that the popular games and physical activities of the Natives would never be "anything more than amusements, recreation."[116] In his opinion only modern Western sports were civilized activities: "If one wishes to extend to natives in colonized countries what we will boldly call the benefits of 'athletic civilization,' they must be made to enter into the broad athletic system with codified regulations and comparative results, which is the necessary basis of that civilization."[117] It is understandable that Coubertin was embarrassed by the St. Louis Anthropology Days and the "savage games" of the indigenous, who were not ready to participate in such a prestigious event as the Olympic Games. He regarded the Olympic Games as the flagship of his "athletic civilization mission." The legacy of this mission is still manifest in our times: despite what Coubertin considered to be "the fundamental rule of the modern Olympiads, which fits into two words: *all games, all nations,*" the program of the Games remains dominated by Western sports.[118]

In the colonies Coubertin believed sports to be "a vigorous instrument of the disciplining" of the indigenous people to be colonized.[119] Sport should help to keep social peace in the colonies, because "sport not only strengthens but also calms."[120] Commercial exchange between the Western world and the colonies, but also the civilizing mission, would have been troubled without social peace among the Natives and the colonizers. The colonies became an experimental field for social engineering in the home country, where Coubertin tried to use sport as an instrument to foster mutual understanding between different social strata.[121]

Anti-Semitism

Coubertin openly took a position against Dreyfus and Zola during the Dreyfus affair, which split the Third Republic into two adversary camps. At the end of the nineteenth century, the wrongful conviction of the young Jewish officer Alfred Dreyfus for treason deeply divided France into two adversarial camps: on the one hand were the *anti-Dreyfusards,* generally journalists and politicians belonging to the right wing, who displayed openly anti-Semitic opinions; and on the other hand were the *Dreyfusards,* mostly socialists, Republicans, anticlericalists, and intellectuals, like Émile Zola, who supported the erroneously accused officer. In the middle of this political turmoil, which caused one of the severest crises of the French Third Republic, Coubertin openly took a position against Dreyfus and Zola.[122] Was it a sign of his racism or was he just conforming to the general attitude of the conservative milieu to which he belonged?

Already in 1901 he showed a somewhat more moderate position toward the Dreyfus affair, when he praised Emile Loubet's neutral attitude to the incident.[123] Loubet, one of the presidents of the Third Republic, kept his distance from the adversaries of Dreyfus as well as from his defenders. However, at the end of the nineteenth century, Coubertin also published some comments about Jews that can indeed be considered as racial stereotyping. In 1900, in an article on the German empire published in the *American Monthly Review of Reviews*, he complained that the wealthy Jews were responsible for the high costs of living in certain districts of Berlin: "The Jews, who are many in number—as many, I believe, as in the whole of France—and very wealthy, have by degrees driven the nobility out of their old homes or have erected costly mansions where they entertain their friends and feast among themselves. Thus the court is on one side and the money on the other, with a ditch between them."[124]

Even after the First World War, in his *Universal History*, he has a stereotypical view of Jews: "You know them almost only through the money amassed by some of them. Rough and persevering in winning, skilful and tricky in business, they often rendered themselves detestable, but their vices hide an obstinate and untamed idealism that had been reinforced by the mad persecutions of which they have been victims, and that had served much with the arriving of democracy."[125] But at the same time he criticized the "German error" and Nietzsche, who treated the Jews as a "*rebel race* that substituted the morality of leaders, elitist men, strong and beautiful, with the *morality of slaves*, the morality of the masses."[126] He was convinced that "Jewish blood" had a "primordial power" and that "some drops sometimes would be sufficient to assure the conquest of a home."[127]

In 1903 Coubertin wrote an article in *Le Figaro* taking a position against Edouard Drumont, whom he accused of "spread[ing] the virus of anti-Semitism."[128] Drumont was a fanatic anti-Semite. In his book *La France juive*, which he published in 1886 and which sold more than a million copies, Drumont claimed that the Jews were responsible for the French social and national "degeneration."[129] In his journal *Revue du pays de Caux* of 1902, Coubertin published an obituary praising the late Rudolf Virchow, a teacher of Franz Boas, who in the 1880s had argued strongly against anti-Semitism in the French journal l'Homme, providing yet another instance of his support for the struggle against anti-Semitism.[130] According to Boulongne, another demonstration that Coubertin was no anti-Semite occurred when he appointed the Hungarian Jew Ferenc Kemény as a representative of the Austrian Olympic Committee, which was composed of many racist members.[131]

Coubertin's Racial Attitude after the First World War

In the first decade of the twentieth century, Coubertin's position toward the racial question was rather ambiguous. Later on, even before the First World War, according to the sense in which we have earlier defined racism in this chapter, his statements can no longer be considered racist. In an article of the *Olympic Revue* from 1912, entitled "Eugenics," Coubertin criticized vehemently "the belief in the natural sovereignty of a specific race, designated to dominate all the others."[132] He treats the defenders of this theory, like Georges Vacher de Lapouge, as *demi-savants* (half-scientific) and regards their ideas as *âneries* (nonsense).[133]

After the First World War, his attitude toward colonized people became more compassionate and humane. Writing about the African Games in his *Olympic Memoirs* he argues against the old "colonial spirit" and pleads for the emancipation of indigenous people.[134] There may be different reasons for Coubertin's ambiguous attitudes before the First World War. One explanation could be that he took a more cautious position in the *Olympic Review*, which was addressed to a worldwide public, while he could express his harsh racial position when writing for reviews like the *Revue du Pays de Caux*, the *Revue pour les Français* or the *Revue des Deux Mondes* as the readership of these publications was in general in favor of ruthless colonial politics.

In addition, the heroic and selfless devotion of the African soldiers serving in the French army during the Great War contributed to a somewhat less racist attitude toward the Natives in the French colonies. An example of the respect toward these soldiers was the attitude of General Lyautey, Coubertin's close friend and one of the great figures of French colonial activities, who demanded that all kinds of racist exhibitions should be forbidden during the 1931 Colonial Exhibition in Paris.[135]

In his writings after the First World War, Coubertin has a monogenetic perception of humanity even though he thinks that there is no historical evidence to back up this theory. In the preface of his *Universal History* he presents different ways to classify human beings according to skin color, language, or cranial measurement, and he demonstrates that, depending on the methods, the resulting race categories are different.[136] Regarding the question of the equality of the different races, he states that arguments favoring the superiority of the "white group representatives" are not corroborated. Like Montesquieu, Coubertin thinks that the influence of the milieu, the context, is clearly proven, and for him the "climate has been the real stonemason of the races, it gave them their physiognomy and their distinctive traits."[137] "The vast land and the vivifying climate" contributed in his opinion to producing a "strong race" in the United States.[138] In emphasizing the impact of climate and the environment, Coubertin's ideas still fit the racial concepts of Gobineau. However, the huge difference between the two men is that Coubertin no longer believes in the racial superiority of the white race and does not share Gobineau's pessimistic view about the evolution of human races.[139] Sport too plays a role for Coubertin in modeling the "races." Admiring the stoicism of English and American people dying in the shipwreck of the Titanic he states "that their race had gotten such habits by contact with violent exercises."[140]

Yves-Pierre Boulongne notes that there is a rupture in Coubertin's conception of race and that after the First World War he completely changed his mind.[141] Indeed, Jean-Marie Brohm, the harshest critique of Coubertin, who claims that the founder of the modern Olympic Movement was definitely a racist, based his assessment of Coubertin's racist attitude almost exclusively on texts published before 1915. The only text he quotes that was written after 1915 concerns the Chinese and Coubertin's warnings against the "yellow danger."[142] This was quite a common term in Coubertin's time and seems to have had a geopolitical meaning rather than a racist one.

After careful analysis, it must be concluded that the evolution of Coubertin's racial attitude is a little bit more complicated. We can distinguish three different time phases in Pierre de Coubertin's conception of race. First, there was a period of empathy, where class differences were perceived to be more troubling than racial differences. During this time Coubertin believed in the existence of different races with different cultural levels due to environmental conditions, but the "inferior" races were able to improve and to catch up with the dominant ones; see his comments on African Americans.

The next phase in the development of Coubertin's thought may be seen as an ambiguous racist period from 1900 to the end of the First World War, with many racist statements claiming the innate inferiority of nonwhites on the one hand and on the other hand statements considering the educability of "races" other than the white race. The change in Coubertin's attitude toward nonwhite people was probably influenced by the International Congress of Colonial Sociology ("Congrès International de Sociologie Coloniale") held during the 1900 Paris Universal Exhibition. This congress can be considered as a turning point. It favored segregation politics, arguing that there are fundamental and definitive differences between the races.

Finally, Coubertin's attitudes reveal a change back to an assimilationist position after the First World War, in a quest for social and international peace, according to his Olympic and educational ideas. His writings evidence a changing focus from national education and improvement of the French "race" to improvement of humankind. Taking into consideration this evolution of his conception of race throughout these different life periods, we can evaluate his comments on the 1904 Olympic Games in St. Louis from a new perspective. Even though he tried to be polite, Coubertin made statements about Anthropology Days that clearly established a hierarchy of different cultures. As such these commentaries can be regarded as racist, especially if we take into consideration Coubertin's racial attitudes during this time period.

Coubertin made his first comments on Anthropology Days in a phase of his life when he showed in his writings ambiguous but often clearly racist attitudes toward nonwhite people. In this time he was probably influenced by the widely promulgated "scientific" racial paradigm of the Third French Republic. But instead of judging Coubertin solely on this period of his life we should take into consideration his whole work and the evolution of his thoughts and ideas. From 1900 on, Coubertin's writings shifted from the class-as-race discourse to an emphasis on cooperation between classes, education of the lower classes, and to a biological concept of race claiming natural hierarchies between civilized and uncivilized peoples. This shift was parallel to a general evolution in Europe after 1900 toward "the efficient working together of all for the greater cohesion and strength of the nation locked in struggle with other states."[143] After the trauma of the Great War and the shock of the Russian October Revolution, he changed profoundly, focusing his efforts on popular education.[144] He probably realized that neither social peace nor international peace would be possible while major groups of people were dominated by others and deprived of education.

It seems that Coubertin's fervent colonialism, patriotism, and nationalism contradict the evident universalism of his Olympic ideals. According to Frederickson, Alexis de Tocqueville, one of the key thinkers who influenced Coubertin, faced almost the same contradiction "between a professed universalism and a covert racism and ethnocentrism."[145] Frederickson argues that the contradiction is one between theory and practice: "The theorist may be a cosmopolitan advocate of principles that apply to humanity in general, but the locus of liberal politics is the nation-state. . . . As long as nation-states govern the world, universalist liberalism will be unable to realize its ideals."[146]

Coubertin's work was characterized by the will to improve humankind. First, at a national level, he focused on the moral, intellectual, and physical education of the French aristocratic and bourgeois society, while next he expanded this uplifting mission to the whole of mankind. His efforts on behalf of educational reform in France, his fervent philhellenism, his enthusiasm for the colonial endeavor, his engagements in popular education were all part of his "great work" of keeping social and international peace and of "uplifting mankind."[147] He considered the "civilized part" of mankind to be threatened by moral and physical degeneration, while he saw the rest still in a state of "primitive" and inferior civilization. The Olympic Games, which brought together the finest youth of the whole world every four years, were a symbol of an eternal spring of humankind, a symbol of the eternal striving to better humanity. In Coubertin's mind, peoples at the stage of "half-savages" were not ready yet for this noble and elitist meeting. Also their games were not serious enough to be included in the Olympic Games that were to accomplish the athletic part of the civilizing mission. Today, the Olympic Games, as a legacy of the civilization mission, still promote Western or westernized sports exclusively, even though they claim to be a universal movement.

Notes

1. Pierre de Coubertin to Jiři Guth-Jarkovsky, March 13, 1904.

2. Etienne de Crussène, the hero of Coubertin's largely autobiographic novel *Roman d'un Rallié*, falls in love with Mary, a beautiful young American girl, who symbolizes the American dream. Coubertin showed a critical but all in all a very positive attitude toward the United States, and admired the action- oriented American lifestyle. With his numerous French articles and books on the United States and his English publications on France, he tried to foster understanding between the two countries.

3. Boulongne, *International Olympic Committee*. There were probably different reasons for Coubertin's absence. One was certainly the fact that the Games, like the Paris 1900 Games, were associated with a fair; another may have been that the main organizer was James E. Sullivan, who had tried to replace the IOC by an International Union. See Coubertin, *Une Campagne de vingt-et-un ans*; Chappelet, *Le système olympique*, 101; and Mousel Knott in this volume.

4. Coubertin, *Olympism*, 402–3. There is a translation error in the English version of *Olympism*: the original states that the Turks were *not* flattered.

5. Coubertin, *Olympism*, 402–3.

6. Coubertin, *Olympism*, 408–9.

7. Coubertin, *Olympism*, 695.

8. Hache, *Jeux Olympiques*, 38.

9. Guttmann, *Olympics*, 26.

10. Quel Corps? "Coubertin, l'Olympisme et Berlin '36," 32.

11. Fredrickson, Racism, 70.

12. Boulongne, Pierre de Coubertin; Durry, Le vrai Pierre de Coubertin; Brohm, Le mythe olympique; Brohm, Jeux Olympiques à Berlin; Brohm, "Pierre de Coubertin et l'avènement du sport bourgeois," 283–300; Brohm, "Olympisme et national-socialisme," 223–39.

13. Schantz, "Sport und Leibesübungen als Erziehungsmittel bei Pierre de Coubertin," 111–24.

14. More than fifteen thousand printed pages. See Müller and Schantz, Bibliographie des oeuvres de Pierre de Coubertin, xviii.

15. Sammons, "'Race' and Sport," 206.

16. See, for example, Ruffié, De la biologie à la culture; Jacquard, Éloge de la différence; Langaney, Les hommes; Cavalli-Sforza and Cavalli-Sforza, Chi siamo; Eberhardt, "Imaging Race," 181–90.

17. Holt, The Problem of Race, 21; also Loveman, "Is 'race' essential?" 891–98.

18. Go, "'Racism' and Colonialism," 37.

19. Higginbotham, "African-American Women's History," 253.

20. MacMaster, Racism in Europe, 27.

21. Holt, The Problem of Race, 8.

22. Balibar, "Gibt es einen Neo-Rassismus?" 28.

23. Encyclopaedia Britannica, s.v. "Racism."

24. Arendt, Origins of Totalitarianism, situates the beginning of anti-Semitism at the start of the nineteenth century, but there is much evidence that this kind of racism started much earlier. See Delacampagne, L'invention du racisme. Probably the first antiracist text can be found in Aristotle's Metaphysics, book Iota, chapter 9.

25. Marten, "Racism, Social Darwinism, Anti-Semitism and Aryan Supremacy," 23–41.

26. Until the middle of the twentieth century, psychology was considered to be a kind of subdiscipline of philosophy in France; see Reynaud Paligot, République raciale, 155.

27. Fouillé, Psychologie du peuple français, 20.

28. Taine, Histoire de la littérature anglaise, xxiii.

29. See Sowell, Race and Culture, 6.

30. For example, in 1887 he wrote, that "the French blood is not older than that of the races which are around us" (Le sang français n'est pas plus ancien que celui des races qui nous entourent.) Coubertin, "Un programme: Le Play," 547. During the First World War, for example, he praised the "traditional elegance of his [French] race" (Coubertin, "1870–1914," 1). When analyzing the political evolution in Belgium, he talked about the two different races (Flamands and Wallons) of this country (Coubertin, "La Belgique devant l'histoire," 2).

31. Coubertin, "Sources et les limites," 13.

32. See Geulen, Wahlverwandte, 47–50. Another example for the use of the term race in

the sense of aristocracy or nobility can be found in an article about the neomonarchists, where he argues against the monarchy, but claims more "race" within the administrators and diplomats. Coubertin, "La Thèse des Néo-Monarchistes," 116–19.

33. See Schantz, "Französische Festkultur," 64–85.

34. Reynaud Paligot, République raciale, 2.

35. See Dozon, Frères et sujets; Vergès, "'Le nègre n'est pas. Pas plus que le blanc,'" 45–64.

36. Manceron, "Les 'sauvages' et les droit de l'homme," 399–405.

37. See Coubertin, "Sources et les limites," 13.

38. From 1900 to 1903 Coubertin published a series of articles called "Letters of an Independent" in the Belgian journal L'Indépendant Belge. See Müller and Schantz, Bibliographie, 54–64.

39. See Coubertin, Lettre aux électeurs; see Auger, "Pierre de Coubertin," 41.

40. Coubertin showed a certain sympathy for socialism as an ideology driven by "the notion of justice and the impulse of goodness" (Coubertin, "Que faut-il penser?" 137). After the First World War he focused his work on popular education in order to keep social peace.

41. MacAloon, This Great Symbol, 112.

42. See Schantz, "Französische Festkultur," 72.

43. See Coubertin, "L'athlétisme," 193–207.

44. See Coubertin, L'Education des adolescents; Schantz and Müller, "Préface," 1–22.

45. Coubertin, Une campagne de vingt-et-un ans, 218.

46. Toqueville, Démocratie en Amérique, 127–35.

47. Coubertin, Qué es el Olimpismo? 27; see Coubertin, "Chronique pour après," 1.

48. Roosevelt, "Strenuous Life," 269. Roosevelt entirely supported Coubertin's efforts to promote utilitarian gymnastics for every young man, as "in our modern highly artificial, and on the whole congested, civilization, no boon to the race could be greater than this acquisition by the average man of that bodily habit which you [Coubertin] describe." Roosevelt to Pierre de Coubertin, June 15.

49. Matthew, "Liberal Age," 567.

50. Coubertin, "Aux jeunes Français," 3.

51. See Coubertin, L'Évolution française.

52. Hobsbawm, Nations and Nationalism.

53. MacMaster, Racism in Europe, 56.

54. See Geulen, Wahlverwandte, 34.

55. See Schantz, "Sport und Leibesübungen," 117.

56. See Foucault, Les mots; Geulen, Wahlverwandte, 22.

57. Coubertin, Histoire universelle, xv.

58. Coubertin, "L'Eugénie," 163–66; see Schantz, "L'oeuvre pédagogique," 101–17.

59. Coubertin, "Lettre Olympique," 2.

60. Coubertin, "Fille sauvage," 38.

61. Coubertin, *Olympism*, 630.

62. Geulen, *Wahlverwandte*, 30.

63. Renan, "Qu'est-ce qu'une nation?" 27.

64. See Rétat, "Renan," 322.

65. MacAloon, *This Great Symbol*, 47.

66. See Lennartz, "Parade of Nations," 99–111.

67. Coubertin, "Géographie sportive," 51.

68. See Brownell, "'Athletic Geography,'" 5.

69. French original version: "Loin d'étouffer les passions nationales, tout ce faux cosmopolitisme les exaspéra." Maurras, *Lettres des Jeux Olympiques*, 13.

70. Coubertin, *Olympism*, 265.

71. Coubertin, *Olympism*, 265.

72. Coubertin, *Olympism*, 265.

73. In a talk given in 1929 Coubertin pretends that the first Parade of Nations already took place in 1896 in Athens. Coubertin, *Olympie*, 9.

74. Coubertin, "Art, lettres et sport," 211–15; Coubertin, "L'ouverture de la 4e Olympiade," 103–5; Coubertin, "Une Olympie moderne," 41–44.

75. French original version: "'Le respect des patries' était à la base de ma conception des temps nouveaux. C'était l'article 1er de mon Credo." Coubertin, "Mes mémoires," 459.

76. "Honteuses distinctions"; Coubertin, *Universités transatlantiques*, 257.

77. Coubertin, *Universités transatlantiques*, 257–58.

78. Coubertin, *Universités transatlantiques*, 259.

79. Coubertin, *Universités transatlantiques*, 259.

80. Coubertin, "La question nègre," 1.

81. Coubertin, "La question nègre," 1.

82. Coubertin, "La question nègre," 1.

83. See Gobineau, *Essai sur l'inégalité*, vol. 1.

84. Coubertin, "La question nègre," 1.

85. Coubertin, "Mes mémoires," 460.

86. See Callebat, *Pierre de Coubertin*, 233.

87. See Gershovich, "Collaboration and 'pacification,'" 139–46. According to Fabrice Auger, it seems that Coubertin had some influence on Lyautey and other important persons such as Théophile Delcasé, Jules Simon, and the president Marie François Sadi Carnot. Auger, "Une histoire politique du mouvement olympique," 190.

88. Quoted in Bancel and Clastres, "Pierre de Coubertin et Hubert Lyautey," 59.

89. See, for example, Mommsen, *Imperialismustheorien*.

90. See Arendt, *Origins of Totalitarianism*.

91. See Bancel, Blanchard, and Vergès, *République coloniale*, 68.

92. Bancel, Blanchard, and Vergès, "Zoos humains," 13.

93. See Lidchi, "Poetics and Politics," 151–223.

94. A similar ethnic village was displayed four years later at the 1893 Chicago World's Columbian Exposition.

95. Lidchi, "Poetics and Politics," 198.

96. Picard, *Exposition Universelle*, 4:352.

97. Boulongne, *International Olympic Committee*, 1:121.

98. Coubertin, *Une campagne de vingt-et-un ans*, 389.

99. See Bancel et al., *République coloniale*, 96.

100. Coubertin, *Chronique de France*, 2:194.

101. Coubertin, "Le drame sud-africain," 69.

102. Coubertin, "Le drame sud-africain," 69.

103. See Loomba, *Colonialism*, 126.

104. Coubertin, "France on the Wrong Track," 449.

105. Coubertin, "Fille sauvage," 38–39.

106. Coubertin, "Fille sauvage," 38–39.

107. Coubertin, "Fille sauvage," 39.

108. Coubertin, "Fille sauvage," 38.

109. Coubertin, *Pages d'histoire contemporaine*, 4.

110. Ashcroft, Griffiths, and Tiffin, *Post-Colonial Studies*, 201.

111. Coubertin, "Colonisation sportive," 12.

112. Coubertin, "L'urgente Réforme," 386; see Coubertin, "Collège modèle," 379–99.

113. Coubertin, "Collège modèle," 379–99.

114. Pierre de Coubertin, "Le Sport et la Société moderne," 383.

115. See Deville-Danthu, *Le sport en noir et blanc*, 24.

116. Coubertin, "Colonisation sportive," 12–14. Quoted from Coubertin, *Olympism*, 704.

117. Coubertin, *Olympism*, 704.

118. Coubertin, "La géographie sportive," 51.

119. Coubertin, "Les sports et la Colonisation," 9.

120. Coubertin, "Discours prononcé par le président du Comité," 5.

121. Auger, "Histoire politique"; Bancel and Gayman, *Du guerrier à l'athlète*; Schantz, "Le 'Gymnase de la Cité'," 15–27.

122. See Coubertin, "Present Problems and Politics of France," 187–94.

123. See Boulongne, *La vie et l'oeuvre pédagogique*, 163–64; Coubertin, "Emile Loubet."

124. Coubertin, "French View of the German Empire," 179.

125. Coubertin, *Histoire universelle*, 2:25.

126. Coubertin, *Histoire universelle*, 2:26.

127. Coubertin, *Histoire universelle*, 2:26.

128. See Boulongne, *La vie et l'oeuvre pédagogique*, 164.

129. See Mosse, *Towards the Final Solution*.

130. Coubertin. "Le professeur Virchov," 135; see Reynaud Paligot, *République raciale*, 91.

131. Boulongne, *La vie et l'oeuvre pédagogique*, 164.

132. Coubertin, "L'Eugénie," 164.

133. Coubertin, "L'Eugénie," 164.

134. Coubertin, *Olympic Memoirs*, 119; see Callebat, *Pierre de Coubertin*, 234.

135. Bancel et al., "Zoos humains," 11.

136. Coubertin, *Histoire universelle*, 1:xi.

137. Coubertin, *Histoire universelle*, 1:12.

138. Coubertin, "Ce qu'il y a de changé aux Etats-Unis," 41.

139. See Gobineau, *Essai sur l'inégalité*, vol. 1.

140. Coubertin, "Chronique du mois," 77.

141. Boulongne, *La vie et l'oeuvre pédagogique*, 173.

142. Coubertin, *Où va l'Europe?* 17–18.

143. MacMaster, *Racism in Europe*, 56.

144. See Schantz, "Le 'Gymnase de la Cité,'" 15–27; Cholley, *Pierre de Coubertin*.

145. Fredrickson, *Comparative Imagination*, 116.

146. Fredrickson, *Comparative Imagination*, 116.

147. See Osterhammel, "'The Great Work of Uplifting Mankind,'" 363–425.

Chapter 4. Anthropology Days, the Construction of Whiteness, and American Imperialism in the Philippines

GERALD R. GEMS

Inquiries into the nature of "race" and "difference" began with early European characterizations of Native Americans as "Indians," children of nature who possessed the conflicting qualities of stoicism, courage, cruelty, cunning, and ignorance. Debate ensued over the nature and origin of difference with monogenists assuming a common descent for humankind and one human species. Polygenists proposed multiple lines of descent and the development of separate human species. Some believed blacks to be subhuman, and they were stereotyped as such in grotesque cartoons and minstrel shows. In the early nineteenth century, American scholars embarked on linguistic studies of Native American tribes to determine the course of divergence. By 1842 they founded the American Ethnological Society.[1]

Scientific rationalizations for the construction of difference began soon after the publication of Charles Darwin's *On the Origin of the Species by Means of Natural Selection* in 1859, an influential treatise that sparked evolutionary theory. Lewis Henry Morgan, an early American anthropologist, suggested three evolutionary stages with concomitant moral characteristics. He claimed that "primitive" societies were also promiscuous ones; while "barbarians" moved toward the "civilized" stage characterized by monogamy. Morgan advocated selective breeding between whites and Native Americans to improve the stock of the latter. The scientific revolution of the nineteenth century

189

thus assumed racial, social, and religious qualities that soon drifted into pseudoscience that purported to rationalize human differences. In the first half of the nineteenth century, phrenologists, such as Samuel G. Morton, studied the bumps and protrusions of the skull to determine mental capacity and levels of intelligence, and physiognomists analyzed facial features to ascertain one's character. Stereotypes became rationalized, justified, and entrenched. While the phrenologists and polygenists lost credibility by mid-century, Morgan assumed the presidency of the American Association for the Advancement of Science in 1879, the first anthropologist to hold the esteemed position. Thereafter, cultural anthropologists, such as Franz Boas, contended with the evolutionists in an ongoing debate over the nature of the human species.[2]

The Concept of Whiteness

Over the last two decades anthropologists and historians have asserted the concept of whiteness as a social and historical construct. Whiteness meant more than skin color. It included the adherence to a white, Anglo-Saxon, Protestant (WASP) middle-class value system, with its particular tenets of morality, discipline, and work ethic. The attainment of whiteness accorded an ethnic group particular rights and privileges as well as social respect. Nonwhites who failed to obtain the necessary standards faced ostracism and ridicule. Marked by their "difference," such groups became "Others," situated at lower positions on the hierarchical racial ladder.

Religious differences also fostered suspicions and distrust as Catholics and Jews brought alternative rituals and practices, and a seeming loyalty to a countervailing theocracy. Nativists assumed that Catholics' greatest allegiance lay with the pope, and therefore, they could never adhere to the American constitutional proviso of the separation of church and state. While German Jews readily assimilated, but did not gain full acceptance in the mainstream culture, their eastern European, Orthodox brethren faced greater hurdles in American society. Yiddish culture subjected all Jews to the WASP gaze of difference. A *New York Times* report of 1893 described Jewish neighborhoods as "perhaps the filthiest place on the western continent. It is impossible for a Christian to live there because he will be driven out, either by blows or the dirt and stench. Cleanliness is an unknown quantity to these people. They cannot be lifted up to a higher plane because they do not want to be."[3] Eugenicist Madison Grant further emphasized the racial connotations in 1916 when he declared that "the cross between any of the three European races and a Jew is a Jew," and a clear pollution of the white gene pool.[4]

Blacks, originally imported as slaves, occupied the lowest rung of the social order. A Supreme Court case of 1857 had determined that "Negroes (were) beings of an inferior order with no rights which any white man was bound to respect."[5] But in the South, where slave bodies had greater monetary value, Irish laborers undertook the most grueling tasks. As late as 1874 an African American doctor described the Irish in derogatory terms.

> These people are remarkable for open, projecting mouths, prominent teeth, and exposed gums, their advancing cheek bones and depressed noses carry barbarism on their very front. . . . Degradation and hardship exhibit themselves in the whole physical condition of the people . . . giving such an example of human degradation as to make it revolting. They are only five feet two inches, upon an average, bow-legged, bandy shanked, abnormally featured, the apparitions of Irish ugliness and Irish want.[6]

The characterization of most Irish had improved little by 1896 when an *Atlantic Monthly* author claimed that "a Celt . . . lacks the solidity, the balance, the judgment, the moral staying power of the Anglo-Saxon."[7] The Irish eventually superseded blacks through political and athletic successes that brought them into the mainstream culture and provided a measure of social mobility. Asians, Native American Indians, and southern and eastern European immigrants resided somewhat higher than blacks, but well below the dominant WASPs.[8] The Chinese, who posed a seeming labor threat to whites in California, were exoticized and vilified. As early as 1877 a congressman asserted that "there is not sufficient brain capacity in the Chinese to furnish motive power for self government. Upon the point of morals, there is no Aryan or European race which is not far superior to the Chinese as a class."[9] Five years later the U.S. Congress passed a Chinese exclusion act barring immigration.

Professor Daniel Brinton, the first anthropology professor in American colleges, and the president of the American Association for the Advancement of Science in 1896, stated that "the black, brown, and red races differ anatomically so much from the white . . . that even with equal cerebral capacity they never could rival its results by equal efforts."[10] General Leonard Wood, a colonial warrior in the Philippines, military governor of Puerto Rico, and later a presidential candidate, was even more explicit in a 1910 letter to the Episcopal bishop of the Philippines. He asserted that "no one . . . can question the inadvisability of the introduction of any other alien race, of a black, brown, or yellow strain into this country. We must make it a white nation."[11] As the United States' belief in its own Manifest Destiny fostered the accumulation of new lands and even colonies by the late nineteenth century, whiteness rationalized and justified imperial ventures both on the mainland and abroad.

The March of American Imperialism

The missionary zeal of the Christian proselytizers, and their use of sport to accomplish their missions, had been long underway. The early comparisons of whites, blacks, and Native Americans paralleled the American belief in Manifest Destiny. By 1820 American missionaries traveled to Hawaii, coercing the monarchy to Christianity and imposing standards of whiteness on Hawaiian children in residential boarding schools. They introduced baseball in the 1840s as a means to inculcate the proper cultural values.

As Americans pushed ever westward they confiscated Native lands, characterizing the previous inhabitants as unworthy, uncivilized heathens, or noble savages at best. In the 1830s Anglo settlers moved into the Texas region of Mexico and soon declared their independence from a Catholic people that

they considered to be a mongrel race and less than white. The U.S government annexed the territory in 1845, prompting the Mexican-American War
that garnered California and the Southwest. Chinese, deemed nonwhite,
soon faced exclusionary immigration laws.

Native Americans fared marginally better. As noble savages they possessed
some redeeming values for progressive reformers. In 1879 the U.S. government founded Carlisle Indian School in Pennsylvania, the first of many such
residential boarding schools designed to impart whiteness in its subjects
by forcing them to adopt the English language, Anglo clothing, short hair,
vocational trades for a capitalist economy, and American sports that reinforced WASP value systems.

Sport and American Imperialism

G. Stanley Hall, first president of the American Psychological Association,
theorized that societies recapitulated evolutionary stages in their forms of
play. The tag games of young boys, for instance, replicated the more primitive hunt- and-chase societies. Civilized groups played more complex and
strategic games. His play theory suggested that inferior groups might then
be raised from their savage states by education, physical education in particular, and especially through the proper sports and games. The Young Men's
Christian Association (YMCA) trained young men to teach a WASP version of
"muscular Christianity" through sport and soon embarked on a worldwide
mission of conversion and character development.[12]

Following the successes of American missionaries in Hawaii, Congre-
gationalists, Baptists, Episcopalians, and Methodists headed for China in
search of converts. A baseball club appeared in Shanghai by 1863 and the
YMCA established itself in Shanghai a decade later. Some of the Chinese
students who traveled to the United States before the immigration ban of
1882 returned to their homeland as baseball players. While the missionaries
were able to introduce other Western sport forms with some success, they
accomplished little in the way of religious conversion.

A similar fate awaited the missionaries in Japan. The Japanese government quickly adopted a modernization movement after Commodore Matthew Perry forced an end to isolationism in 1853. The reform efforts included industrialization, technological improvements, Western governmental forms and educational practices, as well as new sport forms. Baseball, in particular, appealed to the Japanese; but they adapted it to their own cultural characteristics. With the abolition of the samurai warrior class in 1876, baseball provided an alternative means of displaying masculinity and martial spirit. White racist practices injured Japanese pride and led to a series of baseball challenges by the 1890s. Japanese victories in such contests led to racial comparisons and a growing sense of nationalism. The Japanese soon embarked on more militaristic campaigns in the contest for Asian leadership. Within such an atmosphere American missionaries failed in their proselytizing efforts, as the adoption of Western sport forms allowed the supposedly inferior Japanese to question and challenge the established tenets of Social Darwinism.

The use of sports in the civilizing mission overseas mirrored their use at home. The famous Carlisle Indian School football team paraded around the country, exhibiting newfound skills, and often victories, against elite institutions such as Harvard. Carlisle games became progressive spectacles of assimilation, played before huge crowds in the largest cities. The adoption and display of white sport forms provided evidence to white administrators and policymakers that their efforts to educate and civilize were achieving the desired results.

The Display of American Imperialism at the
Chicago World's Columbian Exposition

The work of John MacAloon on the ritual, festival, and spectacle of the Olympic Games and their ability to symbolize power relationships, as well as the scholarship on world's fairs, has demonstrated the force of public exhibitions as pageants of cultural dominance.[13] The 1893 World's Fair, held in Chicago, heralded the celebration of a European-inspired "civilization" in the United States. Famed architect Daniel Burnham led the construction of an eloquent and stunning "white city," illuminated each night by innovative electric lights that proclaimed American technology and modernity to the world. The classical architecture further symbolized the order, discipline, grandeur, and harmony of the idealistic bourgeoisie. The fairgrounds occupied a former marshland, demonstrating the ability of Americans to transcend the natural environment with a manmade lagoon, canal, and basin surrounded by monumental exposition buildings. Such exhibition palaces featured construction materials of a temporary nature, such as stucco facades; but even that signified Anglo abilities to fashion and refashion the environment to one's needs, creating an artificial utopia by design. This grandiose vision marked the emergence of the United States as a world power, and the American economy soon surpassed Great Britain as the foremost industrial nation in the world.[14]

The program planners for the 1893 exhibition assumed whiteness as the norm for civilized society. Utilizing the anthropologists' three stages of development, they depicted African tribes as most primitive and white Europeans and Americans as the most advanced societies. Despite their protests, African Americans faced exclusion except for an Education Department display that extolled the benefits of schooling for nonwhite groups. The *Columbian Exposition Album* "hoped that the Dahomans would take back the influence of civilization to West Africa."[15]

The Beginning of an American Empire: the Philippines, Anthropology, and the Rationalization of White Rule

The Philippine archipelago came to the United States as bounty in the aftermath of the Spanish-American War of 1898. Filipinos had been scrutinized long before their conscription within the American domain. As early as 1887, a University of Michigan zoology professor, Dean Worcester, had traveled to the Philippine Islands in search of specimens. A second expedition from 1890 to 1893 and his forays into physical anthropology established him as an

12. Negrito from the Philippines in the archery contest. From J. Sullivan, ed., *Spalding's Official Athletic Almanac for 1905: Special Olympic Number, Containing the Official Report of the Olympic Games of 1904*, 250. From the LA84 Foundation Digital Archive.

"authority" on Filipino tribes. Consequently, President McKinley appointed Worcester to the First Philippines Commission in 1899. He supervised the final report, recommending U.S. rule, despite the fact that the revolutionary movement that preceded the American intervention had already established a provisional government. Worcester returned to the Islands in 1900, serving as secretary of the interior, a post which made him wealthy until his resignation under scandalous conditions in 1913. Throughout his life, which ended in

13. Moro throwing the javelin. From J. Sullivan, ed., *Spalding's Official Athletic Almanac for 1905: Special Olympic Number, Containing the Official Report of the Olympic Games of 1904*, 250. From the LA84 Foundation Digital Archive.

Manila in 1924, Worcester engaged in lucrative publications, lecture tours, and photographs that depicted Filipinos as half-naked savages, headhunters, and primitive tribesmen.[16]

Robert Bennett Bean, a University of Michigan anatomist, emphasized racial differences and, combined with the works of Worcester, depicted the Filipinos as genetically inferior and unable to govern themselves without proper American guidance. As late as 1913 Worcester stated that the Negrito tribe "are probably the lowest type of human beings known and have been described as not far above the anthropoid apes." He classed the Ilongots as a "tribe so primitive that they are unable to count beyond ten"; and Moros, who inhabited the southern islands, "are unexcelled pirates and slave traders, treacherous and unreliable to the last degree."[17]

The Debate Over American Imperialism

The acquisition of the Philippines in 1898 fostered vitriolic debate in the United States. Along with Cuba, Puerto Rico, Guam, American Samoa, and the annexation of the Hawaiian Islands, the largesse created an instant American empire and placed it among the imperial world powers of Europe. Anti-imperialists charged that a true democracy could not, and certainly should not, colonize subject peoples. The fact that Puerto Rico and the Philippines already had provisional governments in place when American forces arrived further questioned American legitimacy. The Philippines offered a particular dilemma for the United States. Unlike Hawaii, American citizens had no sugar plantations in the Philippines and, unlike the Caribbean islands, the location of the Asian archipelago offered no strategic necessity for the safeguard of American coastlines.

Less egalitarian anti-imperialists feared the incorporation of nonwhites in the American polity. Such acquisitions also entailed the acceptance of the "white man's burden" to uplift, educate, civilize, and Christianize such subject populations. Protestant missionaries and the YMCA embarked for the new territories, eager to convert the already Catholic masses to their better form of Christianity. John Procter, a member of the U.S. Civil Service Commission, argued that "the Tropics are peopled with millions of low social efficiency; and it seems to be the fate of the black and yellow races to have their countries parcelled [sic] out and administered by efficient races from the Temperate Zone. . . . In the interests of civilization and humanity, this country should retain the Philippines."[18]

Where Christian imperialists saw a moral duty, capitalists perceived a need for foreign markets for American goods, especially after the economic depression of 1893. Military strategists coveted the harbors of Hawaii and the Philippines that might allow the United States to wrest control of the seas from Great Britain and Germany, and the Islands might also provide a buffer for the imperial designs of the Japanese in the Pacific. John Barrett, the former American ambassador to Siam (Thailand), invoked Social Darwinian rights when he claimed that "[t]he rule of the survival of the fittest applies to nations as well as the animal kingdom. It is a cruel, relentless principle being exercised in a cruel, relentless competition of mighty forces."[19] Senator Albert Beveridge likewise declared that "we are a conquering race . . . we must obey our blood and occupy new markets, and, if necessary, new lands.

American factories are making more than the American people can use. American soil is producing more than they can consume. Fate has written our policy for us: the trade of the world must and shall be ours."[20] President William McKinley and the Republican Congress ultimately sided with the imperialists. But unlike the Native American Indians and the African Americans already residing on the mainland United States, the imperialists had no clear vision as to if and when any colonial subjects might be incorporated into the American citizenry. The Philippines would present an opportunity for social experimentation.

The Display of American Imperialism in the St. Louis World's Fair

In 1901 Chicago was awarded the bid for the third version of the resurrected modern Olympic Games, but ultimately declined when St. Louis, site of the 1904 World's Fair and Louisiana Purchase Exposition, scheduled a rival competition for the same period. In 1904 St. Louis combined both festival and spectacle in a public exhibition of white American might. Fair organizers doubled the size and cost of the 1893 Chicago Fair and highlighted the technological advancements of American society. Though few outside of the United States attended or took note, middle-class white Americans reveled in their own sense of racial and cultural superiority, with great ramifications over the next century.[21]

Michel Foucault has demonstrated the role of language and discourse in establishing power. By identifying itself as the "greatest of World's Fairs" and establishing the "primitive" nature of others, the fair clearly asserted the Anglo claim to superiority. The Louisiana Purchase Exposition, the World's Fair of 1904, portrayed a benevolent American imperialism through "living exhibits" that displayed the different races in "a sequential synopsis of the developments that have marked man's progress."[22] Frederick Skiff, director of exhibits at the fair, stated that "over and above all is the record of the social conditions of mankind, registering not only the culture of the world at this time but also indicating the particular plans along with which different races and different peoples may safely proceed, or in fact have begun to advance towards a still higher development."[23] WJ McGee, head of the Anthropology Department at the fair, concurred. "The aim of the Department of Anthropology at the World's Fair will be to represent human progress from the dark prime to the highest enlightenment, from savagery to civic organization, from egoism to altruism."[24]

Exhibits at the fair portrayed the modes of transport, living conditions, and recreational practices of inhabitants of artificial "villages," with the contrasting Anglo structures, technology, and practices symbolic of a more refined culture and higher intelligence. While "others" traveled by donkey, camel, or rickshaw, whites moved by means of railroads, electric boats, automobiles, and even hot air balloons. By such measures the dominant group asserted its superiority and attempted to inculcate that belief among the subordinate groups. The official exposition album stated in its foreword that "[m]uch attention is given to the artistic grace of the Exposition . . . and other features of this greatest of World's Fairs. Scarcely less interesting than the buildings are the types of primitive people to be seen at the fair. Here we have them from every part of the globe where primitive people dwell."[25]

Throughout the exposition photo album the terminology of WASP whiteness prevailed. In the "living ethnology" exhibit, a writer marveled at the "giant Patagonian, nearly seven feet high"; but his photograph in guanaco skin, long hair, and head scarf marked him as less than the Anglo ideal of civilized masculinity. The writer left no doubt as to his intentions in the adjoining photograph of a younger male by indicating that the sixteen-year-old was a

> prototype of his aged kinsman, . . . nothing being discernible in his dress or conduct that would indicate any racial reform in the fifty-five years' time that marks the difference in their ages. The youth delights in the half-savage life of his forefathers, and, wrapping his wild skins closer about his massive shoulders, shakes his bushy black head negatively when civilization becks [sic].[26]

14. Igorot throwing the javelin. From the St. Louis Public Library Online Exhibit "Celebrating the Louisiana Purchase."

The Philippines Exhibit

While WJ McGee organized the exhibition of various others, such as African Pygmies, Argentinean Patagonians, the Ainus of Japan, and various Native American contingents, the U.S. government undertook the display of the Filipinos for Americans' edification in an area officially termed a "reservation" rather than a village—an attempt to encompass Filipinos within the same civilizing framework applied to Native Americans.[27] The depiction left little doubt of the need for American guidance. The Filipino habitation included five divergent classes ranging from the "Negritos, who are so primitive that they have no fixed habitation," to the cultured and civilized Visayans. "The Moros, who rank next to them in intelligence, are Mohammedans and are truly piratical in instinct . . . fearless fighters, and many of them are religious fanatics."[28] The Igorots were classified as "spirit-worshiping barbarians," with tattooing as a means of showing "their record of lives taken" on "transparent copper-brown skins." Some of the Igorot tribes built "rude houses of planks, thatched with straw"; while others engaged in headhunting.

Americans flocked to the Philippines exhibit, curious to see the changes wrought by six years of colonial administration. The Igorot dances by men clad in loincloths proved especially attractive to fair patrons. The *St. Louis Post-Dispatch* ran a tongue-in-cheek caricature of a young chief of the Bagobo tribe, extolling the physical beauty of the "Bronze skinned . . . Adonic savage"; whose less than masculine demeanor in the Western sense of gender construction was "akin to that of a pretty woman primping before a mirror." An adjoining cartoon portrayed Filipino tribesmen as cannibals fattening up a missionary for a feast.[29] Even the more civilized tribes were portrayed by their differences with Anglo norms. The writers claimed that Moros lived upon the seas or in trees, and admitted that they had

> *caused Uncle Sam much annoyance in his effort to conquer them. . . . Some of them have developed into noted pirates and the coast country has been pillaged by their roving bands. The tree dwellers are less designing, but more hostile. Cannibalism is practiced among them. When the Sultans and their attendants are dressed for occasions of state . . . they compose a setting that for color would do justice to a comic opera. Their costumes are fashioned of the flimsiest of silk and are draped about them without regard to fit.*[30]

The exposition album writers admitted that such savage tribes were a minority and would be an anomaly in Manila; yet educated Filipinos took umbrage at the characterization. One wrote to the *St. Louis Post-Dispatch* that "the Igorottes were no more representative of the Philippines than the most savage Indians are representative of Americans."[31]

The Philippine Constabulary Band

The World's Fair also exhibited the results that American tutelage had already achieved in the Philippines. The exposition album applauded the Philippine Constabulary Band by quoting the prominent bandleader John Philip Sousa.

15. The Philippine Constabulary Band. From the Louisiana Purchase Exposition Corporation, *The Greatest of Expositions*, 226.

"I am simply amazed. I have rarely heard such playing." The caption declared: "the little brown men are natural musicians and capable of the highest training." The use of the diminutive further exemplified the Filipinos' physical inferiority, and their need for training minimized their own capabilities. Americans later reinforced such beliefs in the caption of a *National Geographic* article that claimed that the members of a boys' band were unable to play a note upon entering school, but were now playing ragtime and light opera. Another photo of the Philippine Constabulary, which served as a rural police force, claimed that "large crowds of spectators" gathered to watch the soldiers conduct their rifle drills and calisthenics, which were an "innovation since their arrival in America."[32]

The transformation of the Manobo warriors of Mindanao and their adoption of the Western styles of clothing marked their transition to modernization under WASP guidance. Previously slaveholders, with a "passion for killing," who occasionally indulged in human sacrifice, they accepted "civilization."[33] Americans thus took credit for Filipino successes, both at home and abroad.

Anthropology Days

At the fair in general, sport and play were displayed as means of educating both youth and the nonwhite groups. The fair incorporated a model gymnasium and playground where throngs of children used gymnastics equipment, ropes, and climbing poles, as well as engaging in a variety of ball games. Luther Gulick, a referee for the Anthropology Days events, had initiated the Public School Athletic League in New York only the year before and by 1906 he became cofounder and president of the Playground Association of America. He founded the American version of the Boy Scouts in 1910. A former instructor at the YMCA Training School, Gulick, like other progressive reformers, believed deeply in the powers of "muscular Christianity" to transform lives. The YMCA would become thoroughly involved in the rehabilitation of the Filipino youth; and at the 1904 fair a "shoot the chutes" slide was constructed within the Filipino village to allow Moro children the thrill of a watery splash. The exposition album claimed it "is now their principal pastime and the sport will be carried with them back to the Philippines."[34]

To further accentuate the physical debility of nonwhites, the organizers initiated competitive sports preceding the Olympics in St. Louis. They labeled the spectacle "Anthropology Days," as a comparative scientific experiment. The numerous groups from the Philippines, as well as African Pygmies, various Native American tribesmen, the Patagonians of Argentina, and the Ainu tribe of northern Japan were among those who participated in various events. The activities included typical track-and-field contests, such as running and jumping events, a shot put, javelin and weight throws, as well as archery, and a tug-of-war. Other activities measured baseball throws for both distance and accuracy; while only the Patagonians engaged in bolo throwing. Pseudo-athletic affairs such as a greased pole climb and a mud fight clearly implied Anglo cultural superiority. Native Americans, with a quarter century of exposure to the white activities, "won" thirteen of the eighteen events. Winners earned a small American flag for their efforts. The unfamiliarity

16. Mangyan from Mindoro Island, the Philippines, with American flag. He has boar bristles inserted into his left thigh to make him run faster. From the St. Louis Public Library Online Exhibit "Celebrating the Louisiana Purchase."

of the foreigners with Western sport forms resulted in comparatively poor performances, presumably proving Anglos' relative physical prowess. The victory of Basilio, a Filipino Negrito, in the pole climb, reinforced racist stereotypes as American soldiers in the Islands often referred to the inhabitants as monkeys. The official history of the fair declared the "savage and uncivilized tribes" to be inferior athletes, "greatly overrated." Another history of the exposition stated that the Anthropology Days competition destroyed the "common belief that the greatest natural athletes were to be found among the uncivilized tribes in various parts of the world."[35]

Henning Eichberg's study of the Anthropology Days detected a lack of effort by the competitors, negating the seriousness of the American intentions, and obviously, it seems, to all but the organizers, discrediting the results. A Pygmy chased a photographer during the pole climb, while another attempted to remove his clothing, and they generally found great hilarity in the contests, thereby inverting a serious spectacle into frivolous festival. The Native American Arapaho tribe dressed in finery and feathers for the tug-of-war and hardly intended to get dragged through the dirt. Another mark of only three feet in the weight throw portrayed an obvious disdain for the activity. Such a variety of responses also signified the multiplicity of choices by subordinate groups when confronted with the cultural impositions of Western sport forms mandated by the dominant whites. Some mocked the proceedings, while others performed with little or no determination, unaware or unwilling to contribute to the American pretense. Moreover, Native Americans, all too knowledgeable of their territorial losses, could hardly have been expected to glorify an exposition of the Louisiana Purchase that commenced the destruction of their traditional lifestyles.[36]

Nor was Pierre de Coubertin, a founder of the modern Olympic Movement, pleased with the American experiment in racialization. Though not present in St. Louis, Coubertin received a report from one of the Olympic Committee representatives. Appalled at the desecration of the Olympic ideal of brotherhood and fraternity, he stated: "As for this outrageous charade, it will of course lose its appeal when black men, red men, and yellow men learn to run, jump, and throw, and leave the white men behind them."[37] Despite such remonstrations the fair served American political and psychological purposes by providing the government with a venue to rationalize its actions, justify its assumptions of the "white man's burden," despite antidemocratic criticism, and soothe the national psyche regarding the morality of imperialism. For Americans who witnessed the display of primitive nonwhite debility, the need for WASP guidance and direction on the path to civilization would seem inevitable.

Postscript to 1904: Daniel Burnham Builds a "White City" in Manila

In the fall of 1904 Daniel Burnham, architect of the 1893 World's Fair, set sail for the Philippines to reconstruct Manila in the American likeness. He designed wide boulevards named after American heroes, constructed monumental neoclassical buildings similar to those in Washington DC, and established parks worthy of the City Beautiful movement; but the best waterfront land rested in the hands of whites and recreational facilities remained segregated. In Baguio, the summer capital located in the cooler mountains of northern Luzon Island, Burnham designed the town according to American ideals of aesthetics and social order. The business district rested upon a meadow, while the municipal building stood upon a hilltop. Burnham stated that "every section of the Capital City [sic] should look with deference toward the symbol of the Nation's [sic] power."[38] He further proclaimed that "the two capitals of the Philippines, even in their physical characteristics, will represent the power and dignity of this (U.S.) nation."[39] The governmental complex enjoyed "preeminence over all other buildings of the city."[40] An architectural journal extolled the designs that intended to "develop civilizing influences side by side with commercial development."[41] His selection of sites and monumental structures established and objectified United States and white dominance in a fashion similar to the social pageant of the World's Fair.

Sport as a Means of Education, Assimilation, and Social Control

Sport became an integral tool of education and indoctrination in the occupied Philippines. The American military forces introduced the Filipinos to baseball and boxing as early as 1898, and colonial administrators soon banned cockfighting, gambling, and lotteries as immoral. They hoped to replace such pastimes with American sports and games, particularly baseball. General Franklin Bell, commander of the U.S. forces in Manila, stated that "baseball had done more to 'civilize' Filipinos than anything else."[42] Worcester, too, urged baseball as a means to "strengthen muscles and wits."[43] The American-owned *Manila Times* even claimed that "[b]aseball is more than a game, a regenerating influence, a power for good."[44] The American national game meant to teach a wholesome form of entertainment while inculcating particular values. Filipinos learned the concepts of individuality within a team framework, making sense of seemingly contradictory practices. For example, on defense, all nine players had to contribute to the welfare of the team and self-sacrifice for the good of the whole, just as in a democracy. Yet when at bat, each player might gain recognition for his individual accomplishments. Moreover, practice required a strong work ethic and time discipline, and competition served as the basis for a capitalist economy. Perhaps most importantly, they learned deference to authority in the form of a captain, coach, or umpire. An American educator and coach remarked: "An American umpire would have an easy time of it in Luzon, for the players never treat the arbiter of the game to the criticism and the sarcasm that he receives in America. The umpire's decisions are always received without kicking, and the official is accorded a respect that would seem impossible . . . in the United States."[45] Baseball thus channeled rebellious sentiments into the more docile qualities of a compliant workforce. The latter proved especially important as Filipino insurgents maintained a guerrilla war against the American occupiers until 1916.

Just as the Anthropology Days served as an experiment in the social construction of race, the American occupation of the Philippines became "a laboratory for reform" that merged imperialism with Progressivism. While the Filipinos opposed the American forces in their homeland in guerrilla warfare and through the Nacionalista political party that clamored for independence, American educators imposed the English language and tried to acculturate the Natives, and sports became a primary means of instruction. The Bureau of Education organized interprovincial competition between schools in 1904 and required physical education for both boys and girls the following year. Under Governor-General W. Cameron Forbes, a former Harvard football coach, interscholastic athletic competitions permeated the public schools' curriculum. The comprehensive program of competition soon encompassed the Islands and surpassed even the most ambitious programs in the United States.

The colonial masters even found a way to redirect the Filipinos' nationalism into sport. When the Waseda University baseball team arrived from Japan for a series of games in 1905 the contests approximated a surrogate war. The Japanese victory in the Russo-Japanese War that year signaled Japanese imperial intentions of their own, and Filipinos assumed the role of American protégés. One American reported that "the rivalry was spirited. Once or twice, it bordered on bitterness. In short, the game was for blood. Having defeated a white foe in war, no doubt the Japs could not brook defeat by their neighboring islanders."[46] A thousand spectators witnessed a close win by the Filipinos in Cebu and five thousand turned out for the match in Manila, which gave the Filipinos a slight one-game edge in the series. Baseball thus offered a common denominator of cultural comparison and presumed supremacy in the Pacific as the athletic rivalry continued over the next three decades until the onset of actual hostilities.[47]

The Far Eastern Games: Sport and the Redirection of Filipino Nationalism

Such comparisons and racial rivalries assumed greater importance with the initiation of the Far Eastern Games. The Manila Carnival, organized in 1908 as commercial fair, also served as the national athletic festival that marked championships in men and boys' baseball, basketball, volleyball, and track and field, as well as girls' basketball by 1912. It included open competition in swimming, tennis, running, golf, polo, soccer, football, and bowling. With the inclusion of the Waseda University team in the baseball tournament, the spectacle assumed the moniker of the Far Eastern Olympiad.

Elwood Brown, who had arrived in the Philippines in 1910 to direct the Manila YMCA, assumed a primary role in the organization and promotion of sport, not only in the Philippines but throughout Asia. A year after his arrival Brown prepared the official recreation manual for the schools and a YMCA staff member served as the acting director of public education. Brown soon trained the playground directors as well, and by 1913 he served on the Playground Committee. Shortly thereafter the YMCA garnered support from the board of education; in effect, operating as an unofficial arm of the supposedly secular government.[48]

The YMCA operated not only with the support of but in close cooperation with the colonial administration. When Brown founded the Philippines Amateur Athletic Federation in 1911, he served as the secretary-treasurer, while Governor-General Forbes presided over the organization. Forbes took a great interest in promoting sport throughout the colony. He spent part of his personal fortune constructing a polo field and a golf course at Baguio, the summer capital. He supplied complete uniforms to the best baseball and basketball teams and awarded trophies for the track- and-field competitions. Even provincial level teams won prizes. By the end of his tenure more than 1,500 baseball teams competed for the awards and 95 percent of enrolled students participated in the sports and games. The wholesale organization of sport moved beyond the Philippines when Brown invited both Japan and China to join in a Far Eastern Athletic Association, and soon extended the membership to other Asian nations. He reported that "nothing previous to this meeting has shown so clearly the departure of the Oriental nations from the old conservative standards, for the interest of the East in organizing athletic sports is only recent."[49] Such declarations assumed that the newer cultures of the West, and the United States especially, had much to teach the older civilizations of Asia.

Pierre de Coubertin grew alarmed at yet another American attempt to besmirch his Olympic ideals and the possibility of an Asian rival to the modern games. He cautioned:

> We are now in possession of curious accounts of the beginnings of athletic exoticism. In truth, these are not really its beginnings. The festivities recently held in the capital of the Philippines did have a precedent. During the competitions held at the Third Olympiad, held in St. Louis in 1904, one or more days were reserved for performances by Asians. The Americans clearly see themselves as athletic preceptors in the Far East. The day-long festivities in St. Louis were hardly flattering for the people in that part of the world. These descendants of such ancient and refined civilizations were called on to compete with the representatives of peoples scarcely refined out of their original barbarism. This was a mistake. The International Committee, which is at times reproached for having too aristocratic a membership, is certainly more democratic in its procedures. It seeks to spread athleticism throughout the world without cataloguing races.[50]

Despite his initial misgivings, de Coubertin granted approval to the new venture once Brown agreed to drop the Olympic designation, changing it to the Far Eastern Games.

The Legacy of Imperial Whiteness

The American efforts to educate and "civilize" the Filipinos did not encompass racial equality, however, as stateside attitudes carried over to the Islands. As early as 1899, an African American soldier stationed in the Islands wrote home that "[t]he whites have begun to establish their diabolical race hatred in all its home rancor in Manila, even endeavoring to propagate the phobia among the Spaniards and Filipinos so as to be sure of the foundation of their supremacy when the civil rule that must necessarily follow the present military regime, is established."[51]

In Manila the recreational facilities of the YMCA and the American Army-Navy Club were segregated. Filipino men were racialized and emasculated as house servants for American women, who referred to them as "monkey-like coolies."[52] The American-owned *Manila Cablenews* declared that "[a]ll of us who have lived in the Far East know that in practice these yellow and brown peoples must be guided and often driven in a forward direction so that they do not obstruct the progress of the world nor infringe on the rights of other nations."[53]

In Baguio, American employees and tourists reveled in the construction of difference, accentuating such in photographs that proclaimed Anglo moral and physical superiority. The Americans favored naked Igorot women at work in the fields, and even paid boys and young men to pose accordingly. The Baguio dog market, where locals could buy "a highly appreciated article of diet," emphasized cultural and presumably civilizational differences. *National Geographic* editors drew attention to the "narrow waisted" men of the Kalinga tribe, who dressed in bright, gaudy colors and bedecked their hair with bright feathers and flowers, a clear indication of effeminacy in Western minds.[54] That public exhibition of difference, constructed during the 1904 World's Fair, carried lasting effects.

The YMCA's promotion of sport and its proselytism of an evangelical Protestant Christianity reached global proportions, with mixed results. It had great success in establishing both basketball and volleyball, two sports it had invented in the 1890s, and both were eventually included in the Olympic program. It found few converts in its religious mission, however. Likewise, Christian missionaries who employed sport as a means of proselytism in China and Japan, surrendered to their fate and departed Asia by the 1930s with only a handful of conversions (they were more successful in Korea).

The American racialization of nonwhite immigrant groups proved to be more entrenched and enduring. In 1911 the Dillingham Commission on immigration concluded that there were forty-five separate races of varying desirability. Immigration restrictions ensued and citizenship became limited to those who could achieve the necessary standards of whiteness. Chinese, Japanese, and Filipinos all faced exclusion from the ranks of citizenship or segregation for those already in the continental United States. The Ku Klux Klan resurrected itself in the enforcement of its own version of a racist white ideology and segregated schools became a reality for Asian Americans and African Americans until overturned, albeit technically, by the Supreme Court in 1954. The attitudes displayed in the Anthropology Days thus affected American society for generations.

More subtle forms of racialization endure and the role of sport continues to grow as part of the imperial process. As early as 1922 the American Olympic Association planned to "sell the United States to the rest of the world" through its sporting enterprises. Within a decade the federal government had enacted a global marketing plan to interest non-Americans in American sport forms in order to sell sporting goods.[55] In a new kind of corporate imperialism, Nike and other companies have far exceeded their wildest dreams. More recently, American military personnel have transported their footballs, basketballs, volleyballs, bats and baseballs, as well as golf clubs to the deserts of the Mideast. Boys in Afghanistan are learning baseball, just as Filipinos did more than a hundred years ago. A century after the 1904 Anthropology Days, ethnocentrism and the adherence to the belief in an American Manifest Destiny still prevail. Like the imperialists of that era, American government officials of the early twenty-first century maintain that the United States has not only a right but a duty to bring its version of order, justice, and civilization to the regions of the world that it has deemed despotic. As in the Philippines, it is a mission beset with racial and religious overtones.

Notes

1. Bieder, *Science Encounters the Indian*. See Joyce, *Shaping of American Ethnography*, for an account of a transitional era in American ethnography and racial comparisons with Polynesian groups.

2. Bieder, *Science Encounters the Indian*, 68, 232, 235, 244–45, 250; Gould, *Mismeasure of Man*; Baker, *From Savage to Negro*; Tucker, *Science and Politics of Racial Research*; Jacobson,

Barbarian Virtues. See Regna Darnell, *And Along Came Boas,* for a comprehensive treatment of the transitions in American anthropology.

3. Brodkin, *How Jews Became White Folks,* 29.

4. Guterl, *Color of Race in America,* 29.

5. Blum et al., *National Experience,* 334.

6. W. Brown, "On Race and Change," 56–57.

7. Merwin, "Irish in American Life," 289, 294–95, 298, cited in Jacobson, *Whiteness of a Different Color,* 49.

8. Among the early whiteness studies, see Horsman, *Race and Manifest Destiny;* Forbes, "The Manipulation of Race, Caste, and Identity"; Allen, *Invention of the White Race;* and Roediger, *Wages of Whiteness.* On the construction of a dominant and hegemonic social group, see Hoare and Smith, *Selections.*

9. Jacobson, *Whiteness of a Different Color,* 159.

10. Baker, *From Savage to Negro,* 27.

11. Leonard Wood to Bishop Brent, March 24, 1910.

12. Mrozek, *Sport and American Mentality.*

13. MacAloon, *This Great Symbol;* Benedict, *Anthropology of World's Fairs;* Badger, *Great American Fair;* Rydell, *All the World's a Fair.*

14. Hines, *Burnham of Chicago,* 74–124; Badger, *Great American Fair,* 91–2, 104, 120–23; Rydell, *All the World's a Fair,* 47, 52, 64, 67; Neufeld, "Contribution of the World's Columbian Exposition."

15. *Columbian Exposition Album* (Chicago, 1893), 98, cited in Ziff, *American 1890s,* 4.

16. Findling, "Chicago Loses the 1904 Olympics"; Barney, "Born from Dilemma."

17. *The Greatest of Expositions,* 2, 214–24.

18. Rydell, *All the World's a Fair,* 159.

19. Rydell, *All the World's a Fair,* 159.

20. Rydell, *All the World's a Fair,* 162.

21. Rydell, *All the World's a Fair,* 189; see Rydell, *All the World's a Fair,* 167, on the Philippines "reservation."

22. Procter, "Isolationism or Imperialism," cited in Welch, *Imperialists vs. Anti-Imperialists,* 25.

23. Barrett, "Problem of the Philippines," cited in Welch, *Imperialists vs. Anti-Imperialists,* 66.

24. Wolff, *Little Brown Brother,* 63.

25. Dean C. Worcester Papers, Bentley Library, University of Michigan.

26. Rydell, *All the World's a Fair,* 189.

27. Fossett and Tucker, *Race Consciousness,* 237–41; Worcester, "Non-Christian Peoples of the Philippine Islands," 1157–1256, 1180, 1182, 1189 (quotes, respectively.)

28. Rydell, *All the World's a Fair,* 163; Louisiana Purchase Exposition Corporation (LPEC), *Greatest of Expositions,* 230 (quotes).

29. Rydell, *All the World's a Fair*, 233, 236; cartoon in St. *Louis Post-Dispatch*, October 23, 1904, courtesy of Susan Brownell.

30. St. *Louis Post-Dispatch*, June 19, 1904, cited in Kramer, "Pragmatic Empire," 235.

31. LPEC, *Greatest of Expositions*, 238.

32. R. Sullivan, *Olympics*, 18; Hoffmann, "German and German-American Contribution to the 1904 Olympic Games," 2; Renson et al., "Olympism and Colonialism"; Matthews and Marshall, St. *Louis Olympics 1904*, 126; Eichberg, "Forward Race," 115–31.

33. Eichberg, "Forward Race," 117; Matthews and Marshall, St. *Louis Olympics 1904*, 125.

34. Mallon, *1904 Olympic Games*, cited at http://www.aafla.org/6oic/OfficialReports/Mallon/1904.pdf.

35. Hoffmann, "German and German-American Contribution to the 1904 Olympic Games," 1; LPEC, *Greatest of Expositions*, 239 (quote).

36. Worcester, "Non-Christian Peoples of the Philippine Islands," 1250 (quotes); LPEC, *Greatest of Expositions*, 226–27.

37. Worcester, "Non-Christian Peoples of the Philippine Islands," 1173.

38. Hines, *Burnham of Chicago*, 203.

39. Moore, *Plan of Chicago*, 29.

40. Hines, *Burnham of Chicago*, 209.

41. Hines, *Burnham of Chicago*, 210.

42. Seymour, *Baseball*, 324–25.

43. Worcester, *Philippines*, 2:515.

44. Gleeck, *American Institutions in the Philippines*, 39.

45. Reaves, *Taking In a Game*, 96.

46. Frederic S. Marquardt Papers, Bentley Library, University of Michigan; National Baseball Hall of Fame Archives, Foreign: Philippines file; Wooley, "'Batter Up' in the Philippines," 313–14 (quotes).

47. Kramer, "Reflex Actions," (quote); Marquardt Papers, Bentley Historical Library, University of Michigan, and Wooley, "'Batter Up' in the Philippines," 313–14, on baseball games.

48. Beran, "Americans in the Philippines"; Governor-General Harrison, Executive Order 79, Sept. 16, 1914, National Archives, R 350, Box 931, on Brown's appointment; Philippines Correspondence Reports, 1911–1968, YMCA Archives, Administrative Reports file, University of Minnesota; Gleeck, *American Institutions in the Philippines*, 74–75.

49. Frederick Starr Papers; E. Brown, *Annual Report* (quote).

50. Coubertin, "An Olympiad in the Far East (May 1913)," in *Olympism: Selected Writings*, 695, courtesy of Susan Brownell.

51. John W. Galloway to *Richmond Planet*, Nov. 16, 1899, cited in Gatewood, *"Smoked Yankees" and the Struggle for Empire*, 252.

52. Rafael, "White Women and United States Rule," 658.

53. *Manila Cablenews*, August 8, 1907, cited in Stanley, *Nation in the Making*, 107.

54. Worcester, "Non-Christian Peoples of the Philippine Islands," 1167, 1192, 1200; Bulosan, *America Is in the Heart*, 40–69.

55. Dyreson, "Globalizing American Sporting Culture."

Chapter 5. "From Savagery to Civic Organization"

The Nonparticipation of Canadian Indians
in the Anthropology Days of the 1904 St. Louis Olympic Games

CHRISTINE M. O'BONSAWIN

In August of 1904, organizers from the Departments of Anthropology and Physical Culture of the Louisiana Purchase Exposition (LPE) arranged an athletic event dedicated to displaying the physical prowess of "primitive" peoples of the world. This event was termed "Anthropology Days" and has since been described as "an unusual set of 'athletic' events," that took place on August 11 and 12 during the Olympic Games.[1] This athletic competition of "surpassing" interest was to be organized "under the auspices of the Department of Physical Culture, participated in by representatives of all the tribes of strange people at the Fair."[2] However, historical records suggest that Canada's assemblage of "strange people," otherwise known as Canadian Indians, remained conspicuously absent from the Anthropology Days athletic event.

To understand why Canadian Indians were not represented as competitors on Francis Field, the site of this two-day "Olympic" event, four areas of analysis are identified for investigation. The first area of study broadly historicizes the participation and showmanship of Canadian Indians, particularly the Mohawks of Kahnawá:ke, in nineteenth-century lacrosse tours. While the growing popularity of world's fairs and Wild West shows in the second half of the nineteenth century relegated lacrosse tours, and thus their spectacle dimensions, to a peripheral position, this did not deter Mohawk Indians from competing in various sporting contests, including the 1904 Olympic Games proper. Accordingly, this examination recognizes Canada's sizeable and successful participation in the St. Louis Olympic Games. The significant representation of Canadian athletes at the St. Louis Games is examined in relation to the contrasting absence of Canadian Indians in the Anthropology Days athletic event. This discussion adopts a holistic analysis of the Department of Anthropology and theorizes that the absence of Canadian Indians from this "Olympic" event is diametrically related to the aims and objectives of this division. In line with American Indian policy objectives and ideological visions, Canadian Indians assumed a nominal role in the anthropological and ethnological exhibits of the Louisiana Purchase Exposition, which consequently led to their absence in the Anthropology Days event of the 1904 St. Louis Olympic Games.

Canadian Indian Showmanship

The appropriation of Indian spectacles can be traced to the landing of Columbus and the initial years of European colonization. The earliest printed reports of the New World not only provided verbal accounts but also ethnographically inaccurate illustrations of the new land's indigenous peoples.[3] In 1999, Christian F. Feest published a compilation of interdisciplinary essays entitled *Indians and Europe*.[4] This edited volume organizes, chronologically, over thirty contributing essays that address the Eurocentric fascination with Indians. The anthology commences with examples of European exposure to stereotypical presentations of North American Indians in the sixteenth century and then sequentially reports on European interpretations and reactions to Indian lore throughout the subsequent centuries, concluding with the twentieth century. Appropriately, in his postscript, Feest concludes, "A simple explanation for the reasons of the special relationship between Europeans and the native populations of North America is that no such relationship exists."[5] Although North American Indians have, in some respects, been characterized throughout history primarily as a homogeneous population, the cultural diversity of Indian societies has been adapted and appropriated to accommodate stereotypical European perceptions of "Indianness" or "Indian exoticism."

The latter half of the nineteenth century and the early years of the twentieth century witnessed a proliferation of Canadian Indian populations serving as prominent public spectacles, particularly in celebrations of national significance. For example, the Kwakwaka'wakw (Kwakiutl) of Vancouver Island, British Columbia, participated in dramatic performances at the 1893 Chicago World's Columbian Fair.[6] At the Quebec tercentenary celebrations of 1908, the inclusion of Native actors in dimensions of spectacular pageantry assisted in the process of deception, thereby presenting a harmonious unification of two culturally diverse populations (the French and the indigenous peoples) and the perceived acceptance of an otherwise marginalized Aboriginal population.[7] In 1927, Native populations enthusiastically participated in the artistic programs of national celebration during the Diamond Jubilee of Confederation.[8] When reviewing the literature on Canadian Indian showmanship, one cannot dispute the longstanding tradition of the Mohawks of Kahnawá:ke in participating in such events.

Kahnawá:ke showmanship did not first appear out of the Wild West–show era, as some believe. To the contrary, its origins are much older. The writers of the *Jesuit Relations*, for example, recorded Jesuit displeasure with the participation of Mohawks in ritual, social, and parody dances prior to the founding of Kahnawá:ke in 1667. The inclusion of Mohawks in such traditional practices troubled the Jesuits on two levels. First, their persistent participation in ritual dance impeded missionary conversion efforts. Second, the entertainment value of social and parody dances provided further evidence of Indian autobiographical pantomime. A process of compromise and negotiation concerning the issue of dance performance occurred between the Jesuits and Mohawks in the eighteenth century. Following a lengthy process of negotiation, the Kahnawá:ke Mohawks willingly brought the competitive elements of their showmanship to the imagination of Europeans in the nineteenth century.[9]

In August of 1860, Albert Edward, the eighteen-year-old Prince of Wales, was the first representative of the British monarchy to visit Canada. Ian Radforth provides a comprehensive commentary on the regal celebration in his 2004 book *Royal Spectacle: The 1860 Visit of the Prince of Wales to Canada and the United States*. Radforth's investigation is based primarily on media reactions to the lavish public spectacles honoring the future king of England. He argues that, in general, scholarship addressing public spectacles primarily concentrates on the formation of national identity through commemoration. However, Radforth suggests that "the 1860 visit looked resolutely *ahead* to further commercial expansion, industrial transformation, moral and social progress, and nation building."[10] Ritualistic commemorative ceremonies performed for the prince focused on new beginnings and a promising future. At this time, the matter of national identity was an uncertainty in the colonies, where proposals for a confederated state were, at best, tenuous. Local identities prevailed as old ties to France, England, Scotland, Ireland, and Wales divided the population. The topic of national unity was contentious as a British cultural chauvinism imposed its white, Protestant, and English-speaking ideologies onto the population at large, some of which included French Canadians, Irish Catholics, English Protestants, and African Canadians.[11]

In regard to Indian spectacles, Radforth dedicates an entire chapter to the popularity of "Performing Indians." The author identifies and provides examples for the inclusion of Canadian Indian spectacles in national celebrations and argues, "However much the Canadian state has robbed, suppressed, patronized, and denigrated First Nations peoples, governments have nevertheless found it advantageous to include Aboriginal people in celebrations that define and affirm an imagined national community."[12] As Radforth correctly acknowledges, the royal tour provided an opportunity for non-Native people to appropriate and display Indians, as well as an occasion for Native peoples to demand public attention. Regardless, the disconcerting issue of representation was brought to the forefront. Non-Aboriginal organizers relied on the "invention of tradition" and therefore drew on Indian cultural resources to impart to the prince a national identity rooted in the country's heritage of colonialism.[13]

Showmanship and Sporting Lacrosse Tours

During this royal tour, the showmanship of various Indian populations was evident in the public exhibition of cultural sporting traditions. In anticipation of the Prince of Wales's royal entry to Halifax, Mi'kmaq men set off in specially decorated birch-bark canoes to greet and escort the prince to the shores of the colony. In his first few days, Mi'kmaq men and women entertained and delighted their royal dignitary by engaging in athletic pursuits, including the grand regatta paddle races and track- and-field competitions held on the commons. Like all competitors, the Mi'kmaq were enticed by declarations informing them that considerable cash prizes would be rewarded in exchange for their participation in such contests. Upon traveling to the Montreal region, the prince was once again met with much-publicized sporting spectacles. With the intention of entertaining their royal guest and attracting ticket-purchasing spectators, the Montreal reception committee had chosen to highlight the city's prominence as a sporting center and appropriately hosted the "Indian games." At this event, at least two lacrosse matches were contested, the first between Algonquin and Iroquois teams, and the second between an Iroquois and non-Native team (the Montreal Shamrocks). Immediately following these matches, spectators were further entertained by "Indian war dances" performed by Mohawk men from the Kahnawá:ke and Kanasetake communities.[14] As Radforth reports, these displays included Indians who were "dressed in buckskin, paint, and feathers," and "the Iroquois warriors danced to the beat of drums and brandished tomahawks and knives, mimicking a bloody battle — complete with the scalping of enemy captives."[15] Furthermore, during his stay in Montreal, the prince was entertained by water spectacles, which were performed by approximately one hundred Iroquois canoeists. This display, which was organized by the Hudson's Bay Company and hosted at Dorval Island in Lake St. Louis, dazzled the royal company by incorporating "colourfully decorated canoes and their rapid and meticulously synchronised paddling."[16] While the Prince of Wales later visited other large congregations of Indian populations, particularly the Ojibwa (Anishinabe) peoples in Sarnia and the Six Nations Iroquois (Haudenoshaunee) of the Grand River, records do not substantiate that he was greeted with such sporting spectacles in Upper Canada.

The exhibition of these sporting displays proved to be inconsistent. The demonstrations of Indians in athletic competitions in Upper Canada suggested to the prince that games such as lacrosse were an admirable example of whites' borrowing from Native peoples. "In its address to the prince, the recently organized Montreal Lacrosse Club recognized the origins of the game, saying it was a 'manly' sport 'peculiar to Canada,' derived from the 'aboriginal Red Man of the forest, and preeminently adapted to test their swiftness of foot, quickness of ear and vision, and powers of endurance.'"[17]

The participation of Indians in "war dances" as well as the encouragement and insistence on the part of the Department of Indian Affairs (DIA) to have these "chiefs" and "warriors" dressed in traditional clothing appears to be an anomaly in itself. At this time, government officials were aggressively pursuing the policies of the DIA, which sought to "civilize" and assimilate Canada's Aboriginal populations. In Upper Canada, particularly in Sarnia and Brantford, Native populations appeased the DIA and greeted the royal entourage in traditional dress and regalia. It is important to note that while many Native people obliged with the requests of the Indian Department, for many, their decision to dress in ceremonial costume was a personal choice with the intention of maintaining and honoring traditional customs. While the endorsement of such exploits proved inconsistent with departmental objectives, it was the intention of the DIA to mount a spectacle for the prince that incorporated paint and feathers. The purpose was to contrast the spectacular and childlike way of the historic "blanket" Indian against the newly conformed patriotic citizen of the colony. Consequently, the majority of chiefs and warriors who attended these gatherings in Upper Canada did so in traditional dress. Unlike the eastern regions of Halifax and Montreal, non-Native citizens in the west detested Aboriginal enthusiasm for sport and games as they were deemed "savage" and objectionable. Halfway through the royal tour an editorial appeared in the *Christian Guardian*, a Toronto-based Methodist newspaper, suggesting that it was deplorable that "the prince had been taken to see Indians playing 'savage games,' where Upper Canada would like to see His Royal Highness and the Duke of Newcastle hear our Christian Indians sing, with their sweet voices, sons of Zion, to them pray to God of heaven."[18] Accordingly, the "Christianized" Aboriginals of Upper Canada were measured against Lower Canada's heathen "savages."

In spite of such opinions, the royal tour of 1860 strengthened a longstanding tradition for the Mohawks of Kahnawá:ke. Throughout the second half of the nineteenth century, this population continued to engage in acts of showmanship, as many families from the community toured various parts of Europe and engaged in assorted games and dance for both royal and public audiences.[19] At the time of confederation, the exhibition of Indian spectacles increased due to political and visionary understandings of post-confederated nationalism.[20] In 1867, two Kahnawá:ke men served in the Canadian delegation at the Paris Exposition Universelle and then traveled to London, England, to demonstrate traits of "Canadianness" to English schoolchildren. The following year, fifteen Mohawk men and women from Kahnawá:ke also traveled to London with the purpose of staging pantomime dance performances and exhibition lacrosse games.[21] The most ostentatious acts of Mohawk showmanship, arguably, took place during the lacrosse tours of 1876 and 1883. Kevin Wamsley identifies that by 1873, Canadian foreign promotional efforts of federal immigration policies proved feeble in comparison to the attractive endorsement campaigns on the part of the United States government. Accordingly, the new Dominion of Canada "[w]ished to supplant the images of backwardness and marginality with images of Canada as a resource-rich land in which state-of-the-art technology offered new kinds of opportunities for 'developed' and for sophisticated living."[22]

At this time, lacrosse tours proved to be an ideal platform to convey "progressive" initiatives of the newly confederated nation. Prior to the 1850s, various Indian populations participated in traditionally significant practices of *baggataway* or *tewaarathon*. While the French understood "lacrosse" in culturally familiar terminology, the British ultimately standardized and popularized this "sport" according to socially accepted ideologies of the Montreal and Toronto middle classes. In 1876, English, Scottish, and Irish crowds were indoctrinated on the allure of Canada. As Wamsley observes,

> An important subtext was being communicated here in the positioning of contrast and distinction between the "savages" of the wildlands of Canada and their "masters," a team of amateur, rule-abiding, honourable white gentlemen. Similar to the projected images of many of the Canadian exhibits at world's fairs at this time, the Native athletes represented an earlier, more civilized era, while the white team signified the march of progress, rationality, and a modern social order.[23]

Naturally, Indians were adorned in beaded outfits, war paint, and petitioned to participate in spontaneous war dances.

At this time, a Montreal dentist by the name of Dr. George W. Beers was shrewdly capitalizing on the nationalist fervor of the confederation craze. In his attempt to promote lacrosse as "the national game of Canada," he sought to stimulate and eventually popularize the sport both home and abroad.[24] In 1883, Beers led a European expedition of middle-class lacrosse teams from the urban centers of Montreal and Toronto. Fittingly, a team of Mohawk Indians from Kahnawá:ke were included in the western journey. The intention was to once again promote the dominion's immigration efforts in England, Scotland, and Ireland. This tour proved overtly political as incidences of Indian pageantry, ceremonies, and demonstrations were complemented by immigration addresses and the distribution of pamphlets promoting all things Canadian. Lacrosse tours proved to be analogous to world's fairs as both served to propagate the culture of spectacle and images of nation-ness.

However, in subsequent years, the tradition of Canadian Indian showmanship would be considerably altered due to various American cultural movements, including the professionalization of American anthropology, the inclusion of ethnological and anthropological exhibits in world's fairs, and the emergent popularity of Buffalo Bill's Wild West shows.

Although the showy attributes of the Kahnawá:ke Mohawks served the emotional and cultural needs of Europeans throughout the second half of the nineteenth century, American progressive and civilizing movements would eventually reject this showmanship and "acculturation" of certain Canadian Indian populations. The theme of the 1893 World's Columbian Exposition was "progress," and the fair was ironically dubbed "The White City." The racial connotations were fitting as "exhibits of human beings representing successive stages of race and civilization were a central aspect of this project."[25] Despite humble efforts to incorporate a human anthropological exhibit at the 1876 Philadelphia Centennial Exposition, Chicago was the first North American international exhibition to fruitfully incorporate such displays. Consequently, curator and professor of Harvard's Peabody Museum and the head of the fair's ethnology department, Frederic Ward Putnam, included "live exhibits" in his anthropology encampment in Chicago.

At this time, the U.S. government was confronted with a multifaceted quandary when exhibiting its Indian populations at international exposi-tions.[26] There existed a paradox between the spectacular attractiveness of America's "old blanket" Indians and the apparent disinterest in the "imita-tion white man with red skin."[27] Consequently, the "1889 Agreement" was employed for the 1893 World Columbian Exposition by Indian Commissioner Thomas J. Morgan. This doctrine ensured that the exhibition of American Indians would contain a comparative component, and the "brutish" ways of Wild West shows would not make a mockery of the civilizing efforts and assimilation program of the U.S. government.

In 1889, promoter J. W. Crawford had attempted to bring a small group of Apaches to a St. Louis trade fair: Capitalizing on the interest in Indians,

> Crawford proposed that the Apaches, "in all their native pride and strength
> . . . give daily exhibitions of their weird dances, ceremonies and incanta-
> tions, and exemplify their modes to savage warfare." To secure federal
> permission for the Apaches to leave their reservation, Crawford discovered
> he had to placate the Indian Bureau. As a result, he struck a deal with
> Secretary of the Interior John W. Noble, whereby the Apaches would "be
> placed in juxtaposition with a band of youths from the Indian school at
> Lawrence, Kansas, so that the visitors may have ocular evidence of the
> refining influence of education on the aboriginal mind." This device fit
> the needs of both sides, permitting the Bureau to sanction Indian exhibits
> as long as they contained a comparative component.[28]

Accordingly, the 1889 agreement stipulated that if "savage" Indians were
incorporated into bureau-sanctioned exhibits in Chicago, they would have to
be placed in juxtaposition with a band of Indian youths who were subjected
to the comprehensive system of U.S. Indian education.[29]

Regardless of fiscal and organizational shortcomings, the failures of the
comparative component in Chicago rested with fairgoers' reverent attraction to traditional Indian culture and their indifference to the unromantic
"wave of the future." Putnam appeased U.S. policy officials by incorporating
comparative dimensions, which pitted "savage" Indians against the government's enlightened Indian products. While the schoolhouse symbolized the
government's civilizing accomplishments, various North American Eskimos,
Crees, Penobscots, Iroquois, Kwakwaka'wakw, Chippewas, Winnebagos,
Sioux, Blackfoot, Nez Perces; South American Arrawacs and Savannah Indians;
and Natives of Bolivia and other states, represented the essence of savagery.
Franz Boas assisted Putman in overseeing the Northwest Coast component
of the exhibit. This section of the encampment, as was consistent with all
aspects of the display, omitted everyday elements of late-nineteenth-century
Kwakwaka'wakw lifestyle in favor of "authentic" representations. For example,
Hudson's Bay Company blankets, common articles in Kwakwaka'waka life

at this time, were removed from exhibit display in preference for "authentic" cedar bark covers.[30] Comparable to the pragmatism of the blankets, the Mohawks of Kahnawá:ke were excluded from Putnam and Boas's exhibit as they were deemed "unauthentic" and "acculturated." As Blanchard argues,

> Franz Boas, in charge of the ethnological exhibits including the importation of Native Americans to the fair, insisted upon strict scientific accuracy in the Ethnology Department. Natives deemed "acculturated," such as the Kahnawake Mohawk, were not invited to the fair to exhibit lacrosse, pantomime dance, or to sell their crafts.[31]

Although the Mohawks of Kahnawá:ke were not officially invited to the fair, they did use their own resources to travel to Chicago. Upon arrival, these people were employed and participated in various private shows and contests that underscored their rich history and involvement in the Indian show trade. While it is unclear whether any men or women from Kahnawá:ke joined Buffalo Bill's Wild West show in Chicago, it is clear that the displays of Mohawk dance, lacrosse, and crafts could not compete with the extravagant allure of Cody's troupe at this exposition. Subsequently, the influence of such shows altered the Mohawks' postexhibition involvement in the entertainment industry, as people from Kahnawá:ke began to participate in various adaptations of Wild West shows throughout the northeast regions of Canada and the United States.[32] By the dawn of the twentieth century, the "primitive" aspects of the less "acculturated" Northwest Coast Canadian Indian populations began to serve the interests of emergent American anthropologists who proved captivated by these peoples' cultural and linguistic variances. Moreover, the perceived state of Northwest Coast "savagery" further supported the political doctrines of the U.S. colonial government, which proposed that its own American Indian populations were well on the path toward civilization and citizenship.

In celebration of the one-hundred-year anniversary of the Louisiana Purchase, St. Louis was imparted with the responsibility of organizing and hosting the centennial celebrations. In recent literature, historians have addressed various issues associated with the inclusion of "primitive" peoples in the Louisiana Purchase Exposition and its "Olympic" related events. In reference to the Indian exhibits, specifically the ethnological encampments and Model Indian School, Trennert argues: "The St. Louis school exhibit, better organized, better financed, more innovative, and generally more impressive [than Chicago], cannot be said to have accomplished its goal, however; No matter what bureau officials stated, traditional Indian displays dominated and overshadowed the model school. Once again the public expressed more interest in old Indian ways than education."[33]

The ethnological exhibits at world's fairs, including St. Louis, proved to be resilient marketing forces that promoted living anachronisms. Despite the government's employment of the 1889 Agreement as well as its efforts to combat the popular Wild West image at the 1904 Exhibition, the public enthusiastically flocked to state-sponsored exhibits to observe America's "old blanket" Indians. Ironically, the U.S. government had also become caught up in the Indian show trade.

Unlike the 1893 World's Columbian Exposition, Canadian Indians proved less prominent in the anthropological exhibits in St. Louis. Nevertheless, exhibition organizers remained allured by the authenticity of Northwest Coast culture and, accordingly, organizers once again solicited the Kwakwaka'waka peoples. Organizers intended to incorporate these people into the anthropological and ethnological displays at the Fair. Comparable to the 1893 Fair, the Mohawks of Kahnawá:ke were not officially invited to play a part as such in 1904. However, historical records suggest that a group of Canadian Mohawk Indians from the Six Nations of the Grand River formally participated as athletes in the lacrosse event of the official 1904 St. Louis Olympic Games.

Canadian Athletes and the 1904 Olympic Games

Despite the various controversies that plagued the 1904 St. Louis Olympics, the participation and successes of Canadian athletes in these Games proved unparalleled. Following a contentious transfer of these third Olympic Games from the city of Chicago to St. Louis, the athletic events were marred with disorganization as a result of their amalgamation with a world's fair. This union resulted in an athletic program that exceeded a four- and-a-half-month period. Further adversities in the swimming pool and on the marathon route have been noted and well documented by respected sport historians.[34] Despite the various debacles associated with the St. Louis Games and the overwhelming dominance of American athletes, Canada successfully fielded its largest contingent to that date. In all probability, this was the result of the geographical proximity of St. Louis to Canada. Regardless, Canadian athletes and teams, including Étienne Desmarteau, George Lyon, the Winnipeg Shamrocks, the Mohawk lacrosse team, the Galt Football Club, and the Toronto Argonauts Rowing Club, successfully competed in St. Louis, thus marking their places in Canadian Olympic history.[35]

Of particular significance to this study is the 1904 Olympic lacrosse event, which saw the participation of two Canadian teams — the Winnipeg Shamrocks and the Mohawk Indians. Initially, four teams had entered the St. Louis Olympic lacrosse event, including the Brooklyn Crescents, the St. Louis AAA (Amateur Athletic Association), the Winnipeg Shamrocks, and the Mohawk Indians. In the end, only three teams participated as the Brooklyn Crescents failed to arrive in St. Louis. The lacrosse event took place on Francis Field on July 2 and 7 and consisted of thirty-six players (twelve players per team) from two nations. To date, sports historians have relied too much on newspaper sources to verify the membership of the Mohawk team. In his conclusive report entitled *The 1904 Olympic Games: Results for All Competitors in All Events, with Commentary,* Bill Mallon reports that the Mohawk lacrosse team was "called the Iroquois Indians by the *Globe-Democrat.* The *Manitoba Free Press* and the *Chicago Tribune* both called them the Mohawk Indians. The team roster came from the *Chicago Tribune.*"[36] To add clarity to Mallon's ambiguous account, it is important to note that this indigenous team, which was recognized as "Canadian" on the Olympic program, was comprised of

Iroquois Confederacy Mohawks. The Mohawk Indians finished behind the first-ranked Winnipeg Shamrocks and second-positioned St. Louis AAA. The lacrosse event of 1904 was credited by Mallon as a tournament of Olympic caliber as it was "contested by amateur athletes of both America and foreign countries with no restrictions placed on them."[37]

The Nonparticipation of Canadian Indians in the Anthropology Days

While the chief of the Department of Physical Culture, James E. Sullivan, was overseeing the organization and administration of this division, and thus the Olympic Games proper, the chief of the Anthropology Department, WJ McGee, was utilizing anthropometry and psychometry laboratories to assess the intellectual, psychological, and physical values of "savage" races at the fair. In addition to organizing the Olympic Games, Sullivan sought to popularize this event with athletic spectacles. In the summer of 1904, Sullivan approached McGee with an enticing offer, proposing that "primitive savages" of the fair compete in athletic pursuits with the purpose of confirming their supposed physical prowess. In honor of McGee and the Department of Anthropology, the Physical Culture Department hosted the Anthropology Days athletic event on August 11–12, 1904. Historians, including Nancy Parezo and Mark Dyreson in this volume, have thoroughly researched and analytically discussed the complexities surrounding the Anthropology Days event, which Parezo (this volume) describes as "a comedy in bad science through the use of a badly flawed anthropometry methodology to prove central premises of Social Darwinian and unilinear evolutionary paradigms." However, the literature and extensive evidence fails to acknowledge the absence of Canadian Indians at this athletic event, despite their inclusion, albeit limited, in McGee's anthropological exhibits and the sizeable participation of Canadian athletes in the Olympic Games proper.

In August of 1904, the World's Fair Bulletin inaccurately reported that an event of surpassing interest was to take place on August 16. This article also suggested that the Vancouver Island Indians were expected to be among those competing in this interracial athletic contest.[38] However, existing records fail to document the inclusion and participation of Canadian Indians in the Anthropology Days event. An article published in the September 1904 edition of the *World's Fair Bulletin*, entitled "A Novel Athletic Contest," reported the top performances at the "Olympic" event. There is no mention of Vancouver Island Indians finishing with award-winning results. In reference to the "most interesting event," the one-mile run, it is stated that "in this race North America finished first, Asia second, Africa third, and a South American not far behind." Once again, no Canadian Indian athlete is identified as having competed. In *The Olympic Century: III Olympiad — St. Louis 1904, Athens 1906* publication of *The Olympic Century* series, it is stated that "of the world's continents, North America was the best represented at the 'Olympic' Anthropology. Days."[39] This statement is followed up with commentary related to the successes of American Indian athletes, including the Sioux, Pawnee, Chippewa, and Crow tribes. However, in this extensive discussion is there no mention of any Canadian Indian athlete having competed in this "Olympic" event. In his summary and commentary on the 1904 Olympic Games, Mallon provides a competitor and results list for the Anthropology Days athletic event — once again Canadian Indians are not listed as having participated.[40] Furthermore, in McGee's "Report of the Department of Anthropology," written on May 10, 1905, there is no mention of Canadian Indians having been involved.[41]

The Aims and Objectives of the Department of Anthropology

Even though the Anthropology Days were to include "not just the savages . . . [and] all those other nonwhites wandering the Pike," McGee was ultimately dismayed by the poor showing for the Anthropology Days athletic event.[42] As published in the *World's Fair Bulletin* in August of 1904, event organizers anticipated that numerous "savages" were expected to attend the athletic event; however, the Vancouver Island Indians remain noticeably absent from the records. It is plausible to qualify the absence of the Vancouver Island Indians in this "Olympic" event based on two general premises. First, for each Native group invited to participate in his anthropological experiments and ethnological exhibits, McGee identified scientific and racial functions. As a result, the second premise is based on the limited number of individuals and groups representing specific Native populations (including Canadian Indians) who were invited to participate in the anthropological and ethnological exhibits.

Dr. William J McGee was selected as chief of the Department of Anthropology upon its formation on August 1, 1903. Director of Exhibits F. J. V. Skiff reported that McGee's selection to this post was due to his eminent note and achievements in the fields of archaeology, anthropology, and ethnology. However, Dyreson (this volume) revealed McGee's frailties and shortcomings, ultimately questioning his credibility in this high profile position: "McGee was an ambitious polymath who lacked the formal credentials increasingly necessary for a career in science. Indeed, the title of 'Dr.' which preceded his name on many of his publications was an honorary award from Iowa's Cornell College."

At the LPE, McGee ultimately aspired to unveil the most comprehensive hierarchical matrix of physical-cultural development. He adopted an evolutionary paradigm that positioned all of humanity on a linear continuum consisting of barbarism, savagery, civilization, and enlightenment. Naturally, McGee positioned the Caucasian "race-type" as an exemplar of man's highest enlightenment. The overall departmental aim was to present to the mass public "man as both creature and as worker."[43] The popular success of the anthropological exhibits was due, in large part, to the living displays within the department's section of ethnology. McGee aspired and evidently succeeded in fabricating an outdoor ethnological exhibit comprised of cultural anomalies. He selected indigenous peoples from various cultures, as he assumed each group possessed a particular scientific and racial uniqueness that would validate the anthropological visions of the department.

> The Ainu, for example, were desired because McGee felt the group was composed of two subtypes divided on sex lines; the men showed their tree-climbing ancestry through "their small statue, their centripetal (or bodyward)

movements, their use of the feet as manual adjuncts, their elongated arms
and incurved hands, and their facility in climbing." As a contrast to the
small Ainu, McGee felt it was crucial to include the Patagonian "giants,"
whom he held to be heroic in statue. The Cocopas were selected to represent
an anomaly: extremely tall men and short women. The Dakota Sioux were
to serve as examples of tallness, powerful body build, and agility, while
the Pueblos would represent short stature. Some groups (for example, the
Pygmies and Negritos) were chosen to represent the world's "least-known
ethnic types," including groups thought to be the "least removed from the
sub-human or quadrumane form." McGee sought still others because they
were closer in development to the mentality of the highest human forms, had
extraordinary creativity, or were members of races that should be studied
more systematically by trained scientists before they disappeared in the
face of Western imperialism.[44]

In terms of the ethnological encampment, various "race-types" erected
and occupied traditional habitations. McGee explained: "While groups were
chosen primarily to represent the human varieties or sub-species, they were
selected also with the view of illustrating the arts, industries, languages, social customs and beliefs prevailing among the various nations and peoples;
i.e., the groups represent both race-types and culture-types."[45] According to
McGee's scheme, then, cultural attributes were also associated with "racial"
groups. The Pygmies of Central Africa were, according to Greek mythology,
one of the most powerful and warlike tribes on the continent; the Cocopas
were recognized for their agricultural endeavors; many Americanized Indians were identified for their unique accommodations, including the earth
lodges occupied by the "picturesque" Pawnee and Navaho groups, and the
aesthetically pleasing quarters of the "refined" Kickapoos.[46] In his report,
McGee acknowledged that the Klaokwaht and Kwakiutl, otherwise known
as the Vancouver Group, were integrated into this living ethnological exhibit
primarily because they possessed "a highly interesting product of aboriginal
culture."[47]

Similar to his evolutionary paradigm, which positioned all of humanity on the linear continuum of barbarism, savagery, civilization, and enlightenment, McGee desired to place the "savage" populations on an analogous scale, which represented "human progress from the dark prime to the highest enlightenment, from savagery to civic organization, from egoism to altruism."[48] The most important section of the anthropology exhibit was the ethnological exhibit, which was primarily supported with federal appropriations.[49] This exhibit encompassed over forty acres of the fairgrounds and incorporated approximately 325 aliens, including indigenous populations from various parts of the world, including Japan, South America, Africa, Canada, and America's "old blanket" Indians.[50] The savage communities were positioned on a linear continuum according to the degree of their development. Fittingly, "exposition grounds may be seen at every stage in industrial progress with the development in arts, languages, social customs, and beliefs characteristic of each stage of human advancement."[51]

The Native peoples were situated within the Anthropology Villages and Indian Village so that visitors would meet the most "primitive" group first—the African Pygmies. The visiting public could then travel up a small hill where they could observe exemplars of the various races that McGee positioned in his evolutionary model. Situated in close proximity to the African Pygmies were the Ainus of Japan, the Patagonians of Argentina, the Cocopas of the southern United States, and the Klaokwaht/Kwakiutl of Canada. Of the twenty-nine groups included in the exhibit (it must be noted that the living ethnological exhibit and allotments were modified from time to time with the coming and going of groups), the Vancouver Group was positioned in the twenty-fifth station—both physically and spatially removed from the American Indians and the Model Indian School. For the most part, the Americanized Indians occupied positions one through twenty-four, as their lodges were clustered outside the Model Indian School. According to McGee, he and Superintendent Samuel McCowan had designed the exhibits with the purpose of displaying "family groups living in the Stone Age, others just at the beginning of metal working, others engaged in primitive pottery-making and basket-weaving, and so on through to civilization."[52] A fabricated evolutionary paradigm was established on the west end of the grounds in order to demonstrate and verify the superiority of U.S. Indian policy and the civilizing effects it was having on its Indian populations. The visitors' journey came to an end when they arrived at the hill's summit where the government's Model Indian School was erected.

On May 22, 1903, approximately four months prior to the establishment of an Anthropology Department, the American federal government had assigned Indian Service Agent McCowan to the position of superintendent of the government's Indian exhibit. The Fifty-seventh Congress of the United States appropriated forty thousand dollars to the exhibit and the Fifty-eighth Congress later financed an additional twenty-five thousand dollars.[53] David R. Francis, president of the LPE, rationalized the involvement and objectives of the U.S. government in association with the Anthropology Department and its ethnological and Indian School sections by stating that "[t]he United States government has performed no worthier function than that of aiding our aboriginal landholders on their way toward citizenship. The means and the ends of purposive acculturation as applied to the American aborigines and the actual processes illustrated by living examples were exhibited in the typical Indian school forming the most conspicuous feature of the department."[54]

With the fiscal and administrative support of the U.S. government's Bureau of Indian Affairs (BIA), the Anthropology Department effectively illustrated the superior means and methods of U.S. Indian policy "and how it had successfully raised the American Indian tribes to the plane of citizenship."[55] The triumphs and achievements of U.S. Indian policy were exemplified by an unambiguous ethnological exhibit that placed the so-called exotic, barbaric, and savage peoples of the world at the farthest end of the continuum. Further on, America's "blanket" Indians were craftily positioned outside the Model Indian School. This testimonial building exemplified the goals of the government, which had triumphantly advanced its "savage" Indian populations along the evolutionary paradigm.

Situated on this linear continuum were five Vancouver Indians: three Klaokwaht and two Kwakwaka'waka. As previously stated, McGee and the Department of Anthropology invited these individuals because they possessed unique cultural attributes. The Klaokwaht clan house, which provided consanguineal groups and families with a fixed place within the structure, was of particular interest. While the Kwakwaka'waka were recognized for their especially light color of skin, they were particularly distinguished for their elaborate totemic or heraldic crests. The Canadian assemblage occupied the Klaokwaht clan house, and a great sea canoe lay alongside their lodging. Their active participation in exhibitions of primitive peoples was noted and reference was made to their distinctive masks and ceremonial costumes. In his final report, McGee made note of Kwakwaka'waka practices of human sacrifice and their physical scars, which were the result of symbolic cannibalism associated with fiducial feasts. McGee concluded his report by annotating the dramatic ceremony that was repeatedly performed by the Kwakwaka'waka priests, with the help of their Klaokwaht neighbors, which involved a cannibal dance performance.[56] However, Parezo suggests that "the Kwakiutl held a Hamatsa ceremony in which they ritually ate a pig dressed as a pygmy. It was a big joke on McGee."[57]

Many questions arise concerning the circumstances of the Canadian Indian contingent. Specifically, considering Canada's geographical proximity to St. Louis, why were only five Indians from Canada represented in McGee's living ethnological exhibit? Furthermore, why was the Vancouver Group positioned in such a remote location on the continuum? The answers rest within the motive and scope of the Department of Anthropology—to trace the paths of human progress. The U.S. government desired to promote the superiority of its Indian policy by positioning its Indian populations furthest along the continuum. In order to accomplish this, the department separated its Indians from the primitive peoples of the world. Canadian Indians were positioned on this evolutionary continuum alongside indigenous peoples who were irreconcilably dissimilar to them.

In reality, the formulation and implementation of U.S. Indian policy, in the later years of the nineteenth century and the early years of the twentieth century, was, arguably, occurring alongside that of Canadian Indian policy. At this time, the Canadian government had also established a reservation system and residential schools. The civilizing effects of policy initiatives were supposedly readily seen among Canadian Indian populations. Although the showy attributes of the Kahnawá:ke Mohawks had served the emotional and cultural needs of Europeans, Americans, and Canadians for nearly a century, U.S. progressive and civilizing movements would eventually reject this showmanship and acculturation of Canadian Indian populations. The perceived primitive aspects of the Northwest Coast populations continued to both captivate American anthropological professionals and further support political doctrines of the U.S. government. According to the president of the LPE, the purpose of the ethnological exhibit and the Model Indian School was to prove that "the United States government [had] performed no worthier function than that of aiding [its] aboriginal landholders on their way toward citizenship."[58] There appeared no place for, or interest in, presenting Canada's civilized Indians alongside that of the civilized and Americanized Indians of the United States.

The nominal role Canadian Indians assumed within the Department of Anthropology's ethnological exhibit is directly related to their absence in the Anthropology Days athletic event of the 1904 St. Louis Olympic Games and Louisiana Purchase Exposition. While Canadian athletes were accordingly represented, due to geographical proximity, within the Olympic Games proper, Canadian Indians were noticeably underrepresented in the ethnological exhibits and conspicuously absent from the Anthropology Days athletic event. Throughout the LPE, the ethnological exhibit was consistently comprised of approximately 325 primitive peoples; only five of which were Canadian

Indians. This diminutive quantity of representatives directly contributed to the absence of Canadian Indians in this athletic event. Since the Anthropology Days were not an obligatory event, the primitive peoples of the fair participated freely. However, the majority of participants were enlisted from the ethnological exhibits of the Department of Anthropology. While McGee chose groups of primitive peoples to represent human varieties or subspecies and cultural types, Canadian Indians proved physically ordinary in relation to Americanized Indians, too controversial for the purposes of U.S. Indian policy endeavors, and undesirable to McGee and the Department of Anthropology. Consequently, the record books overzealously accredit the numerous achievements of Americanized Indians to North American Indians, thereby neglecting to address the absence of Canada's sizeable and adjacent Indian population in this "Olympic" event.

Epilogue

Since 1904, and the participation of the Mohawk team in the Olympic Games lacrosse event, many exceptional Native athletes have successfully represented Canada in official Olympic competition. Some of the more celebrated Aboriginal athletes in Canada include Tom Longboat, the Onondaga distance runner from the Six Nations of the Grand River, who competed in the 1908 London Games and has since been referred to as Canada's most legendary athlete of the twentieth century; Sharon and Shirley Firth, two Gwich'in Loucheaux-Métis from the Northwest Territories, who competed in an unprecedented four consecutive Winter Olympic Games between 1972 and 1984; Alwyn Morris, a Mohawk Indian from Kahnawá:ke, who received gold and bronze medals in kayaking at the 1984 Los Angeles Games; Steve Collins, the high-flying Ojibwa athlete from the Fort William Reserve, who competed in the 1988 Calgary Winter Games; Angela Chalmers, a member of the Birdtail Dakota Nation, who was a three-time Commonwealth champion and Olympic bronze medalist in the 3,000-meter track- and-field event at the 1992 Barcelona Olympic Games; and finally, Waneek Horn-Miller, another Mohawk athlete from the Kahnawá:ke community, who co-captained the Canadian women's water polo team at the 2000 Sydney Olympic Games. Unfortunately, the extraordinary accomplishments of these Native Canadian athletes have not been without incidents of racism and discrimination. Recent efforts in Canada have aimed to eliminate the negative experiences of Aboriginal peoples in sport in order to provide supportive and equitable opportunities for all indigenous athletes.

Shortly after the inauguration of the Canada Games in 1967, "the Fitness and Amateur Sport Directorate recognized that native people in northern Canada did not have an equal opportunity to compete in this event."[59] Consequently, Prime Minister Pierre Elliot Trudeau was on hand to open the first Arctic Winter Games in Yellowknife, Northwest Territories, in 1970. The Games have since been held every two years and have incorporated both Westernized sport and traditional games of northern indigenous populations, including the Dene Games. With the emergence of the North American Indigenous Games (NAIG) in 1990, Native peoples in both Canada and the United States have been afforded a prominent and popular sporting event, which is geographically and culturally inclusive for the First Nations of North America. From a Canadian perspective, the history of the NAI Games reveals a larger struggle for Aboriginal self-determination. In her comprehensive discussion, *From Assimilation to Self-Determination: The Emergence of J. Wilton Littlechild's NAI Games*, Janice Forsyth adamantly concludes: "Littlechild created the NAI Games because he realized that there were few opportunities for sport and recreation in Aboriginal communities; that the mainstream sport system discriminated against Aboriginal athletes; and that Aboriginal rights supported their rights to a distinct sport program that was separate from the mainstream sport system. . . . In this way, Littlechild created NAI Games to overcome the systematic discrimination Aboriginal athletes experienced within the mainstream sport system by expanding Aboriginal opportunities for sport within the all-Indian sport system."[60]

The historic participation of Canadian Indians in nineteenth- and twentieth-century sport was dependent on the greater political, social, and ideological needs of the nation-state. The emergence of Aboriginal athletic competitions, such as the Arctic Winter Games and the NAIG, has confirmed that the struggle for Aboriginal sport is deeply embedded in the politics of Canada's national consciousness. While sport was historically utilized as a tool of Indian assimilation, its function in contemporary Canada has radically altered. In recent years, indigenous populations have actively exploited sport as an apparatus for self-determination. As such, sport has served to dismantle historically appropriated understandings of "Indianness" and has further assisted in the construction of modern "Indian" identities based on resilient and proud tribal, national, and cultural distinctions.

Notes

1. Mallon, 1904 Olympic Games.
2. Louisiana Purchase Exposition Corporation (LPEC)—World's Fair Bulletin, "Of Surpassing Interest," 56.
3. Colin, "Wild Man and the Indian," 5–36.
4. Feest, Indians of Europe.
5. Feest, Indians of Europe, 609.
6. "The tribes today known as the Kwakawaka'waka have historically been referred to by non-Aboriginal people as the (Southern) Kwakiutl. Kwakiutl or Kwagiulth, in fact, more correctly refers to a confederacy of previously four, now three, Kwakwaka'wakw groups who moved to Fort Rupert at its founding, and to their dialect of the Kwak:wala language. Kwakwaka'wakw means roughly 'those who speak Kwak'wala.' It is the term First Nations people from Fort Rupert (Kwakiutl or Kwagiulth), Alert Bay ('Namgis), Cape Mudge (Lekwiltok), Knight Inlet (Mamalilikula), and surrounding areas prefer to use to describe themselves." Raibmon, Authentic Indians, 217. Concerning performances by the Kwakwaka'wakw at the 1893 Chicago World's Columbian Exposition, also see Raibmon, Authentic Indians.
7. Nelles, Art of Nation Building.
8. Radforth, "Performance, Politics, and Representation."
9. Blanchard, "Entertainment, Dance, and Northern Mohawk Showmanship."
10. Radforth, Royal Spectacle, 14.
11. Radforth, Royal Spectacle.
12. Radforth, Royal Spectacle, 206.
13. Radforth, Royal Spectacle.

14. Wamsley and Gillespie, "Prince of Wales Tour."

15. Radforth, "Performance, Politics, and Representation," 10.

16. Radforth, "Performance, Politics, and Representation," 10.

17. Radforth, "Performance, Politics, and Representation," 10.

18. "The Memorial of the Indians to the Queen," *Christian Guardian*, September 5, 1860.

19. Radforth, "Performance, Politics, and Representation."

20. Wamsley, "Nineteenth-Century Sport Tours."

21. Blanchard, "Entertainment, Dance, and Northern Mohawk Showmanship."

22. Wamsley, "Nineteenth-Century Sport Tours," 78.

23. Wamsley, "Nineteenth-Century Sport Tours," 84.

24. Morrow and Wamsley, *Sport in Canada*.

25. Raibmon, *Authentic Indians*, 35.

26. Trennert, "Selling Indian Education."

27. Trennert, "Selling Indian Education," 218.

28. Trennert, "Selling Indian Education," 204.

29. Prucha, *Documents*.

30. Raibmon, *Authentic Indians*.

31. Blanchard, "Entertainment, Dance, and Northern Mohawk Showmanship," 11.

32. Blanchard, "Entertainment, Dance, and Northern Mohawk Showmanship."

33. Trennert, "Selling Indian Education," 217.

34. See Barney, "A Myth Arrested," and "Born from Dilemma"; Barney and Barney, "Angst, Argument, and Antiquity"; Dyreson, "America's Athletic Missionaries," and "St. Louis, 1904"; and Mallon, 1904 *Olympic Games*.

35. Zweig, "Meet Me in St. Louis."

36. Mallon, 1904 *Olympic Games*, 167.

37. Mallon, 1904 *Olympic Games*, 165.

38. LPEC—World's Fair Bulletin, "Of Surpassing Interest," 56. Other articles from the *World's Fair Bulletin* that address the Anthropology Days and the Olympic Games events include: "Novel Athletic Contest"; "Olympic Games of the World's Fair"; and J. Sullivan, "Division of Exhibits: Physical Culture."

39. Lennartz et al., *Olympic Century*, 40.

40. Mallon, 1904 *Olympic Games*.

41. WJ McGee, "Report of the Department of Anthropology."

42. WJ McGee, "Report of the Department of Anthropology."

43. WJ McGee, "Report of the Department of Anthropology."

44. WJ McGee, "Report of the Department of Anthropology"; Francis, *Universal Exposition of 1904*, 527; Parezo, this volume.

45. LPEC, *Official Catalogues of Exhibitors, Universal Exposition*, 9.

46. WJ McGee, "Report of the Department of Anthropology."

47. WJ McGee, "Report of the Department of Anthropology."

48. WJ McGee quoted in LPEC—World's Fair Bulletin, "Of Surpassing Interest," 29.

49. Francis, *Universal Exposition*.

50. Francis, *Universal Exposition*.

51. Troutman and Parezo, "'Overlord of the Savage World'," 17–34, 20.

52. WJ McGee, cited in Parezo, this volume.

53. WJ McGee, "Report of the Department of Anthropology."

54. Francis, *Universal Exposition*, 529.

55. LPEC, *Official Catalogues of Exhibitors, Universal Exposition*, 9.

56. WJ McGee, "Report of the Department of Anthropology."

57. Brownell, "Summary of Discussion," 4. A first-person account of the Hamatsa joke was written by one of the participants, Charley Nowell. See Ford, *Smoke from Their Fires*, 186–90.

58. Francis, *Universal Exposition*, 529.

59. Macintosh, Bedecki, and Franks, *Sport in Canada*, 100.

60. Forsyth, "From Assimilation to Self-Determination," 139.

Chapter 6. "Leav[ing] the White[s] . . . Far Behind Them"

The Girls from Fort Shaw (Montana) Indian School,
Basketball Champions of the 1904 World's Fair

LINDA PEAVY AND URSULA SMITH

On a chilly October afternoon, a steady stream of people made their way across the fairgrounds toward the basketball court marked off on the plaza in front of the Model Indian School. A full hour before tip-off, the human rainbow curving around the sides of the court stretched all the way back to the Navajo, Arapaho, Cheyenne, and Pawnee encampments along the perimeter of "Indian Hill." From the portico at the top of the school's broad steps, referees and school officials assessed the situation, conceded the impossibility of keeping the growing mass of spectators from inching onto the playing field, and called in the Jefferson Guard, the world's fair security corps. Within minutes a contingent of soldiers, unarmed except for the ceremonial swords at their sides, marched onto the plaza, formed a protective cordon around the court, and managed to push the crowd far enough back for play to begin.[1]

The game that had enticed so many fairgoers away from the myriad attractions that vied for their attention was the second in a three-game series between the Missouri All-Stars, alumnae of Central High in St. Louis, perennial state champions, and five teenaged girls from an off-reservation boarding school in Montana who had spent the summer playing exhibition games at the Model Indian School. Stakes were high, for the Indians had soundly defeated the All-Stars in their first meeting a month earlier. Colorful

17. Fort Shaw team in front of the Anthropology Division's Model Indian School at the 1904 St. Louis World's Fair. Standing (*from left*): Rose LaRose, Flora Lucero, Katie Snell, Minnie Burton, Genevieve Healy, Sarah Mitchell. Seated (*from left*): Emma Sansaver, Genie Butch, Belle Johnson, Nettie Wirth. Photo by Jessie Tarbox Beals. From the Missouri Historical Society, St. Louis, World's Fair Presentation Album II, plate 801.

newspaper accounts of that rough-and-tumble contest had helped generate the curiosity and enthusiasm that had drawn hundreds of men, women, and children to Indian Hill for the long-awaited rematch.[2]

At last the referee's whistle signaled the start of what one reporter described as "the most exciting game ever played in Missouri." Exciting, but one-sided, for in forty minutes of play the All-Stars scored but one goal from the field. Lightning speed, dazzling plays, and impeccable teamwork carried the day, and when the final whistle blew, the score stood 17 to 6. The girls from Fort Shaw Indian School in Montana were the "basket ball" champions of the 1904 St. Louis World's Fair.[3]

Who were these young women and how did they come to be at the 1904 St. Louis World's Fair? These five girls so renowned for their teamwork and unselfish play came from four different tribes, some of which had a lengthy history of animosity toward one another. Captain and right guard Belle Johnson was a Piegan from the Blackfeet Reservation. Left guard Genie Butch was an Assiniboine from Fort Peck Reservation, as was the team's center, Nettie Wirth. At forward were Emma Rose Sansaver, Chippewa-Cree and one of Montana's landless Indians, and Minne Burton, a Shoshone from Idaho's Lemhi Reservation.[4]

The team's rise to basketball glory began at an Indian boarding school established in 1892 on the grounds of an abandoned military post in Montana's Sun River Valley. Modeled after Carlisle in Pennsylvania and Haskell in Kansas, Fort Shaw School drew its students from tribes across Montana and from Idaho and Wyoming as well. In keeping with prevailing federal policies, the school's mission was to strip its students of the ways of their people and teach them English, academic subjects, and vocational skills that would enable them to make their way in the "white world."[5]

The members of the Fort Shaw girls' basketball squad—the five who played in the world's fair championship game and the five reserves who accompanied them to St. Louis—were not only superior athletes, they were also well-rounded students who had proved themselves in classroom and workroom and were skilled performers in music, dance, and rhetoric. They were, in sum, model "products" of the government's Indian education system. And as such, they had been brought to St. Louis that summer of 1904, along with 140 other equally outstanding students, to demonstrate to the world the extent to which the prevailing federal policy of acculturation and assimilation through education was meeting its goal of "civilizing" Indian youth.[6]

The Model Indian School was the centerpiece of the Indian exhibit at the Louisiana Purchase Exposition. Its superintendent, Samuel McCowan, head of Chilocco Indian School in Oklahoma, had been appointed by the Office of Indian Affairs (OIA) to work alongside WJ McGee, chief of the fair's Anthropology Department. Their charge was to "demonstrate the progress of races and tribes" while avoiding "all objectionable features of wild west shows."[7] The OIA's edict dovetailed nicely with McCowan's own vision for the proposed exhibit.

Located on the western edge of the fairgrounds, the Indian exhibit abutted the Anthropology Department's other major display, the Philippine Reservation. Assigned a thirty-acre site that was "prominent, semi-exclusive, and a half mile from the Midway," Superintendent McCowan plotted a semicircle of encampments that would house various Native peoples from western North America.[8] At the height of the fair, some two hundred individuals representing fourteen western tribes had constructed and were living in their traditional tipis, hogans, earth lodges, bark huts, and longhouses. Sharing Indian Hill with the indigenous peoples of North America were WJ McGee's imported "exotics"—"Giant Patagonians" from Argentina, "Hairy Ainu" from Japan, and Pygmies from the Congo.[9]

Set against and rising above that panorama was the Model Indian School, an impressive, two-story, "classic revival-style" structure. The front entrance, porch, and balcony overlooked a broad plaza and parade grounds. Massive double doors led into a lobby flanked by two long wings and opening into a sizeable auditorium that accommodated conferences and concerts and served as a chapel on Sundays. Running the length of each wing was a wide hallway that separated a row of booths on one side from a row of open classrooms and workrooms on the other. In these booths, Indians from the surrounding encampments plied their "primitive" crafts—shaping pottery; weaving baskets and rugs; creating drums, flutes, and other musical instruments; and fashioning tools and weapons of stone, flint, and wood—while on the other side of the hallway, students demonstrated their "modern" academic and vocational skills. It was a dramatic display, one intended to leave the public with a lasting impression of the contrast between the old ways of life and the new.[10]

The students representing the "new" were among the 150 boys and girls McCowan had chosen from Indian boarding schools across the West, primarily from those within the Louisiana Purchase Territory. Representing forty tribes and ranging in age from kindergartners through teenagers, these well-prepared and "most deserving" youngsters had been selected for their academic and vocational accomplishments and for their athletic, musical, and literary talents and achievements.[11]

The boys from Chilocco formed the core of the Model Indian School's famed forty-piece band. Young men from Chilocco also ran the print shop that produced a daily paper, the *Indian School Journal*. One group of Chilocco girls formed the seventh-grade "literary" class held each weekday morning; a second demonstrated modern techniques for handling kitchen and laundry work. Boys from Haskell's blacksmithing shop displayed their horseshoes and hammers, and Haskell girls demonstrated the domestic arts of sewing, tailoring, and millinery. Boys from Genoa demonstrated harness making. From the Sacaton Indian School in Phoenix came a dozen little Pima children, ages five and six, to form the kindergarten class.[12]

And from Fort Shaw Indian School in Montana came ten young women who contributed to the literary and musical entertainments held each afternoon in the school chapel, joined their new classmates in club swinging and other gymnastics exercises, and, on two afternoons a week on the parade grounds in front of the school building, engaged in hard-fought intrasquad matches that demonstrated the game of basketball.[13]

That game had come a long way in the dozen years since its invention by James Naismith, an instructor at the National YMCA Training School in Springfield, Massachusetts. Though originally intended as an indoor sport to keep the young men at the YMCA occupied and physically fit during the long, cold Massachusetts winters, the game was soon being played across the country, by women and girls as well as men and boys. The game's popularity among females was understandable, since it was one of the few active sports deemed acceptable for "the fairer sex" at a time when conventional wisdom held that "strenuous activity" was harmful to female health.[14]

Well aware of Victorian sensibilities and fearful that the sport might be banned altogether, Senda Berenson, a physical education teacher at Smith

College, quickly devised a set of "girls' rules" that would allow young women to play basketball in a safer, more decorous manner. The court would be divided into zones. There would be six players on a team—two guards, two centers, and two forwards—and the players could not step outside their respective "zones." By slowing down the game and banning many of the rougher and most exciting aspects of play, these so-called girls' rules so drastically altered the dynamics of the sport that most high school and college women's teams—especially those west of the Mississippi—continued to play by "boys' rules," that is, full-court action, five players to a side.[15]

It was "boys' rules" by which the girls at the Indian School in Montana's Sun River Valley were introduced to the sport. And they were introduced to it within six years of the game's invention, for the first documented game of basketball at Fort Shaw took place at year-end exercises in June of 1897.[16] The sport was likely brought to Fort Shaw by Josephine Langley, a Piegan from Montana's Blackfeet Reservation, who had spent a year at Carlisle Indian School in Pennsylvania before returning to Fort Shaw as assistant matron. Having seen—and played—the game at Carlisle, Josie saw its advantages for the physical culture program at Fort Shaw.[17] She had an ideal facility for the game, for the old military dance hall was of sufficient length—at 125 feet—to allow for indoor play, and its hard-packed dirt floor was ideal for bouncing a ball.[18]

Josephine Langley not only had an ideal space in which to play basketball. She also had an eager group of participants, for almost universally in Indian cultures, unlike in the white world, there was a long history of female participation in sports. Games played by girls—lacrosse, shinny, and double ball—like those played by boys, had been central to the spiritual as well as the sporting life of Indian communities. And girls and women had played their games with as much intensity as men and boys.[19] Now these girls from Fort Shaw, most of whom had grown up hearing of their grandmothers' feats on the field of play, seized upon this new game as an outlet for their energies and their skills. After a semester of drills and scrimmages, Josie Langley was ready to put her team on display.[20]

Though that game at the closing exercises in 1897 was only an exhibition of the new sport, over the next few years, Josie put together two strong scrimmage teams. Acting as player-coach, this enthusiastic young woman kindled the basketball flame in the hearts of many girls at Fort Shaw, several of whom would be among the ten players who spent the summer of 1904 at the Model Indian School in St. Louis.

While the presence of basketball on the campus of Fort Shaw Government Indian Boarding School can be attributed to the efforts of Josephine Langley, the prominence the sport achieved at the school was due to the efforts and influence of Superintendent F. C. Campbell, who assumed his post in 1898. A tireless promoter of the work of the Indian School Service, Campbell was pleased to find that the school's musical and literary entertainments had already begun to impress audiences in several of Montana's major cities. While such events went a long way toward demonstrating the progress being made at Fort Shaw, there was a missing component to this outreach program.[21]

Campbell had been a star catcher during his undergraduate days at the University of Kansas, and he knew from experience the self-esteem participation in sports could impart to young athletes. He was also well aware of the public relations benefits that attached to a strong sports program. Though Fort Shaw School had fielded track and baseball teams, those teams had seldom played beyond campus. Their visibility could be raised, and there was the potential for the development of a football team. And a basketball program.[22]

There was clearly enough talent on the two scrimmage teams Josie Langley had developed over the past few years to create a basketball squad that should be able to hold its own against most of the schools in the state. By fall of 1902, Campbell was ready to put his team to the test, having worked hard to schedule games with the major towns and cities in the western half of the state. He had also convinced the city of Great Falls to provide a home court for his girls, since the dirt-floored gymnasium at Fort Shaw was hardly an adequate place for hosting visiting teams. The Fort Shaw team traveled the twenty-five miles between the school campus and Luther Hall in Great Falls by open, horse-drawn wagon and rail. Rain, snow, sleet, and even a few blizzards never kept them from a scheduled game. Nor did the weather deter the equally intrepid sixteen-piece band, which entertained before and after the games.[23]

Four of the five girls who comprised the team during the school's first year of interscholastic play were still first-stringers on the team that was named champion of the world's fair a year later. Nettie Wirth, by no means the tallest girl on the team, played center, having earned that position by virtue of her prodigious leaping ability. That vertical leap served the team well at a time when a jump ball at center court followed every score. At guard were Josie Langley, described by one reporter as "the heaviest girl on the team," and steady, stalwart Belle Johnson. At right forward was four-foot eleven-inch Emma Rose Sansaver. Known as "the little one," Emma's speed and agility more than made up for her short stature. The tallest girl on the squad, left forward Minnie Burton, was also the team's most prolific scorer and the object of the rallying cry, "Shoot, Minnie, shoot," that rang down from the stands every time the ball came into her hands.[24]

Fort Shaw's starting five chalked up some impressive victories over high schools and colleges within Montana's loosely cobbled girls' basketball league. They defeated the women from the state university in Missoula by a score of 13 to 9 in January 2003, and later that spring they twice trounced the Farmerettes from the state agricultural college in Bozeman, first by a score of 36 to 9 and then by a score of 20 to 0 in a rematch played before a crowd of eight hundred, which, according to a contemporary reporter, was "probably the largest crowd that ever attended a college game." Credited with having "had much to do with making the game so popular," the girls from Fort Shaw Indian School had helped transform girls' basketball from a game for physical culture classes to the most exciting spectator sport in Montana.[25] These ambassadors for women's team sports not only went on to win the unofficial 1902–3 state championship in their first season of competitive play but so endeared themselves to fans that they had, in essence, become "Montana's team."[26]

Racist terms still appeared in headlines as reporters for local newspapers wrote of the "dusky maidens" as invincible and of the "massacres" suffered by their opponents. But, by and large, these young women were shown a deference not extended to any other Montanans of their race. They were entertained at banquets and receptions hosted by community leaders when they came to town to play a game, and they were popular dancing partners of white students at postgame parties.[27]

Never one to miss an opportunity to show how his students were defying stereotypes and breaking down barriers, Fred Campbell, superintendent and coach, made sure his remarks to sports fans gathered in small- town and city auditoriums and halls across Montana emphasized that the outstanding play and exemplary social skills of his girls' basketball team were indicative of the many ways in which students at Fort Shaw Government Indian Boarding School were being prepared to take their place in the white world.[28]

By late spring of 1903, reports of the girls' accomplishments on the court and off had spread far beyond Montana's borders. Realizing at once that this group of young women would be a valuable addition to the student body he was assembling for his Model Indian School, Samuel McCowan invited Montana's champions to spend the summer of 1904 at the world's fair in St. Louis, playing exhibition games before an international audience. Superintendent F. C. Campbell immediately informed his team of the invitation and promised that if they continued to do well in classroom and workroom, and continued to improve their play as they pursued a second state championship, then he would accept the invitation on their behalf and do all within his power to see that they were well prepared for their residency at the Model Indian School.[29]

Though the girls began the fall semester of 1903 with every intention of winning yet another championship, it was not to be. When an official high school league was formed, the Indian School was not among those included in the organization. Racism, which had never been a problem before, does not seem to have played a role in Fort Shaw's failure to make the list. The official reason given for the slight was the school's lack of high school accreditation, though the inclusion of the agricultural college at Bozeman and the university at Missoula calls that excuse into question. The most likely explanation for this unexpected turn of events was voiced by a reporter from the *Anaconda Standard* who said the girls had been "compelled to quit playing [other teams because] . . . no other team in the state could play good enough to make it interesting."[30]

Stung by the rebuff but determined to keep his girls—and his school—in the public eye, Fred Campbell decided to expand the team to ten members so they could continue to tour the state, playing exhibition games and staying sharp for the challenges that awaited them in St. Louis. His first task was to choose a replacement for long-time player Josephine Langley, who had withdrawn from active play because of her age and her approaching marriage. Genie Butch, who had served as the team's substitute during their 1902–3 championship season, was moved to first team as guard.[31]

That task settled, Campbell picked the five girls who would join the starters in playing exhibition games around the state that year, choosing from among the girls who had shown the most promise in scrimmaging against the champions: There were two sixteen-year-olds, Katie Snell, Assiniboine from the Fort Peck Reservation, and Rose LaRose, Shoshone-Bannock from the Fort Hall Reservation in Idaho; two fifteen-year-olds, Genevieve Healy, Gros Ventre from the Fort Belknap Reservation, and Flora Lucero, Chippewa-Cree; and the youngster of the group, fourteen-year-old Sarah Mitchell, an Assiniboine from Fort Peck Reservation.[32]

Through the fall and spring of 1903–4, the ten girls barnstormed the state, staging basketball exhibitions and giving "literary" and musical programs in front of crowds of eight hundred and more who filled auditoriums and gyms in such towns as Great Falls, Butte, Bozeman, Missoula, Helena, Havre, and

Choteau. This colorful display of the success of the government's efforts to "civilize" the Indian also provided many residents with their first glimpse of the game of basketball.[33]

Superintendent Campbell charged fifty cents admission to see his talented students, and the public readily paid for such fine entertainment. The team often traveled with a supporting cast—the sixteen-piece Fort Shaw band, three solo instrumentalists, and two youngsters who gave recitations in the comic and tragic traditions. In addition to providing excitement on the court, the ten basketball players were an integral part of the pregame "entertainments." They generally opened the program with a mandolin selection, followed by a demonstration of barbell drills and club swinging. Then, while their classmates carried on the show, the girls changed into ceremonial buckskin dresses and beaded breastplates for a choral recitation of the famine scene from Longfellow's *Hiawatha*. Again, the other Fort Shaw performers took the stage while the girls traded their buckskins for diaphanous Grecian gowns and returned for a Delsartian interpretation of "Song of the Mystic."[34]

The evening ended with the exhibition game that had drawn the spectators. The girls returned to the court in their basketball uniforms—navy worsted woolen bloomers and middies, striped dickies at the neck, dark cotton stockings, and rubber-soled shoes. The color of the stripes on their dickies and the color of the "F" and "S" embroidered on the collars of the middies enabled the girls—and the fans—to distinguish between the two teams. Always eager to take the court, the "Reds" and the "Blues" never failed to give their audiences more than their money's worth in terms of the razzle-dazzle play, lightning-quick moves, daring "field throws," and smooth teamwork that had come to be associated with their brand of basketball.[35]

And if, during the showcase season of 1903–4, Montana's former state champions missed the intensity of interscholastic competition, there was nothing in their action on the court to indicate that fact. Their sights remained set on the stage that awaited them in St. Louis.

The Louisiana Purchase Exposition officially opened on April 30, 1904, when

President Theodore Roosevelt touched a golden telegraph key in Washington DC, signaling the start of festivities out in St. Louis, but the Model Indian School did not open until June 1.[36] And it opened without the delegation from Fort Shaw, since a series of whistle-stop, fund-raising games along their rail route to St. Louis kept the girls from arriving at the fair until mid-June. Their arrival on Tuesday, June 14, had apparently been anticipated by the press as well as by Superintendent McCowan and his staff at the Model Indian School. According to a reporter from the St. Louis Republic, the arrival of the girls from Montana "attracted more attention than any contingent that has yet arrived at the Indian Building."[37]

Perhaps that reporter was taken by the girls' obvious excitement and enthusiasm—and by their eagerness to stretch their legs and take in the sights. Their first request was to be taken to the fabled Pike, a mile-long stretch of amusements on the northern boundary of the fairgrounds. With Superintendent McCowan as their guide, they wandered up and down the midway—Jim Key, the educated horse; Hagenbeck's Zoological Paradise and Animal Circus; the Temple of Mirth, the Baby Incubators. There was no time to even begin to take it all in. Exhausted from their long rail journey and their abbreviated tour of The Pike, the girls were more than ready for a good night's sleep in the girls' dormitory on the second floor of the school.[38]

The very next afternoon, the group of young women the Indian School Journal described as "the most enthusiastic visitors the Fair has [ever] had" appeared in the first of their scheduled afternoon entertainments at the Model Indian School. The program was similar to the many they had given across Montana, with the Mandolin Club, under the direction of "Miss Nettie Wirth," opening the presentation, followed by a recitation of Longfellow's "The Famine" and the pantomime performance of "Song of the Mystic." The audience received the concert enthusiastically, and the St. Louis Globe-Democrat reported that the "accomplished musicians" and performers "lend picturesquesness to their appearance by wearing the native dress of buckskin adorned with elaborate decorations of beads, elks' teeth, and bone."[39]

Fort Shaw's first exhibition game, played on the plaza in front of the Indian School, took place that same afternoon, immediately after the program in the chapel. The game drew even fuller coverage from the *Globe-Democrat* than had the "literary and musical" program. A team photo appeared with a headline announcing, "Champion Basket Ball Team . . . at World's Fair." The accompanying article identified each of the girls by name and by tribe, though some names were misspelled and some tribes misattributed. Those errors aside, the young women from Fort Shaw were being featured in the press of one of the country's largest cities.[40]

A reporter from the *St. Louis Republic* described their exhibition game as "the fastest thing of the sort ever seen in this city." The girls from Montana were veritable "streaks of lightning," and the excellence of their play that afternoon had more than "justified their title of basket ball champions of the northwest." In his studied opinion, "The natural agility of the Indian maiden has been developed by the training of the Fort Shaw team to surpassing excellence, and . . . plays an important part in the success of the team."[41]

The young women who drew such attention were, indeed, endowed with a "natural agility." But it would take a little more exposure to their play for reporters and observers alike in St. Louis to recognize what Montanans acclaimed as the true hallmark of the team—their flawless teamwork. That teamwork, that almost intuitive interplay with one another, was also evident in their musical and literary performances. The perfect synchronization of movements in their choreographed recitation of the scene from *Hiawatha* and in their "pantomime performance" of "Song of the Mystic" attested to the unity of spirit that characterized their play on the court.

The girls gave a variation on that first performance in the chapel the very next day. And the next. Though they were originally scheduled to perform in literary and musical programs only on Wednesday and Friday afternoons, the popularity of the Fort Shaw group grew so quickly they were soon performing three or four afternoons each week. Their concerts and entertainments helped draw "increasing crowds each afternoon," according to the *Indian*

School Journal. And with the chapel no longer able to accommodate the number of visitors who gathered for the afternoon programs, Superintendent Mc-Cowan announced that hereafter all entertainments would take place on the east porch of the Indian School building, weather permitting.[42]

In very little time, the Fort Shaw contingent was well integrated into life at the Model Indian School. Much of the time not given to practicing their music, recitations, and basketball was given to answering requests for interviews from newspaper reporters. They were also frequently stopped by visitors to the school and asked to pose for photographs, especially when they were wearing their handsome buckskins. In their free time they wandered the school's main hallway, comparing what they observed in the classes and workrooms with their own training back at Fort Shaw, and learning about the crafts of the "traditional" Indians who worked in the booths across the hall.[43]

Busy as they were, the girls had the opportunity to experience life beyond the fairgrounds. Before Superintendent Campbell, who had escorted the team to the fair, returned to Montana in late June, he took the entire Fort Shaw contingent on a riverboat excursion down the Mississippi. That same night they were treated to a performance of *Louisiana*, a musical that all of St. Louis was talking about. The girls were enchanted with the play and with the elegance of the newly opened Odeon Theatre on Grand Boulevard.[44]

Such day-long excursions were the exception, however. For the most part, the girls stayed close to the school. Even so, their fame spread beyond the fairgrounds. Before the month of June was out, they had received challenges from two of the best girls' basketball teams in the area—O'Fallon High School, across the state line in Illinois, and the Missouri state champions from St. Louis's Central High. This was exactly what the girls had hoped for—a chance to play against some of the best of the teams in the Midwest. And though the proposed games were some weeks away, their scrimmages took on new energy as they prepared themselves for the challenges ahead.[45]

The Fourth of July was marked with festive celebrations across the fairgrounds. On Indian Hill the special event was an afternoon game of basketball between the Fort Shaw girls and the girls from Chilocco, their dormmates at the Model Indian School. It was the first match game for Fort Shaw since their arrival in St. Louis, but it was hardly a match in any other sense of that word. Though the Chilocco girls had been watching their opponents play a number of exhibition games, they themselves had never played as a team before. As reflected by the final score: 36 to 0.[46]

While the girls from Fort Shaw were playing exhibition games twice a week on the plaza in front of the Model Indian School, an array of men's and boys' athletic competitions were taking place in the newly erected stadium virtually across the street from the school. Built for the Third Olympiad scheduled for late August and early September, Francis Field was the scene of many AAU, YMCA, college, and scholastic contests throughout early summer. Teams from across the country competed for trophies in such sports as football, basketball, gymnastics, and croquet.[47] And though women in bustled skirts and mutton-sleeved blouses looked on with interest, there was not a single woman on the field of play.

And this despite the seeming openness of the fair's director of Physical Culture, James E. Sullivan, to the idea of adding team sports for women to the competitions in St. Louis that summer. "It would be a great thing for girls' sport," Sullivan had said, "[something] I believe would prove a drawing card at the Fair." *Provided*, of course, that the schools and organizations sponsoring girls' and women's teams were prepared to violate long-standing gender taboos by allowing their players to compete in a public arena before mixed crowds—a requirement for all athletic contests held in conjunction with either the fair or the 1904 Olympics to be staged in conjunction with the fair. Predictably, deep-seated prejudice prevailed, saving Sullivan the need to make good on his offer to open competition to women.[48] And so it was that at the World's Fair of 1904 team sports for "the fairer sex" were exemplified only by the hard-driving intrasquad games played twice a week by the young women from Fort Shaw. And these games, contested in a very public arena on the plaza in front of the Model Indian School, did indeed prove to be "a drawing card."

Back home at Fort Shaw, Fred Campbell received regular reports from Superintendent McCowan regarding the Fort Shaw students, reports he turned into press releases or shared in interviews with reporters around the state. He expressed his pleasure "with the reception accorded the basketball girls at the big fair." The team was "making a great hit . . . and having a fine time," he told the *Great Falls Daily Leader*. The girls were making the most of this educational opportunity by "properly study[ing] the many wonderful and interesting exhibits in the buildings and foreign pavilions on the grounds."[49]

They were also continuing to explore the attractions on The Pike, often after dinner when the temperatures had dropped and the midway was less crowded. With the other residents of the Indian School, they were guests of the management at the various attractions. None drew their interest so much as Cummins' Wild West Indian Congress, a spectacle replete with the stereotypical depictions of Native Americans that Superintendent McCowan had worked so hard to avoid. Within a huge arena, some eight hundred actors played "cowboys and Indians." Chief Joseph, Chief Red Cloud, and Chief American Horse made special appearances. And the Custer massacre was re-enacted daily, with Frederick Cummins himself playing Custer.[50]

The residents of the Model Indian School were well aware that, like the participants in Cummins' Wild West Show—indeed like the "traditional" Indians with whom they shared Indian Hill—they were regarded by the majority of fairgoers as a curiosity. They were frequently exposed to the ignorance and rudeness of people touring the school. Absurd questions were asked of students and adult Indians alike. And even when they weren't the targets themselves, the girls from Fort Shaw felt the embarrassment.[51]

However enlightened or unenlightened visitors to the Model Indian School may have been, they continued to increase in number as the days moved on. "When I leave the hotel in the morning," one fairgoer told Superintendent McCowan, "I am just naturally drawn in this direction. When I go home, people will ask me what I have seen and I will have to say, 'Well, I saw the

Indian School; then I went to the Philippines [Reservation]; then I went back to the Indian School.'"[52]

The Fort Shaw girls were a major reason for the growing popularity of the school. "Those girls in the pantomime are champion basket ball players and have a fine mandolin club," a concertgoer was heard to say one afternoon. "They surely are versatile." A teacher from Boston left her remarks in a visitors' book: "The exercises in the Indian School chapel Saturday afternoon were the finest of the kind I have ever heard." And from another, "I have been on the grounds a week, and that scarf drill is the prettiest thing I've seen."[53]

Not every day was given to performance, nor every evening to entertainment. In late July the girls stepped up the intensity of their scrimmages as the time drew near to meet the challenge offered earlier that summer by the O'Fallon High School girls' basketball team. Publicity surrounding the game promised that the O'Fallon team would "give the Indian girls a taste of the quality of the Illinois girl."[54]

The game was to be played in Belleville, some twenty miles southeast of St. Louis, as a feature of that city's annual YMCA midsummer festival. Accordingly, on Thursday morning, July 28, the Fort Shaw girls departed the fairgrounds in the company of the Indian School band, a coterie of fellow students, and a significant number of other world's fair representatives—including "a group of savage Head Hunters from the Philippines," Bedouins from The Pike's re-creation of the ancient city of Jerusalem, and elephants from Hagenbeck's Zoological Paradise and Animal Circus. The band, "head hunters," Bedouins, and elephants led the parade that opened the festivities at two o'clock that afternoon.[55]

By four o'clock the crowd that had assembled for the game was so great that ropes had to be used to keep the field of play clear. The "court" was laid out on uneven ground in an open field. The goals at either end lacked backboards. But those inconveniences afforded no advantage to either side. The starting lineup for Fort Shaw was the lineup that had carried the team to prominence back in Montana: Minnie Burton, Emma Sansaver, and Nettie

Wirth in the front court; Belle Johnson and Genie Butch in the backcourt. By halftime there was little doubt of the outcome. The fast pace of the game, the agility and teamwork of the Indian girls, their feinting and dodging were too much for the O'Fallon team. Even when Emma turned her ankle at the beginning of the second half and had to leave the game, the girls never lost a beat. With Katie Snell taking Emma's place at forward, the score continued to mount. When the timekeeper signaled the end of the game, the Indians had put up 14 points, the O'Fallon girls 3.[56]

The Illinois state champions accepted their defeat gracefully; the Indian band escorted both teams from the field, and everyone enjoyed the evening concert before the Model Indian School students and the rest of the colorful entourage had to board the train for home.[57] Excited by their convincing win over a highly regarded opponent, the Fort Shaw girls were glad to hear that Superintendent McCowan had wired a report of the game to Superintendent Campbell back in Montana. And the news buzzing around the Model Indian School the following day even reached the ears of the president's three sons—Theo Roosevelt and his younger brothers Kermit and Archie—who were visiting as special guests of McCowan.[58]

McCowan kept his students informed of the public's reaction to the school. On the first Friday of August, he circulated a letter to the editor clipped from the *New York Tribune*. The letter writer, who had recently visited the fair, praised the performance of "the dozen [sic] Indian girls who in long white robes, with flowing sleeves and arms uplifted, gazed heavenward, [miming] "Nearer, My God, to Thee." He wrote of having also taken in an exhibition basketball game and the late-afternoon dress parade on the Indian School plaza. Nothing impressed him so much, he said, as the skills and the discipline demonstrated in those exercises.[59]

The dress parade, held every afternoon at 5:30 in front of the school, was indeed an impressive sight, "a picture for an artist" in the words of one observer. "Imagine," he wrote, describing the scene in some detail, "a vast gathering of people from every clime crowding the school porch and stretching across the grounds . . . and out in the center of the plaza . . . the pupils of the Indian School in military formation." The band and the boys' company are "clad in neat grey uniforms, the girls in blue skirts and white [blouses]." At the sound of the bugle, the band bursts into "a stirring march . . . the two companies pass[ing] to the right in front and back of the band and return[ing] to their places." The spectators marvel "at the grace and ease with which [the marchers] make the turns, at their erect military bearing, at the manly air of the boys, and the modest, yet self-possessed demeanor of the girls, at the sweetness of the music." As the last strains of that music die, the crowd, "no longer able to restrain its feelings," bursts into applause.[60]

Dress parades, basketball exhibitions, afternoon mandolin concerts and literary recitations, and glimpses of visiting dignitaries continued to fill the days of the girls from Fort Shaw Indian School. There were extravaganzas too. One warm evening in early August, they enjoyed an immense fireworks display staged in Francis Field across the street from the school. The girls had not yet learned that just a few days hence they themselves would be center stage in that impressive stadium — as an addendum to the "Anthropology Days Athletic Meet."[61]

The brainchild of WJ McGee, head of the fair's Anthropology Department, and James Sullivan, head of Physical Culture, the meet provided an opportunity to test the purported "natural athletic ability" of "natives from the four quarters of the globe" by pitting these "savages" against each other in such track- and-field events as the 100-yard dash, the 120-yard hurdles, the 440, the mile, the shot put, javelin, and broad jump. Other events on the schedule were intended to test the Natives at "their own games": throwing stones for accuracy, tree climbing, tugs-of-war, and mud fights.[62]

Hence, on Thursday and Friday, August 11 and 12, with virtually no training and little understanding of what they were supposed to accomplish, the men encamped on Indian Hill — Sioux, Cocopas, Cheyennes, Pawnees, Maricopas, Patagonians, Pygmies, and Ainus, along with Filipinos from the neighboring Philippines Reservation and "Kaffirs" from the Boer camp on

The Pike—participated in a two-day track-and-field meet, the "Aboriginal Games."[63] Though described years later as "the low point of the entire summer," the Anthropology Days games were hailed at the time by WJ McGee as having demonstrated "what anthropologists have long known, that the white man leads the races of the world, both physically and mentally" and that Native Americans, winners of the vast majority of the events, more closely modeled the white man's achievements than did any other "aboriginal."[64]

In contrast stands the scathing denouncement of Pierre de Coubertin, founder of the modern Olympics, who called the Anthropology Days games "an outrageous charade" that would "lose its appeal when black men, red men, and yellow men learn to run, jump, and throw and leave the white man far behind them." Egalitarian as he was in matters of race, Coubertin was no champion of women's rights, describing women's participation in sports as "monstrous" and calling for such participation to be "absolutely prohibited." Since he was conspicuously absent from the St. Louis Olympics, there is no way to know whether Coubertin's sexist views might have been altered had he seen the Fort Shaw team in action, living proof that "red men"—or in this case, "red women"—had already learned "to run, jump, and throw" sufficiently well to leave the "white[s] far behind."[65]

The young women who were already fulfilling Coubertin's prediction—and had only a few weeks earlier defeated the white basketball champions of the State of Illinois—were a last-minute addition to the Anthropology Days meet, providing the closing event on Thursday afternoon. Dividing themselves into two teams as equally matched as possible, the girls from Fort Shaw showed the large crowd drawn to these "Special Olympics" how intensely women—Native American women—could engage in sport. The game was hard fought. And close, with the lead changing hands a number of times. In the end the "Reds" overcame the disadvantage of having only two of the first-string players on their team and nudged out the "Blues" by a score of 14 to 12.[66]

A week and a half after that exhibition game, the girls were presented with a handsome silver trophy in an awards ceremony held at the Model Indian School. The gold-lined, mahogany-based loving cup bore the inscription

World's Fair

St. Louis, 1904

BASKET BALL

WON BY

FORT SHAW TEAM

Considering the fact that the other winners in the Anthropology Days games were given small monetary prizes immediately after their events, whereas the girls received their trophy in a special ceremony, the award came to be seen as an indication of the overall excellence of the team's basketball exhibitions at the world's fair.[67] The silver loving cup was put on display in the lobby of the school, there to be admired by the visitors to Indian Hill, who were now numbering more than fifty thousand a day.[68]

As August drew to a close, the girls returned to serious preparation for the one major challenge that remained: the series of three games against the Missouri All-Stars, the series that would ultimately determine the basketball champions of the world's fair. Philip Stremmel, a well-known basketball authority in the area, had put together a team from the best of the recent graduates of St. Louis's Central High. It was time to see how well the best team in the Midwest compared with the best in the West.[69]

Fort Shaw's lopsided victory over the O'Fallon five in July had bolstered the girls' confidence, but they had no way of knowing how they would measure up against the Missouri champions. With the long-awaited series due to begin the first weekend in September, they stepped up their practices. "The girls played basket ball last evening," the Indian School Journal reported on Tuesday, August 23. The exhibition had attracted "a large gathering of spectators. If the Blues enter [the championship series] with as great a determination as they evinced last evening, their opponents will surely meet their Waterloo, although our girls are badly handicapped by [Emma Sansaver's] sprained ankle."[70]

Even as they prized their precious silver trophy and looked forward to their series against the Missouri champions, the girls from Fort Shaw were aware that the "real" Olympic Games were underway in the stadium where they had so recently played. The Third Olympiad of modern times, the first on American soil, opened in St. Louis on Monday, August 29. It was, in truth, an American Olympics. Of the 687 athletes who competed in such standard Olympic events as running, jumping, weight lifting, vaulting, wrestling, swimming, fencing, rowing, boxing, and gymnastics, more than 500 came from the United States. American athletes won every one of the track- and-field events, save the Canadian victory in the 56-pound shot put and the British victory in the decathlon.[71]

On Saturday, September 3 — coincidentally, the last day of the Olympic Games — the Fort Shaw team met the Missouri All-Stars, at Kulage Park in the northeastern sector of the city. The girls playing for St. Louis were protecting an unblemished record that stretched back to their school days at Central High, and over the course of the summer they had given hours to practice under the watchful eye of Coach Phil Stremmel. Stremmel had scouted several of the Fort Shaw exhibition games on the fairgrounds and had taken his girls to Belleville in late July to see the game against O'Fallon High School. Though the St. Louis girls were awed by the level of play they saw in the Indians' defeat of a very good O'Fallon team, Stremmel had used the intervening weeks to bring his players to the peak of readiness.[72]

The third of September dawned delightfully cool, a perfect day for basketball. Up until the tip-off, it was expected that Katie Snell would take Emma Sansaver's place at forward, given Emma's still-swollen ankle. But when the girls took the court at 4:30 in front of several hundred onlookers, Emma stood with her teammates — Belle Johnson, Minnie Burton, Genie Butch, and Nettie Wirth. A trolley-load of supporters had followed the girls from the fairgrounds, and as the two centers moved into position, a cheer went up:

Bum-a-ling! Bum-a-ling!

Bow-wow-wow!

Ching-a-ling! Ching-a-ling!

Chow-chow-chow!

Bum-a-ling! Ching-a-ling!

Who are we?

Fort Shaw! Fort Shaw!

Rah! Rah! Rah![73]

According to the reporter sent by the *Post-Dispatch* to cover the contest, any doubt as to the final outcome was dispelled within minutes of the tip-off. The St. Louis athletes were "not in a class" with Fort Shaw. "The Indian girls were more active, more accurate, and cooler than their opponents" and trounced the All-Stars, 24 to 2.[74]

The *Great Falls Tribune* treated Montana fans to a detailed and colorful account of the game, courtesy of the on-the-spot reporting of Fort Shaw assistant matron Lillie B. Crawford. At the tip-off Nettie got the ball, and "with some brilliant team work [the Indians] rushed it to the western goal but failed to score—handicapped as they were by the sun shining in their eyes." Though an All-Star grabbed the rebound, in seconds Emma recaptured the sphere and "dodging here and there with the rapidity of a streak of lightning," displayed a "fearlessness [that] completely nonplussed her opponents." Time and again "the little one" managed to get the ball into the hands of the right player at the right time. Most often that was Minnie, who scored two "fine field throws" and two foul shots before the end of the first half. In the second half "Nettie made four brilliant field throws," and Belle pulled off "one of the finest plays . . . ever." Genie "was a wonder [at] . . . guard," and she and her teammates held their opponents to 2 points, while scoring 24 themselves.[75]

Having fully expected to win, Coach Stremmel and his girls had, instead, suffered "an ignominious defeat." Yet the game had been so hotly contested that the fans went away satisfied they had gotten their money's worth. "I stayed over one day to see the game," remarked one spectator, "and would not have missed it for $50. The playing of these Indian girls is simply marvelous. They can easily defeat any team in the world."[76]

Excited as they were by their win, the girls from Fort Shaw Indian School were well aware that this was a two-out-of-three championship series. The team captains, Belle Johnson and Florence Messing, agreed that the second game would be played two weeks hence, on Saturday, September 17, on the plaza in front of the Model Indian School.[77]

In the interim the girls from Fort Shaw resumed their regular activities at the Model Indian School. At the invitation of friends from Chilocco, they participated in the celebration of Oklahoma Day at the fair on Tuesday, September 6. "One of the delightful features" of that celebration, according to an article in the St. Louis Republic, was "the entertainment given by . . . girls [who] performed a pantomime of 'Song of the Mystic' with splendid effect." That article was accompanied by a photo of nine Fort Shaw girls clad in their white robes.[78]

Their afternoon exhibition games on the plaza were now drawing even larger crowds than usual, probably due to press coverage of the championship series. Those fans who had waited impatiently for the second game in that series were destined to wait still longer. On September 16, the day before the scheduled rematch, Florence Messing, captain of the All-Stars, contacted Belle Johnson, requesting "a few weeks' delay," but giving no reason. Seeing no other recourse, Belle agreed. So rather than playing a championship game, the girls devoted Saturday, September 17, to appearances in two programs, to opening the morning entertainment at the school with a mandolin prelude and demonstrating club swinging and barbell drills in the afternoon.[79]

The days were growing shorter—and cooler. When they were not in their buckskin dresses, basketball uniforms, or Grecian robes the girls were now attired in uniforms made of slightly heavier navy blue "shirtwaist" material. Turned out by the Haskell girls in the sewing room of the Model Indian School, these outfits were a necessary response to the chill of St. Louis in autumn. The unanticipated cold weather caused other problems less easily solved. The school building, intended from the beginning to serve only one season, had no central heating, leaving students and staff shivering. Unwilling to compromise the health of those in his charge, Superintendent McCowan had begun to consider closing the school sooner than anticipated. Staying on through November seemed less and less feasible.[80]

When cold and rainy weather reduced the flow of visitors to the Anthropology Building located just west of the Model Indian School, scientists in the anthropometric and psychometric laboratories, who had spent the summer taking physical measurements of the fairgoers as well as those of the "primitives" on display, now turned their attention to "scientific measurements" of subjects close at hand. With the test results from thousands upon thousands of "primitives" and "civilized" individuals on file, the experimenters began to use their state-of-the-art equipment to test the students at the school and the other residents on Indian Hill. In addition to determining the strength of their grip and measuring their height, weight, and lung power, the scientists paid particular attention to facial structure, limbs — even feet — in their dedicated effort to characterize the various "races" represented at the fair. There were some curious theories abounding. For instance, the supposition that the Indian, "along with several of the savage race," had little or no perception of the color blue. A color wheel awaited the students in the labs.[81]

On Friday, September 30, Emma Sansaver reported on schedule to Dr. Frank Bruner in the anthropometry lab. After running a battery of tests, he recorded her age as nineteen, her height as 4 feet, 11¼ inches, her weight as 109¼ pounds. Her pulse, resting, was seventy-five. He measured the strength of her forearms, her back, and her legs. Her hearing was "excellent," and her vision was "normal." She was able to distinguish all colors — including blue. And, for whatever use Bruner made of such findings, she liked the color pink and disliked orange. Though the girls had no idea of the significance of the numbers given to the size of their skulls, the distance between their eyes, and the capacity of their lungs, they spent whole evenings in the dorm comparing the measurements on the charts they brought back from the anthropometry lab.[82]

On the first Friday of October, Belle Johnson received the phone call from Flo Messing that the girls had been waiting for. The All-Stars were finally ready to play the second game of the series—the very next afternoon, Saturday, October 8—on the parade grounds in front of the Model Indian School.[83] Belle quickly agreed. Her team was ready to play any time, any place, she assured Miss Messing. Her only concern was whether or not publicity for the game could be generated at this late date.

Belle need not have worried. Within twenty-four hours word had spread across the fairgrounds and out into the city. By now, even the most ardent St. Louisians were fans of the nimble athletes from the Indian school in Montana, and they were aware that this might be their last chance to see the girls play a match game. In addition to those who came from afar were scores of supporters from Indian Hill, few of whom had been able to attend either the game in Belleville, Illinois, or the one at Kulage Park. Even had there been time for more extensive publicity, it is doubtful there would have been room for any more fans. Hundreds of men, women, and children stood shoulder- to-shoulder around the sides of the court. So great was the press of humanity that the eager spectators had to be pushed back from the field of play before the game could begin.[84]

At precisely four o'clock the captains walked to center court where "a coin was tossed to decide goals." The lineups were the same as seen in the first game of the series, with Coach Stremmel depending on his squad's extra weeks of practice to give them the edge they had lacked in the earlier match. Once again, Fort Shaw's color commentator, Lillie B. Crawford, wired the *Great Falls Tribune* a full account of the contest from opening play to final whistle. At the tip-off, as "the leather sphere rose and fell . . . Nettie made one of her phenomenal leaps . . . and sent it spinning far toward the Indian girls' goal" and into Belle's hands. "Skillfully evading her opponent," Belle got the ball to Minnie, "who smiled as she dropped it into the basket, while the audience went wild with enthusiasm." That enthusiasm never flagged. At the end of the first half, the score stood 9 to 3 in favor of Fort Shaw.[85]

The onslaught continued in the second half, as Fort Shaw's teamwork "called forth round after round of applause." The partisan cheering seemed to disconcert the All-Stars, who managed to score only three more points, all on foul shots. Meanwhile Nettie made two "magnificent field throws," and Emma and Belle contributed one apiece. Genie's defensive play was "par excellence" and a major factor in the eleven-point spread in the final score: Indians 17, All-Stars, 6.[86] The girls from Montana were the official champions of the Louisiana Purchase Exposition. In the eyes of their supporters — and Montana journalists — they were even more: They were "the undisputed . . . world's champions."[87]

Though the All-Stars had been confident they would avenge their earlier loss and force Fort Shaw into a third game, Coach Stremmel conceded that the teamwork, skill, and fleetness of foot of the Indians had proven too much for his girls. "Their powers of endurance [were] simply marvelous," he said, and despite their own talents and their diligent preparation for this rematch, the girls from Missouri could not "cope with such formidable opponents."[88]

The girls from Montana immediately resumed their duties at the Model Indian School, though the number and nature of their accustomed literary and musical programs changed as some of the singers and other performers began to return to their home schools. More apparent changes were also underway. By the middle of October, the encampments of the traditional Indians were all but abandoned. In the absence of the varied peoples who had given life to those empty dwellings, Indian Hill became a shadow of what it once was.[89]

As the student body of the Model Indian School continued to thin out, the Fort Shaw girls passed around "memory books" to be inscribed by special friends among the many with whom they had shared their adventure in St.

Louis.[90] Every good-bye was tinged with sadness, but on November 5, when, for the last time, the band boys from Chilocco marched down the steps and out onto the plaza, still in the perfect formation that had marked their performances all summer, a pall fell over the Model Indian School.[91]

A week later, only a handful of students, the Fort Shaw girls among them, remained in the dorms. The staff had been reduced to a few individuals. The hallways so recently alive with activity now echoed with emptiness. It was hard to imagine that this same building had hosted over three million visitors in the weeks between the first of June and the last of October.[92]

As mid-November approached, the girls from Fort Shaw began crating up their gear and outfits—ceremonial buckskins, Grecian gowns, and basketball uniforms. After a round of good-byes to remaining residents of Indian Hill, and heartfelt thanks to faculty and staff, the girls boarded the intramural railway for the last time. At the entrance to the fairgrounds, they caught a downtown trolley and headed for Union Station to begin the journey home. As the train rolled across the country, through Chicago, St. Paul, Fargo, and more familiar towns beyond, there were no games, no entertainments, just the growing anticipation of a triumphant return to the campus where their odyssey had begun. On Friday, November 18, five and a half months after their departure, the team arrived in Montana, holding their trophy high and greeted by cheers, applause, and the music of their own school band, a fitting welcome for the basketball champions of the 1904 World's Fair.[93]

On December 1, two weeks after the girls' departure, the city of St. Louis staged the closing ceremonies for the Louisiana Purchase Exhibition. That morning, William Reedy editorialized in his popular magazine the *Mirror*, "[I]t is over—the Fair—Yet much of it remains with us . . . [including] a broader tolerance [and] a keener appreciation of the good in all the world. . . . We have learned to be humble before the achievements of other peoples whom we have fancied we long ago left behind in the march of progress."[94]

Perhaps no other group at the fair had contributed to that appreciation as much as had the students at the Model Indian School, including the ten young women who had gone to St. Louis to demonstrate their talents and skills in the concert hall and on the basketball court. To S. M. McGowan and his superiors, the girls from Fort Shaw were first and foremost a key component of the living exhibit designed to prove to the world the effectiveness of the U.S. government's Indian education policies. Yet McCowan's goals and those of the Indian girls he put on display were hardly mutually exclusive. Seizing the opportunity for travel, adventure, and their moment in the sun, these ten young women easily turned their world's fair experiences to their own advantage. And they returned to Fort Shaw in triumph, leaving the white athletes of Illinois and Missouri "far behind them" and savoring memories no one could ever take away from them.

The girls cherished those memories, and pieces of the story of their grand adventure have been handed down through generations of family and tribal kin. There is no disputing the influence these ten women had on the aspirations of their own daughters and granddaughters, sons and grandsons. And there is every reason to believe that their legacy extends beyond their descendants and tribal kin to the thousands of other Native American young people fortunate enough to observe—or hear about—their accomplishments on and off the court.[95]

Yet in the early years of the twenty-first century, as women's basketball is drawing the attention of sports fans around the globe, few of those fans realize that at the dawn of the twentieth century, girls' teams playing full-court "basket ball" were already challenging long-held assumptions about women and sports. And at a time when indigenous peoples around the world are reclaiming their heritage and celebrating their history, few Indians—or non-Indians, for that matter—have ever heard how the best of the best, a team one Missouri reporter described as ten "aboriginal maidens . . . from the Fort Shaw Reservation [sic]" in Montana overcame racial and gender barriers to emerge as basketball champions of the 1904 St. Louis World's Fair.[96]

Notes

1. *Great Falls (Montana) Daily Tribune*, October 14, 1904.

2. *St. Louis Post-Dispatch*, August 27 and September 4, 1904; *St. Louis Republic*, October 9, 1904; *Great Falls Daily Tribune*, September 9, 1904. The October 9 *Post Dispatch* carried lineups for both teams; starters for the All-Stars were forwards Florence Messing and Lillian Randal, A. "Birdie" Hoffman, center, and guards Laura Strong and Pauline (Paula) Fisher.

3. *Great Falls Daily Tribune*, October 14, 1904. The *St. Louis Republic* of October 9, 1904, gave the final score as 17 to 5.

4. Register of Pupils, Record Group 75, National Archives, Denver (hereafter RG 75, NAD), entry 1358. The expanded story of the girls and their experiences as a team is told in Peavy and Smith, *Full-Court Quest*.

5. Founded in 1869 to protect Montana's settlers and transportation routes from "marauding Indians," Fort Shaw was decommissioned in 1891. Miller and Cohen, *Military and Trading Posts*, 76–79. Many excellent books about Indian education in government boarding schools have appeared in the last dozen years, including D. Adams, *Education for Extinction*; Lomawaima, *They Called It Prairie Light*; Child, *Boarding School Seasons*; and Archuleta, Child, and Lomawaima, *Away from Home*.

6. *(Helena) Montana Daily Record*, March 4, 1904; S. M. McCowan to Commissioner of Indian Affairs (hereafter CIA), March 20, 1903, Record Group 75, National Archives, Washington DC (hereafter RG 75, NAW), Letters Received 1903, entry 18545.

7. Bradfield, "A History of Chilocco Indian School," 61–62; C. H. Spencer to Secretary of the Interior, February 2, 1903, RG 75, NAW, Letters Received, 1903, entry 11457. For a comprehensive overview of the Indian presence at the fair, see Parezo and Fowler, *Anthropology Goes to the Fair*.

8. McCowan to CIA, April 17, 1903, RG 75, NAW, Letters Received 1903, entry 23155; "World's Fair Indian Exhibit," 114.

9. *Indian School Journal*, June 1 and June 14, 1904.

10. McCowan felt his school was located on a "splendid site." McCowan to CIA, June 25, 1903, RG 75, NAW, Letters Received 1903, entry 39333; David Francis article in LPE, *World's Fair Bulletin* 6:43; *Indian School Journal*, June 16, 1904; Trennert, "Selling Indian Education," 214.

11. McCowan to CIA, March 20, 1903, RG 75, NAW, Letters Received 1903, entry 18545; *Indian School Journal*, June 6 and 16, 1904; October 1904.

12. *Indian School Journal*, June 6 and 16, 1904; October 1904.

13. *Indian School Journal*, June 16, 1904.

14. James Naismith, "Basket Ball," [YMCA] *Triangle*, January 1892, 145–46.

15. Full-court action would not be restored to women's basketball for seventy years, with the implementation of Title IX. For an excellent overview of the development of

women's basketball and the evolution of "girls' rules," see Spears, "Senda Berenson Abbott"; and Davenport, "Tides of Change," 19–36; 83–108. See also Grundy and Shackelford, *Shattering the Glass*, 9–33.

16. *Great Falls Daily Leader*, June 12, 1897.

17. Register of Pupils, 1892–1908, and Roster of Employees, 1892–1910, RG 75, NAD, entry 1358; interview with Patricia Deboo, great-niece of Josephine Langley Liephart, November 2004.

18. Baldwin, "History of Fort Shaw," 5.

19. Culin, "Games of North American Indians," 647–64.

20. Double ball, a "women's game" played by Minnie Burton's paternal grandmother, was not banned from the Lemhi Reservation until after Minnie transferred to Fort Shaw School in 1901. Madsen, *The Lemhi*, 154, 156.

21. Baldwin, "History of Fort Shaw," 9; Roster of Employees, 1892–1910.

22. *(Helena) Montana Record-Herald*, February 18, 1939; F. C. Campbell, personal statement, January 24, 1922, in possession of Fred DesRosier, grandson of F. C. Campbell.

23. The long wagon ride from Fort Shaw to the railhead at Sunnyside, present-day Vaughn, Montana, was made in uncovered farm wagons, though after the 1902–3 championship season, Campbell sought, likely unsuccessfully, to raise money for a covered conveyance in which to transport his students, in particular his basketball team and band. *Great Falls Daily Tribune*, May 7, May 8, 1903.

24. Register of Pupils, 1892–1908. Nettie's jumping ability derived from various newspaper reports and from granddaughter Winona Weber. *Great Falls Daily Tribune*, January 30, 1903. Emma's height and other "anthropometric" statistics are listed on an official document from the fair in the possession of Emma's granddaughter Beverly Braig. Unfortunately, the heights and weights of most of the girls cannot be known since, ironically, such measurements of all the Fort Shaw students (the first taken in several years) were made on June 1, 1904, while the team was en route to St. Louis. The team's rallying cry was first printed in the *Bozeman Avant Courier*, June 27, 1903.

25. *Great Falls Daily Tribune*, January 30, 1903; "Fort Shaw Wins Again," undated news clipping in Nettie Wirth Mail scrapbook in the possession of Mail's great-niece Terry Bender; *Bozeman Avant Courier*, April 3, 1903; *Anaconda (Montana) Standard*, March 24, 1904.

26. *Great Falls Daily Tribune*, April 25, 1903; *Great Falls Daily Leader*, July 2, 1903.

27. Newspapers in Great Falls, Butte, and other cities across the state covered the games that year, as well as college newspapers. See, for instance, *Butte (Montana) Inter Mountain*, November 28, 1902; *Great Falls Weekly Tribune*, January 22, 1903; *Great Falls Daily Tribune*, January 30, 1903; *Kaimin*, newspaper of the University of Montana (then Montana State University) in Missoula, April 1903; *(Montana) Missoulian*, January 31, 1903; *Exponent* (Montana Agricultural College), April 1903.

28. Campbell's use of student "entertainments" and athletic events to champion the cause of the government's Indian education program in general and Fort Shaw School in particular is evident long before the girls' basketball team's rise to prominence gave

him an additional platform for his cause. See, for example, *Anaconda Standard*, December 9, 1900.

29. *Great Falls Daily Tribune*, June 27, 1903.

30. *Great Falls Daily Leader*, January 15, 1904; *Anaconda Standard*, March 1, 1904.

31. Josie Langley's playing days ended in late June of 1903. She was married to school employee Harvey Liephart at Fort Shaw School on Christmas Day of that year. *Great Falls Leader*, December 26, 1903.

32. (*Helena*) *Montana Daily Record*, February 26, 1904; Register of Pupils, 1892–1908. The identities of the five girls added to the roster for the state and St. Louis intrasquad exhibition games have been determined through newspaper articles in Montana and Missouri papers and through interviews with descendants of the ten young women who composed the full team.

33. *Great Falls Weekly Tribune*, January 22, 1903; *Great Falls Daily Tribune*, January 31, 1903; *Bozeman Avant Courier*, April 3, 1903; *Havre Plaindealer*, June 27, 1903.

34. *Anaconda Standard*, March 1, 20, and 25, 1904; *Great Falls Daily Tribune*, May 31, 1904; *Montana Daily Record*, May 6, 1904; *Great Falls Daily Leader*, February 5 and 8, 1904. Louis Youpee, a ten-year-old Chippewa, performed the comic routines; Gertrude La Rance, an eight-year-old Chippewa, recited the melodramatic pieces.

35. "Three Survivors in This Area of Famous Girls' Team," undated *Phillips County News* clipping in possession of Donita Nordlund, granddaughter of Genevieve Healy Adams. The uniforms as described in this passage can be seen in the team photo taken at the world's fair and published in Fox and Sneddecker, *From the Palaces*, 185. The caption for this photograph incorrectly identifies the girls as being from "Fort Smith."

36. Fox and Sneddecker, *From the Palaces*, 37; McCowan to CIA, June 2, 1904, Letters Received 1904, RG 75, NAW, entry 36905; *Indian School Journal*, June 2, 1904.

37. *Great Falls Daily Leader*, June 2, 1904; *Great Falls Daily Tribune*, June 11, 1904; *Indian School Journal*, June 15, 1904.

38. *St. Louis Republic*, June 15, 1904. For a contemporary description of The Pike, see chapter 7, "Wonders of the Glorious Pike," in Marshall Everett's *The Book of the Fair*. Published by P. W. Ziegler, circa 1904, the book is out of print but can be accessed on the Web under Jim Zwick's site on World's Fairs and Expositions.

39. *Indian School Journal*, June 15, 1904; *St. Louis Republic*, June 15 and 16, 1904; *St. Louis Globe-Democrat*, June 16, 1904, page 111, in Louisiana Purchase Exposition (hereafter LPE) scrapbook, Missouri Historical Society (hereafter MHS), St. Louis.

40. *St. Louis Globe-Democrat*, June 17, 1904, LPE scrapbook, 113.

41. *St. Louis Republic*, June 16, 1904.

42. *Indian School Journal*, June 16, 18, 28, and 30, 1904; *Official Daily Program*, June 21, 1904, LPE Collection, Box 30, Folder 6b, MHS, St. Louis.

43. *Indian School Journal*, June 16, 1904.

44. *Indian School Journal*, July 2 and September 12, 1904.

45. *Indian School Journal*, July 1, 1904.

46. *Indian School Journal*, July 6, 1904; *Great Falls Daily Leader*, August 1, 1904.

47. Dyreson, *Making the American Team*, 80–81.

48. *Colorado Springs Telegraph*, September 6, 1903.

49. *Great Falls Daily Leader*, July 13 and 23, 1904; *Indian School Journal*, June 13, 1904.

50. *Mandan (North Dakota) Pioneer*, July 10, 1904.

51. Anecdotes related by Donita Nordlund, granddaughter of Genevieve Healy Adams.

52. *Indian School Journal*, July 21, 1904.

53. *Indian School Journal*, July 20 and 25, 1904.

54. *O'Fallon (Illinois) Progress*, July 22, 1904.

55. *O'Fallon Progress*, July 22, 1904

56. *O'Fallon Progress*, August 5, 1904; *Indian School Journal*, July 29, 1904; *Great Falls Daily Tribune* of August 10, 1904, quoting from St. Louis Republic of July 29, which gave the score as 13 to 3.

57. *O'Fallon Progress*, August 5, 1904.

58. *Indian School Journal*, July 29, 1904.

59. Letter quoted, without signature, in *Indian School Journal*, August 22, 1904.

60. *Indian School Journal*, October 1904, 51–52.

61. *Indian School Journal*, August 12, 1904.

62. *Official Daily Program*, August 11 and 12, 1904, LPE Collection, Box 30, Folder 6b, 2; *St. Louis Globe-Democrat*, August 13, 1904, LPE scrapbook, 206.

63. *St. Louis Globe-Democrat*, August 13, 1904. Though others have cited August 12 and 13 as the dates for the Anthropology Days games, the contemporary media—including the official report of the Department of Anthropology, pages 42–44, LPE Collection—cite Thursday and Friday, August 11 and 12.

64. Guttman, *Games Must Go On*, 19; LPE—World's Fair Bulletin, "Novel Athletic Contest," 50.

65. Coubertin, *Olympic Memoirs*, 43.

66. *Indian School Journal*, August 13, 1904.

67. *Indian School Journal*, August 25, 1904. The trophy was modeled on the loving cups given to the winners of the official Olympic events. Other winners in the Anthropology Days meet were taken into the Physical Culture building immediately after their events and given a cash prize—three dollars for first place, two for second-place finishers, and a dollar for third place. LPE—World's Fair Bulletin, "Novel Athletic Contest."

68. *Indian School Journal*, August 23, 1904.

69. *St. Louis Post-Dispatch*, August 27, 1904.

70. *Indian School Journal*, August 23, 1904.

71. J. Lucas, *Modern Olympic Games*, 54. Archery was the only women's event on the 1904 Olympic Games schedule.

72. *Indian School Journal*, July 29, 1904. Fort Shaw's lineup was the same as usual; the All-Star starters were Flo Messing and Pauline Fisher at forward, Lillian Randall at center, and Laura Strong and A. "Birdie" Hoffman at guard. *St. Louis Post-Dispatch*, August 27, 1904.

73. *Great Falls Daily Tribune*, September 9, 1904.

74. *St. Louis Post-Dispatch*, September 4, 1904.

75. *Great Falls Daily Tribune*, September 9, 1904.

76. *Great Falls Daily Tribune*, September 9, 1904.

77. *Indian School Journal*, September 12, 1904.

78. *St. Louis Republic*, September 12, 1904.

79. *Indian School Journal*, September 17, 1904.

80. McCowan to Frederick Skiff, August 18, 1904, in WJ McGee, "Report of the Department of Anthropology,"

81. *Official Daily Program*, May 25, 1904, LPE Collection, Box 30, Folder 6b, 3.

82. Emma Sansaver's assessment by Dr. Frank Bruner, September 30, 1904, record held by Beverly Braig, Emma Sansaver Simpson's granddaughter. No other such assessments for the Fort Shaw girls have been found.

83. *Great Falls Daily Tribune*, October 14, 1904.

84. *Great Falls Daily Tribune*, October 14, 1904.

85. *Great Falls Daily Tribune*, October 14, 1904.

86. *Great Falls Daily Tribune*, October 14, 1904. The *Post-Dispatch* reporter attributed the improved play of the All-Stars to Coach Stremmel's having shifted positions for his starting five, with all girls doing well in their new assignments and "Miss Hoffman" shining at center. *St. Louis Post-Dispatch*, Sunday, October 8, 1904.

87. "Basketball Champions," undated *Great Falls Daily Tribune* article in Nettie Wirth Mail scrapbook, in possession of Terry Bender, Mail's great-niece.

88. "Basketball Champions," undated *Great Falls Daily Tribune* article.

89. McCowan to CIA, October 15, 1904, Letters Received 1904, entry 72479, RG 75, NAW; McCowan to Captain Sayer, October 30, 1904, McCowan files, Oklahoma Historical Society.

90. Memory book held by Barbara Winters, Emma Sansaver Simpson's granddaughter.

91. Memory book of Emma Sansaver Simpson.

92. Report of W. C. Buskett, special agent in charge at St. Louis, January 30, 1904, Manuscript Collection 35, Folder 10, Box 315, Montana Historical Society; WJ McGee, "Report of the Department of Anthropology," 22.

93. Travel vouchers for November 10 and November 21, 1904, in McCowan files, Oklahoma Historical Society; *Great Falls Daily Leader*, November 21, 1904.

94. Reedy, "End of the Fair," December 1, 1904.

95. Interviews and correspondence with more than fifty descendants of the team and of other Fort Shaw students (transcripts, notes, audio and video tapes, and letters in possession of authors) attest to the ways in which the girls on that team inspired their kith and kin, plus their Fort Shaw and Model Indian School classmates.

96. *St. Louis Republic*, June 15, 1904.

Chapter 7. Germans and Others at the "American Games"

Problems of National and International Representation at the 1904 Olympics

SUZUKO MOUSEL KNOTT

Referred to as the "American Olympics" by chroniclers and historians today, the 1904 Olympic Games remain inextricably linked to the Louisiana Purchase Exposition. The official moniker—the third modern Olympics, held under the auspices of the Department of Physical Culture at the 1904 Louisiana Purchase Exposition in St. Louis, Missouri—points to the central problem associated with these Olympic Games, namely the conflict of national and international representation on the field of play. Held under the auspices of a committee formed for the world's fair, the Olympic designation was in many ways appropriated by its American organizers. The athletic contests in St. Louis exhibited more homegrown than foreign talent, begging the question, To what purpose were the third modern Olympics organized if not to bring international athletes together in competition? Whose Olympic vision was realized in St. Louis, and who did the individual athletes competing in these Olympics represent? And more importantly, whose identity was misrepresented? These questions hinge upon the complex interplay of competing notions of nationality in an international context, represented at the level of the individual athlete competing in the 1904 Olympics.

In an effort to address the question of national representation in an international context, this chapter will examine the participation of individual athletes, whose national and cultural affiliations have been blurred by circumstance, misread by historians, or simply denied by their contemporaries. The discussion begins by examining the participation of individuals representing Germany, and then moves to examine the participation by those individuals denied the right to represent themselves according to their self-identification, or whose performance was staged to express a dominant culture's hegemony over colonized peoples. In the case of German participation, organizational confusion and club affiliation result in a rather benign mistaking of national identity, colored by the perception of local audiences and reporting by newspapers. In stark contrast, politically motivated practices of exclusion and ghettoized sporting events express the hegemony of the fledgling and aged empires of the United States and Great Britain. The examination of these two seemingly disparate situations, the experience of the German athlete, and that of the political or racial "other," in fact reveals a common origin—a shifting notion of nation and nationality vis-à-vis a politics of race and racial classification, which plays out in the international context of Olympic competition.

Athletes and the Question of Representation at the "American Games"

Reflecting on the Olympics in his book *Lion of the Valley*, St. Louis historian James Neal Primm comments: "The 1904 Games . . . were the last to adhere to the original Olympic ideal."[1] Primm's understanding of an Olympic ideal emphasizes individual athletic performance, as opposed to a focus upon the athletic prowess demonstrated by a nation as a whole, where "instead of national 'teams' marching under flags into chauvinistic combat, the athletes entered as individuals, or in the case of team events, as clubs."[2] This interpretation of the 1904 Olympics rings brighter than that of most historians, who have deemed them "a dismal failure."[3] It also remains unclear to what extent the 1904 Olympics lived up to an "original Olympic ideal," for what Pierre de Coubertin had intended to be an internationally organized and staged event had been co-opted by local St. Louis organizers of the world's fair and transformed into the "American Games."

On May 14, 1904, something akin to an opening ceremony was held at the Olympic Interscholastic Meet.[4] President David Francis arrived at the stadium, now called Francis Field, on the campus of Washington University in St. Louis, with U.S. Secretary of State John Milton Hay. Together they led a line of officials and commissioners and proceeded to their box seats in the grandstand. "The Star Spangled Banner" was played and Francis, Hay, and James Sullivan, head of the exposition's Department of Physical Culture, walked down to the starting line, where Sullivan called the athletes to the start. David Francis fired the pistol at 3:00 p.m. What athletes had, however, managed to make it to the line? Many international athletes were unable to afford the trip to St. Louis; other athletes simply chose not to bother.[5] Countries would have sent more delegates had they been allotted enough time to make the necessary financial arrangements.

Germany and its athletes comprise one of the few countries who did take pains to travel to the 1904 Olympics. Participation was hard fought, as Germany's Olympic committee worked feverishly to find, fund, and house its athletes for the third modern Olympics. Karl Lennartz writes in *Die Beteiligung Deutschlands an den Olympischen Spielen* that up until the departure of the first group of athletes to St. Louis, the gymnasts, the imperial commission had, above all, money problems.[6] The budget proved far too short for the travel costs of the fifty athletes they had planned to send. Letters were sent to rich Americans of German decent requesting financial assistance.[7] Dr. Willibald Gebhardt's request to find housing for German athletes was fulfilled, although not by any International Olympic Committee (IOC) action. There was no official housing provided for international athletes; however the German gymnasts were later guests of a certain rich German-American in St. Louis, the brewer Adolphus Busch of Anheuser-Busch.[8] Gebhardt's frustration with a lack of accommodations was only one of many organizational challenges the German Olympic Committee faced. Establishing when athletes should arrive for competition was equally vague. In the summer of 1903 Gebhardt was already criticizing the organization of events, writing that one thing was to be regretted: the international events are timed somewhat askew.[9] By October the German committee members expressed regret that the program was still not available in enough detail to allow the subcommittees to do concrete work.[10] If one assumes that transatlantic travel arrangements were to be made for as many as fifty different athletes, then the mounting frustration of the German Olympic Committee may well be understood.

Facing the logistical difficulties presented by the Olympics in St. Louis, Gebhardt chose to send only athletes in those events deemed important. In an effort to maximize a German presence, Lennartz relates, Gebhardt then addressed the chances of the German athletes. He felt it necessary to send athletes for the competitions in athletics, swimming, fencing, tennis, and soccer. He had particularly high expectations of the German rowers and gymnasts.[11] However of these six important categories, athletes for only four (athletics, gymnastics, fencing, and swimming) competed at the third modern Olympic Games. Another example of the organizational chaos Gebhardt faced: while already in America, he was informed of a student soccer team willing to travel from Germany to compete in St. Louis. Gebhardt was then informed that no further team could be sent for financial reasons.[12] The result was that only twenty German athletes traveled to St. Louis, of which only seventeen actually participated.[13]

The athletes who traveled to St. Louis as part of the German delegation performed well in the Olympic events, ranking high in swimming and dominating gymnastics. However, not all the athletes who competed for the German delegation were in fact German nationals. Adolf Spinnler, a citizen of Switzerland, competed for the German team.[14] A member of the Esslinger Turnverein near Stuttgart, Germany, Spinnler's club membership, rather than nationality or citizenship, determined which country he would represent in St. Louis. Otto Wahle is another example of an athlete whose club

281

affiliation superseded his national identity in international competition.[15] In 1897 Wahle was the European Champion in the mile and had been a member of the Austria Wien Club in Vienna. Despite having immigrated to the United States shortly after the 1900 Olympics in Paris and having joined the New York Athletic Club, which he represented in St. Louis, Wahle apparently retained his Austrian citizenship. Nonetheless, Wahle competed in St. Louis as a member of the German delegation.

Individual athletes and their nationalities appear to have been subsumed into the national representation of their athletic clubs in the 1904 Olympics. Julius Lenhart won a gold medal for the United States, despite the fact that he was not a U.S. citizen. Dr. Ferenc Mező counts Lenhart among the American gymnasts, representing the Philadelphia Turngemeinde of Pennsylvania. Mező points out, however, that "the American gymnasts were either Germans living in the United States, or actually Americans of German descent."[16] Lenhart was, however, neither a German living in the United States, nor an American of German descent. Karl Lennartz uncovers that Lenhart was an Austrian citizen, who had learned gymnastics in the T. V. Mariahilf Wien Club and had gone to the United States for work-related reasons, where he lived until 1905. He became a member of the Turnverein Philadelphia and the club's star gymnast. Austrian historians and statisticians have since tried to claim Lenhart as their Olympian.[17] Lennartz comments that Lenhart had also lived in Paris and Switzerland, where he had won gymnastics prizes, which prompted the *Deutsche Turn-Zeitung* (German Gymnastics Newspaper) to question if Lenhart were a mercenary prize gymnast.[18] Indeed, in 1903 Lenhart lived and worked in Munich, competing in the Deutsches Turnfest (German Gymnastics Festival) in nearby Nuremburg, winning second place. Austria's attempt to reclaim Lenhart as an Austrian gymnast today demonstrates a point of national pride that didn't yet exist in 1904 and lays bare a shift in meaning of sport that took place after the 1904 Olympics.

Reading National Representation

International competition, which Coubertin wished would replace the battle-ground, only fulfills its function if the athletes are accepted and recognized by the spectators as representations of a nation. One of the fundamental questions posed by the modern Olympic Games would become, Whom were the athletes to represent? Pierre de Coubertin's conception of the Games envisioned athletes who carried clear national signification. Athletes would represent the nations from which they hailed to an end seemingly incongruous with the nationalistic representation they signified: representing their respective nations, the athletes would foster peace between nations by engaging in symbolic battles in competition among sportsmen.[19] Allen Guttman notes: "The modern games were, in fact, revived to propagate a political message. In the eyes of Pierre de Coubertin and in the men who succeeded him as president of the IOC, the political purpose of the games — the reconciliation of warring nations — was more important than sports. They were merely the competitive means to a cooperative end: a world at peace."[20] An individual athlete would in this vision become a representation of the nation as a whole.

Athletic contest, and its political representations, relies upon an audience's perception of the event to impart meaning. The very nature of competitive sport demands the interpretation of an athlete's actions in a public space in order to determine and assign cultural value to the spectacle, be it national or international in scope. Writing on the relationship of spectator to sporting events, David Kanin explains:

> International sport is a form of cross-cultural activity which attracts the interest of, and is understood by, a mass public. Most have their contact with athletes and fans from other states second hand, via the mass media. Modern communications technology makes matches of national interest immediately available to anyone who wants to watch or listen. It enables the mass public, which tends to identify with the athletes, to take notice

of contests against teams or individuals from friendly or hostile states.
Governments can use this identification when sporting events are staged
to demonstrate the temper of relations between the states represented by
the athletes.[21]

What Kanin describes is true of the Olympic Games today; however the
Olympic Games in St. Louis reflected international sport in transition. Mass
communication technologies, such as the telegraph and newspaper circulation, were slow and not readily available to all in 1904. Consequently, the
international appeal of sporting events had yet to truly develop by the third
modern Olympics. There was, nonetheless, a public in attendance at the
1904 Olympics, and it is through their perception that the representation of
nations and national identity played out.

In the minds of the spectators and readers of press coverage, individual
athletic performance becomes the abstracted signification of a nation. Without
the audience to extrapolate "nation" from "athlete," no international contest
could be represented in a sporting event. However, the prerequisite to such
an association is the belief in an "imagined community" — a nation.[22] Only
through the complex process of identification with an imagined and idealized cohesive whole does the idea and belief in nation become fixed in the
individual. It is therefore necessary to consider how the audience of the 1904
Olympic Games defined "nation," and what competing, even contradictory,
interpretations of community and belonging shaped their perception of the
athletic contests viewed.

Major "Olympic" events held in St. Louis such as gymnastics and athletics drew very few crowds and only specific communities with a vested
interest in the results viewed or reported on the contests.[23] In this case, the
audience was overwhelmingly German-American, representing a large and
vibrant immigrant population in St. Louis.[24] Local turnvereine (German-
American gymnastics clubs) and turnvereine throughout the Midwest sent
delegations to compete in gymnastics. Their leaders, members, and families

18. German turners who competed in the international gymnastics championships in the 1904 Olympics. From J. Sullivan, ed., "The Olympic Games of 1906 at Athens."

were intensely interested in the competitions, following the contests in local German-language publications such as the *Westliche Post*, a newspaper published for the large German-American population in the city of St. Louis and its surrounding communities.[25] Articles in the *Westliche Post* provided extensive coverage of German participation in the world's fair, especially of events associated with the turnvereine, and bemoaned thin crowds and a lack of support shown to athletes. Meanwhile, local American papers such as the *Missouri Saturday Republican* hardly took notice of the events.[26] Anticipating the arrival of the German delegation, the *Westliche Post* reported on May 29, 1904, that twelve German turners would be boarding a ship in Hamburg on June 11.[27] On June 30, their arrival was announced: "There was great excitement at the St. Louis train station last night, as participants in the upcoming World's Fair Turnfest arrived."[28] The article further includes detailed coverage of the athletes' reception, including lodging and dining information. There was comprehensive coverage of the meets themselves, with lists of athletes and their club affiliation, results, and editorials by local turnverein leaders about their sport.[29]

The primary audience of the 1904 Olympics read nationalism in terms of a pan-Germanic fantasy, based on the writings of Johann Gottfried Herder and informed by the nationalistic polemic of "Turnvater" Friedrich Ludwig Jahn, the founder of the German Turner movement. Herder "was a proponent of an experience- and tradition-based particularism, of communal identities, and of linguistic nationalism" that need not be confined in one nation-state.[30] Herder's concept of Volk coalesced a nationality within and without the confines of the arbitrary borders drawn by a state and called for the creation of a nation-state. After Herder, "a nation no longer simply meant a group of citizens united under a common political sovereign," his was a nationalism based on specific cultural and linguistic characteristics.[31] Friedrich Jahn's writings pushed Herder's formulation of Volk from a philosophical realm into everyday practice, calling for the founding of a pan-Germanic country in his 1808 manifesto Deutsches Volkstum, encompassing present-day Netherlands, Germany, Austria, Switzerland, and parts of Denmark and defended by a standing army of turners.[32]

Founder of the turnverein movement in Germany, Friedrich Jahn continued to have influence on the clubs in both Germany and abroad.[33] Among the many German cultural institutions available to the German-Americans living in St. Louis in 1904, the turnvereine were very active in the community. Fifteen thousand turners participated in the Turner's Day at the world's fair, an event coordinated apart from Olympic activities by the German-American community in St. Louis.[34] Given Jahn's conception of Deutschheit (being German), it is not surprising that athletes like Otto Wahle and Adolf Spinnler would have been received as "German" by the local German-American community that welcomed them to St. Louis. Reports published in the Missouri Blätter (the Sunday edition of the Westliche Post) refer to Swiss Spinnler as one of their German guests.[35] Although historians would later count him as an

American, on July 3, 1904, the *Missouri Blätter* again reported that a "German guest," this time Austrian Julius Lenhart, had won gold in the gymnastics meet.[36]

While members of the German-American community and turnvereine in St. Louis would certainly be familiar with the work of Friedrich Jahn, the lumping of athletes hailing from Switzerland and Austria into one "Germanic" group may also be explained according to the community's own ambiguous cultural and national identity. The German-American community of St. Louis "was not an isolated and enclosed ethnic ghetto," but rather formed "an ill-defined and even amorphous group of people of German ancestry who harbored certain attitudes about German culture."[37] Comprised of various generations of German-Americans, turnvereine facilitated interaction with other St. Louisians who claimed a German heritage and served as a site of German cultural preservation in the face of Americanization. Some scholars have read a form of cultural schizophrenia within German-American communities, where members "considered themselves to be loyal to the American political and economic system, but at the same time they were loyal to American cultural values only to the extent that such loyalty did not impinge upon their sympathy for and attachment to German cultural values."[38] Surrounded by Americanizing forces and values, particular or regional beliefs conflate into a united front of "German cultural values," be they Bavarian, Saxon, or in the case of athletes at the 1904 Olympics, Swiss or Austrian.

The athletes competing at the 1904 Olympics were recognized first and foremost by club affiliation. What, however, of the athletes who competed in individual events? Or of those who asserted their nationality? Adolf Spinnler, the Swiss member of the German Esslinger Turnverein, insisted that the Swiss national anthem be played in addition to the German anthem during his award ceremony.[39] How is this action, a celebration of self-identified nationality and the willful differentiation from a pan-Germanic ideal, to be read in the context of an Olympics dominated by the presence of club-organized sports?

E. J. Hobsbawm, writing on the transformation of the popular understanding of nationalism during the period 1870–1918 in *Nations and Nationalism Since 1780*, cautions that "nations do not make states and nationalisms but the other way around," and that "national identification and what it is believed to imply, can change and shift in time."[40] Until 1870 there had existed, so Hobsbawm asserted, the heterogeneous state comprised of aggregate nationalities: "[N]obody ever denied the actual multinationality or multilinguality of the oldest and most unquestioned nation-states, e.g., Britain, France, and Spain."[41] This historical situation of empire remained, however, relatively unreflected upon until the popular crystallization of new views on nationalism. It was not until "the map of Europe was, for the first—and as it turned out for the only—time redrawn according to the principle of nationality, and when the vocabulary of European nationalism came to be adopted by new movements of colonial liberation or Third World assertion," that the prioritization of multinationalities on the level of the individual forced a rethinking of nationalism within the nation-state.[42]

By analogy, the sport club to which the athletes belonged and which they represented during the third modern Olympics in St. Louis may be viewed as a governing body much like a political state, comprised of aggregate nationalities within seemingly arbitrarily drawn borders. When Adolf Spinnler made his nationality visible to the public in attendance by insisting the Swiss national anthem be played during his award ceremony, he asserted a right to recognition. This model, which privileged club affiliation over the individual athlete's national affiliation, would soon no longer hold as a transformed notion of "nationality" began to take shape in the minds of the athletes and spectators. Nationality had long been an integral facet of individual identity, yet how these nationalities and their attendant politics would relate to sport on an international scale was still in flux at the time of the 1904 Olympics.

The 1906 Intermediate Olympic Games, held in Athens, Greece serve as a turning point for the understanding of national representation in an international context at the level of the individual athletes' bodies. Although not recognized by the IOC as "official" to this day, Allen Guttmann counts 887 athlete participants representing twenty countries in the 1906 Intermediate Games in Athens.[43] For the first time, these 887 athletes engaged in a ritualized signification of nationalism that would become a "permanent, symbolic feature of the Olympic Games," namely the Parade of Nations in the opening ceremony.[44] Alexander Kitroeff notes that "[p]rior to St. Louis, nation-based teams retained their own particularisms," whereby athletes were more readily identified by club affiliation.[45] The athletes after 1906 would now march under the flag of their country from the outset of the contest, thereby exhibiting a direct link to country that would eventually overshadow athletic club affiliation. The parade spectacle would thereafter facilitate the spectator's ability to at once imagine a nation comprised of individuals but unified as a whole (team) and nations pitted against one another in contest.

In two short years following the 1904 Olympics, "[s]port was so closely tied to politics by 1908 that the Olympic host that year (Great Britain) defined 'country' as 'any territory having separate representation on the International Olympic Committee or, where no such representation exists, any territory under one and the same sovereign jurisdiction.'"[46] That the IOC would find it necessary to define what constitutes a country and how it may represent itself in an Olympic context speaks to the historical moment from which the statement stems. Kanin points to the problems of Finnish and Bohemian representation between 1906 and 1914, the Finns then a part of the Russian Empire and the Bohemians part of the vestige Austro-Hungarian Empire, necessitating official IOC guidelines to define the parameters of "country."[47] As questions of nationality and nationalism intensified on the European continent, erupting in the violence of World War I, the IOC had no choice but to address the representation of former colonies and sub-states at the end of the "age of empire." Coubertin concedes at this point in history that "The Olympic Games are becoming an affair of State. Royal Families were becoming involved and governments, too."[48] Kanin further comments: "Questions concerning sub-state Olympic participation also cropped up in 1908. Although sport representation does not always mean political independence, separate status for India and South Africa before a British Olympic audience in 1908 confirmed the change in relations within the British Empire."[49]

Recognition afforded former colonial holdings reflects on one level the mounting call for political independence of India and South Africa from the crown and on another the progressive, albeit tenuous, potential of the IOC to redress the nonrepresentation of minority nationalities within larger states. This gesture speaks to what Charles Taylor has termed "a politics of recognition," where a minority group within a nation-state demands political recognition.[50] However, recognition resonates on the individual level as well. Taylor notes, "The demand for recognition . . . is given urgency by the supposed links between recognition and identity, where this latter term designates something like a person's understanding of who they are, of the fundamental defining characteristics as a human being."[51] What then of the athletes who are meant not to represent a sovereign state or people, but rather a belief in one culture's superiority over another's? What of the athlete stripped of the right to represent his or her nationality and made to represent the racist discourse of eugenics and Social Darwinism?

Representation and "Anthropology Days"

Although ambiguity surrounding German athletic participation offers insight into the reception of European athletes by their immigrant populations in the United States, a more troubling question of national representation is revealed by examining the lowest point of the third modern Olympics: the "Anthropology Days," which consisted of athletic competitions among "primitive peoples." Where athletes of the Western world positively represented their clubs and nations, the participants of the Anthropology Days were meant to represent something altogether different. Stemming from cultures conquered by emerging nation-states and not recognized as members of sovereign nations in their own right, the participants of the Anthropology Days reflect the misrecognition of minority cultures within a pluralistic

19. Ainus from Japan competing in the archery contest. From the St. Louis Public Library Online Exhibit "Celebrating the Louisiana Purchase."

society and what would now be termed a postcolonial problem of Olympic categorization. The Anthropology Days were meant to stand in contrast to the Olympic Games, to underscore the belief that the nations competing in the Olympics would remain superior to the "savages and foreigners" competing in the "Anthropology Days." Kanin states of the Olympics:

> Political identification led to state teams, and soon no athlete could compete as an individual, or appear in Olympic events out of national uniform (these rules still apply). However, "citizenship" and "nationality" are terms synonymous in parts of Western Europe and the United States (and this unity shows signs of cracking). Using state teams as units meant that the Olympic system would be a part of Western political culture. Other peoples entering the system would be forced to conform to Western structures even if artificial state boundaries did not reflect the actual borders of ethnic identification.[52]

Therefore if an Ainu tribesman were to compete at the modern Olympics today, he would have to compete under the national sign of Japan. What transpired at the third modern Olympics was far worse, for the Ainu tribes-man competed in what constituted a dehumanizing sideshow carnival, Anthropology Days, meant to cast a garish spotlight on the perceived otherness of those who resided within the same political borders, but were viewed as belonging to another Volk or people.

An article in the World's Fair Bulletin, titled "A Novel Athletic Contest," reports: "All the tribes appeared in their native costumes and many of the events were of a special nature suited to their habits. The Pygmies engaged in a realistic mud battle; the Cocopas kicked the baseball; the Negritos climbed the fifty-foot pole; the Moros threw the javelin, and the Ainus and Patagonians engaged in archery contests."[53] Accentuating tribal affiliation, no individual names are given to the athletes in the introduction of the report. Instead, the athletes are meant to represent their tribes or people as a whole. Later in the article, the names of some competitors are listed: "The race (one mile run) was won by the Crow Indian, Black White Bear, in fairly good time, 5 minutes and 38 seconds. Yousouf Hana, a Syrian, finished second, while Letrouw, a Kaffir who had led up to the last stretch, came in third. In this race, North America finished first, Asia second, Africa third, and a South American not far behind."[54] The effect of naming the athletes in this fashion has very little to do with celebrating the talents or skills of an individual, but rather serves to further exoticize the participants. Each individual is linked to a particular ethnic group, and no athletes are given the opportunity to represent the nation-state within which they reside. The victories are pronounced in terms of continents, mirroring the denial of place, belonging, or citizenship of those differentiated, colonized groups, all the while asserting the hegemony of a perceived racial order: white, yellow, black, and so on.

The Anthropology Days were not sanctioned by the IOC, nor did its president approve. Coubertin noted: "As for that outrageous charade, it will of course lose its appeal when black men, red men, and yellow men learn to run, jump, and throw, and leave the white men behind them."[55] Nonetheless, the Anthropology Days have been viewed in relationship to the Olympic Games held in St. Louis, in part because their organizers hoped to showcase the superior ability of the athletes competing in the Olympics and to demonstrate a hierarchy of races based on athletic performance. The official results of the Anthropology Days were published in the *World's Fair Bulletin*. WJ McGee, reflecting upon the event, wrote: "I am very much pleased with the results of the meet. It demonstrates what anthropologists have long known, that the white man leads the races of the world, both physically and mentally, and in the coordination of the two which goes to make up the best specimen of manhood. . . . Of course, primitive peoples are experts in certain directions in which their habits and environments enable them to excel, but in all-around development no primitive people can rank in the same class with the Missouri boy.[56]

It is clear from McGee's assessment of participant performance that the Anthropology Days were meant to bolster a belief in white (or in this case Missourian) supremacy. This sentiment was not limited to the writings of WJ McGee but extended also to James Sullivan, chief of the Department of Physical Culture. The *Bulletin* goes on to remark that "the meet was the greatest thing of the kind in the world and could be held nowhere else but here" and that Sullivan pronounced: "'From a scientific standpoint, it proves conclusively that the average savage or foreigner is not equal to the white man. The savages are not even strong, to say nothing of skill.'"[57] Previous chapters have discussed the spurious nature of the scientific findings, but here I would like to point out that the conclusions of organizers Sullivan and McGee reveal a calculated staging of the Anthropology Days to reinforce the practice of misrepresentation of minority cultures and nationalities within the dominant discourse of the ruling powers.

The article reveals that "Old Geronimo of Apache fame," was also in attendance. The *Bulletin* notes, he "was a sullen spectator of the contests" and "stood against the railing separating the track from the field with bow and arrow in hand, and silently looked on."[58] The Negritos of the Philippines and the Native Americans exhibited at the Anthropology Days constitute what Robert Rydell has referred to in "The Culture of Imperial Abundance" as the acquired goods and commodities available to the general population in an emerging American empire.[59] They represented the lands conquered by the U.S. government. In order to uphold the "justice" of its actions, the dominant culture must maintain the appearance of its supposed superiority over the colonized people. It does so here through continued misrecognition of the individual, as Charles Taylor states: "The thesis is that our identity is partly shaped by recognition or its absence, often by the misrecognition of others, and so a person or group of people can suffer real damage, real distortion, if the people or society around them mirror back to them a confining or demeaning or contemptible picture of themselves. Nonrecognition or misrecognition can inflict harm, can be a form of oppression, imprisoning someone in a false, distorted, and reduced mode of being."[60] The participants in the Anthropology Days were indeed misrecognized, reduced to an essentialized ethnic identity and denied entrance into the signification of nation-state. No Negrito would represent the United States in the third modern Olympics.[61]

People of "inferior races" were, however, allowed to participate in some of the main Olympic events. How exactly this came about, we are not sure. Notably, two men identified as Lentauw and Yamasani participated in the marathon, although neither actually represented the country of South Africa at the time. Chroniclers have since assigned Lentauw and Yamasani South African representation, despite their ambiguous national affiliation (see Susan Brownell's afterword). African American athletes George Poage and Joseph Stadler won medals in track and field for the United States. One of two Canadian lacrosse teams to compete in the third modern Olympics was the club team Mohawk Indians of Canada. As members of clubs, Poage, Stadler, and the Mohawk Indians were likely able to compete in the Olympics because their club affiliation trumped whatever individual ethnic or racial identity might have been ascribed to them at that time. In contrast, Karl Lennartz notes that the individual athletes Lentauw and Yamasani had traveled to St.

Louis as laborers from South Africa, and they appear to have had no club affiliation in South Africa or the United States. Lennartz reveals that the names "Lentauw" or "Lehouw" are misspellings of Len Tau and that "Yamasini" actually refers to Jan Mashiani.[62] Len Tau and Jan Mashiani were the first South Africans to finish the marathon, which proved most embarrassing during apartheid and the exclusion from the Olympic movement.[63] It is difficult to reconstruct how or why Len Tau and Jan Mashiani were able to compete in the IOC-sanctioned event when neither were affiliated with clubs. The case of Len Tau presents a further complication, as he participated in both Olympic and Anthropology Day events. While competing in the marathon, Len Tau represented South Africa; while competing in the Anthropology Days, he was erroneously presented as a Zulu tribesman. Lennartz notes that he and Jan Mashiani were in fact Tswanas.[64]

The Meaning of Representation Today

The work to recover the true identity of these South African athletes by later historians speaks to a change in attitude toward minority cultures and nationalities within a multicultural society. Engaged in what Edward Said has called "contrapuntal reading," researchers strive for the "simultaneous awareness both of the metropolitan history that is narrated and of those other histories against which (and together with which) the dominating discourse acts."[65] Yet as one follows the threads of nationality, representation, and recognition, one uncovers the great paradox of this contemporary multicultural discussion on the metatextual level: to call attention to difference, be it cultural, ethnic, and so on, has at once the potential to both exclude and to celebrate the individual based upon her or his difference. Adolf Spinnler, the Swiss gymnast, celebrated his difference by requesting the Swiss national anthem be played at his awards ceremony. Len Tau, however, was not given the opportunity to control the presentation of his difference; rather, his difference was manipulated by Sullivan and McGee to propagate the specific, exclusionary message of Anthropology Days. Charles

Taylor reminds us, "With the politics of equal dignity, what is established is meant to be universally the same, an identical basket of rights and immunities; with the politics of difference, what we are asked to recognize is the unique identity of this individual or group, their distinctness from everyone else."[66] One might argue that Len Tau and Jan Mashiani's inclusion in the Olympic marathon might be read as a step in the direction of a "politics of equal dignity," but the cost in their case was the loss of a unique or distinct identity in the history books. As Olympic athletes, their names are misspelled, they are today recorded as representing a state, South Africa, which denied them the right to citizenship, and their tribal identity is incorrectly recorded. Today this loss continues, as nation-states still wrangle with the questions posed by multiculturalism. How can we maintain "this distinctness that has been ignored, glossed over, assimilated to a dominant or majority identity" without slipping down the slope to exclusion, discrimination, and misrecognition?[67]

It would be difficult to view the third Olympics as truly "international," as the list of official participants and the nations they have come to represent reveals. Though teams from other nations were not openly discouraged to compete, lack of interest abroad and the difficulties and costs associated with transatlantic travel at that time resulted in low international representation. Closer analysis of individual participation reveals contrasting functions of the Olympic contests. In the case of the German turnvereine, athletes from various Germanic and German-American backgrounds competed together in a sport spectacle to fulfill the fantasy of an "imagined" pan-Germanic community in the minds of its spectators and speak to the desire of total inclusion. In stark contrast, the athletic competitions of the Anthropology Days demonstrate the extreme exclusionary function of sport in a double refraction. Designed to pit an illusory "us" versus "them" and reinforcing a polarized worldview of colonizer and colonized, the contests of the Anthropology Days show the divisive politics of race in an American context.

Between these formulations of nationalism the third modern Olympics took place, for as the Games were held firmly within the age of American empire, the problems of cultural pluralism within political boundaries were only beginning to be recognized as potential threats to the romantic notion of an imagined homogenous national identity, "American." And in Europe, the Herderian notion of Volk was mobilizing nationalities within larger states to assert their right to political recognition.

The third modern Olympic Games in St. Louis were indeed the "American Games," not only because of the number of victories in sanctioned events, but rather because the Olympic name was appropriated to advertise state and national sporting events and to demonstrate American athletic prowess to the nations and conquered peoples in attendance. The Anthropology Days stand as a dark testament to colonial expansion, its justification resting upon pseudoscientific thought. Previous American involvement and athletic success in the Olympic Games of Athens and Paris had given Coubertin hope that the first Games hosted by America would be a greater success than those of the Paris Exposition. The IOC's desired theme of international reconciliation was, however, lost in America. Coubertin noted: "I wanted Olympism, after its return from the excursion to utilitarian America, to don once again the sumptuous toga, woven of art and philosophy, in which I had always wanted to clothe her."[68] The United States had recognized the role international competition could play in the representation of a nation and used sport to demonstrate and promote its own imagined image of power and colonization at the 1904 Louisiana Exposition in St. Louis.

Notes

1. Primm, Lion of the Valley, 386.
2. Primm, Lion of the Valley, 386.
3. Kanin, Political History of the Olympic Games, 31.
4. Mallon, 1904 Olympic Games, 11.
5. In 1904 the Olympics did not yet represent the pinnacle of sporting events. To many, they were still considered an oddity.

6. All translations by the author.

7. Lennartz, *Beteiligung Deutschlands*, 107.

8. Lennartz, *Beteiligung Deutschlands*, 112.

9. Lennartz, *Beteiligung Deutschlands*, 84.

10. Lennartz, *Beteiligung Deutschlands*, 87.

11. Lennartz, *Beteiligung Deutschlands*, 86.

12. Lennartz, *Beteiligung Deutschlands*, 131.

13. According to Lennartz. He cites participation by the following number of athletes: "10 Turnern, 2 Leichtathleten, 7 Schwimmern, und einem Fechter" (*Beteiligung Deutschlands*, 131).

14. Lennartz, *Spiele der III. Olympiade*, 235–36.

15. Lennartz, *Spiele der III. Olympiade*, 212.

16. Mező, *Modern Olympic Games*, 72.

17. Lennartz, *Beteiligung Deutschlands*, 116.

18. Lennartz, *Spiele der III. Olympiade*, 236.

19. According to Allen Guttmann's chapter "The Baron's Dream" in *Olympics: A History*.

20. Guttmann, *Olympics: A History*, 1.

21. Kanin, *Political History of the Olympic Games*, 1–2.

22. From Benedict Anderson's *Imagined Communities*.

23. The *Missouri Saturday Republic* reported that gymnastic events had been held, but failed to ever print the results. In contrast, the *Westliche Post* printed daily updates on Olympic events and athletes (July 2, 1904).

24. According to David Detjen, 184,404 of the total 687,029 inhabitants of St. Louis in 1910 claimed a direct relationship to Germany, either by birth or parentage (*Germans in Missouri*, 9).

25. Detjen notes, "In 1910, the *Westliche Post* . . . had a circulation of thirty thousand in the city, while the Sunday edition of the paper, called the *Missouri Blaetter*, had a circulation of sixty thousand" (*Germans in Missouri*, 12).

26. The *Missouri Saturday Republican* reports "The results of yesterday's exercises will not be announced until today . . . ," without ever reporting the results in subsequent editions (July 2, 1904).

27. *Westliche Post*, May 29, 1904.

28. *Westliche Post*, June 30, 1904.

29. The *Westliche Post* ran articles covering all events associated with the world's fair, beginning in May 1904, for the duration of the exhibition, on page five of every edition.

30. Blickle, *Heimat*, 51.

31. Barnard, *Herder's Social and Political Thought*, 59.

32. Jahn, *Deutsches Volkstum*, 90.

33. Testament to which is the statue of Friedrich Ludwig Jahn that stands to this day

in Forest Park, site of the 1904 World's Fair.

34. Detjen, *Germans in Missouri*, 15.

35. *Missouri Blätter*, July 3, 1904.

36. *Missouri Blätter*, July 3, 1904.

37. Detjen, *Germans in Missouri*, 6.

38. Detjen, *Germans in Missouri*, 23.

39. Lennartz, *Spiele der III. Olympiade*, 236.

40. Hobsbawm, *Nations and Nationalism*, 10, 11.

41. Hobsbawm, *Nations and Nationalism*, 33.

42. Hobsbawm, *Nations and Nationalism*, 3.

43. Guttmann, *Olympics: A History*, 27.

44. See Kitroeff's chapter in this volume, "Greece and the 1904 'American' Olympics," 14.

45. Kitroeff, "Greece and the 1904 'American' Olympics," 8.

46. Kanin, *Political History of the Olympic Games*, 27.

47. Kanin, *Political History of the Olympic Games*, 27.

48. Coubertin, *Olympism: Selected Writings*, 463.

49. Kanin, *Political History of the Olympic Games*, 35.

50. Taylor, "Politics of Recognition," 25–73.

51. Taylor, "Politics of Recognition," 25.

52. Kanin, *Political History of the Olympic Games*, 27.

53. LPEC—World's Fair Bulletin, "Novel Athletic Contest," 50.

54. LPEC—World's Fair Bulletin, "Novel Athletic Contest," 50.

55. Mallon, *1904 Olympic Games*, 12.

56. McGee, "Novel Athletic Contest," 50.

57. McGee, "Anthropology," 50.

58. McGee, "Anthropology," 50.

59. Rydell, "Culture of Imperial Abundance," 191–216.

60. Taylor, "Politics of Recognition," 25.

61. The United States appears to have had an ambiguous approach to its territories, allowing some to have their own Olympic representation, while denying it to others. Kanin notes that in 1908, for example, Hawaiian Duke Kahanamoku was made a member of the American Olympic swim team, thereby denying Hawaii separate Olympic representation on the IOC. Puerto Rico, in contrast, would eventually have an Olympic team of its own, which served "to rally advocates of political independence" (Kanin, *Political History of the Olympic Games*, 35).

62. Lennartz (*Spiele der III. Olympiade*, 156). Lennartz writes "Mashiani" as Mashianu," but this appears to be a mistake since the original research by van der Merwe reconstructed the name as Mashiani. See the discussion in Parezo's chapter of this volume.

63. Lennartz, *Spiele der III. Olympiade*, 156.

64. Lennartz, *Spiele der III. Olympiade*, 156.
65. Said, *Culture and Imperialism*, 51.
66. Taylor, "Politics of Recognition," 38.
67. Taylor, "Politics of Recognition," 38.
68. Guttmann, *Olympics: A History*, 28.

Chapter 8. Greece and the 1904 "American" Olympics

ALEXANDER KITROEFF

The leaders of the small Greek delegation to the St. Louis Olympics of 1904 viewed the Games through an ethnocentric and nationalist lens. The so-called revival of the ancient Greek Olympic Games and the decision to hold the first modern Games in Athens, in 1896, suddenly thrust Greece into the international limelight. The Greek hosts had failed in their bid to keep the Games permanently in Athens every four years. But a compromise with the International Olympic Committee (IOC) paved the way for Athens to organize "interim" Games, to be held in between the quadrennial regularly scheduled Olympics. The decision was taken over the objections of the head of the IOC, Pierre de Coubertin, and he retaliated by ensuring that those interim Games would never be granted the status of an official Olympics.[1] The first of these interim Games (which turned out to be the only ones, because Greece was unable to continue to hold them) was scheduled for 1906, two years after the St. Louis Games. Therefore the Greek sporting establishment was far more concerned with planning for the interim Games of 1906 than it was with participating in the 1904 Olympics. Nonetheless, as far as the Greeks were concerned, the St. Louis Games were an important test of the IOC's concept of rotating the Games among international venues that had prevailed over the Greek view that the Games ought to be held permanently in Greece. Thus, the leaders of the Greek delegation in St. Louis looked at those Games in order to elicit an affirmation of their own particular perspective on the Olympics. The initiatives they took in framing the organization of the interim Games of 1906, generally considered as an important turning point in the history of the modern Olympics, echoed their reactions to what they witnessed in St. Louis.

The Greek View of the Olympics

Greek attitudes to physical exercise and sport in the nineteenth century were colored by a very strong sense of a cultural continuity between modern and ancient Greece. This claim was one of the cornerstones of modern Greek identity from the time Greece gained political independence in 1830. That the modern Greeks were the heirs of classical Greece was a concept that legitimized Greece in the eyes of the European powers and offered the Greeks themselves a sense of national worth that offset any sense of inferiority at their small country's obvious shortcomings in relation to the more developed European states. Public life and cultural practices, therefore, were permeated by recourse to modern Greece's ancient heritage.[2] This was also true of the value placed on physical exercise and sport. The socioeconomically developed European nations were transforming informal games into a form of discipline and socialization into the norms of an industrialized society, and in some cases they promoted physical exercise as a way of training young men for military service. In contrast, Greece saw physical exercise and sporting activities as a way of affirming its ties with the classical past and celebrating its heritage. This was because although Greece became an independent sovereign state relatively early by European standards, in 1830, unlike Western Europe, it did not undergo the type of industrialization and social changes that helped generate a rationalized and utilitarian sporting culture. Nor did the country's dominant religion, Greek Orthodoxy, experience the type of embrace of physical exercise that Protestantism did with the rise of "muscular Christianity." Greek Orthodoxy's reflective and metaphysical characteristics militated against any such development. Accordingly, organized sports made their appearance in the late nineteenth century in Greece as part of a social trend that produced a range of cultural associations led by intellectuals and which is considered as the emergence of a "public sphere" in Athens, the country's capital city.[3]

Greece's own revival of the ancient Olympics, in the form of the Zappas Olympics, named after Evangelis Zappas, a Greek diaspora merchant who provided the funds, reflected the Greek sense that modern sport was in practice an imitation of ancient sports and in terms of their cultural meaning a celebration of ancient Greece. The Zappas Olympics, held four times between 1859 and 1889, included a range of sports, many of which were "ancient" sports, such as throwing the javelin, the discus — according to the way it was depicted by artistic representations of athletes in antiquity — and the stone throw. All of these were not considered as sports in other countries but the Greeks considered them essential elements in their own revival of the Games. In short, while Coubertin would conceive his revival of the Olympics as a celebration of sport colored by ancient traditions, "the Zappas Olympics were a celebration of ancient traditions colored by sport."[4]

Greek sporting culture's reliance on the "ancient connection" that formed part of Greek identity meant that it was implicated if only indirectly in the country's nationalist program that aimed to incorporate within Greece's borders outlying areas inhabited by Greek populations. This plan of national unification, known as the "Great Idea," shaped Greek political life through the end of World War I.[5]

The Baron de Coubertin's revival of the Olympics and his inclusion of Greece by way of holding the first modern Games in Athens helped crystallize the ties between Greek sport and nationalism in the minds of the Greek intellectual and political elite. Hosting such an international event in its capital city offered Greece a chance to earn prestige and to showcase its recent economic development before the eyes of the world. For a small country whose nationalist goals relied on the goodwill of the Great Powers, this was a rare opportunity. The royal family spearheaded the Greek initiative to begin preparations and helped overcome the political naysayers. With the great majority of the population of Athens rallying to the cause, and with a serious commitment of government resources and donations from the wealthy Greek merchant diaspora, the 1896 Games were a success. They were also a celebration of Greek nationalism. The hosts decided that the opening day of the Games would be March 25, which was Greek Independence Day.[6] In his speech on the opening day, Crown Prince Constantine evoked national pride and Greece's sense that holding the Games in Athens affirmed Greece's claim to be the heir of ancient Greece. He was echoing what was by now an impressive array of Greek intellectuals who had portrayed the hosting of the Games in Athens as proof of modern Greece's ancient heritage.[7] His father, King George I, concluded his formal announcement of the opening of the Games with the cry "Long Live the nation! Long Live the Greek people!" These are examples of how Greek national pride suffused the Athens Olympics of 1896. This peaked when the Greek Speros Louis won the marathon race and culminated with the king's proposal, at the conclusion of the events, that the Games should be held permanently in Greece because they were, after all, an ancient Greek institution.[8]

Coubertin's rejection of the Greek proposal is well known and has been well documented, but it is worth mentioning here that he also did not share the Greek view that the Olympics could be considered as a national institution either by invocations of continuity with the ancient past or by dint of hosting the Games. Coubertin's philhellenism was rooted in the early-nineteenth-century romantic notion that the landscape of modern Greece could evoke the "spirit of the place" and embodied ancient traditions. But according to this romanticist perspective the "landscape" was not per se modern Greece or its people, a more literal view of antiquity that was the foundation of the modern Greek perspective on the ancient past.[9] By the same token, Coubertin did not share the type of nationalism that underpinned the understanding of the past and of sport evident in the views of the Greek intellectual and political leaders at the time. Those views conformed to the vision that many nationalities shared in what is known as the age of nationalism, but Coubertin's ideas were quite different. Coubertin espoused a unique form

20. Nikolaos Georgantas, shown throwing the discus "Greek style" in the 1906 Athens Olympic Games, in which he placed second in both the "Greek style" and "free style" discus. From J. Sullivan, ed., "The Olympic Games of 1906 at Athens," 88.

of humanist internationalism that acknowledged the existence of different countries and national characteristics but did not give these the precedence accorded to them by nationalist thinkers.[10] He was an internationalist who embraced patriotism but not nationalism. In the words of his biographer, John MacAloon, Coubertin believed the Olympics were a venue at which "real cultural difficulties were discovered and celebrated" leading "foreigners to true experiences of common humanity."[11]

The Greeks also viewed sports in general, not only the Olympics, in national terms. Several of the main figures in the Greek athletic establishment suggested that if the modern Games were a revival of the ancient Games then it behooved athletes to revive and imitate the ways athletes used to compete in the ancient era. This entailed pressure to include "ancient" sports such as the stone throw and to adopt the so-called classical style of discus throwing, and it absorbed a great deal of energy within the fledgling Greek sports movement and, moreover, caused friction between the purists and the more Western- oriented administrators who were less enthusiastic about imitating ancient Greek styles. This split notwithstanding, there emerged a conventional wisdom around the 1900s that asserted that sports tournaments that included ancient sports or styles were, by definition, more "Greek" while similar events that did not include such sports were considered "foreign." This was part of a more general pattern of labeling various athletic systems and practices according to their country of origin. Gymnastics, for example was described by sports officials and the Greek newspaper writers as belonging to either the "German" or the "Swedish" system.[12]

Looking Ahead to St. Louis

The ethnocentric and nationalist Greek sporting culture shaped the country's preparations for the St. Louis Olympics. The most obvious sign was how little interest was generated in sending a strong team, indeed almost any team at all. Four years earlier, Greece had sent only five athletes to the 1900 Games in Paris at a time when it was only gradually abandoning its claim as the rightful permanent host of the Games. On the eve of the 1904 Olympics the Greeks were far too focused on the forthcoming interim Games of 1906 in Athens to spend too much time over their participation in St. Louis. On both those occasions the Greek sporting establishment evinced a reluctance to become fully invested in Games being held outside Greece. An article in a Greek sports publication, the only one of its kind, reflected the grudging acceptance of the Paris Games in Greece. It mentioned that athletic games would take place as part of the 1900 world's fair in Paris organized by the fair's executive committee, adding that those games would be considered part of the Olympic Games of which the first had taken place in Athens.[13] In the end Greece participated with only five athletes, two of whom happened to be studying in Paris. That was a time when the Greeks considered their claim to hold the Games permanently to be still viable. The government had established the Greek Olympic Committee in 1899; its official name was "Committee of the Olympic Games" and one of its responsibilities according to its government-approved charter was to organize the Olympic Games every four years.[14]

By the time the 1904 Olympics came around, the IOC and the Greeks had struck the compromise that allowed Greece to organize interim Games, so attitudes toward the St. Louis Games were slightly less dismissive though hardly enthusiastic. What little coverage existed of the Games echoed the national perspective. For example, the reputable Athens daily *Hestia* began referring to the St. Louis Games as the "American Games" in its reports of the Greek preparations in 1904.[15] The preparations themselves were not going very well. The newly constituted Olympic Committee was dragging its feet so it fell to the major track- and-field club, Panhellenios, to plan for St. Louis. Initially, the club envisioned sending five athletes to St. Louis, a small number equal to that Greece sent to Paris four years earlier. By all accounts, Panhellenios had difficulties raising funds to cover the travel expenses of the five athletes. After passing the hat around, it collected funds from a variety of sources including the Ministry of Education, the Municipality of Athens, the Hellenic Olympic Committee, the Greek Track and Field and Gymnastics Federation, the National Bank of Greece, the Bank of Athens, the Athens Stock Exchange, and a private donor. The sum of 3,225 drachmas was sufficient for the travel expenses of only two or three athletes and ultimately only two of them made the trip. The only reliable source provides no information about why the Greek delegation was so small. There seems a stark contrast to sending two athletes to the United States when, in the same year, 11,343 Greek citizens immigrated to the United States.[16]

It was, in fact, thanks to the presence of Greek immigrants in the United States that the total number of Greek athletes participating in the St. Louis Games was fifteen, because thirteen Greek Americans participated as part of the Greek team. They were enlisted thanks to the efforts of the Greek Consular authorities in the United States.

The decision to include Greek immigrants living in the United States as part of the Greek team is another sign of the national-colored attitudes to sports. It is true that at the time most Greek immigrants were recent arrivals who retained their Greek citizenship and maintained close ties to Greece.

21. Seated (*from left*): D. Jannopoulo, Greek consul in St. Louis; H. E M. Pasmezoglu, Greece, Secretary. Standing (*from left*): Perikles Kakousis and Nicholas Georgantas [spelling in original caption], medal winners from Greece. From C. Lucas, *The Olympic Games 1904*, photo insert after p. 22.

Yet it is unlikely that the Greek Consular authorities who located these athletes stopped to consider such details. The charter establishing the Olympic Committee in Greece called for the establishment of annual track- and-field games known as the "Panhellenic Games" and these were open to Greeks living outside Greece. This was irrespective of their citizenship, a moot point since Greek nationality was determined in large part on the basis of culture and, in the case of certain areas, those lands were claimed as part of Greece anyway in the context of the "Great Idea."

Later accounts of those early games have confirmed the nationalist connection. Mihail Rinopoulos, a member of the Greek Olympic Committee from 1924 through 1938 and its general secretary from 1924 to 1935, wrote in 1940 that the early Panhellenic Games "were not merely athletic games, they were games of a strong national character, at which all the occupied Greek lands" were present "in the capital of free Greece."[17]

The inclusion of Greek immigrants into the Greek team participating in St. Louis was successful and unproblematic in the sense that there are no Greek reports of objections on the part of the organizers. This must have certainly encouraged the Greeks to go forward and apply the model they had adopted at the Panhellenic Games in the interim 1906 Olympics. In 1906, athletes and teams made up of Greeks living in the Ottoman Empire and Egypt—where there existed a large Greek community—participated as Greeks, irrespective of their citizenship, although officially they were considered representatives of their city.

This was a time when national affiliations were still in flux. Prior to St. Louis, nation-based teams retained their own particularisms, as, for example, the Americans who competed in Athens in 1896 considering themselves members of the Boston Athletic Association and were cheered by cries of "B-A-A!" by their fellow Americans.[18] By 1904 the organizers regarded national teams in cultural-national terms; and it is not surprising, given the hostile attitudes to southeastern European immigrants, that the American authorities allowed the immigrants to participate in the team of their homeland. This was the first step toward making the teams conform primarily to nationality *and* citizenship that became the norm in the period between the two World Wars.

Greek Reflections on the St. Louis Games

Greek observers greeted the conclusion of the St. Louis Olympics with a flurry of admiring and laudatory comments. The 1904 Games appeared to confirm the Greek view of sports, and the lessons they drew clearly encouraged them in applying those views to the organization of the interim Games in Athens two years later.

The Greeks were reacting more to the organizational aspects of the Games rather than to the performance of the Greek athletes, which was more than satisfactory. Pericles Kakouses came first in weightlifting, and Nikolaos Georgantas came second in the discus throw. There was elation in Greece over those results, especially since Georgantas had gone up against a very strong field of American "champions," Martin Sheridan, Ralph Rose, and John Flanagan. Demetrios Veloules, one of ten Greek immigrants who took part in the marathon, placed fifth out of a relatively strong field of thirty-two. Christos Zekhouritis came in tenth and Andrew Oikonomou fourteenth.[19] The head of the Greek delegation, Panhellenios Club member Vaselios Antonopoulos returned to Athens and submitted a report to the Olympic Committee singing the praises of the Games, which made a great impression.

In a work published much later, Ioannes Chrysafes explained how the Greeks perceived the St. Louis Games. Chrysafes was an important figure in Greek sports up until his death in 1932, and was the proponent of the "purist" tendency that favored the strictest possible adherence to sports as they were practiced by the ancient Greeks, and he combined this with an admiration for the Swedish gymnastic tradition. He was also a committed Greek nationalist and had fought as a volunteer in a Greek uprising in the Ottoman-controlled island of Crete in 1896, returning briefly to Athens to attend the Olympic Games. The next year he fought in the short-lived Greco-Turkish war. After that he dedicated his life to promoting Greek sports, and

22. Perikles Kakousis wins the weightlifting competition; R. Tate McKenzie is the judge on the right. From C. Lucas, *The Olympic Games 1904*, photo insert after p. 76.

he advocated including the so-called classical tradition as much possible in sports events in Greece and also in the Olympic Games.[20]

Chrysafes "read" Antonopoulos's report of the St. Louis Games as an affirmation of the Greek sporting culture, its attachment to ancient Greece and its nationalist dimension. Chrysafes was also predisposed to a certain degree of admiration of all things American, something that was prevalent among many in relatively underdeveloped southern and Eastern European countries, whose emigrants returned with stories of wonder and awe at the achievements of the United States in the late nineteenth and early twentieth centuries. So when Antonopoulos reported that the Games had been run extremely efficiently, Chrysafes saw the organization of the Games as "most practical and truly wise in its conception" and "admirable" in the way it was enacted because the Games were run by experts. Chrysafes goes on to write that in his opinion "the American organization was technically far superior to the two previous ones," which included the Athens Games. Demonstrating the elitism of Greek sports administrators, who were all connected to the

University of Athens, Chrysafes noted that three-quarters of the members of the various committees running the St. Louis Games were made up of "personalities from the university world."[21]

Yet Chrysafes's high opinion of the 1904 Games was not due to what he considered a smooth and sophisticated level of organization—as a purist, his main concern was with the reflection of the ancient spirit of the Games in their modern revival. And this he saw in abundance in the 1904 Olympics. Chrysafes believed that despite the criticisms leveled by Europeans, the St. Louis Olympics were a watershed in the history of the modern Olympics—in contrast to the Paris Games that he believed had distanced themselves from the original neo-Olympic direction. Chrysafes took issue with Carl Diem's critique of the 1904 Games that appeared in Diem's report of the 1912 Stockholm Games.[22] The Greek sports administrator discounted the negative influence of the world's fair on the Games that bothered Diem and other European observers, whom he did not mention by name. He believed that despite the coincidence of the two, the Games had existed autonomously and were not negatively affected by the fair.[23]

In Chrysafes's view there was a great deal about the Games that was praiseworthy, and most of it, inevitably, related to his own strong belief that the modern Olympics should echo the spirit of the ancient Olympics. Perhaps the best example for Chrysafes was the predominance of American college student athletes at the Games. This he saw as an echo of the ancient Greek pedagogical ideals of creating healthy and strong persons, balanced and coordinated, both physically and mentally. Chrysafes noted with great admiration and pleasure the prominence of American students at the St. Louis Games. He saw their presence as the outcome of the encouragement of "American intellectuals who are inspired by ancient Greek pedagogical ideals."[24] Chrysafes drove the point home further on in his discussion of results of each event at the St. Louis Games. He noted that the greatest number of American winners were students and reiterated his belief that American universities bred all-around persons in the tradition of the ancient Greek pedagogical ideals.[25]

Chrysafes was also full of praise for the Olympic Lecture Course that took place in conjunction with the Games. He believed that the nineteen lectures, along with an exhibition that displayed the progress of physical education in American schools and universities, were a more practical and effective showcasing of the athletic idea than the international congress that had taken place in Paris in 1900.[26]

Most surprising of all perhaps is that both Antonopoulos and Chrysafes regarded the "Anthropology Days" in a positive light. While Antonopoulos mentioned them without comment, Chrysafes seized the opportunity to draw analogies with ancient Greece. He regarded the inferiority of the performances of the "wild tribesmen" in comparison with the Western athletes as corresponding to the superiority of the ancient Greeks over the barbarians. The ancient Greeks, he noted, had reached perfection through training, as had the Western athletes, and in both those cases training overshadowed brute force. Thus for Chrysafes, the Anthropology Days confirmed the validity of ancient Greek sporting practices. Chrysafes was surprised at the criticism leveled by European observers over the inclusion of the Anthropology Days, which he believed was clearly a "scientific experiment" carried out under ideal circumstances.[27]

Chrysafes's unambiguous though selective praise of the St. Louis Games, including the Anthropology Days, reflected the narrow perspective of the Greek intelligentsia that was focused in maintaining the principle of continuity between modern and ancient Greece. Greece was not a colonial power, nor was it the victim of modern colonialism. In general, then, attitudes toward colonized peoples were either indifferent or tended to side with the colonizers as a sign of Greece's own civilized and developed status, which was not always conceded by the more developed world. To regard the contrast between American athletes and the "tribesmen" in terms of the relationship of the ancient Greeks to the barbarians was to put the best face possible on a topic that Greek intellectuals preferred to avoid as they distanced themselves from certain Western anthropological concepts at the turn of the century.

This attitude dates back to the 1830s when Jakob Philipp Fallmerayer, a scholar of Tyrolean origin, disputed the modern Greek claim of ancestral continuity with classical Greece. Although Fallmerayer's evidence was historical and cultural rather than genetic, his views were formulated in such a way as to suggest that the population of Greece at the time was of entirely non-Greek racial origin. This constituted an attack on the core element of the identity of newly independent Greece, and it elicited a sharp reaction that included the launching of Greek folklore studies and the production of a series of studies furnishing cultural and historical data designed to verify Greek continuity with the ancient past and to refute the theories "of the German historian."[28] In what was a strategic collective decision, Greek intellectuals limited their engagement with racial and evolutionary anthropological theories, preferring instead to focus on ethnographies and folklore studies, which they considered the most reliable means to shore up the assertion of modern continuity with the ancient past.[29]

Chrysafes, though not a folklorist himself, would have been familiar with their work because it was so central to Greek intellectual and public life at the turn of the century, and by the same token he would have been uncomfortable with concepts of evolutionary anthropology. There were certain Greek militant, nationalist spokesmen who described the Greeks as a civilized nation pitted against the barbarism of the Turks—this was the era when Greece was claiming that historically Greek territories and peoples under Ottoman rule should be incorporated within Greece. Yet by the turn of the century theirs was a decidedly minority voice, increasingly drowned out by less derogatory and even positive views of the "Turk."[30] Under those circumstances, the inclusion of a Turk and a Syrian in the Anthropology Days would have been likely to cause great unease for Chrysafes and the rest of the Greek delegation. The Turks after all were neighbors of the Greeks so their "orientalization" opened the possibility that the Greek might suffer the same fate, conjuring up images of an unwelcome return of the Fallmerayer thesis. Moreover, debates over the racial purity and stock of incoming southeastern European immigrants in the United States included the Greeks.[31] It is unclear how much of this would be known to the Athens-based sports officials, but the Greek diplomatic representatives were monitoring those exchanges—all the more reason, therefore, not to dwell too extensively on the potential meanings of the Anthropology Days.

Greek attitudes toward the United States, finally, may have also contributed to the Greeks not reacting negatively to the Anthropology Days. We have already seen that the Greek press described the St. Louis Olympics as the "American Games" as a function of the national lenses through which the Greeks saw sporting activities. The wider cultural connotation of "American" in Greece at that time was certainly positive. Stories describing the wealth of the United States by the Greek immigrants who began arriving there in the 1890s, and earlier newspaper and magazine articles describing the wonders of America in the post–Civil War "Gilded Age," created a favorable impression on Greek public opinion. The New World, many Greeks believed, was a rich land in which many wondrous but also strange things happened.[32]

From St. Louis 1904 to Athens 1906

The conventional Greek master narrative of the history of the Olympic Games describes the interim Games of 1906 as the moment Greece saved the Olympics following the dismal failures of the Games in Paris in 1900 and St. Louis in 1904.[33] It is based on the generally accepted all-around success of the 1906 Games in terms of participation, attendance, and overall organization. Several non-Greek accounts echo the view that the interim Games rescued the newly established institution of the Olympics.[34] Other non-Greek accounts, however, ignore the interim Games, in part because they have never been recognized as "official" by the IOC, and describe the next regular Games, held in London in 1908, as the turning point in the fortunes of the Games.[35]

Going beyond the question of how "official" or not the 1906 Olympics were, we can certainly point to a different approach to the Olympics compared to the St. Louis Games, one that was reflected later on in the London Olympics of 1908. The differences between the ways in which the 1904 and the 1906 Games were organized go beyond the obvious point of the 1906 Games not being part of a world fair. They also entail the removal of the Anthropology Days and their colonial division of civilized and uncivilized peoples and, at the same time, the reinforcement of the national dimension of the Games that was at the core of the Greek understanding of the Olympics. Both those developments occurred largely through the initiative of the Greek organizers of the interim Games, who enjoyed considerable autonomy in planning the Games because Coubertin was unhappy about holding them and this prevented the IOC from becoming too closely involved.

The removal of the Anthropology Days was perhaps inevitable following the criticisms leveled by Coubertin and other European observers. But Greece's own lack of engagement with the evolutionary categories underlying the Anthropology Days, its "neutral" position toward imperial conquests and civilizing missions, and the absence of a world's fair, which was, at the time, a venue showcasing Western "progress," also contributed to keeping the Games focused on athletic competition. To be sure, there was a surfeit of references to the classical past, as was the case with the first Games in 1896, but this reinforced rather than weakened the athletic character of the Games—they were after all supposed to be a revival of ancient sports. And as we have seen, Chrysafes saw enough echoes of the classical tradition in St. Louis to encourage him and the other Greek sports administrators to emphasize the ties with antiquity in 1906.

The emphasis on the ties with classical Greece was, as we have seen, connected with national identity in the minds of Greek administrators, and this was reflected in the preparations for the Games. Concerned about its ability to raise funds for the Games as well as attracting enough competitors from abroad, the Greek government established "preparatory committees" abroad. Wherever there was a large and wealthy Greek element, such as in Alexandria, Cairo, and Istanbul, those committees were asked to raise funds for the Games in an appeal to the patriotism of the Greeks in those cities that unfolded in a markedly nationalistic climate. In other countries, such as the United States, for example, the committees worked toward raising the awareness of the athletic community about the forthcoming Athens Games, toward generating national pride about the country's participation, and also toward raising funds to help the athletes travel to Athens. The "American Committee of the Olympian Games at Athens, Greece, 1906" was especially active thanks to the efforts of James Sullivan, one of the country's leading sports administrators.[36]

The most important evidence of the national concept of the Olympics that the Greeks applied to the 1906 Games was the first-ever parade of national teams marching behind their flags at the opening ceremony.[37] Also for the first time the flags of the athletes placed second and third were raised alongside the winner's national flag at the awards ceremony.[38] In the first Parade of Nations, the Germans marched first and the Greek hosts brought up the rear. The parade would be repeated in London in 1908 and became a permanent, symbolic feature of the Olympic Games. Coubertin, who was in Athens in 1906, wrote in his *Olympic Memoirs* that the first parade of teams marching behind their national flags took place at the London Games of 1908.[39] But the first time was in Athens in 1906 and there is good reason to credit the organizers of the interim Games with the idea to introduce a formal Parade of Nations. Prior to the 1906 occasion, parades of athletes had routinely taken place in Greece during the national track-and-field tournaments, the Panhellenic Games, with domestic clubs marching alongside the various Greek clubs based in the Ottoman Empire. The organizers evidently regarded the parade as proof that the Panhellenic Games included Greeks from within Greece as well as the lands outside its borders that were considered culturally Greek, an affirmation that this event conformed to the nationalist desiderata of unifying the Greeks of the Ottoman Empire with Greece.

Parades had been a staple of nationalist celebrations since the French Revolution and became common practice in Greece beginning with the commemorations of the fiftieth anniversary of the Greek revolution, in 1871.[40]

23. Entrance of the royal party into the Panathenaic Stadium in the opening ceremonies of the 1906 Athens Olympic Games. From J. Sullivan, ed., "The Olympic Games of 1906 at Athens," 58.

Their incorporation into the Panhellenic Games, a celebration of the unity of Greeks, is no surprise. The vision of a "Greater Greece" may not have been feasible in practical terms, but it could be achieved symbolically by including all of its constituents in a parade of athletes. Several years earlier, Chrysafes had been angry at a Greek administrator in charge of the Panhellenic Games who had prevented the parade being held because that was not the custom in Britain, where he had spent some time observing sporting practices. And naturally, a Parade of Nations figured as part of the opening ceremonies of the 1906 Games. That the Greek hosts saw these Games as a "Greek," and therefore nationally colored, event is no surprise. Nationalism, according to George Mosse, one of its most perceptive analysts, "made symbols the essence of its politics."[41]

The "nationalization" of the 1906 Olympics by the Greek organizers was also evident in their decision to officially recognize certain competitors and teams that can be best be described, in present terms, as representing ethnic groups in the Ottoman Empire and, in the case of the Irish, the British Empire. In another extension of the practices of the Panhellenic Games, the Greek Olympic Committee had held Greek trials in Alexandria, Egypt, as well as in Istanbul and Smyrna, which were part of the Ottoman Empire. Thus, in 1906, aside from the Greek team, teams competed that were made up of Greeks from the Ottoman Empire, Egypt (a semi-independent region of the Ottoman Empire under informal British control), Cyprus (a British colony), and two soccer teams from two cities within the Ottoman Empire — Thessaloniki, which was made up by Greeks, and Izmir (Smyrna), which included players who were listed as being Armenian, British, and French. The Irish athletes who were part of the British teams were also listed both together and separately from the British teams.[42]

Finally, one can get a better sense of Greece's role in this shift from the Anthropology Days of 1904 to the Parade of Nations in 1906 by examining Coubertin's views on the role of the nation in the Olympics during that time. We have already noted that Coubertin regarded the nation as an element contributing to a humanistically understood internationalism, and that he reacted positively to the Parade of Nations in the London Games of 1908. Had he been able to bring himself to acknowledge the contribution of the "interim" Games in 1906 he may have remarked positively on the Parade of Nations there, as well. Nevertheless, the initiative of the Greek hosts in 1906 conformed to Coubertin's positive views of the role of the nation in the Olympics because the Parade of Nations evoked the value that Coubertin placed on internationalism, a crucial element of the Olympic movement.

The parade itself also conformed to Coubertin's strong preference for pomp and circumstance surrounding administrative as well as sporting events that were part of the Olympics. In general, advocates of the Olympic Movement and of nationalism have shared a strong sense of ceremonial practice and ritual performance designed to produce a meaningful spectacle.[43] One can think of the shift from the Anthropology days of 1904 to the Parade of Nations of 1906 as a realization of this affinity that has been present ever since.

To be sure, beyond its ritual form, the "nationalization" of the Games soon raised several difficulties, obliging Coubertin to adopt a less starry-eyed view that nations competing in sports join in a spirit of internationalism.

The London Games of 1908 witnessed a great deal of friction between the British hosts and the United States team. The British accused the Americans of overeager competitiveness and the Americans responded by claiming that the British judges were blatantly biased against their athletes.[44] Coubertin had to acknowledge that the grandiose excitement surrounding the Games gave rise to "a few short sharp clashes" but he added, "even so, the Games do not seem to have suffered."[45] Another problem had to do with the definition of a nation and its eligibility to compete. This became especially acute at the time of the 1912 Stockholm Olympics when nationalist rivalries increased, a reflection of rising tension in Europe on the eve of World War I. Coubertin sought to defuse the situation by offering his own sporting-based definition of nationalism. He suggested the "undeniable existence of a 'sports geography,' quite distinct from a political geography," and this, he believed, justified the inclusion of teams of nations that lacked political independence over the objections of independent sovereign nation-states.[46]

Many of the particular issues that plagued the 1912 Games would be resolved thanks to the collapse of the Austro-Hungarian Empire and the emergence of several nation-states in its place following the end of the Great War, but other national rivalries would emerge in the future. The Olympics, by becoming "nationalized" in practice, reflected Coubertin's vision of competing nations with a broader framework of human internationalism.

There is a touch of irony in the current Greek conventional wisdom that considers the interim Games in Athens in 1906 as having saved the Olympic Movement from the near oblivion it was consigned to following the Games in Paris in 1900 and St. Louis in 1904. In contrast to the present official Greek narrative a closer look at Greek reactions at the time indicates that Chrysafes and the other Greek Olympic administrators felt empowered to "Hellenize" the 1906 Games in the wake of the so-called American Games.[47] To be sure, as the Anglo-American friction in 1912 demonstrated, the spread of nationalism on the eve of World War I would have caught up with the Olympics sooner or later. The Greeks were the precursors of that trend, in a somewhat similar way to their more militant nationalistic Balkan neighbors operating in Sarajevo during the Archduke's fatal visit there in 1914, who are said to have triggered World War I.

Greece's role was at least partially scripted by Coubertin, who saw modern Greece's involvement in the early phase of the revival of the Olympics as a legitimating factor given that modern Greece was generally regarded as the heir of the ancient Greek civilization that generated the Olympic Games. The Greeks accepted that role because it corresponded to and indeed confirmed the way in which they regarded themselves, namely as heirs to that civilization, thanks to a core belief in the cultural continuity between ancient and modern Greece. When the Greeks hosted the 1896 Games their particular understanding of the Olympics as part of their national heritage was hard to miss. But it is important to underline that the ceremonies surrounding those first Olympics had a dual meaning for the Greeks, on the one hand harking back to ancient Greece and on the other hand underscoring a sense of modern Greek nationhood by doing so.

Yet the subsequent two Olympics and especially the Games in St. Louis in 1904 were organized according to a different concept, one that included a modernist- oriented celebration of civilization over barbarism, and which, at the same time, attenuated the nationalist symbolism evident in Athens in 1896. In the aftermath of the St. Louis Games, the coincidence of the discrediting of the Anthropology Days and the return of the Games to Athens, and, as we have seen, the cultural meaning the Greeks attached to the 1904 Games brought about a nationalist turn in the organizational structure of the Olympics. Thus it is not the current Greek conventional wisdom about 1904 that is accurate but rather that of the Greeks who were in St. Louis, and especially Chrysafes, who interpreted those Games from a Greek perspective in retrospect and who understood that the "American" St. Louis Olympics of 1904 were a turning point in the history of the early, modern Olympics.

Notes

Research for this article was assisted by Haverford College's faculty support funds that included a research fieldtrip to Greece by my student assistant Constantinos Vassiliou (Haverford class of 2006).

1. The debates among administrators over the status of the 1906 Games ended when the IOC rejected a proposal that they be recognized as "official Olympics" at its forty-third session, held in Rome in 1949.

2. Kitromilides, Enlightenment; Herzfeld, *Ours Once More*.

3. Koulouri, "Voluntary Associations."

4. Kitroeff, *Wrestling with the Ancients*, 9. For a discussion of the Zappas Olympics see pp. 11–23, and for more detailed accounts see Georgiades, *Olympic Revival*, 51; and Young, *Modern Olympics*, chapters 1–4.

5. Skopetea, *To "Protypo Vasilio."*

6. Unlike most of the participant countries that followed the newer Gregorian calendar, in which that day was April 6, Greece still followed the older Julian calendar.

7. Georgiades, *Olympic Revival*, 206–9; Kokkinos, "Greek Intellectual World."

8. Kitroeff, *Wrestling with the Ancients*, 45–52. See also Smith, *Days of 1896*.

9. Kitroeff, *Wrestling with the Ancients*, 29–31. Coubertin would adopt a more utilitarian view on modern Greece and its role in the Olympic Movement after World War I.

10. Coubertin, *Olympism*, 45n.

11. MacAloon, *This Great Symbol*, 267; see also 256–69.

12. Koulouri, *Athlitismos*.

13. Skiadas, *100 Chronia*, 147.

14. Kitroeff, *Wrestling with the Ancients*, 60.

15. *Hestia*, August-September 1904.

16. See 61st Cong., 3rd sess., Senate Document no. 747, Abstracts of the Reports of the Immigration Commission, II Washington, 1911.

17. Skiadas, *100 Chronia*, 145.

18. Curtis, "High Hurdles and White Gloves."

19. Mallon, *1904 Olympic Games*, 49–108.

20. Skiadas, *100 Chronia*, 253–55.

21. Chrysafes, *Oi Sygchronoi*, 410.

22. Diem, *Die Olympische Spiele 1912*.

23. Chrysafes, *Oi Sygchronoi*, 416, 431–33.

24. Chrysafes, *Oi Sygchronoi*, 416–17.

25. Chrysafes, *Oi Sygchronoi*, 420.

26. Chrysafes, *Oi Sygchronoi*, 421–23.

27. Chrysafes, *Oi Sygchronoi*, 423–28.

28. Herzfeld, *Ours Once More*, 75–81.

29. Kirkiadou-Nestoros, *E Theoria tis Hellenikes Laografias*, 94–97.

30. Kitroeff, "Greek Images of the Ottomans and Turks."

31. Anagnostou, "Forget the Past."

32. Saloutos, *Greeks in the United States*; Tuckerman, *Greeks of Today*.

33. Skiadas, *100 Chronia*, 155–81.

34. Mallon, "Athens 1906," 41–49, describes the Games as well as the efforts of Olympic historians, including Karl Lennartz and David Wallenchinsky, to persuade the IOC to recognize the Games as official Olympics. In his study of turn-of-the-century U.S. involvement in the Olympics, Mark Dyreson discusses the 1906 Games at length in his *Making the American Team*.

35. Guttmann, *Olympics: A History*, 27–28; Senn, *Power, Politics, and the Olympic Games*, 28–29.

36. Kitroeff, "International Dimension."

37. This information is provided in the official report of the Games, *Lefkoma ton en Athinais B' Diethnon Olympiakon Agonon*.

38. Georgiadis, "Olympic Ceremonies in the Athens Games," 87–89.

39. Coubertin, *Olympism*, 424.

40. Skopetea, *To "Protypo Vasilio,"* 215–16.

41. Mosse, *Nationalization of the Masses*, 7.

42. Mallon, *1906 Olympic Games*, 26, 32–33, and appendix 4, reproduces the data published in the Greek language report of these Games, *Lefkoma ton en Athinais*.

43. MacAloon, "Olympic Games and the Theory of Spectacle"; Mosse, *Nationalization of the Masses*; Cannadine, "Context, Performance, and Meaning of Ritual."

44. Senn, *Power, Politics, and the Olympic Games*, 29–30.

45. Coubertin, *Olympism*, 421.

46. Coubertin, *Olympism*, 437.

47. For example, Skiadas, *100 Chronia*.

Chapter 9. From the Anthropology Days to the Anthropological Olympics

JOHN BALE

If one wishes to extend to natives in colonized countries what we
boldly call the benefits of "athletic civilization,"
they must be made to enter into the broad athletic system with codified
regulations and comparative results,
which is the necessary basis of that civilization.

Pierre de Coubertin

In this chapter I want to explore some themes, related to the Olympic Games and international sport in general, that have been provoked by a reading of the report of the 1904 Anthropology Days in *Spalding's Official Athletic Almanac for 1905*.[1] The first of these themes is that of the "natural athlete," a major (if illusory) figure in the 1904 "Anthropology Days"; the second is the "contact zone" within which the allegedly "natural athletes" encounter "cultural athletes" of the global sports system. I conclude by suggesting that while the relationship between the "natural" and the "cultural" differ within various contact zones, this dualism has continued well beyond the early twentieth century and is evidenced in the early twenty-first century in a variety of Olympic and sub-Olympic contexts. In other words, the Anthropology Days of the 1904 St. Louis Olympic Games were similar in several ways to other cultural contacts and displays that were performed before and after 1904. The events of 1904 were simply one example of "the Native" being exposed (or subjected) to a culture of display, scrutinized by a colonial gaze.

The "Natural" Athlete

John Hoberman has suggested that while admiration for "Native" physicality had existed during the nineteenth century, in Germany (at least) it was not until the 1920s that "the African" was seen as a potential Western-style athlete.[2] It is clear, however, that reading the Native as an athlete occurred rather earlier than that—even in Germany. For my purposes the Anthropology Days, held in association with the St. Louis Olympics in 1904, form the starting point for reading the ways in which the "natural athlete" has been both described and invented. In particular, the Anthropology Days may have been the first occasion when the "natural athlete" came to be seen as a potential Olympian.

The Anthropology Days have been relatively well documented and need little introduction here.[3] In brief, members of ethnic groups from the "living displays" on the grounds of the Louisiana Purchase Exposition, of which the Olympics were a part, were presented to the public as athletes and put through tests (i.e., modern sports events) designed for the trained athletes of Europe and North America. I must admit that I have never seen a definition of the term "natural athlete." Given the contentiousness of the terms "natural" and "cultural," a satisfactory and generally consensual definition is unlikely to be forthcoming, especially at a time when the binaries of social science are steadily being deconstructed.[4] The "historical and conceptual entanglement" of nature, culture, and race, for example, upsets the nature-culture binary.[5] Nature—in the form of "natural athletes"—can be understood as the natural being derived from the cultural, in the sense that the "natural athlete" is a form of cultural representation.

For my purposes I accept that "natural" athletes were represented and read as being able to perform at a high standard in athletic events that they had not previously encountered and for which they had not previously been trained. In other words, they had not been physically "cultured" in such events. On the evolutionary scale of Social Darwinism, the natural athlete could be associated with the initial stage of "savagery"—close to "raw animal existence."[6]

The rhetoric of the "natural athlete" or "savage" featured prominently in the report of the Anthropology Days at the 1904 Games.[7] For example, it was noted that "startling rumors and statements" existed "in relation to the speed, stamina and strength of each and every particular tribe" represented at the Games.[8] More explicitly the report observed that we "have for years been led to believe from statements made by those who should know and from newspaper articles and books, that the *average* savage was fleet of foot, strong in limb, accurate with the bow and arrow, and expert in throwing the stone, and that some, particularly the Patagonians, were noted for their great size and strength, and owing to the particular life that many have been called upon to lead, they have been termed *natural* athletes."[9] Specific athletic qualities were quoted—those of the Indian runner, the stamina of the "kaffir" [sic], and "the *natural* all-round ability of *the savage* in athletic feats."[10]

But, I suggest, this was nothing new. Explorers and anthropologists had recorded and measured a variety of corporeal feats by Africans and other Native peoples before and after the more formally experimental approach at St. Louis. After all, athletics and anthropology came together in the frantic desire to observe, measure, and quantify human morphology and physical performance. Examples from the end of the nineteenth century serve as illustrations.

In the early 1880s events that were presented in the Jardin d'Acclimation in the Bois de Boulogne in Paris were said to have established a "balance between scientific education and entertainment." This distinction typified many of the displays of physical performance at the time. In this case Native peoples were put "on display and routinely examined and measured by leading anthropologists."[11] Included among the activities that were subjected to "anthropological" surveillance were dances and wrestling matches. Rather more reminiscent of St. Louis Anthropology Days was an event organized in Paris in 1893 when a special exhibition was set up "to take advantage" of a party of Dahomeans en route to the Chicago World's Fair. As part of the publicity, the Dahomeans were invited to take part in a 100-kilometer steeplechase against several French sports stars. This was the famous Baggage

Porters' Race, so named because participants were required to carry a 100-kilogram sack on their backs.[12] The objective of the race was to demonstrate the superior physical qualities of the European runners. The well-known French professor of anthropology, Charles Letourneau, declared that "the white race" led "the 'steeple chase' of human groups," a similar assumption to that held by the St. Louis anthropologists.[13] But the "moment live people are included in such displays, the issue of what they will do arises" and unpredictable outcomes are possible.[14] In this case, the winner turned out to be a Dahomean unknown to the French observers, called Ahivi, who became an overnight celebrity. The anthropologists continued to regard the Dahomeans as ignorant and immoral but satisfaction was gained "from the evidence that their superior strength made them worthy opponents."[15] The scientists seemed happy enough to reject their implicit hypothesis and acknowledged that it required revision.

The events described above were formally organized. A large number of informal recordings of the innate athletic abilities of Native peoples can be readily unearthed as well. For example, the French geographer, Elisée Reclus, noted that the Masai of Kenya "generally have slim, wiry figures, admirable for running"; the nineteenth-century German adventurer Ludwig Krapf praised the club-throwing ability of the Masai, stating that they hurl the club "with the greatest precision" and "at a distance of from fifty to seventy paces they can dash out the brain of an enemy"; and in 1902 Captain Richard Meinertzhagen, of the King's African Rifles, had put his Kenyan soldiers through their paces in a two-and-a-quarter-mile cross-country race in which the winner recorded a time of "exactly 14 minutes."[16]

That these results were measured and recorded reveals an embryonic process of "sportization" of body-cultural practices — a desire to organize (bureaucratize), record, quantify, and compare athletic displays, performances, and results.[17] The quasi-sportized events noted above supplied the kind of data that the St. Louis anthropologists could have used in formulating their hypothesis. However, such praise and idealization contrasted with a parallel mode of colonial rhetoric that negated the "Native" as the "lazy savage."[18]

Hypothesis Testing

The Anthropology Days, I suggest, adopted a more scientific approach (though not one that matched the modern anthropological research model) than the kinds of (often impromptu) displays of athletic performance noted above.[19] A scientific basis of the study was implied in the language of the report and by the fact that Dr. WJ McGee, chief of the Department of Anthropology at the St. Louis Exposition, had aided the establishment of the Anthropology Days. Also involved were Dr. Stephen Simms of the Field Museum, Chicago, and, more significantly perhaps, the well-known physical educationist and eugenicist Dr. Luther Gulick, who was to become a member of the American Olympic Committee.[20] These gentlemen, it is noted, paraded themselves as "Doctors," serving to aid their legitimacy as "scientists." The events were held in August so that "gentlemen interested in scientific work could be present."[21]

The Anthropology Days were seen as a "scientific" experiment, extending to the athletic field the ideology of anthropometric quantification. The scientists would seek proof or disproof of their hypothesis.[22] They followed the scientific method: their hypothesis was derived from an a priori model of the world that drew upon images of Native peoples such as those outlined above. They classified and measured athletic performances (i.e., collected data). However, their hypothesis could not be verified and such a lack of success resulted in negative feedback—that is, a need to reconstruct their images of the real world. It is not made explicit in the report that the scientists "meant to degrade" the Natives, as has been suggested, nor that the Anthropology Days "were designed [specifically] to show the superiority of whites and thus confirm racial evolutionary theory."[23] However, other chapters in this book go beyond the rhetoric of the report and suggest that its relatively benign view of indigenous peoples was a cover-up for alternative visions (see, for example, the chapter by Nancy Parezo).

In the track- and-field events the "savages" turned in results (measured to the nearest tenth of a second and half inch!) that were, according to the report, poor "for even an ordinary man in a healthy condition"; the "ridiculously poor performances" of the shot putters could have been bettered by high school boys; and the jumping results of "Pigmies," the Ainus, and some of the Indians were "really ridiculous."[24] From these results the scientists could prove "conclusively that the savage is not the natural athlete that we have been led to believe."[25] Nevertheless, in the spirit of scientific method, the Anthropology Days were regarded as a success. "It taught a great lesson," the report stated, and concluded by stressing that "[l]ecturers and authors will in the future please omit all reference to the natural athletic ability of the savage, unless they can substantiate their alleged feats."[26] This was a sensible conclusion and though some observers, such as the Baron de Coubertin, might have felt the "events" to be scandalous and racist, it was recognized by McGee that the Natives' "utter lack of athletic ability" (that is, lack of ability in European sports) resulted from their lack of training and that if coached they "would become as proficient as many Americans."[27] They were clay waiting to be molded into the Occidental model.

I will return to some aspects of the rhetoric of the report later, but, for the moment, will take its conclusions seriously and examine some other examples of how the representatives of the world of modern sport reported the athletic performances of indigenous "others." In other words, the experiments of the Anthropology Days were far from unique, even though they were more formally organized and more explicitly couched in scientific and athletic terms than the reports of other such "nature-culture" contacts during the early twentieth century.

"Natural Athletes": Some African Examples

It is unlikely that the German Adolf Friedrich, Duke of Mecklenburg, the leader of the first major anthropological expedition to Rwanda in central Africa in 1907, had read the report of the St. Louis Games, even though he was later to become a member of the German National Olympic Committee.[28] However, if anyone could put an alternative gloss on the athletic performances of Natives and "natural athletes," it was Mecklenburg. A graduate in anthropology from the University of Dresden, he followed a similar approach to the scientists at St. Louis. He reported that in Rwanda he had witnessed (and photographed) fantastic athletic performances and results achieved by Rwandan Tutsi.[29] He wrote that such high jumping (gusimbuka urukiramende) was "native to the Tutsi" and hypothesized that they "must have always been excellent jumpers."[30] He was also quoted as saying: "We came with our expedition to see the Tutsi. At the sight of their stature a thought came to me. I suggested to my adjutant that these men should know how to perform the high jump."[31] To test their hypothesis, the Germans arranged a jumping event, their apparatus approximating to the European gymnastic style with makeshift vertical uprights, a rope, and a takeoff mound.

The results were measured and recorded. The best jump was claimed by Mecklenburg to be 2.5 meters (about 8 feet, 2½ inches). He did not name the athlete who performed this feat but noted that a number of other jumpers achieved similar results. Additionally, "young boys" were said to have achieved heights of 1.5 to 1.6 meters (around 5 feet).[32] Assuming the same model as that used at St. Louis, Mecklenburg compared the heights achieved by Rwandans with results from the world's sport system, that is, he took the body culture of the Western sports system as his norm and noted that the existing world's best performance in the "sportized" high jump was 1.94 meters by the American Michael Sweeney.[33] Part of the (admittedly fractured) discourse of the "Tutsi high jump" was that the jumpers were untrained and the implication was that the African "Natives" could easily outperform the Western sportsman in an athletic event that they had never previously encountered.

Travelers in the African colonies adopted a similar rhetoric to the organizers' conclusion with respect to the Anthropology Days. "Conversionist" or "interventionist" fantasies found expression in sports. The notion that the

Native could be readily transformed into a star athlete was well illustrated in a cartoon published in the French sports magazine L'Auto in 1923. A semi-naked African Native holding a spear and shield was shown with palm trees in the background. A second image, showing what that Native would look like two years later, was of a modern athlete, clad in athletic uniform and track shoes, and adorned by garlands and trophies. He is placed on the familiar cultural terrain of the running track. To paraphrase Mary Louise Pratt, the interventionist fantasy completely displaced the reality of the Native's body and became the content of the colonialist's vision.[34] In effect, this was the message found in the conclusion to the report of the St. Louis "experiment."

In the 1940s and '50s attempts to appropriate (physically rather than textually) the Rwandan athletes for the global sports system included suggestions by Africanists such as Ellen Gatti, Mary Akeley, and the sports scientist Professor Ernst Jokl (coauthor of a so-called cultural anthropology of the 1952 Olympics), that Rwandan high jumpers should be invited to compete in the Olympic Games.[35] This would have proved bureaucratically difficult as Rwanda did not possess a national Olympic committee and was a trust territory of the League of Nations but, in any case, Native Rwandans appeared to have no desire to take part in such an event. This was hardly surprising in view of the fact that their "high jumping" was a totally different body culture from that sanctioned by the international governing body for achievement sports. Yet it again mirrored the mind-set of the St. Louis anthropologists who saw in the Native a natural sportsman.

As late as the mid-1950s Track and Field News reported that a missionary was seeking to train one of these athletes and send him to the 1956 Olympics at Melbourne.[36] U.S. track coaches were also reported to be seeking college recruits in Rwanda, such had become the fame of the "Tutsi high jumpers."[37] Predictions were made that the Rwandans could jump higher than the records reported by Mecklenburg and they would overwhelm the "West" at the Olympics.

The anthropologists at St. Louis were putting the Natives through the same events as the Olympic athletes who competing in the official Games. The same was not true of Mecklenburg and those of his followers who rhetorically appropriated an indigenous body culture by describing it in the language of modern achievement sports. Even so, it was felt that those taking part in the display of Rwandan "folk" high jumping would, like the Igorots, Ainus, and Patagonians at St. Louis, seamlessly become converts to the practices of Western sport. As with the long distance runners of the Tarahumara Indians of Chihuahua, Mexico, who appeared to be potential Olympians, the "language" of modern European sports made little sense to them.[38]

Eventually Rwandans adopted the ideology of Western sports. Rwanda became a member of the global bureaucracy, the International Association of Athletic Federations (IAAF) and the international form of high jumping was introduced, along with the notions of quantitative measures, standardized conditions, competition, and records. Today the Rwanda high jump record, validated by the IAAF, is 1.9 meters (about 6 feet, 2¾ inches). The prophecy made by Professor Ernst Jokl that Tutsi athletes were "bound to play an increasingly important role in the Olympic Games in the future" has never been reflected in actuality.[39]

The ability to jump or run in a particular way is meaningless outside a particular socialized experience and function. Here, I think, it is appropriate to quote the words of the British sociologist Brett St. Louis: "The perception of sport as a set of universalized physical activities endows it with intrinsic and naturalized properties that ignore the given and interested social contexts [and] their particular rules and regulations."[40] Jumping, like walking and running, is multiple and complex and there is no one essential form. Clearly, there is no such thing as "jumping in itself," no certain physical motion which is, as it were, elementary, universal, or pure. There are only varieties of jumping. From a postcolonial perspective, the rhetoric illustrated earlier reveals that anthropologists and explorers were unable to read African body culture without the use of a European lens.

Let me now move on a few years to the 1920s. Also traveling in East Africa,

F. A. M. Webster, a captain in the King's African Rifles, English javelin-throwing champion, track- and-field coach, and prolific writer of training manuals during the 1920s and '30s, encountered spear-throwing Natives in what was then Kenya Colony. He observed that "one would imagine [i.e., hypothesize] that spear or javelin throwing would be a physical feat at which the African native is bound to excel."[41] However, to his surprise—like that of the anthropologists at St. Louis—he found that "using a spear of the weight and length of approximately the Olympic javelin I could beat any native I ever took on, whereas with their own casting spears they could always beat me by yards."[42]

This engagement between African and European is similar to an event that took place in August 1925, when two English missionaries in Rwanda asked the "king," Mwami, if he had any good runners or jumpers. One of them, Geoffrey Holmes (a former captain of the British ice-hockey team), asked if he could "try one out" in a 100-yard race. Two Rwandan boys were selected. One beat Holmes "by about a foot" and he beat the other by about the same margin. Several Rwandan high jumpers performed for the spectators, one making a leap of "about 6 feet, 2 inches."[43] Holmes did not compete; there was no point in him doing so as the African was obviously superior. In the 100-yard dash, bicultural participation was considered workable. But the Rwandan and Western high jumps, on this occasion and (as far as I know) on most other occasions, seemed sufficiently different to put the European well and truly in his place. It had been recognized as a Native event. The Rwandan had performed or exhibited his jump but had not engaged in a competition with the Europeans. It should have been a reminder that jumping did not take place as a universalized form. As with Mecklenburg, the Europeans were there simply to gaze at the display performed before them. In this case it was acknowledged that this body-cultural practice was something different from that of the missionary. It may have looked similar but it was not the same.

It was only when the universal cultural and sporting currency of the result or record became familiar to both the African and the European that meaningful comparisons could be made. At St. Louis, the Europeans were better at their events than the Africans could possibly be, given quite different ideologies and philosophies. Likewise, the Rwandan was better at the Rwandan high jump and the Kenyan was better with his spear. This, too, should not be surprising. The problem facing the anthropologists, Webster and others, was that they failed to distinguish between different body-cultural configurations.[44] To them, running and jumping were, well, running and jumping. The "folk" tradition of the Native was simply not recognized as being a different practice from that of the sportized, serious competitors at the Olympics. However, Coubertin did recognize the configurational differences between African and sportized jumping (for example). In a 1931 article on "Sporting Colonization" he accepted that "native athletics" will "never be anything more than amusements, recreation."[45]

There are a number of other such meetings or contacts that could demonstrate the labeling of the African athlete as "natural." Perhaps the most notorious was the view of Adolf Hitler when, in the contact zone of the Berlin Olympic Stadium, he averred that in subsequent Olympics the Africans should be excluded because of their unfair *natural*, animal advantages. It was the misperceived congruence of Native body cultures with those of the West that lead a prominent German physician to ask: "What, then, will be left of our world records?"[46]

Less than twenty years after the Berlin Olympics, a further example of the contact zone was illustrated in the White City Stadium in London. The occasion was the 1954 championship of the (English) Amateur Athletic Association. It was the first time that a group of Kenyan athletes had taken part in this august event, and most publicity (such as it was) was focused on a Kenyan high jumper and a javelin thrower. There happened to be two long-distance runners also entered for the championships, but it was widely believed that these would fail to achieve the slightest success. At the time, black athletes were said to possess "great speed but little stamina," a hypothesis that could be "confirmed" by spurious statistical data.[47]

On the first day of the championships the 6-mile race was contested. The spectators were surprised to see a bare-footed Kenyan entrant, named Lazaro Chepkwony, at the starting line. He set off at a fast pace, intermittently slowing down and then repeating his faster efforts. This bemused the fans and, to an extent, upset the British athletes. But after fifteen laps he dropped out with an injured leg and the British runners fought out the race for themselves. His performance confirmed the stereotype: black Africans were not long-distance runners. The following day the 3-mile event took place and again a Kenyan faced the best runners that Britain could offer. His name was Nyandika Maiyoro. Like his compatriot he set off at a fast pace, which, if sustained, would have produced a world record. He led the field for much of the race. In the final stages the experienced British runners, Chris Chataway and Fred Green, overtook him and went on to break the world's record. Maiyoro faded but still finished in third place, a most unpredictable result.

The response to the two Kenyans in the subsequent press reports was fractured. On the one hand the editor of Athletics Weekly stated that "it was the unusual and unexpected form by some of the coloured [sic] runners in the distance races which provided much food for thought. Never again shall we nurse the idea that the coloured races are no good at anything beyond a mile." Echoing WJ McGee, he added that Maiyoro "would, with the right training, be a match for any runner in the world."[48] On the other hand, two of the major British newspapers were somewhat negative in their reactions to the Kenyans. One stated that the Kenyans had ruined the races because of their naiveté and inconsistent pace. The six miles had been "bedevilled" by the unevenness of Chepkwony's running and the three miles had been "made confusing" by Maiyoro's "ludicrously fast pace."[49]

Several decades later, Kenyan and Ethiopian middle- and long-distance runners had indeed been recognized as outstanding athletes, possessing both speed and remarkable stamina. However, there remained the strong implication that they were "natural athletes"—that if they had stamina in one sport, it could be readily converted into another.[50] The Nike sports goods corporation set out to experiment with some Kenyan runners to establish if they could transfer their running skills into the world of cross-country skiing. The unwritten text is almost the same as that from St. Louis in 1904: "We have been led to believe that the average Kenyan is fleet in foot and strong in limb and have been termed natural athletes." In the mid-1990s two Kenyan runners were taken to Finland, invited by a Finnish coach in some way affiliated with Nike. It seems that few people in Finland took the idea seriously, though there was considerable curiosity at such exotic skiers. The media presented the skiers as figures of fun. The Kenyans took part in the 1998 Olympics but failed to perform as expected and produced results that, in relative terms, were similar to those of the Patagonians and Pygmies at St. Louis. As a result, in 1999 Nike withdrew their support and the two skiers returned (were sent back) to Kenya.[51] In 2003 it was established that one of them, Henry Bitok, had become a farmer but the other, Philip Boit, had not given up his skis. He had already participated in the 2002 Winter Games, but with no success. However, Nike resumed supplying him with funds and he represented Kenya in the 2006 Winter Olympics in the 15-kilometer cross-country skiing event. He finished ninety-second out of ninety-seven entrants. A recent report stated that he had been training for skiing in South Korea instead of Finland, this time funded by the IOC as part of their global "development" program. Was the experiment carried out on Boit very different from that of the anthropologists at St. Louis in 1904? If Bitok and Boit were good runners they must surely be good skiers, the men from Nike hypothesized.

The Contact Zone and the Culture of Display

In this final section I want to situate the displays of body-cultural practice exemplified above in the context of what Mary Louise Pratt has termed a "contact zone." By this she refers to spaces of "colonial encounters, the space in which peoples geographically and historically separated come into contact with one another and establish ongoing relations, usually involving conditions of coercion, radical inequality, and intractable conflict."[52] This is a somewhat overgeneralized statement, and "coercion" and "intractable" conflict were not necessarily present. I use the term to explore incidents or meetings in "contact zones" within which non-Western people engaged with representatives of colonial nations who possessed a mind-set influenced by Western sports. To be sure, in many of these contacts expectations were that the Natives were natural athletes and would outperform Western athletes. But the context of such interaction has varied considerably over time and space.

For explorers, missionaries, and anthropologists the contact zone was to be found in colonized lands of Africa, Asia, Oceania, and Latin America. For those living in the "mother" countries, contacts with, and displays of, Native peoples were to be found in the growth in international exhibitions or expositions that grew rapidly in number from the mid-nineteenth century. Later, these would be joined by homologous international sporting contests. The display was a surrogate for travel, and in these fairs, noted Walter Benjamin, crowds were conditioned to derive pleasure from the spectacle alone.[53] While many of the exhibitions displayed Native peoples, Benjamin contrasted the international expositions and the Olympic Games by noting that whereas the former displayed the latest in industrial machines, the latter displayed "the fittest in human bodies," or more appropriately today, perhaps, the latest in human machines.[54] John MacAloon has also suggested a link between the exhibition (and the contemporaneous circus and geographical society) and the Olympics: "In the very decades during which 'scientific' ethnology and cultural studies were being organized by intellectual elites, 'popular' or 'mass' culture was formalizing and elaborating its own means to the same end. . . . [T]he appeal of the Olympic Games is based in no small part upon the continuing tradition of popular ethnography."[55]

There was, I suggest, a fine line to be drawn between "popular" and "scientific" ethnography at the time of the early—and, indeed, later—Olympics. Perhaps it is no accident that Gulick and Mecklenburg, each of whom claimed a sort of anthropological affiliation, were also members of their respective national Olympic committees. However, as Johannes Fabian has noted, many early twentieth-century explorers and anthropologists were less scientific than might have been expected and "rationalized frames of exploration" were often ignored.[56] Often, it seems, they were more like spectators than scientists, more passersby than ethnographers. Both the expositions and the Olympics projected live specimens and different physiognomic types to the audience. However, "the inherently performative nature of live specimens" tends to blur the lines between curiosity and scientific interest, theater (e.g., synchronized diving) and living ethnographic displays (e.g., the 10,000 meters), staged recreation, and cultural performance.[57] Exhibitions and Olympics share other similarities. They are ephemeral constructions, catalytic and celebratory at the same time, involving economic risk in expectation of future returns; they can each be carnivals and communal activities.[58] Olympics are surely exhibitions.

So, too, was the Mecklenburg "event"; and, in effect, the javelin and spear throwing by Webster and his Kenyan "other." Likewise Maiyoro was exhibited at the White City and Bitok in the Winter Olympics. These were, surely, cultures being exhibited or "objects of ethnography." If they weren't watched by thousands of people in situ, their photographs were exhibited in the books of international publishers. They became "things to be seen."[59] A culture of display and the European gaze characterized the anthropological events, the explorers' photography, and the more formal spectatorship of the exhibitions and Olympics. In addition to the gaze and the spectacle, however, sports performances had the added attractions of the result and the record.

The main aim of this chapter has been to situate the Anthropology Days of 1904 in the much broader practice of the exhibition of body cultures to audiences brought up with Western norms of athletic performance. To the display of peoples in theaters, exhibition halls, museums, circuses, and zoos — identified by Kirshenblatt-Gimbett as contact zones — can be added the open spaces of Native African settlements and the modern Olympic stadium. Additionally, of course, "natural athletes" can today be mediated via the technology of television.[60]

It has been suggested that in a televisual world we are "all rather like anthropologists, in our own living rooms, surveying the world of all those 'others' who are represented to us on the screen."[61] Nowhere can this be more apparent than in the television coverage of the Olympics. Here the long-standing stereotype of the "natural athlete" can be recast and broadcast in familiar terms.[62] Indeed, Edward Said has suggested that in an electronic age stereotypes have been reinforced rather than removed.[63]

Epilogue

In 2004 I was invited to join a group of scientists at Glasgow University who had established an International Center for East African Running Science. I was impressed by the fact that the group consisted of scholars from the humanities and social sciences as well as from the "hard" sciences of biology, nutrition, and genetics. The objective of the center was not quite the same as that of the anthropologists at St. Louis. Since 1904 it had become established that some of the Africa Natives could, as WJ McGee (and, to be fair, Coubertin and Ernst Jokl) had predicted, become as good as the Americans once they were trained to run in the sportized manner of Europe and North America. By the 1920s, African athletes were being described as natural sprinters; from the 1960s they had also become, some believed, "natural" long-distance runners. However, the Glasgow group had taken the step beyond accepting a hypothesis; their job was to find an explanation. They had visited Kenya, examined hundreds of runners, taken blood and DNA samples, undertaken genetic analysis, established whether the boys they interviewed ran or walked to school, and checked the athletes' diets. The runners' bodies were measured and analyzed. I was reminded of the anthropometrical antics of the nineteenth-century explorers. Back in Glasgow a conference was held where the results were presented to an excited

339

audience of trainers and scholars. Additionally, an international road race was held in which it was demonstrated that the first six finishers were from East Africa. A Kenyan runner of world-class standard was invited to make a short presentation to the conference and to answer questions from the audience. One of her responses was: "Why are you studying me? Why don't you study the British world-record marathon runner, Paula Radcliffe?" I felt uneasy about being one of the group's members.

Notes

Pierre de Coubertin, "Athletic Colonization," in *Olympism*, 704 (italics added).

1. J. Sullivan, *Spalding's Official Athletic Almanac for 1905*.

2. Hoberman, *Darwin's Athletes*, 104.

3. In addition to standard works on the history of the Olympics, see also Eichberg, "Forward Race"; and Goksyr (misspelling of Goksøyr), "'One certainly expected a great deal more.'"

4. See, for example, Cloke and Johnston, *Spaces of Geographical Thought*.

5. St. Louis, "Sport, Genetics, and the 'Natural Athlete,'" 84.

6. Laska, "Revisioning the Millennium."

7. J. Sullivan, *Spalding's Official Athletic Almanac for 1905*, 249–66.

8. J. Sullivan, *Spalding's Official Athletic Almanac for 1905*, 249.

9. J. Sullivan, *Spalding's Official Athletic Almanac for 1905*, 249, italics added. Confusion seems to have arisen in this quotation about "natural" and "cultural"; that is, is a "particular life" "natural" or "cultural"?

10. J. Sullivan, *Spalding's Official Athletic Almanac for 1905*, italics added.

11. Maxwell, *Colonial Photography*, 19.

12. Maxwell, *Colonial Photography*, 20.

13. Maxwell, *Colonial Photography*, 20.

14. Kirshenblatt-Gimblett, "Objects of Ethnography," 405.

15. Maxwell, *Colonial Photography*.

16. Quoted in Bale and Sang, *Kenyan Running*.

17. The "sportization" of body-cultural practices has been thoroughly explored by Eichberg, *Body Cultures*; and Guttmann, *From Ritual to Record*.

18. Laziness was often attributed to climate. See Bale, "Lassitude and Latitude."

19. MacAloon, "Anthropology at the Olympic Games." In this "overview," MacAloon inexplicably omits the Anthropology Days of the 1904 Games.

20. Winter, "Luther Halsey Gulick."

21. J. Sullivan, Spalding's Official Athletic Almanac for 1905.

22. J. Sullivan, Spalding's Official Athletic Almanac for 1905, 249.

23. Laska, "Revisioning the Millennium."

24. J. Sullivan, Spalding's Official Athletic Almanac for 1905, 251.

25. J. Sullivan, Spalding's Official Athletic Almanac for 1905, 253.

26. J. Sullivan, Spalding's Official Athletic Almanac for 1905, 259.

27. J. Sullivan, Spalding's Official Athletic Almanac for 1905, 257.

28. Duke of Mecklenburg, In the Heart of Africa. On this subject see Bale, Imagined Olympians.

29. Quoted in Bale, Imagined Olympians, 31.

30. Bale, Imagined Olympians, 96.

31. Duke of Mecklenburg, In the Heart of Africa. The official ethnographer in the Mecklenburg party, Jan Czekanowski, claimed the height jumped was 2.35 meters; Jan Czekanowski, letter to Carl Diem, November 22, 1958 (Mappe 478, Diem Archive, Deutsche Sporthochschule, Cologne).

32. Duke of Mecklenburg, In the Heart of Africa, 59.

33. In fact Sweeney's "world record" was 1.97 meters.

34. Pratt, Imperial Eyes, 209.

35. See Bale, Imagined Olympians, 78; Jokl et al., Sport in the Cultural Pattern.

36. Dozier, "Tribesman Jumped 7' 6"," 4.

37. Bale, Imagined Olympians, 79.

38. MacAloon, "Olympic Games."

39. Jokl et al., Sport in the Cultural Pattern, 35–36.

40. St. Louis, "Sport, Genetics, and the 'Natural Athlete'" 84. Note also, MacAloon, "Olympic Games," 278n42.

41. Webster, Science of Athletics, 384.

42. Webster, Science of Athletics, 384, italics added.

43. See G. Holmes's untitled article in Ruanda Notes.

44. Eichberg, Body Cultures.

45. Coubertin, "Athletic Colonization," in Olympism, 704.

46. Quoted in Hoberman, Mortal Engines, 46.

47. Wiggins, "'Great speed but little stamina'"; McWhirter, "Unusual facts and fallacies," 205.

48. Athletics Weekly 8, no. 29 (1954): 8, italics added.

49. Manchester Guardian, July 12, 1954; London Times, July 12, 1954.

50. See Bale and Sang, Kenyan Running.

51. Vettenniemi, "Kato neekeri hiihtää!," 151–66, 238–39.

52. Pratt, Imperial Eyes, 26.

53. Kirshenblatt-Gimblett, "Objects of Ethnography"; Buck-Morss, Dialectics of Seeing, 85.

54. Buck-Morss, *Dialectics of Seeing*, 324.

55. MacAloon, *This Great Symbol*, 136.

56. Fabian, *Out of our Minds*, 8.

57. Kirshenblatt-Gimblett, "Objects of Ethnography," 397.

58. Hinsley, "World as Marketplace," 344–45.

59. In this sense, the Rwandan high jumper could be said to be taking part in a "spectacle": see MacAloon, "Olympic Games," 242–43.

60. Kirshenblatt-Gimblett, "Objects of Ethnography," 403.

61. Morley and Robbins, *Spaces of Identity*, 133.

62. See, for example, Blain, Boyle, and O'Donnell, *Sport and National Identity*.

63. Said, *Orientalism*, 28.

Chapter 10. Olympic Anthropology Days and the Progress of Exclusion

Toward an Anthropology of Democracy

HENNING EICHBERG

The Games of 1904 in St. Louis were exceptional in the series of modern Olympics in establishing a link between sport and anthropology. They displayed the problematic relationship between the Western pattern of sport and the body cultures of "other" people. This connection is still worth some deeper reflection in our times — and maybe more than ever before. The Games of 1904 included a special "pre-Olympic" annex, called Anthropology Days, sometimes also Tribal Games.[1] As the term *anthropology* indicates, the event was scientifically inflected, based, as it was, on the cooperation between an anthropologist and a physical educator. William John McGee, who acted as the chief of the world fair's Department of Anthropology, was the founding president of the newly established American Anthropological Association and former director of the federal government's Bureau of American Ethnology. And James Edward Sullivan, the head of the fair's Department of Physical Culture, had founded the Amateur Athletic Union (AAU) in 1888 and led it for many years. These two powerful persons joined to send indigenous people from Africa, Asia, the Americas, and the Pacific onto the racetrack of sport competition.

Expectations for the "anthropologic" event were remarkable. Newspaper headlines announced: "Barbarians meet in Athletic Games."[2] The event revealed much more than a merely "scientific" character. The Olympic Games had at that time become a sideshow of the world's fairs. And the "ethnological zoo" was a well-known genre around 1900, linked to world's fairs, zoological gardens, and traveling exhibitions. At the St. Louis World's Fair, officially called the Louisiana Purchase Exhibition, African Pygmies, Argentine Patagonians, Japanese Ainus, "Red Indians" from Vancouver Island, Manguins, and Eskimos were all "displayed" to Western spectators. In particular, groups of "Red Indians" from the United States were presented to the public of the fair—Arapahos, Chippewas, Chiricahua Apaches, Kickapoos, Kiowas, Maricopas, Moquis, Navajos, Nez Perce, Pawnees, Sioux, Wichitas, and Zunis. The most prominent participant was Goyathlay (One Who Yawns), known as Geronimo, the former legendary war chief of the Apache. The new imperial aspirations of the United States in Asia were represented by tribes from the recently conquered Philippines: Bagobos, Igorots, Moros, Negritos, and Visayans. Each of these groups was exhibited with their typical utensils, weapons, clothing, materials for habitation, crafts, and objects for everyday use, as well as some animals associated with their subsistence. Sport was regarded as a part of this set of ethnoculture. Thirteen of the represented "savage tribes" were to compete in races linked with the Olympic Games.

The "anthropological" competitions were held over two days in eighteen different sport events. There were seven running events, two types of jumping, and different forms of throwing—javelin, baseball, shot put, 56-pound weight, and bolo. Further events were archery, tug of war, pole climbing and mud fights. Most of the events were arranged after the pattern of Western Olympic competition and record production. They had an experimental character in that they were imposed by the organizers on the colonized human beings who had no links to these practices by their own cultural tradition or self-determination. Some of the "indigenous" competitions, however, had native roots—and were arranged without rivals. Bolos were thrown by Patagonians only. Pole climb was done only by Africans and Filipinos. And in the mud fight, it was only Pygmies who participated.

Whether the St. Louis event really was as exceptional as it appears at first glance should be examined in greater depth, the longer lines of the historical "before" and "after" being the topic of this chapter. This requires a clearer picture of what "really" was happening there in 1904. The very different and contradictory comments of contemporary observers — as well as of later researchers — show that this task may not be easy.

Ranking the Peoples: The Games as Laboratory

Official voices analyzed the measured results of the Anthropology Days as poor, even shameful (thus contributing to the title of "shambles," as the St. Louis Games more generally have been called), but shameful for whom?. According to James Sullivan's report of the Olympic Games of 1904, "One certainly expected a great deal more from the savages."[3] The official Olympic report saw the event as proof of the inferiority of the Natives and ridiculed them. It pointed out that some of the "records" in the throwing events could easily be beaten by schoolchildren, or that a result in the running long jump could be bettered by top American athletes doing the standing long jump. There were also some positive exceptions. An Igorot named Basilio gave, for instance, "the most marvelous performance of pole climbing ever witnessed in this country."[4]

But other records were really representative: "Never before in the history of sport in the world were such poor performances recorded for weight throwing."[5] This remark deserves special attention, because it is one of the few cases in the history of modern Olympic sport that a "negative record" was recorded. Maybe it is the only case. In this respect, the Anthropology Days represented a remarkable exception in the development of the modern way of conceptualizing the "record." The poor results of the participants were held against what one characterized as the traditional view in anthropology: "We have for years been led to believe from statements of those who should know and from newspaper articles and books, that the average savage was fleet on foot, strong of limb, accurate with the bow and arrow and expert in throwing the stone."[6] This assumption had now been proven to be incorrect.

The Anthropology Days shattered the romantic myth of the "noble savage" as a natural sportsman. The measured records proved that Western Olympic athletes were just plain better. "Lecturers and authors will in the future please omit all references to the natural ability of savages."[7]

The competitions confirmed the opposite myth, which McGee—like other dreamers of Western supremacy—had already developed for a long time: the evolution of human history as an upward process. In a lecture about "The Trend of Human Progress," McGee had in 1899 proposed to order the development of mankind in four stages: savagery, barbarism, civilization, and enlightenment. The last stage was led to perfection by, in racial terms, "the Caucasian": "The burden of humanity is already in large measure the White Man's burden—for, viewing the human world as it is, white and strong are synonymous terms."[8] The classical work about the "progress" from the "savage" stage via "barbarianism" to "civilization" had been written by Lewis Henry Morgan some decades before and had had a remarkable impact on both bourgeois and Marxist theories.[9]

All this was not just a dream. It was also a matter of method. The arguments and the empirical procedures witnessed a positivist way of obtaining knowledge. People could be classified, and their ranking should best be done on the basis of quantified data, thus trusting in the "objectivity" of "facts." The results tell the true story. Sport served as an experimental laboratory for a sort of "anthropometry of bodily movement"—side by side with the anthropometry of bodily structure, which was used by the race science of that time. Sport as laboratory gave reason to scientific, methodological pride. One could, as McGee stated, "obtain for the first time what may be called interracial athletic records."[10]

Discourse on culture could be based on metric comparison—this was the progress of knowledge. Progress demanded sacrifices. Two Filipinos died on the way to the exposition in a freezing railroad car. This was deplorable, to be sure—expressed in the actual language of globalization, it was "collateral damage." However, the dead bodies could be used for scientific purposes, the "soft parts" and skeletons, as McGee proposed, for the university and the brains for the anthropologist's museum. The corpses would, thus, serve progress, nevertheless.[11]

Developing the World: The Games as Progressive Education

An opposite perspective, though in the framework of the same progressive dream, was expressed by Pierre de Coubertin, the founder and philosopher of the modern Olympics. For him, the Anthropology Days themselves were contemptible, not just their results. They were not only vulgar, offending his aristocratic taste, but also they were opposed to his fundamental conviction of progress: "As for that outrageous charade, it will of course lose its appeal when black men, red men and yellow men learn to run, jump, and throw and leave the white man far behind them. Then we will have progress. But these races! Now tell me that the world has not advanced since then and that no progress has been made in sporting spirit."[12]

The main interest of Coubertin's Olympic idea was not to compare "savages" and "civilized" men, but to develop humanity as a whole. Coubertin's method was evolutionist and moral educational. Sport is a way of moral learning. Sport is part of a positive colonial process, spreading better life over the whole world—a better life after the Western pattern, of course. The educational impetus was what Coubertin had in common with the anthropologist McGee, but their educational perspectives were different. For McGee, the anthropological parts of the St. Louis Fair had the educational value of displaying the otherness of "the others." The exhibition of other people stimulated observation and scientific inquiry into rare ethnological types. For Coubertin, in contrast, the world was not broken down into two (or more) types of human beings, "savage" and "civilized," but it "advanced" as such: the world as a whole is in "progress." Sport expresses this advancement in an ideal form, and thus it can function as the ritual of human progress— and as character building. Coubertin's Olympism was a humanistic and a colonial project at the same time.[13]

If one searches for a bodily practice that would positively correspond to the evolutionist question—How can "we" develop those "indigenous" others?—one finds, however, not one single answer. Competitive sport was just one of the answers, and not the most obvious one in those years of "the white man's burden." What fitted best to Coubertin's point of view in the 1904 event was the triumph of Indian girls in basketball as world champions of the world's fair.[14] But this championship was an exception and a surprise—being neither part of the official St. Louis Olympic Games nor of the Anthropology Days. The mainstream of body-cultural evolutionism gave at that time—still—quite another answer: The "Natives" should be developed by gymnastic exercise. For the "indigenous people" it was foremost calisthenics, military rifle drills, gymnastic exercises in rank and file, and similar rituals of discipline, which were applied. In the world's fair, this was represented by the highly applauded display of the Philippine Constabulary Band.[15]

The Anthropology Days were definitively *not* a part of this world of gymnastic training and educational evolutionism. Furthermore, they were placed outside the ritual festivity of Olympism (whose ceremonial character was not yet developed in 1904, but took its actual form between 1912 and 1936). This case of body-cultural practice illuminates what the Coubertinian model of Olympism in its core consisted of: a fusion of the sportive and the ritualistic.

Entertaining by Zoo and Carnival: The Games as Attraction

Other perspectives, again different, were applied by the newspapers. The papers took greater delight in the Anthropology Games, displaying them as a spectacle of curiosities. The spectators, too—though they were probably not many in number—seem to have been more amused than the educator Coubertin. The positive valuation by the public had more to do with popular entertainment than with sporting "progress."

The interest of entertainment in itself had different sides. The one side was linked to the taste for "the strange." Here it met with contemporary anthropology and its focus on "Strange Races of Men."[16] This opened the

24. Pygmy laughing after putting the shot. Patagonian and Cocopa Indians are seated in the background. From J. Sullivan, ed., *Spalding's Official Athletic Almanac for 1905: Special Olympic Number, Containing the Official Report of the Olympic Games of 1904*, 258. From the LA84 Foundation Digital Archive.

flank toward a sort of popular racism: The "others" are a sort of freaks — isn't this amusing? The Anthropology Days had elements of a freak show.[17] However, there was another side, too. Some positive, surprising, and amusing situations emerged in the St. Louis competition — and they were of quite another type than that esteemed by the experimental anthropologist McGee. A Pygmy suddenly interrupted his pole climb to chase photographers away. Another athlete wanted to take his clothes off for the competition and was dissuaded only through much effort by the puritanical organizers. The Pygmy participants distinguished themselves in particular by their laughter and ability to grasp the humor of a situation. When they made false starts in the running events, they were quick to laugh, and they made fun of other competitors when these made false starts, too. They went into convulsions when a Japanese competitor took a tumble in his attempt at a long jump. This was not freakish, it was carnivalesque.

What the media of the entertainment industry saw as charming curiosities actually illustrated something else: an intercultural encounter—and a conflict of cultures. The "amusing" situations indirectly told a story about what Olympic sport had lost: the quality of laughter and popular carnival. A tumble on the Olympic track is not a part of the game, but a disturbance, maybe even a catastrophe. And a false start is nothing to laugh at.

The reported situations could thus be read as a subversive narration. In this respect the enthusiasm of the newspapers about the "most unique athletic meeting in the history of the world" held a certain truth, indeed.[18]

This is why some later critical evaluations must be seen from a relative perspective, too. From the side of the physical educator, it was remarked that reporters and recorders had "overlooked" some relevant facts: the absence of high-level sport "motivation" among the indigenous athletes, the absence of "training" among them, the problems of translation, and so on.[19] This critique was justified insofar as it aimed to defend the dignity of the participants against racism, against the derision aimed at the "half-naked natives."[20] And yet, by thinking in terms of an "absence" one tends to reproduce the colonial inequality on a new level: modern sport remains the measure—the others "don't have it yet." The recognition of "the other" implies a deeper revolution inside, not least inside anthropological analysis. The laughter of the Pygmies leads us to the "trickster," who exposes the grotesque sides of the dominant power.

The Future Is No Longer What It Has Been

From the events of 1904, then, questions of a more general character arise that concern anthropology as a way of understanding human being(s): Is anthropology a story of evolution and progress (as expressed by Coubertin and his Olympism)? Is anthropology an attempt at classification, experimental measurement, and ranking (as was expressed by McGee and the concept of the Anthropology Days)? Is it a mix of nostalgia and the spectacular, of freak show, zoo, and carnival (as was the perspective of the popular entertainment industry)? Or is anthropology a narrative of encounter, of conflict— and of laughter?

In any case, observation is not innocent. It is linked to patterns of respect and disrespect of the "other," to the recognition of "otherness" — or non-recognition. Recognition has become a central cultural term for the theory of democracy, especially for the inclusion of different ethnic identities.[21] The culture and psychology of democracy has recognition of the other as its first precondition. But what makes things still more complicated is that this relation is not only dual—recognition versus nonrecognition—it is a complex configuration of diversity, difference, and inner contradiction. Furthermore, if the St. Louis Games have been called "a polyglot circus," today this no longer automatically has a derogatory sound.[22] The idea of "polyglot sport" may even have undertones of utopia.

Likewise, we no longer automatically comprehend the laughter of the Pygmies on the athletic field as a lighthearted disturbance of the serious project of sporting education. With the roaring of "postmodern" sports in our ears, it will be heard in another way. What has won out in the longer run of history is not (or not only) the serious strategy of sporting religion, but (also) the more playful "happening" as it is displayed in event culture.

In its time, indeed, the Anthropology Days may have represented "the ghost of the past" while the Olympic Games represented "the wave of the future."[23] But today we doubt these linear categories. Maybe the future is no

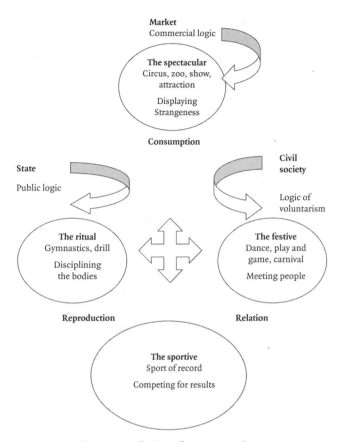

Fig. 1. Contradictions of movement culture

longer what it has been. All this requires a deeper, theory-related analysis. What is chosen here is the focus on the cultural relativity of achievement, that is, on the configurations of production.

The Ritual of Productivism

Before examining the later actuality of the "tribal games," let us consider the history of the production, recording, and comparison of achievements that preceded the 1904 Anthropology Days. The discourse about records—as in modern sports—treats human movement mainly as a way of producing results. This story had forerunners inside modern science, reaching back to the origins of modern industrial culture at the turn of the eighteenth century.

In 1800–1804, François Peron, a French scientist, traveled to Southeast Asia and the Pacific in order to study the physical abilities of indigenous peoples. With a dynamometer, an apparatus to measure physical strength, he registered the abilities of three types of people: Tasmanians, Australian Aboriginals, and Malays from Timor. He arranged his findings in tables, and from these tables he calculated that the average bodily strength of these peoples corresponded exactly to what he called their "stage of civilization." This he compared to data from French and British people, which confirmed the picture. Peron concluded that the more "savage" the people, the weaker was their physical force. Correspondingly, the higher the level of strength, the more one found a corresponding "perfection of civilization." Reports from other peoples from America and the Pacific gave Peron reason to generalize that there was no part in the world where savage peoples by their physical perfection and their development of strength were not "by far minor than the great European nations."[24]

Peron's studies documented that anthropological research was not at all as romantic as McGee assumed in 1904. The reification of human movement had become a mainstream Western modern method, and the quantification of "primitivity" was an accepted strategy to reveal that "savages" and "barbarians" were inferior to "the civilized." Soon it became evident that this growing mainstream of knowledge not only developed in the airy world of ideas but was also linked to concrete bodily practice, to the experience of sport. The positivistic ranking—from Peron to McGee and Sullivan—can be seen as an intellectual superstructure imposed on a "material" process of body-cultural practice. Since the late eighteenth century, Western societies have developed a sport practice that allows the categorization and ranking of human movement along a continuum of bodily production: the production of results, the quantification of records as a way of translating movement to data, the comparison of results, and the gradation of achievement. This was an innovation in the rich history of popular games, festivities, folk competitions, and bodily rituals. It was only by this transformation that "sport history" was generated as a narrative of the one continuous process from lower to higher achievement.

This productivist practice of modern movement culture delivered a model for placing peoples into a hierarchical order, the pinnacle of which was called "civilization." Sport served as a sort of living dynamometer—a laboratory for achievement production and productivistic ranking.[25] It is only with this background in mind that one can really understand the shock that the success of the twentieth century's black athletes aroused in the Western world and especially in America.[26] This emotional commotion cannot be grasped from the "rational" concept of the record, but it touched instead on the deeper layers of ritual practice: the ritual of record, which is linked to the "monotheism of production" as a central myth of Western modernity.[27] The shock was prefigured by the success of African American boxers in the years after 1900, but became more aggravating when the dominance of "the black athlete" became visible on the running track in the 1950 and '60s. The running track traditionally held iconic status among sports, and the 100-meter run can be seen as the modern ritual par excellence.

With this perspective of productivism in mind, we turn to the concrete "anthropological" activities of 1904 and their body-cultural signification.

Running, jumping, and throwing, the classical Western contests, were placed at the center of the 1904 Anthropology Days, and the activity of pulling casts further light on the process.

Running

Among the Olympic events of the Anthropology Days, running events dominated. This corresponded to the fact that the runner is the classical icon of modern sport—and of modern behavior more generally. The runner on the running track expresses through bodily practice the streamline of personal "career" and societal "progress." Career and progress—these keywords of modern life—construct only a meaning with the human being as projectile in mind, the human runner on the racing track under the control of the stop watch.

From the anthropological perspective of body culture, however, the configurations of running are more complex. Racing is more than and other than simply moving forward along a straight line from start to finish.[28] This is shown by the ritual running events of Native American people.[29] The wandering movement of the Aboriginals of Australia along their "song lines" provides further contrast.[30]

This rich variety is not just true for footraces. Chinese boat races, accompanied by drums, were fundamentally different from the Western sporting race, and drum and rhythm play in general a more remarkable role in "anthropological" racing competitions than the Western sportive mind will accept.[31] A special configuration of racing or running—also dancing, limping, and riding—was arranged in the labyrinth, which was used in different historical and "anthropological" cultures for movements going forward to the center and back again to the entrance.[32]

Jumping

Jumping is, at closer anthropological glance, much more complex than one would assume from observing the Olympic versions, which reduce the jump to the production of data on height or length, measured in centimeters.[33] Even in modern Western body culture, the sport model of jumping with its English origins has not been the only one. The Nordic gymnastic model of jumping stressed the aesthetic of symmetrical bodily posture and of the movement flow in its totality. It was part of a system of pedagogical rules aiming at harmony and personal fitness, correctness and the equality of all participants on a collective level as high as possible. In other words, the modern human being can do the jump either as a productive activity—producing results—or as a reproductive exercise, reinforcing health, fitness, and social integration.

There exist, however, many forms of jumping in the world that do not fit into the dual pattern of sport versus gymnastics because they neither display

355

the raising of achievement standards nor the fulfillment of the rule. On the Melanesian isle of Pentecost in Vanuatu, men jump from a high tower down to the earth during traditional festivities. They tie themselves by lianas or vines to the tower, which has different levels for different age groups, and throw themselves down to the ground, encouraged by the chanting, stamping, and dancing of the villagers. In the 1970s and '80s, this Pacific "land diving" inspired the invention of bungee jumping.[34] In Rwanda, certain young men had the tradition of jumping over a high installation in the context of aristocratic court ceremonies, typically jumping one after the other in quick succession.[35] And still nowadays, Mexican Indians fascinate us with their game of los voladores in which men "fly" around a high pole.[36] All these events were or are related to ritual folk festivities.

European folk culture knows the artistic jump at the fair as well as the comical jump of the clown in the circus. Children practice gambol as game. Since the 1970s and '80s, bungee jumping has spread internationally as a risk sport, as a means of psychological self-testing and peak experience. And hip-hop dancers are jumping in their own way. Jumping is a rich world of movement, near to the human impetus "to fly."[37] This deserves deeper analysis.

Throwing

Like running and jumping, throwing is normally regarded as an "elementary" and "natural" activity, which, by modest cultural refinement, was developed further as a sport. Although the activity of throwing can be, and has been, designed in such a way that measurement of the distance of the object thrown is the primary goal (practiced in the 1904 Anthropology Days by means of the javelin throw, shot put, ball, weight, and bolo), this arrangement has not played an important role in traditional popular games. There, the decisive outcome is hitting a certain target and is the origin of popular games such as bowling, quoits, and curling.

What is unique about these games is that one can literally "hear" them—they have the "intonation of laughter." Laughter is provoked by the game of hitting "the point." If an athlete throws the ball or the discus as far as she or he can, there is nothing to laugh about in this instance. But in the case of aiming for and hitting a target—or failing to hit the target—or in obtaining a new and unexpected configuration of balls created by the next cast, we are confronted by diverse opportunities for surprise and laughter. This structure of "hitting the point" corresponds to the fact that jokes have a certain "point," too. Laughter is expressed as a bodily and psychic explosion—the burst of laughter (in French, éclat du rire; in German, Gelächter ausbrechen). Thus, throwing is not just a "natural" technique of obtaining distance, it is, perhaps foremost, a way of making or hitting the point and provoking laughter.

Likewise, the activity of running has been not simply a matter of obtaining a certain distance within a certain amount of time. It has also been, through long periods of human play and gaming (and is still today in children's games) a part of a more structured activity of run- and-catch. Running thus has a point, too—to be caught or to evade being caught. And again this can be "heard" by the laughter that accompanies it.

All of these observations show how problematic it is to construct a progression of development from "elementary" forms of movement to sport. What we find, instead, are diverse cultural activities, which are complex from the very beginning and in fact are often "reduced" by modern sport. This can be seen clearly in the case of "pulling" and its modern manifestations.

Pulling

Somewhere between the Olympic competitions and the "ethnologic" folk practices one finds tug-of-war, as it was practiced both in the Anthropology Days and in the "real" Olympics of 1904.[38] Variations of pull and tug are present in many folk cultures all over the world, but its inclusion into the Olympic program has in the long run been more problematic than one would have thought in 1904.[39]

In Inuit cultures, pulling seems to be especially developed, in the form of

25. International tug-of-war competition in the 1904 Olympic Games. From Bennitt and Stock-bridge, eds., *History of the Louisiana Purchase Exposition*, 568.

stick tug; pulling rope or smooth seal skin; arm pull, finger, wrist or hand pull; neck pull; ear or foot pull; elbow pull; and wrist press. For competitive pleasure, people may tug or turn each other's nose or ear. Even mouth pull, arse pull, and pulling testicles are documented. Traditional games in Scandinavia make up a further province of pull. The multiplicity of forms there include simple actions involving finger, arm, and neck pulling, tug-of-war, and stick pulling, along with more complex variations like the Danish game "to pull the calf from the cow" and "to tie up the peewit," where the opponents try to topple each other by means of a rope connecting their feet. In "to cut out Palle's eye," the two competitors try—backside to backside—to pull a stick between their legs toward a candle, which they try to extinguish. Old Nordic so-called hide games were variations of pulling hide or skin—this could resemble ball games—but also the belt pull, belt wrestling, and rope pull. A variation of the latter was "ring pull," where two men, normally in a sitting position, pulled a rope that formed a ring. In "four men's pull" this could be played as a group game in which each of the pullers tried to reach a certain object, while the others prevented this from happening by their tricky rhythmic pulls, trying at the same time to reach their own respective objects. The pulling games were often connected with joking, so that the physical action exploded into shared laughter. This is also true for the pub game of the Alps where strong men, laughing and drinking beer, challenge each other to *Fingerhakeln*. This finger pulling became an element of modern Bavarian folklore.

The parallels between the different popular cultures of pull and tug should,

however, not be overemphasized. The medieval Danish historian Saxo Gram-
maticus tells about two men who pulled the rope after having wagered their
lives. When one of them finally won after a hard fight, he neither dismissed
the loser with noble "sporting" generosity, nor did the competition dissolve
into laughter in the Inuit manner. But he put his foot on the back of his opponent, breaking his backbone and, to be quite sure of his victory, broke his
neck, too, accompanying this with insulting words.

Whether we believe this story or not, and however representative it may
have been, it bears witness to a warrior culture that placed brutal pull- and-
tug games in the context of competing and killing. This was fundamentally
different both from the sociability of the Inuit winter house, from Bavarian
folklore, and from the modern sport of tug-of-war.

Yet tug-of-war is not an unambiguous modern sport, either. It met with
some serious problems, which have hampered its recognition as an Olympic sport. On its way toward modern sport, tug-of-war passed through the
Scottish Highland Games. In 1822 there was reported an event of "tearing
cows limb from limb after they had been felled."[40] Maybe this game of tug
had its roots in older Scottish practices, based on the cattle raids of the clans.
Maybe, it was an artificial, romantic reinvention of folklore. These origins
remain an open question. In any case, in the 1840s tug-of-war appeared
on the programs of various Scottish Highland Games and soon became a
specific feature—side-by-side with tossing the caber—of their particular
athletic culture. In the Scottish Highland Games that were held in Paris in
1889, the combination of tug-of-war, caber tossing, Highland dancing, and
tartan fashion already resembled an ethno-pop show, organized as it was
side-by-side with Buffalo Bill's Wild West show.[41] It was not a big step from
this to the 1904 Anthropology Days.

During the early phase of modern sport, popular traditions of tug also
existed in English villages and towns. At the London market place, rope pull
was held annually on Shrove Tuesday. It was said that up to two thousand
people participated in the tug event and held a festival afterward in which

the rope was sold. Furthermore, from the late eighteenth century onward, philanthropic educators on the European continent had rediscovered the popular tugging games. They integrated pull and tug into their handbooks of exercises, gymnastics, and games, often in an abstract and systematic way, and adding health-related and moralistic recommendations. In spite of this pedagogization, pulling games were often "overlooked" in the gymnastic literature of the nineteenth century, until tug-of-war reappeared as sport at the end of the century.

As a competitive sport, tug-of-war was adopted around 1880 by the Amateur Athletic Association (AAA) in England and seemed by the beginning of twentieth century to be on its way to being established as an Olympic discipline. From 1900 to 1920, there was rope pulling at the Olympic Games, and at the 1900 Paris Games, a mixed Danish-Swedish team won the first gold medal in this event. After 1920, however, the event was excluded from the Olympic canon, since it was regarded by serious athletes "as something of a joke."[42] Since 1958, the Tug of War International Federation (TWIF) has been working on a regular system of championships with weight classes and detailed rules for their competitions. They have tried to get tug-of-war back onto the Olympic program, but so far in vain.

The exclusion of tug-of-war from Olympic sport is, from the standpoint of body-cultural analysis, at least as interesting as its reverse, the modern integration of the game into sport. Historically, rope-pulling competitions took their place somewhere between the eccentricity of the folkloric mouth pull and the rationality of modern sport. Sport was not just an extension of popular competitions, but an alternative.

New "Tribal Games" in the Age of Globalization?

The relationships between Western Olympic sport and the "anthropological" competitions of 1904—seen in a broader historical and ethnological horizon—were not so simple. They become still more complex when we focus on the specifically "indigenous" activities of the event and take a step forward in time toward the age of "globalization." The history of modern sport shows a shifting rhythm of exclusion, inclusion, and transformation of folk practices.

When modern sport started with the illusion that competitive sport was an extension of popular games and exercises, several attempts at inclusion were undertaken. In 1900, tug-of-war entered into the Olympic program, but Nordic books of sport also included snowball fights and other folk games. Tug-of-war, along with the bolo cast, pole climbing, and mud fights in the 1904 Anthropology Days can be seen in this connection.

Subsequently, however, the "other" types of movement were excluded, and the Anthropology Days were one step on this way of exclusion. They clearly demonstrated that Olympic sport was not an extension or perfection of folk games, but something different. Modern sport in its core was not festivity and game, but work and production, though the myth of "the Games" as "games" is alive and well, not only in the popular ideology of Olympism but also in the scholarly discipline of "sports history."[43]

Later on, however, new attempts at inclusion were undertaken. Games from manifold folk traditions were "rediscovered" and integrated into sport events in different ways. This inclusion was prefigured by certain initiatives in the Soviet Union and China.[44] Soviet "ethnological" games started with the first Central Asian Games in Tashkent in 1920 and were included into the first Workers' Spartakiad of 1928. Folkloric sports and dances as colorful demonstrations became a part of the ceremonies around the "real" sports, thus illustrating the general tendency of state monopolism to use folklore as a "soft" decoration for "hard" contents. The People's Republic of China imitated this model, but took it further. From the first National Minority Games in Tianjin 1953 to the Chinese National Minority Games of 1982, and since then quadrennially, the "ethnological" games—connected with ethnographic fieldwork and classification—served a strategy of integration. Though this happened in large and powerful countries, the state monopolistic character of the "anthropological" strategy—half recognition, half suppression—has remained rather marginal to the global process. The recent wave of inclusion has followed other types of logic. Among different rationales, we can distinguish a logic of Special Games, a logic of Sport for All, and a logic of Social Indignation.

Special Games

The idea of Special Games is derived from the rationale of Olympic sport, the problem of which was and is the relation to "the other." In the hierarchical order of classical competitive sport, the top was the place of the young white man (eventually woman), typically Protestant, middle class, and representing one of the large sport nations. The place for "the other"—people outside Europe, religious and ethnic minorities, working class, sexual minorities, elderly people, children, and so on—was "down there," where the declassified athletes are huddled together in their relative misery as losers. The pyramidal order of sport expresses the idea, We are all united in the same striving for excellence, but some are better, and the rest is not really important. This is what the classical model of sport would dictate—if ways of broader inclusion were not found.

It was exactly this that Coubertin had already planned in the cases of the African and Asian Games, and that he had accepted in the case of workers' Olympiads. For "the others," pyramids of the same Olympic type should be constructed so that they could enter into their own hierarchical systems of striving. Already in 1904, the pattern began to unfold. Though still mostly specialized along disciplinary lines, Sullivan summed it up: "We have had in St. Louis under the Olympic banner handicap athletic meets, interscholastic meets, Turner's mass exercises, baseball, international gymnastic championship competitions, championships for public schoolboys, lacrosse championships, swimming championships, basketball championships, one of the best rowing regattas ever contested, bicycle championships, roque tournaments, fencing tournament, [and] a special week for the Olympic Young Men's Christian Association championships."[45]

The specialization toward target groups was differentiated more and more during the twentieth century, until a principally unlimited panorama of Special Games has appeared—with Paralympics in one corner and anti-Olympic Olympics as the Games of the New Emerging Forces (GANEFO) in another corner.[46] In 2000–2002, the following special events were registered on the agenda of sports: Student Games (for the young), World Masters Games (for the elderly), Games for the Disabled, Transplant Games, Games for Athletes with Cerebral Palsy, Games for the Blind, Games for the Deaf, Games for Catholic Students, Games of the Small Countries, Island Games, Francophone Games, South East Asian Games, Games of Non-Olympic Sports, Gay Games, and World Dwarf Games.

In this way, each otherness can finally get its little box. Though the Special Games are organized along the patterns of Olympic competition, they open up into a larger multitude of activities. These steps became especially visible during the 1980s. In May 1985, the Games of the Small States of Europe was for first time held in San Marino with participants from Andorra, Cyprus, Iceland, Liechtenstein, Luxemburg, Malta, Monaco, and San Marino. The Games were sanctioned by the International Olympic Committee (IOC), followed the Olympic ritual, and had exclusively Olympic standard sports on their program. In July 1985, the first Inter-Island Games took place on the Isle of Man. The participants came from Åland, Anglesey, Faeroe, Froya, Gotland, Guernsey, Iceland, Isle of Man, Isle of Wight, Jersey, Malta, Orkney, Shetland, and St. Helena. Again, the program consisted of the Olympic standard sports, but traditional Manx dances and the ancient Celtic *triskell* as the logo indicated possible directions of future development.

In both cases, the "dwarfs" among the large Olympic sports nations got their special opportunity to excel. Though this was arranged in accordance with Olympic premises, the regional logic could have more far-reaching consequences. In September 1985, the first Eurolympiad of Small Peoples and Minorities was hosted by Friesland in the Netherlands. The participants came from Brittany, Cornwall, Elsass-Lothringen, Belgian Flanders, and French

Flanders, Friesland, Lapland, the Molucs, and Räto-Romania, that is, from peoples without states of their own. They competed not only in standard classical sports, but also in traditional folk sports (Celtic wrestling, Frisian regatta, Frisian *streifvogelen*) and cultural competitions (singing).

In November 1988, a seminar in Villa Real, Portugal, discussed the matter of "Traditional Games" under the aegis of the Council of Europe and proposed plans for a general inventory of their registration.[47] Folk games had achieved "status." Since these beginnings in the 1980s, a rich variety of international festivals of traditional games has developed. Folk games gained an increasingly autonomous place in sport culture, and also in the world of sport research.[48]

Sport for All and Traditional Games

The recent expansion of folk game festivals must also be seen in connection with what is called Sport for All. Sport for All was launched as a concept for mass involvement in sports by European ministers and sport organizations in the late 1960s. Though the concept downplayed the principle of competition, the IOC joined this strategy, trying to control its development. Among the rich panorama of activities, which were proposed for the healthy and socially integrating Sport for All, ethnic games, traditional sports, and folk games soon received special attention. Even leaders of established sport discovered that competitive sport might be a Western-style one-way street and exclude many people who should be embraced by healthy sports. Concerns of this type were expressed by prominent speakers at an international congress of Sport for All in 1986 where traditional sports and movement practices like African dances and Burmese tug-of-war, Chinese tai chi and dragon boat races, Inuit games, Korean seesaw, and Portuguese stilt-walking were named as alternatives or supplements.[49]

One result was that in June 1992 the festival of Traditional Sports and Games of the World was arranged in Bonn, organized by the German Sport Federation together with Trim and Fitness—International Sport for All Association

(TAFISA) and sponsored by Volkswagen and Lufthansa. In the name of "sports culture" and "cultural identity," the festival presented a broad panorama from Danish village games to Brazilian fighting dance, *capoeira*, and from the Chinese martial art *wushu* to Flemish pub games.[50] The festival became a success and was later on repeated in Bangkok, in 1996, and again in Hanover, in 2000, in connection with the World Exposition. Thus, world's fairs and "indigenous" games had met again, though on another historical level.

Popular Movements and Social Indignation

The administrative actions from the top by ministries and sport organizations, which favored traditional games, must be seen in the context of social and regional movements, which developed outside the systems of the state and the market. Alternative youth cultures, regional nationalism, and social indignation from below, from civil society, contributed a new agenda.[51]

Impulses for the discovery of folk sports came in the early 1970s from the so-called New Games. New Games were an outcome of the "new movement culture," which had begun in California. In connection with the movement against the war in Vietnam and with hippie culture, young people engaged in noncompetitive play and game, developed new sports, and rediscovered existing games.

At about the same time, in several regions of Europe there arose a new interest in reviving and preserving traditional folk sports. Among the first to engage in this field were people from Flemish *volkssport. Volkssport* consisted typically of urban pub games and traditional sports organized by local clubs. Having been neglected for a long time, they received new attention in a situation of social and national tension. The youth revolt of 1968 expressed itself in ethnic national strife from the Flemish side, directed against the Belgian central state. Sport for All was launched in Belgium as a democratization of sports, parallel with the federalization of the state, and in this connection folk games received academic status.[52] Also Basque competitions of force and Breton folk games profited from ethnic unrest.[53]

Another new phenomenon was the spread of folk sports from Third World countries to the Western metropolis, which often happened in the context of youth cultures. *Capoeira*, a traditional Afro-Brazilian sport, became popular among young people in European cities such as Amsterdam, Berlin, and Paris. Tai chi and *wushu*—historically based on Chinese warrior training and magic folk practices—were now practiced worldwide. The Indonesian martial art *pencak silat* became a Western sport.[54] Even Japanese sumo wrestling, with its display of the extreme body, appeared in Western countries. Immigrant cultures (re-)invented new movement forms like the *bhangra* dance of South Asians in Britain.

Anticolonial movements in the third world joined the game, stimulated by the "spirit of Bandung" (1955) of African and Asian nations. Radical countries among the nonaligned nations—such as Libya and Algeria—tried to develop traditional games as an alternative to Western "colonial" sport.[55]

Seen in body-cultural perspective, these diffusions of folk sports were contradictory. On the one hand, "ethnic" patterns were sometimes transformed after the Western model into specialized sports of achievement with tournaments, bureaucratic organization, and the controlled production of results. On the other hand, the diffusion of "exotic" folk sports also created new practices in the Western world that are alternatives to modern standardized sport. And a third effect was that new activities developed that cannot any longer be placed in the traditional categories of sport. Bungee jumping is one such innovation, based as it is on the Melanesian folk ritual of "land diving."

In an inversion of the process, Western practices have also given birth to new folk practices in Africa, Asia, and the Americas. Trobriand cricket became the most well-known example, transforming a colonial sport into a Melanesian folk festivity of dance, sport, carnival, and gift exchange.[56] Disco dance appeared in China as *disike*, old people's disco, which became especially popular among elderly women.[57] Danish sport-development aid supported a local folk culture of dance and festivity, *ngoma*, in Tanzanian villages, while at the same time Sukuma drumming appeared in Danish youth culture.[58]

Some of the sharper political edges of modern folk sports were exposed when the Soviet Union broke down, at around 1989–91, under the pressure of democratic movements and ethnic nationalism. Folk sports and people's festivals, which had been repressed in the Soviet era, were now revived in many parts of the former empire. The Kazakh New Year's festivity Nauryz reappeared with its dances and games. Mongolians returned under the sign of Genghis Khan to ancient festivities with nomad equestrianism, belt wrestling, and bow and arrow. Siberian Buriats united by their festivity the Sukharban traditions of Buddhist Lamaism, Soviet sport, modern state folklore, and sponsored market fashion. Tatars held their springtime holiday Sabantuy again, with belt wrestling korash at its center.[59] The Baltic peoples assembled at large song festivals, which gave their political transformation the name of the "singing revolution." And Inuit people from Siberia and Alaska met in the drum dance and winter festivity of Kivgiq.

In post-Franco Spain, folk sports accompanied the process of democratic federalization, too. In Basque country, Catalonia, and on the Canary Islands, folk sports became active factors in the marking of regional identity.[60] In August 1992, the Olympic Games of Barcelona were supplemented by — or contrasted with — a festival of Spanish folk sports displaying forty activities of force, goal throwing, traditional wrestling, and the pelota ball game. This happened in the context of Catalan nationalism, which expressed itself not only in a "war of the flags," but also in the Catalan traditional dance, the sardana, and folk acrobatic gymnastics, castells de xiquets, building human towers, which were incorporated into the Olympic ceremony.[61]

Thus after ninety years, a few new types of "tribal games" have appeared in the context of the Olympic program again. In this perspective, 1904 was not a singular episode. Special Games and Sport for All as strategies from above reflect the dynamics of peoples' cultures from below.

This calls into question our categories of "forward" and "backward" in history. What once had been a "progressive" forward run in 1904, would now look backward, while popular movements "back to tradition" have pushed developments "forward" — even toward democratic revolution.[62] What was happening was structural change.

The structural change also concerned anthropology as a field of knowledge. As the Anthropology Days in 1904 indicated, anthropology at that time was mainly physical anthropology, knowledge of "race" as a one-way street from the white observer to the "tribal" object. One century later, anthropology has become a field of cultural studies unfolding in a complex interplay between the different "tribes" of the world (including Western observer cultures).[63] From anthropometry to cultural anthropology, the popular movements of decolonization have contributed to this shift.

Rethinking the Categories of Movement Culture

The paradoxes of exclusion and inclusion, of racing "forward" and "backward" on the path of change, are processes that are neither accidental nor internal only to the world of sports. They result from an interplay between the folk of civil society, the state with its public logic, and the market with its commercial logic. What is new about the recent wave of "tribal games" is that they grew out of the social movements of civil society, which the Anthropology Days of 1904 did not.

This shows that the analysis of an event (like the Anthropology Days or the Olympics more generally) may not be reduced to its ideas and its organizational framework. It must be based on a theory of "the people," which includes the sociological dimension of civil society, the psychological dimension of identity, and the praxeological dimension of bodily activity.[64]

This gives rise to some philosophical reflections about anthropology and ethnology more generally. Anthropology asks, Who is the human being? But the human being is not alone in the world.[65] "The human being" is an abstraction of the human beings existing in plural. That is why anthropology is related to ethnology, which asks, Who are the folk? Who are the people?

In the case of the Anthropology Days of 1904, we met the peoples of the Pygmies, American Indians, Japanese Ainus, and so on. These "savage" people encountered other people, so-called civilized people, who were following their own strange rituals of Olympism, "production," and sport (whether expressed along the line of McGee and Sullivan or of Coubertin). But there was also a further type of people engaged in the encounter: the enthusiastic spectators and media-journalists of the anthropological spectacle. These "unserious people" are often overlooked by the "serious" scholars of sport, who still often have problems moving beyond the Olympic colonial thinking of the early twentieth century.[66]

The event of 1904 was significant in calling to our attention the "other" ways of body and movement culture. This was, or can be, in some way subversive. On the level of reflection, the Anthropology Days teach a subversive lesson as well. They urge us to rethink the fundamental categories of what we are talking about when we analyze sport and movement culture. When placing the Anthropology Days of 1904 — as well as the possible "tribal games" of the future — into the context of body cultures (in plural), we have to think along different axes: the sportive, the ritual, the spectacular, and the interpopular, or festive, encounter.[67] These may be different genres (as a sort of empirical "ideal typology" in the sense of Max Weber) or models of practice (with some normative undertones) or sheer analytical categories.

The Sportive

Sport represents the unilinear track of progress, according to Western premises. Translating movement into records, sport follows the logic of achievement production by bodily effort. As a machine of monocultural sameness, sport "conquers" the world. The Anthropology Days placed "the others" onto the Olympic style of racetrack — "progress," "career," "development" — and, thus, into the public logic of the colonial state. Sport offers to those others the track of integration and colonization, of inclusion — or exclusion. Sport

is the one mainstream track, and there is nothing else besides certain pock-
ets of "resistance."[68] We all want results, we want records. In other words,
by sportive movement, human beings compete for results. This is production by movement. Olympic monoculturalism of this sportive type was the
background of the 1904 Anthropology Days. The event supplied the sportive
production of records with the production of "indigenous" records (such as
pole climbing), and with the "negative" record of the "weak savages."

But an Olympic record, for example, is not the same as the kind of record
documented by the *Guinness Book of World Records*, which does include world
records of sport, too, but here the sport result is only one chapter inside a
much larger narrative. The category of the Guinness record is more comprehensive and configurationally different from sport records. It collects strange
records. Among these are the slowest tug-of-war (1889, in India), the largest
gymnastic presentation (Czech Spartakiad with 180,000 participants), the
earliest account of girls to play ball in history (at 2050 BCE in Egypt), the
quickest pole climbing (Alaska 1988), the longest side jump, the strongest
weight lifting with one finger, the lift of bear barrel, and many more—some
of these ethnic in character, others just "strange."[69] Recently, C. Manoharan
from India was reported worldwide for his attempted record of running a
live cobra through his nose and out of his mouth for the *Guinness Book of
World Records*; Manoharan had earlier set a record by gulping two hundred
earthworms in thirty seconds.[70] The Guinness record not only witnesses
standardization but also (foremost) unlimited variation in an open horizon.
This is not unlike the circus.

The Spectacular

The circus, the zoo, and the *Guinness Book of World Records* have a different relation to "the other" from sports. They put otherness on stage. Circus makes
the spectacular "strangeness" of human bodies visible, whether more as freak
show or more as carnival. The entertainment industry lives off of the display
of "the other" for the modern gaze, for the show.[71] The logic of the market can

use the taste of the strange, giving the anthropology of "the strange races" a commercial opportunity. Anthropology can be good to consume.

Thus, by spectacular movement, human beings display and experience strangeness. This is a sort of consumption of movement.

Both models — the sportive and the spectacular — may very well entail humanist endeavors: to develop humankind (the human body can do more) and to call the extreme body to our attention (the human body can do quite different things). But both models of body culture also have racist potential. There is the progressivist racism of the colonial type, and there is the racism of the freak show.

The Anthropology Days of 1904 were situated in between these two models. This intermediary position made them useless for "pure" Olympic sport, as it was represented by Coubertin. Mud fight, bolo casting, and pole climbing would never enter into the Olympic program. And tug-of-war was excluded again. This expressed the Olympic politics of monoculture, of non-recognition and progressive exclusion. But for McGee as a promoter of anthropometry by spectacular display, the combination of sport and the "theater of strangeness" was an ideal solution — anthropology with market appeal.

The Ritual

By synthesizing the sportive and the spectacular, the Anthropology Days event in 1904 distanced itself from a further genre of activities, which in a tacit way was present by being absent: the ritual of the disciplined body. The body can be disciplined in another way than by the production of results — in centimeters, grams, seconds — namely, by being subjected to certain rules of "scientific," social geometrical, or aesthetic order. The classical model of this ritual of integration was delivered by gymnastics.

Indeed, what was absent in the Anthropology Days — though not in the world's fair and its adjacent programs more generally — were forms of gymnastic exercise. This is surprising as it was generally the most favored body culture in the colonization of "indigenous people": the "savage" body should be integrated into the new dominant order by exercises in rank and file, by military drill on one hand and gymnastic calisthenics on the other. This model was applied in the Indian Schools, which should educate the Native Americans for "civilization," as well as in the Philippine Constabulary Band, which demonstrated its "civilizing" success at the world's fair. For the McGee method of anthropometry, however, this genre had the disadvantage of being difficult to measure, as it does not produce quantitative results.

In contrast to the model of production, the gymnastic type of movement can—if one uses the terminology of modern productivism—be characterized as reproductive: it is healthy, educative, and socially integrative. The Anthropology Days were in this respect not reproductive, they ranged outside the world of gymnastic training and educational evolutionism. Another indicator of the lack of ritual of the "Tribal Games" was that they were placed outside the ritual wholeness of Olympism. They were only "pre-Olympic." Though the ceremonial character of the Olympic Games was not yet developed in 1904, the "inner ritual" of solemnity evidently already existed. What was expressed by the Olympic ceremonies, as they were developed between 1912 and 1936 simultaneously with fascist ritualism, was already present in the 1904 distinction between the Olympic Games on one hand and the world's fair and Anthropology Days on the other. The Olympics have kept the quasi-religious seriousness of the ritual frame until our days, though the ritual during the last decades has entered into new syntheses with the spectacular gala show.

By ritual movement, then, we mean that human beings enter into common patterns of rhythm, disciplining their bodies for the integration into a larger whole. This may appear as a sort of reproduction by movement. What sport and ritual—whether gymnastic or ceremonial—had and have in common is the culture of sameness. This is what fitted well to the integrationalist intentions of the colonial state, but it was in tension with the commercial taste for the "strange"—and with the popular culture of variety.

This contains a reality that deserves some attention for a broader interpretation of the 1904 case. Actually, sumo wrestling is going from "indigenous" to international, *pencak silat* likewise, as well as *capoeira, wushu,* tai chi, kendo, aikido, arnis escrima (a Filipino martial art), gouren (a Breton wrestling tradition), and Yagli gures (the national wrestling sport of Turkey) — the language of movement culture becomes polyglot.

What is "strange" under these circumstances? In the 1990s, an average Danish family was exhibited with their household, tools, and daily life in the Zoological Garden of Copenhagen. "Normal" human life in the cage was the object of the usual gaze that the human being directs toward the primates. The zoo perspective was turned around. In a paradoxical way *Verfremdung* as a technique of "producing the strange display" calls attention to alienation as an existential experience under modernity, *Fremmedgørelse, Entfremdung.*

The Festive

However, there was more in the encounter of 1904 than sport and spectacle (and the absent ritual) — and this "more" developed on a somewhat subversive level. African Pygmies met American Indians and Japanese — and laughed. And modern popular culture met folk culture — and was fascinated. People met people. This constitutes a further category of movement culture: the festive encounter.

So we meet a genre that is different from sport, circus, and gymnastics, and which demands other categories than the sportive, the spectacular, and the ritual — also other categories than production, consumption, and reproduction. People meet people in play and game, in dance, in popular festivity. They meet the other as other — in encounter.[72] Human existence is variety, and identity is dialogical. Encounter happens in civil society, through popular movements from below. People meet in social community and in social indignation. In building relations to each other, people have fun. There is not only colonial sport, but also Trobriand cricket as a colorful festivity of identity: We are the others! There is not only soccer and baseball on the market but also American exceptionalism.[73] And there were Olympics in China, which challenged the Western colonial understanding of "the other." The encounter of identities is also the place where gender really matters as a relationship.

Thus, by means of festive movement, human beings meet people. This is relationship in movement. The festive has different sides as well—serious ones and lighter ones. Encounter may become deeply serious as a "politics of recognition." Recognition of difference is the fundament of democratic life.[74] In this respect, the anthropological study of "tribal games" as encounter—or "dis-encounter"—may contribute essentially to the self-reflection of democracy.

But encounter may also explode in laughter. Folk festivity is where there is fun and joking, where there is carnival. Laughter may be an important criterion of whether festivity is basically popular or just a show "for the people."[75] This is what the Pygmies expressed bodily in the 1904 event. The popular encounter is also the place of the trickster, who turns serious things upside down. Maybe all this important stuff—identity, social movement, festivity, civil society—is not so serious at the same time. In any case, colonial "race" studies and Olympic sport also have their ridiculous features.

"Race" Show, Olympic Sport, and the Laughter of Pygmies

The genres characterized above should not be regarded as fixed categories. The sportive, the spectacular, the ritual, and the festive are not like closed boxes. But they are categories to describe relations and tensions inside movement culture.

These relations are contradictory, or they can be. The case from 1904 shows how different genres came into conflict with each other. The tensions between Coubertin's Olympic sport on one side and the "race studies" of Sullivan and McGee on the other were related to a conflict between the sportive and the spectacular. The absence of gymnastics in McGee's anthropometry revealed a tension between the disciplining ritual and the sportive tendency of quantification. And the laughter of the Pygmies expressed contradictions between the sportive event and the popular encounter.

Thus the intention of constructing categories like this is not to build a system, as John J. MacAloon (1984) has attempted. And a cultural phenomenon, even an elaborated cultural invention such as the Olympic Games, can never be expected to embrace "the whole."[76] But the meaning of categories is to qualify our thinking of contradictions: to think dialectically (or "trialectically").[77] Models or genres are interesting just because they may exclude each other, and thus can generate cultural clashes.

It would be highly illustrative to analyze in more depth how the different dimensions of human movement are more exactly related to the logics of modern society, to the "trialectics" of state, market, and civil society. This cannot be unfolded here in detail, but by our empirical analysis of the 1904 event, enough affinities have become visible so as to stimulate more theory-oriented anthropology in the future.

The Anthropology Days as a spectacular show, arranged by the gifted promoter McGee, had an affinity to commercial logic. They thus showed a closer relation between the spectacular, its consumption, and the market. The St. Louis Olympics, linked as they were to the world's fair, followed commercial rationality to a great degree, which was not in the spirit of the inventor, Coubertin. In the longer run, however, and especially since the 1980s, under the presidency of Juan Antonio Samaranch, Olympism has been reoriented in this direction.

The rival model of 1904, the—aborted—Chicago Olympics, was characterized by the engagement of professors, students, and idealistic philhellenism, and so was nearer to Coubertin's ideas.[78] The Coubertinian model was also more nation-state oriented in its promotion of internationalism, thus following a public logic. And it was more ritualistic, integrating gymnastic performance and ceremonial rebinding. The colonial ritual of military drill and calisthenics, of healthy, educational, and integrative exercises, was logically related to the state pattern of discipline. This shows a closer affinity between the ritual, the reproductive, and the state rationales.

What the carnivalesque elements of the 1904 event revealed—Pygmies meeting Japanese and Native Americans in laughter and fun — was related to a third order (or disorder). This was neither an expression of state discipline nor correlated with commercial logic, but subversive folk practice. Popular culture entered the scene, joking at the colonial event. It was here that links become visible between the festive encounter, the relational, and the popular, which in today's sociology we call civil society. If this analysis is not to be misunderstood, it requires some methodological clarification.

The discourse of the sportive, the spectacular, the ritual, and the festive does not try to segregate segments or (sub)systems. But it is about different types of "logic of practice." The distinction is not an attempt to put reality into boxes but to enable the analysis of *relations*. The spectacle is not commercial "as such," it appears in the historical process also as the fascist spectacle, that is, a spectacle of statism. The spectacular world's fair was a state project. And sport can very well be analyzed as ritual — as a ritual of production. And yet there are some more striking affinities.

The correspondence between the genres and the varieties of societal logic is not a question of social "law" and determination. But we may talk about *Wahlverwandtschaften* in the terminology of Max Weber (and Goethe), about *affinities* and complex inner connections. And, last but not least, the distinction does not shut down the analysis with a final "explanation" but rather hints toward open questions. If the trialectical tension between market, state, and civil society is fundamental for an understanding of modern society and modern movement culture, we must especially ask, What is the place of the sportive, the productive?

Contradictions of Movement Culture at the Athens Games of 2004

Some new images were added to the anthropology of the Games by the 2004 Olympics in Athens. The opening ceremony of the Olympics presented, as usual, the repetitive actions of ritualism. The Olympic speeches (with their boring pathos), demonstrations of "sacred" symbols, slow-motion pomp around the flag, high-tech fire, the expected pyrotechnics — what had once been invented by the masters of ceremony of the age of fascism was now restaged by the designers of "postmodern" event culture.

This was in striking contrast with other parts of the ceremony such as the parade of "the nations." One saw the people in folkloric display, some in stiff uniforms, others in "native" costumes, dancing and swinging in spontaneous joy, waving flags and displaying their national symbols. These folks represented states whose names were rarely known to the spectator. Many of them were from "tiny" nations, others resulting from recent revolutions or devolutions, such as Palestine and East Timor. And with the perspective that there will be more in the future: Tibet, Chechnya, Aceh, Maluku, Kurdistan, Samiland, and so on. Will there come a day in the future when there are too many nations to take their place in an Olympic ceremony that is still manageable?

In any case, the overall clash became visible: postfascist solemnity, with its attempts to unify "the world" through high-tech and sacral pathos, met colorful life in all its multiplicity. Globalization met the peoples — to be sure, not globalization itself, but its glittering representation — and not the peoples themselves, but the folkloric display of states.

By contrast, the sportive activities of the Olympic Games were not at the forefront of this demonstrated multiplicity. In Athens, too, the configuration of competitive sport was still what it was in colonial times. In this respect, Olympism misused once more the "tribal" touch, just as it had misused the "savages" in 1904. But the body language of ceremonies pointed far over the horizon of the competitive event, toward a politics of recognition. So, what the 1904 Anthropology Days have to tell us is not just historical or of value for theoretical reflection only. Rather, it has an actual political point.

The Folk as Trickster: "Imagine all the people . . ."

The case of the Anthropology Days 1904 tells us about encounter and "disencounter" between peoples, about *Begegnung* and *Vergegnung*, in the words of Martin Buber. The "folk" as peoples in plural, as cultures, were constructions of Western anthropological science. And yet they were more than constructions. They prefigured the actual processes of tribalization and neotribalization in the age of "globalization."[79]

This raises questions that are fundamental for anthropology: Who are the folk of folk cultures and folk sports? Who are the people of popular culture, of popular festivity, and of popular movements? Who are the ethnic people (*ethnos*) of self-determination? And how are they related to the people (*demos*) of democracy?[80] Thus the pre-Olympic Anthropology Days contribute not just to the history of sports, and not just to the history of anthropology. They cast light on the anthropology of democracy, on the tensions between colonial dominance and popular practices, on folk encounters and questions of peace. In a paradoxical way, the study of a racist event of 1904 contributes to an understanding of the recognition of cultures, and to the culture of recognition.

Last but not least, the case tells us about laughter. "Folk" is not a category of classification in the way that the physical anthropology of the early twentieth century treated it. "Folk" is the life of the trickster. Where the McGees of the world permanently try to construct order, popular life answers by convulsions of laughter, by surprising disappearance and reappearance, by the disorder of the carnival.

Notes

1. Stanaland, "Pre-Olympic 'Anthropology Days'"; Goksøyr, "'One Certainly Expected a Great Deal More'"; Lennartz et al., *III Olympiad*, 7–9, 31–43.

2. *St. Louis Post-Dispatch*, August 13, 1904, quoted in Stanaland, "Pre-Olympic 'Anthropology Days,'" 103.

3. J. Sullivan, *Spalding's Official Athletic Almanac for 1905*, 249, 259, quoted in Goksøyr, "'One Certainly Expected a Great Deal More,'" 302.

4. Goksøyr, "'One Certainly Expected a Great Deal More,'" quoted in Lennartz et al., *III Olympiad*, 42.

5. Lennartz et al., *III Olympiad*, 42.

6. J. Sullivan, *Spalding's Official Athletic Almanac for 1905*, 249, quoted in Stanaland, "Pre-Olympic 'Anthropology Days,'" 103.

7. J. Sullivan, *Spalding's Official Athletic Almanac for 1905*, 249, quoted in Goksøyr, "'One Certainly Expected a Great Deal More,'" 302.

8. Quoted in Lennartz et al., *III Olympiad*, 31–32.

9. Morgan, *Ancient Society*.

10. Lennartz et al., *III Olympiad*, 39.

11. Lennartz et al., *III Olympiad*, 38.

12. I quote this statement from Nancy Parezo. In a shortened version, it can be found in the edition of Coubertin, *Olympic Memoirs*, 43.

13. MacAloon, *This Great Symbol*; Alkemeyer, *Körper, Kult, und Politik*.

14. See Linda Peavy and Ursula Smith in this volume.

15. Gerald R. Gems, in this volume. About corresponding colonial practices in Africa see Bale and Sang, *Kenyan Running*; and Bale, *Imagined Olympians*.

16. This was the title of an article by WJ McGee in *World's Work*. See Goksøyr, "'One Certainly Expected a Great Deal More.'"

17. Goksøyr, "'One Certainly Expected a Great Deal More,'" 300.

18. *St. Louis Post-Dispatch*, August 14, 1904, quoted in Stanaland, "Pre-Olympic 'Anthropology Days,'" 104.

19. Stanaland, "Pre-Olympic 'Anthropology Days,'" 105.

20. Also Goksøyr, "'One Certainly Expected a Great Deal More.'"

21. Taylor, "Politics of Recognition."

22. Mandell, *First Modern Olympics*, 168.

23. In the invitation letter for the conference organized by Susan Brownell, 2004.

24. Peron, *Voyage de Découvertes*, 1:475.

25. For more detail see the following works by Henning Eichberg: *Leistung, Spannung, Geschwindigkeit*; "Produktion des 'Unproduktiven'"; "Three Dimensions of Playing the Game." See also Guttmann, *From Ritual to Record*. This is controversially debated in Carter and Krüger, *Ritual and Record*.

26. Hoberman, *Darwin's Athletes*.

27. This challenges Guttmann's formula in *From Ritual to Record*.

28. Bale, *Running Cultures*.

29. Nabokov, *Indian Running*; Dieckert and Mehringer, "Mit 147 kg durch die Savanne."

30. Chatwin, *Songlines*.

31. Yang, "Dragon Boat Race"; Liu, "Dragon Boat Racing."

32. Eichberg, "Racing in the Labyrinth?"

33. More detail on jumping and its "trialectic" variety: Bale, *Imagined Olympians*; Eichberg, *People of Democracy*, 108–10.

34. Muller, "Land diving with the Pentecost Islanders."

35. Bale, *Imagined Olympians*.

36. Bertels, *Das Fliegerspiel in Mexiko. Historische Entwicklung und gegenwärtige Erscheinungsformen*. Münster: Lit.

37. Behringer and Ott-Koptschalijski, *Traum vom Fliegen*.

38. A picture of two Native American "tribes" in tug-of-war; Lennartz et al., *III Olympiad*, 41. For the results of the Olympic tug-of-war, see Lennartz et al., *III Olympiad*, 159.

39. For more detail about pull and tug, see Eichberg, "Three Dimensions of Pull and Tug."

40. Novak, *Schottische "Highland Games,"* 43. See also Jarvie, *Highland Games*.

41. Novak, *Schottische "Highland Games,"* 71.

42. Arlott, *Oxford Companion to Sports and Games*, 1058. The official explanation of why tug-of-war was excluded from the Olympic program was of a formal character, concerning its unclear organizational place between track and field, athletics of strength, gymnastics, and fighting sports. Personal communication from Karl Lennartz.

43. An elaborated defense of the theory of "the one sport" as festivity and game through the whole of history was tried by Carter and Krüger, *Ritual and Record*.

44. Brownell, "Anthropology."

45. Quoted in Lennartz et al., *III Olympiad*, 39.

46. The GANEFO of the 1960s were predominantly African and Asian games with an anticolonial background; Sie, "Sports and Politics."

47. Dufaitre, "Traditional Games."

48. Pfister, Niewerth, and Steins, *Spiele der Welt*; Pfister, *Traditional Games*; Pfister, *Games of the Past*.

49. Baumann, *Fundamentals of Sport for All*.

50. Hafner and Crombach, *Spiele, Tänze, und Sportarten der Welt*.

51. Ramirez, Nunez, and Mendoza, *Luchas, deportes de combate, y juegos tradicionales*; Barreau and Jaouen, *Éclipse et renaissance*; Barreau and Jaouen, *Les jeux traditionnels en Europe*; Eichberg, *Body Cultures*, chap. 8; Liponski, *World Sports Encyclopedia*; Liponski and Jaouen, *Ethnology of Sport*.

52. Renson and Smulders, "Research Methods."

53. This differs from the Danish traditional games movement, which began in the 1980s without features of ethnicity, though with links to the *folkelig* gymnastic movement. See Møller, *Gamle idraetslege i Danmark*; see also Jørn Møller in Amador et al., *Luchas, deportes de combate, y juegos tradicionales*, and in Pfister, *Games of the Past*.

54. Cordes, *Pencak Silat*.

55. For Algeria, see Fatès, *Sport et Tiers-Monde*. About Libya, see Eichberg, *Body Cultures*, chap. 5.

56. The famous film by Jerry W. Leach (*Trobriand Cricket*) has been regarded as the most fascinating film of sports anthropology and can be seen as a peak of film anthropology in general.; see also Leach's chapter, "Structure and Message in Trobriand Cricket," in *Anthropological Filmmaking*.

57. Brownell, *Training the Body for China*, 277–88.

58. Larsen and Gormsen, *Body Culture*.

59. Kuznezova and Milstein, "Traditions of the Tatar Cultural Minority." See also Krist, "Where Going Back Is a Step Forward."

60. Amador et al., *Luchas, deportes de combate, y juegos tradicionales*.

61. Hargreaves, *Freedom for Catalonia?*, 89–95, 101–4.

62. Recently, even a new interest in bodily retro movements has arisen, which may be regarded as a bodily equivalent of the "postmodern" forward-backward confusion: http://www.backward-running-backward.com/.

63. That physical anthropology may, however, be revitalized by actual tendencies of (Olympic) movement culture, especially by the success of African runners, is shown by John Bale in this volume.

64. Here we may profit from looking back to the historical and sociological discussions of "the popular" from the 1970s: Samuel, *People's History and Socialist Theory*. But the program is broader today, concerning both anthropology and the theory of democracy.

65. This is unfolded in the monumental philosophical study by Peter Sloterdijk, *Sphären: Plurale Sphärologie*.

66. That sport is a part of popular culture is not always acknowledged in sport science, in spite of the great achievements of the Birmingham School. Sport can, indeed, be seen in the context of key words such as: action, adventure, advertisement, circus, clown, comic, concert, fan, festivity, film, flipper, glamour, graffiti, hero, horror, image, media, museum, music box, radio, sex, show, star, television, theatre, and violence, in other words, in the context of popular culture. See Hügel, *Handbuch Populäre Kultur*, 430–41. This contributes quite another meaning than that normally realized in the mainstream knowledge of sport, which typically places sport in the context of achievement, education, ethics, fitness, health, morale, pedagogy, physical abilities, physiology, science, school, self-discipline, social integration, social learning, spiritual strength, striving, training of body and mind, and so on.

67. The following analysis has profited from the anthropological analysis of genres, as it has been presented by MacAloon, *This Great Symbol*; and MacAloon, *Rite, Drama, Festival, Spectacle*. Some relevant differences of analysis will be indicated below.

68. Guttmann, *Games and Empires*.

69. *Guinness Book of Records 1990*.

70. *Copenhagen Urban*, September 3, 2004.

71. Bale, *Imagined Olympians*.

72. "All real life is encounter." Buber, *Ich und Du*.

73. About baseball: Zurcher and Meadow, "On Bullfights and Baseball"; Guttmann's chapter, "Why Baseball Was Our National Game" in Guttmann, *From Ritual to Record*, 91–116. About soccer: Markovits and Hellerman, *Offside*; Cogliano, "Baseball and American Exceptionalism."

74. Taylor, "Politics of Recognition."

75. Bakhtin, *Rabelais.*

76. Concerning Olympism, it is therefore illuminating to compare the "ramified performance" hypothesis of MacAloon 1984 with the more conflict- oriented perspective of John Hoberman, "Towards a Theory of Olympic Internationalism."

77. On the trialectical method, see Eichberg, *Body Cultures,* "Three Dimensions of Pull and Tug," and *People of Democracy.* Also Bale and Sang, *Kenyan Running,* 18–21; and Bale, *Imagined Olympians,* 173–85.

78. John J. MacAloon's comments at the International Congress on the 1904 Olympic Games and Anthropology Days, in St. Louis, September 10–11, 2004.

79. Maffesoli, *Les temps des tribus.*

80. The questions of the people of democracy are unfolded more in detail in Eichberg's *People of Democracy,* and Møller, *Folk.* About "people" and "folk" in the studies of popular culture, see also Hügel, *Handbuch Populäre Kultur,* 56–61, 83–89, 342–51.

Chapter 11. The Growth of Scientific Standards from Anthropology Days to Present Days

JONATHAN MARKS

Anthropology is by its very nature a reactive science. It arose as an academic specialty largely in opposition to late-nineteenth-century racism and Social Darwinism—whence E. B. Tylor's assertion, from the last page of *Primitive Culture* (1871), that anthropology is "a reformer's science." A generation later in America, Franz Boas established academic anthropology largely in opposition to hereditarian thought, publishing *The Mind of Primitive Man* the same year as Charles Davenport's *Heredity in Relation to Eugenics* (1911). Davenport's book was the first major post-Mendelian text of human genetics in America, and proceeded to explain class, civilization, and individual intelligence in terms of the global distribution of genetic factors, with particular reference to a major gene for "feeble-mindedness." Boas would wage a decades-long intellectual war to establish anthropology in the face of such powerful scientific opposition.

Anthropology in the early twentieth century existed in a small handful of universities; to the extent that it was acknowledged as a field of scholarship, it was located in museums. The most intellectually progressive museums were in Germany, but the museums with the most ready access to the materials of "savage man" were in America, where the indigenous peoples had been "pacified" for a generation and could now be examined as the objects of dispassionate scientific study.

Franz Boas entered the American anthropological scene in the 1880s, one of a few practitioners equipped with a doctorate—since the advanced degree was still quite rare in America. His experience with the German conception of museum anthropology clashed with the established practice of American anthropology, and Boas leveled a sharp criticism of that practice in the pages of the journal Science in 1887. Boas had found the Smithsonian's collections nearly useless for his interest in peoples of the Northwest Coast, not because the museum lacked materials, but because the materials were organized according to their degree of advancement in relation to similar objects, and not by what we would now call "cultures." The Smithsonian's senior anthropologist defended the scheme on the grounds that cultural evolution proceeds everywhere similarly, since "like causes produce like effects," but Boas argued that this approach was unhistorical, since commonly "unlike causes produce like effects."[1]

Boas was employed at the time as the geography editor for Science. Later thwarted by the Smithsonian's securing an anthropology position for one of their own in Chicago in 1894, Boas would only find permanent academic employment at Columbia in 1896. He was appointed lecturer in physical anthropology (his research expertise lay in "collecting" Eskimo bones and measuring schoolchildren).

In 1902, the Smithsonian bypassed WJ McGee as the successor to John Wesley Powell as the head of the Bureau of American Ethnology, a position for which McGee had been groomed for nearly a decade. Boas published a strong letter in Science in protest, to no avail. McGee, however, became the first president of the American Anthropological Association that year, and shortly thereafter directed the anthropology exhibit at the Louisiana Purchase Exhibition. The paper Boas composed for the occasion was published in 1904 as "The History of Anthropology," and somewhat notoriously situated anthropology as an outgrowth of German philosophy, entirely ignoring the intellectual contributions of the American practitioners. And although those same American practitioners had instituted the simultaneous study of physical form, material remains, activities, and languages as the basic constituents of anthropological research, Boas's 1904 paper is one of the earliest documents to articulate in a formal way the constitution of anthropology as "the biological history of mankind in all its varieties; linguistics applied to people without written languages; the ethnology of people without historic records, and prehistoric archaeology."[2] At the time Boas wrote, the American Anthropological Association was but two years old, and the dominant figures of its first generation were all recently deceased (Lewis Henry Morgan, John Wesley Powell, and Daniel Garrison Brinton). It was an opportune time to write a mythic history for the discipline, which already had little theoretical coherence.

Boas was an innovator in using local history and intellectual integration as an anthropological framework. This was tied to his innovation of using "culture" as a plural noun, and to his suggestion "that civilization is not something absolute, but that it is relative, and that our ideas and conceptions are true only so far as our civilization goes."[3] Nevertheless, the discipline was still not very far removed from crude racism. Scarcely a few decades earlier, American anthropology was principally represented as the craniological studies of Samuel J. Morton, and of Josiah Nott and George C. Gliddon, intended to justify slavery through the demonstration of distinct cerebral physiologies and separate origins of the races. The first generation of American physical anthropology essentially became obsolete after the Civil War.

One can easily perceive the tensions in nascent anthropology shortly before the turn of the twentieth century. In the pages of *Science*, Brinton had lamented a pendulum swing among European anthropologists "[to] deny the existence of any such things as racial or ethnic traits, tendencies, or capacities." Brinton categorically denied that other peoples possessed the same level of intelligence as Europeans. "The mental traits of races and peoples," he wrote, "are as much their peculiar characteristics as are their bodily idiosyncrasies, and are just as impossible to change by any quick process."[4]

A year later, D. K. Shute, a Washington-based physician, read a paper before the Anthropological Society of Washington, subsequently published in the *American Anthropologist*, that presented a roster of ostensibly apelike or "simioid" features possessed differentially by human races. "Measured by these criteria," he wrote, "the Caucasian stands at the head of the racial scale and the Negro at the bottom." This analysis and conclusion provoked some heated discussion, principally from the Washington-based anatomist Frank Baker, the sitting editor of the *American Anthropologist*. Baker observed that the physical differences reported among the races were overblown and "misunderstood." And to the extent that there are racial characteristics by which whites differ from blacks, "as a matter of fact there does not seem to be adequate ground for the conclusion that his racial peculiarities are remarkably simian." Baker drew on first-hand dissecting-room experience of blacks to support his contention that "ape-like characters are no more common among them than among whites." The next commentator, however, agreed more with Shute and asserted that "the negro is an example of retarded or arrested development."[5]

WJ McGee, Boas's new ally in 1904, held ideas about human diversity that were somewhat unsophisticated, but were still a far cry from those of the racist physicians who still comprised much of the anthropology community. He found popular racial classification to be typological and unrealistic, pointing to "the objection that certain peoples hardly fit any one of the five classes." At the same time, however, he argued that the separate origins of different peoples was still an open question and envisioned biocultural evolution as a set of intertwined phenomena, which yielded a four-stage developmental series no matter what was being analyzed, with its European expression at the summit.[6] Thus, "[w]hen the world's peoples are classified by culture-grade, or in terms of progress from the lowest to the highest stages, it at once becomes manifest that they are arranged . . . in accordance with general physical development, including strength, endurance, and viability." And finally, he believed that race mixture was a good thing (a contentious point at the time), with "the world's strongest blood being the world's most-mixed blood," which would seem to place melting-pot America above all other nations.[7]

386

He saw the Louisiana Purchase Exhibition as an opportunity to bring "the field" home, and to study indigenous peoples without the inconvenience of having to travel to them.[8] Torn from any relevant context or environmental setting, these people could nevertheless hopefully be the objects of study in somatology (bodily form), psychology, arts and industries, languages, law and society, faiths and philosophies, general ethnology, general anthropology ("the comparative study of primitive and advanced peoples in an unexampled assemblage of race-types and culture-grades"), and as subjects for scientific, photographic, or artistic record.

Odd as that may sound today, it was only a few years earlier that Boas himself had asked Robert Peary to bring back some Eskimos from Greenland, to be studied in New York. The outcome was tragic, as were the personal histories of Ota Benga and (under quite different circumstances) Ishi.[9] Without cultural context, however, the people and their possessions turned out to be largely valueless anthropologically, and the psychosocial and biomedical consequences of transplanting people were generally overlooked or naively rationalized at the time.

The people brought to the Louisiana Purchase Exhibition would nevertheless be the objects of scientific study, as closely as one could approximate the dispassion of a chemist studying the properties of boron. Natural science would afford the most appropriate role model for the study of "man," and the differences in kind between their subject matters would be minimized as far as possible.[10]

Today, such an idea seems ludicrous for its internal contradiction: To pretend humans are not cultural in order to study them "scientifically" is to begin by denying the most salient natural fact about the human species. Moreover, it is now commonplace in genetics to acknowledge that since a phenotype is the product of a genotype expressed in a specific context, there can be no phenotype independent of the environment that produced it. In the case of humans, obviously, that context is biocultural—with complex environmental, motivational, and experiential components contributing to the development of human bodies and behaviors. Consequently, it is meaningless to try to regard human bodies and behaviors—their states, performances, and products—independently of the circumstances in which they arise, perform, and produce. Those were clearly premodern times in anthropology.

The Return of Racial Pseudoscience

Flash forward a hundred years. We pass the elaboration of cultural relativism by Boas's students after World War I; the vain struggle of Earnest Hooton to differentiate good American racial studies from bad German racial studies between the wars; Sherwood Washburn's reinvention of physical anthropology in the 1950s.[11] We pause by the British physical anthropologist J. S. Weiner's characterization of the biological structure of the human species "as constituting a widespread network of more- or-less interrelated, ecologically adapted and functional entities"—implying that the constituent units of the species are local populations, not para-continental clusters.[12] We note the elucidation of the cultural aspects of race—from studies of immigrants (pioneered by Boas), cultural history, the submerging of former racial identities (e.g., Irish, Jewish), the elaboration of new ones (Latino, Middle Eastern), and the invention of the racial category "multiracial."

And yet, along with the erosion of the idea that race constitutes a natural, biological human category, a backlash develops. In the early 1960s, the Columbia University psychologist Henry Garrett, anatomist Wesley Critz George of the University of North Carolina, and businessman-author Carleton Putnam published articles and books arguing that science supported segregation.[13] Moreover, they maintained that the emerging consensus about race was simply an antiscientific political doctrine imposed by a conspiracy of Jewish communist anthropologists, led by Franz Boas.[14] Similar sentiments were even held by the prominent anthropologist Carleton Coon, who was circumspect enough in public, but would share the Jewish-communist-anthropologist theory in correspondence. Coon, as sitting president of the American Association of Physical Anthropologists in 1962, was clandestinely corresponding with, and aiding, the segregationists.[15]

Indeed, in a 1960 letter to his cousin Carleton Putnam, Coon assured him prophetically, "The tide is turning. Heredity is coming back into fashion, but not through anthropologists. It is the zoologists, the animal behavior men, who are doing it, and the anthropologists are beginning to learn from them. It will take time, but the pendulum will swing." (Putnam later quoted that letter anonymously in his notorious *Race and Reason*.)[16] And fifteen years after Coon wrote those words, *Sociobiology* proved him right.

But actually heredity and sociobiology are non sequiturs, if the question at hand is race. How do they converge? The hereditarian believes that genetic variation underlies behavioral or mental variation. The racist believes that humans are divisible into a number of natural groups, each with different endowments. The interests of the hereditarian and the racist coincide *if the behavioral or mental variation under consideration is specifically that which differentiates groups from one another.*

This may seem like an obscure point, but it gets to the heart of many contemporary misunderstandings involving racism, genetics, and evolutionary psychology (i.e., sociobiology, version beta). The question, Does genetics influence behavior? has a trivial answer. So does the question, Does culture influence behavior? And so, too, does the question, Does personal experience influence behavior? To address the relationship between genetics and human behavior at all rigorously requires that we examine their fundamental patterns of variation. That variation is not random; it has structure.

Genetic variation—approximately 85–95 percent of it—is principally found within groups, that is, as polymorphism.[17] Paradigmatic is the ABO blood group system, in which virtually all human populations have some A, some B, and some O—and only differ from one another in the relative proportions of each allele. Only a small proportion of genetic variation exists as alleles that one group has but another does not.

Behavioral variation in the human species—defying comparable quantification—is principally found between groups, that is, as culture. Regardless of the analytic problems with the concept of culture, we traditionally take it to refer to group-level differences in behavior. That certainly is what the Boasian concept of culture was intended to convey—locally normative ways of experiencing the world, existing in it, and making sense of it. And yet, obviously, the differences between cultures have a basis entirely in social history. If cultural difference constitutes the principal structure of human behavioral diversity between groups, and if those differences are not genetic, then it follows that the great bulk of between-group human behavioral variation must have a nongenetic etiology.

Can genetic differences in mind and act be found? Of course, but they cannot constitute any significant part of "the big picture." These genetic differences will be polymorphisms—like the great bulk of genetic variations are—and thus will be identifiable from person to person within a population. In addition to factors like life experiences and familial traditions, there may well be genetic reasons for why one person tends to think or do one thing and another person tends to think or do another—as long as we understand that we are talking about mental and behavioral differences *within a single population*. In other words, human behavioral variation and genetic variation are structured so differently that the latter cannot reasonably be considered a significant cause of the former. The great bulk of human behavioral/mental variation occurs *between* groups and is the product of historical forces; the great bulk of genetic variation occurs *within* groups, and may indeed comprise part of the causal nexus of someone's life trajectory.

It is consequently anthropologically trivial to discover a genetic variant that influences thought, mood, or deed. Anthropology is concerned principally with the different things that different *groups* of people do; psychology, perhaps, is the science concerned with why people in the same group do different things. Consequently, the discovery of genetic variations in neurotransmitters and receptors is trivial in the scope of human behavior. Imagine a Yanomamo and a Harvard professor, who share an allele that makes them a bit happier (or unhappier, or smarter, or more violent) than their peers. There is no reason to think that their lives, experiences, or perceptions would converge significantly as a result of having the allele. One would still be living the life of an Amazonian horticulturalist and the other would be leading the life of an urban American intellectual. Each would be a little happier (or unhappier, smarter, or more violent), but the genetic similarity they share would be completely submerged by the cultural difference they do not share.

The reason for this digression is that without the analytic partitioning of behavioral diversity into between-group (i.e., cultural) and within-group (i.e., psychological) domains, the hereditary factors that affect the latter may be improperly posited to explain the former as well. This distinction is crucial in genetics. Consider two identical plots of soil. A handful of seed (from the same source, so there is no difference between the handfuls) is scattered in each. One plot receives plentiful sunlight and water; the other receives only a little. In a few weeks, each plot has plants of varying heights. In one, the plants vary a bit, but are generally tall and robust; in the other, the plants also vary, but are generally short and stunted. Genetic differences are certainly at work dictating the range of variation of plants in either plot, but the big difference is between the two plots and is entirely nongenetic.[18]

Looking at the variation within either set of plants, one can calculate a statistic called heritability, which will estimate the extent to which the variation in plant height is related to variation in genes. But that statistic is inapplicable to understanding the difference between the two plots, which is considerably larger and has no genetic basis. Yet that is precisely what hereditarians, from Arthur Jensen through Philippe Rushton, have purported to do: use a study of within-group variation to explain differences between groups.[19]

The Human Genome Project seemed to bring a new legitimacy to hereditarian explanations for human behavior, which the human genetics community was itself slow and somewhat reluctant to criticize.[20] In the 1990s, the "genotype" that helped rouse public support for the Human Genome Project subtly became conflated with the scholarly analysis of heredity itself. As possible niche markets for pharmaceutical companies, races are being actively reinscribed by a strange new breed of epidemiologists and population geneticists.[21] Evolutionary psychology appropriates the authority of Darwin to analyze imaginary cognitive modules as if they were biological imperatives.[22] Thus, old-fashioned racism—the idea that human groups are natural divisions, and are possessed of unequal talents—is back as well.

All four of these research areas—behavior genetics, population genetics, evolutionary psychology, and scientific racism—tend to cite the same core works. These include Derek Freeman's claim to have refuted Margaret Mead's conclusions about Samoan adolescence—and by extension, the importance of culture in human behavior; Napoleon Chagnon's claim to have identified a reproductive bias for Yanomamo warriors, and by extension, for prehistoric warriors; Daly and Wilson's claim that stepparents are more prone to infanticide than genetic parents, thereby rooting human kinship in natural relations, rather than in cultural forms; and David Buss's claim to have identified species-wide propensities in human mate choice.[23] That none of these claims has held up well under scrutiny, and the fact that none is taken seriously in mainstream anthropology does not seem to matter. Like the footprints of human and dinosaur by the Paluxy River in Texas that creationists still cite to confute anthropology, these works are brandished at face value for the sole purpose of—well, confuting anthropology.[24]

Certainly the most bizarre work in this arena is that of Canadian psychologist J. Philippe Rushton, who argues that Africans have evolved high reproductive rates and low intelligence, Asians have evolved low reproductive rates and high intelligence, and Europeans have struck a happy balance of both; and uses brain size, crime rate, sex drive, and penis length, as surrogate measures of intelligence and reproductive rate. Rushton's work was cited by Richard Herrnstein and Charles Murray in *The Bell Curve* (1994), along with a preemptive appendix defending its seriousness. Rushton's work is also cited favorably by Sarich and Miele (2004).

Jon Entine's work complements the lot, and is cited with admiration by Rushton (2000) and Sarich and Miele (2004). Entine's book, *Taboo: Why Black Athletes Dominate Sports and Why We're Afraid to Talk About It*, argued for innate racial differences in athletic ability, and even revived a variant of the old Jewish-Communist-anthropologist conspiracy as his explanation for "why we're afraid to talk about it." In fact, many of us working in human variation talk about it all the time. What we say is something like: (1) human achievements arise in cultural environments and cannot be separated from them; (2) quality of achievements is not a reliable indicator of the quality of innate abilities; (3) professional over-representation is not a reliable argument for the existence of special endowments; (4) the qualities of the population cannot be inferred from the qualities of its most extreme members; and (5) sources of within-group variation are not reliable explanations for differences between groups.

This reflects a scholarly, indeed a scientific, consensus: that there is no rigorous scientific basis on which to infer the presence of group level endowments. To argue in a modern intellectual context that group-level endowments exist requires controlled data (anecdotes and life-histories do not suffice); a means of separating from the analysis the traditions, expectations, and stereotypes that track people into certain venues; and the statistical recognition that one cannot generalize about large populations from their most outstanding members.

As I explained to Jon Entine when he sent me the manuscript, the issue at hand is scientific evidentiary standards. Either you meet them, in which case a dialog can proceed, or you don't—in which case, why are you even bothering to pretend to raise a scientific issue? The fact is that the pseudoscientific arguments for black athletic superiority directly parallel the pseudoscientific arguments for black intellectual inferiority. Entine expressed indignation at my lumping him with the authors of The Bell Curve, went on to disparage my skepticism in the book itself, and then actually wound up as an adjunct fellow at the American Enterprise Institute, Charles Murray's professional base. Small world!

Science and Humanity

The argument that racial endowments are at the root of racial achievements is beset by an epistemological problem. Humans are biocultural animals; everything we do, or think, or say, or achieve is brought into existence and rendered meaningful in a cultural context. There is no human thought or behavior external to culture. Culture indeed precedes our species, which means that every human being that has ever been born has been born into a cultural environment. One cannot analytically remove humans from culture any more than one can analytically remove the eggs from a cake. One can talk no more sensibly about humans without culture than one can talk sensibly about pigeons without feathers.

Why are some "races" over-represented in some sports? The prominence of blacks in modern track and field is paralleled by the prominence of Latin Americans in baseball. Moreover, the prominent Latin Americans in baseball run a wide "racial" gamut, since the very category "Latin American" itself cross-cuts "race." Do blacks in track and field and Latin Americans in baseball require two different explanations, or will the same one suffice?

When a demagogue like Entine generalizes about "the body of the black athlete," we are minimally obliged to wonder what black athletic body he has in mind. Basketball guard Kobe Bryant's wiry body? Baseball slugger David Ortiz's enormous body? Speedy Carl Lewis? Lanky Jerry Rice? Stocky Joe Frazier? Unless we can identify a common biological thread linking them (aside from pigmentation), we are obliged to consider the possibility that the physically diverse group of prominent black athletes are united more by the social filters that tracked them into professional sports than by the possession of a common biological gift.

To the extent that native differences in "abilities" exist, they must be patterned like most genetic variation: that is to say, principally *within* group. Some people will indeed have the eyesight, coordination, and reflexes to be able to hit a fast-moving ball with a piece of wood more reliably than others can. But the unlikely constellation of genes that makes such a feat possible will not be greatly over-represented in one population relative to another. Moreover, like all other human endowments, the genes involved will be expressed in a highly specific context.

To argue, then, that a specific athlete is "naturally" endowed is trivial. To argue that a group is "naturally" endowed, with any degree of rigor, simply requires a lot of well-controlled data. Without those data, the argument is sophistry, not science—and sophistry with an incredibly bad track record. And if those data are impossible to collect, that means that the question itself was not framed scientifically in the first place. Science, after all, is not so much about asking questions, as it is about asking questions *that can be answered*. Posing a question that cannot be answered rigorously, and then pretending that it can be, is pseudoscience.

Except in rare cases, unfortunately, pseudoscience is only identifiable as such in retrospect. But every recent scholarly generation has been saddled with combating the idea that somehow social inequalities or hierarchies are merely expressions of natural hierarchies, or racial endowments. This stretches from the Social Darwinists of the 1890s through the eugenicists of the 1920s, Nazis of the 1930s through '40s, segregationists of the 1950s and '60s, and their inheritors today.

There is no conspiracy of silence on the study of human diversity—although that suggestion, originally made by the segregationists, can still be identified in the writings of some modern scientists, who should know better.[25] The intellectual progress we have made in the study of human diversity over the last century has involved the development of standards for pronouncing scientifically on the nature and existence of human groups. They were needed because of the muddled thought, ignoble goals, and conflicted interests that have pervaded the scholarly and popular literature. Intellectual standards, however, are ultimately what permit a science to mature.

Notes

1. Boas, "The occurrence of similar inventions"; Mason, "The occurrence of similar invention."
2. Boas, "History of Anthropology."
3. Boas, "Museums of Ethnology."
4. Brinton, "Current Notes on Anthropology."
5. Shute, "Racial anatomical peculiarities."

6. WJ McGee, "Current Questions in Anthropology."

7. Provine, "Geneticists and the Biology of Race Crossing"; WJ McGee, "Anthropology at the Louisiana Purchase Exposition."

8. WJ McGee, "Opportunities in Anthropology."

9. Bradford and Blume, Ota Benga; Starn, Ishi's Brain; Harper, Give Me My Father's Body; Kroeber and Kroeber, Ishi in Three Centuries.

10. Mason, "Scope and Value of Anthropological Studies"; Topinard, Anthropology.

11. Hooton, "Plain Statements about Race"; Haraway, "Remodeling the Human Way of Life"; Marks, Human Biodiversity.

12. Weiner, "Physical Anthropology."

13. J. P. Jackson, Science for Segregation.

14. Garrett, "Equalitarian dogma"; George, Biology of the Race Problem; Putnam, Race and Reality.

15. Marks, "Human Biodiversity As a Central Theme"; J. J. Jackson "'In ways unacademical.'"

16. Letter of C. S. Coon to C. Putnam; Putnam, Race and Reason.

17. Lewontin, "Apportionment of Human Diversity"; Barbujani et al., "Apportionment of Human DNA Diversity"; Rosenberg et al., "Genetic Structure of Human Populations."

18. Lewontin, "Race and Intelligence."

19. Jensen, "How Much Can We Boost IQ?"; Rushton, Race, Evolution, and Behavior; Rushton and Jensen, "Thirty Years of Research on Race Differences."

20. Herrnstein and Murray, Bell Curve; Andrews and Nelkin, "The Bell Curve: A Statement."

21. Kahn, "How a Drug Becomes 'Ethnic'"; A. F. Leroi, "A Family Tree in Every Gene," New York Times, March 14, 2005; Koenig et al., Revisiting Race.

22. Pinker, Blank Slate; Rose and Rose, Alas, Poor Darwin.

23. Freeman, Margaret Mead and Samoa; Chagnon, "Life Histories"; Daly and Wilson, Homicide; Buss, Evolution of Desire.

24. Wrangham and Peterson, Demonic Males; Hamer and Copeland, Living with Our Genes; Pinker, Blank Slate; Sarich and Miele, Race.

25. O. Judson, "The Subject is Taboo," New York Times, June 28, 2006, http://judson .blogs.nytimes.com/.

Afterword

Back to the Future

SUSAN BROWNELL

In 1884 Chang Yu Sing, "The Chinese Giant and the Tallest Man in the World," led P. T. Barnum's Ethnological Congress into the big top. When he had joined the circus in the early 1880s, Chang was presented as a representative of the erudition and wisdom of Chinese civilization; an 1881 ad described him as "the Chinese Giant, not the ogre of Fairy Tales, but Gentleman, Scholar and Linguist—the tallest man in the world."[1] This mode of representation was a common one in freak shows of the time. Robert Bogdan calls it the "aggrandized mode" of presentation. A person with a physical anomaly was presented as an upstanding, high-status citizen with conventional, prestigious talents—representative of the best of his society in every way but for the physical anomaly.[2]

What is the difference between Chang Yu Sing in 1881 and NBA basketball star Yao Ming today? The online version of the Chinese *People's Daily* introduced the publication of Yao's autobiography by stating, "Smashing stereotypes forged over centuries and bearing the burden of being an inspiration to a billion compatriots is a mighty tall order. China's seven-foot, six-inch NBA sensation Yao Ming is up to the task. With one foot rooted in the ways and wisdom of the Chinese civilization and the other size-eighteen sneaker planted in the jet-setting world of the NBA, Yao shares his story simply and powerfully in a new, 290-page memoir, *Yao: A Life in Two Worlds*."[3]

The answer to this question hinges on notions of "representation." If they are both seen as representative of China, then what do they represent, to whom, and how? The Chang-Yao comparison above is particularly interesting because the passages are separated by 123 years, the first was written by an American and the second by a Chinese person, and yet each giant is said to represent the same essential core wisdom of Chinese civilization.

Representation has been extensively theorized from multiple angles, particularly by poststructuralists in the last few decades. I will not enter into this theoretical debate here, other than to mention that I find the succinct and accessible overview by Stuart Hall to be a useful formulation.[4] In accord with the approach laid out in my introduction, I would like to conclude this volume by pulling together concrete examples from this book that illustrate how the problem of representation entered into the interpretive frames of anthropologists and sportspeople at the turn of the last century. I concentrate on the problem of representation because, as was demonstrated by Marks and Parezo in particular, and by the other chapters more generally, a contradictory logic of representation was at the core of the "bad science" of race as expressed in ethnological displays and sports events, particularly the Olympic Games. Moreover, this contradictory logic is still at work today. In fact, as MacAloon argues, it is probably the self-contradiction and confounding of classifications that is part of the basic appeal of the Olympic Games.[5]

Barnum's "Perfect Types" versus "Extraordinary Peculiarities"

Chang Yu Sing represented two contradictory trends in Barnum's shows: sometimes Barnum sought to represent nations by "perfect types" that fit existing stereotypes and thus might be considered "average," while at other times he sought those with "extraordinary peculiarities." I would like to pay attention to the specific vocabulary that he used. In his biography, he recalled that his idea for his Congress of Nations was "an assemblage of representatives of all the nations . . . a man and woman, as perfect as could be procured, from every accessible people. . . . I had actually contracted with an agent to go to Europe to make arrangements to procure 'specimens' for such a show."[6] In 1882 he requested the aid of the U.S. government in forming a "collection, in pairs or otherwise," of "not only human beings of different races, but also, when practicable, those who possess extraordinary peculiarities, such as giants, dwarfs, singular disfigurements of the person, dexterity in the use of weapons, dancing, singing, juggling, unusual feats of strength or agility, &c."[7] He described his 1884 Ethnological Congress as "representatives of notable and peculiar tribes."[8]

It is not clear that Barnum ever seriously tried to think through the difference between the average and the extraordinary. In fact, there is some evidence that he recognized that the confounding of familiar categories was precisely what captivated his audiences, and so he played to it. This can be seen in his practice of exhibiting people, whom he labeled "What is it?" One such star attraction at the American Museum was probably a black dwarf, but was exhibited in 1860 as a being captured by gorilla hunters in Africa with advertisements asking "What is it?—or Man Monkey."[9] Bluford Adams notes that as the century progressed, Barnum increasingly used "peculiarities" to mark race, since this meant that the bodily Otherness of the peoples on display was indisputable at a time when anthropologists were attempting to define race in terms of bodily measurements and statistical averages—and failing to develop definitive measures.[10]

If we analyze Barnum's notion of representation, we can see that on the one hand he viewed "specimens" as "perfect types"—something like what we might now conceptualize as an "average" or "normal" person in statistical terms. On the other hand there were people with "extraordinary peculiarities," but what is notable is that these could be of two types. One type could be a physical anomaly such as height or shortness, the absence of arms, or a face covered in hair. The other could be excellence in an acquired skill, such as feats of strength and agility, juggling, singing, use of weapons, and so on. The conflict between "perfect types" and "extraordinary peculiarities" is also interesting because Adams's analysis suggests that when the racial or ethnic differences of his "perfect types," as defined by ethnological science, seemed too mundane to attract his audience, he spiced them up with "extraordinary peculiarities."

The distinction is important because it reveals that for Barnum there were different answers to the question, What does it really *mean* to "represent" a nation, a race, or a tribe? It reveals that in the popular ethnography of the time, it was possible to conceive that a person represented a nation, race, or tribe because he or she was an average type; it was also possible to conceive the opposite, that he or she represented a nation, race, or tribe because she was a peculiarity so extraordinary that only one nation, race, or tribe could have produced it.

In Barnum's scheme, athletes should fall into the category of individuals who are extraordinary because they possess impressive physical skills. If, at the same time, they happen to be very tall or very short or otherwise extraordinary in appearance, then they crosscut both of his extraordinary categories. However, as will be discussed below, McGee and Sullivan tended to view Anthropology Days participants as "types," not "extraordinary" people. Their viewpoints were pseudoscientific conceptions that departed only slightly from Barnum's way of seeing things. From today's perspective, Barnum's view seems more accurate than theirs, since it represented a more- or-less commonsense view, while their views were skewed by pseudoscience (McGee more than Sullivan). The tension between the "perfect" and the "peculiar" modes of representation is evident in pseudoscientific discourses in the realm of sports to the present day, but participants in the discourse rarely distinguish them.

The fate of freak shows is illustrative of what science did to the Barnumesque worldview over time. Science was linked with the displays in order to make them more interesting and less frivolous—and more believable. Scientists were invited to study them and were declared to have made decisive pronouncements about their nature.[11] In Bogdan's analysis, as physicians became professionalized, human differences became increasingly medicalized as pathological. This occurred in the 1930s. When freaks came to be known as people who were sick they lost their appeal.[12] There were critics of freak shows already as early as 1908, when the Greatest Show on Earth eliminated the freak department, ostensibly due to critical letters, but this decision was "reversed" due to public outcry and turned out to be merely a publicity stunt.[13] This suggests that U.S. public sentiment contained some antagonism toward the dehumanizing character of such displays only four years after the St. Louis World's Fair, but not enough to lead to the decline of the market for "freaks."

McGee's and Sullivan's Flawed Science

Fast forward from Barnum's congresses of the 1870s and 1880s to the 1904 St. Louis World's Fair. In defining the objectives of the Anthropology Department, the first two of McGee's five stated goals with respect to the people he assembled were to bring to St. Louis: (1) "a representation of a limited number of the world's least-known ethnic types (i.e., races or sub-races defined on a physical basis); (2) a representation of a few of the world's least-known culture types (i.e., of peoples defined on an activital or mental basis)."[14]

With respect to the first category, he used the label "physical types" to describe the people chosen. Examples were Philippine Negritos, Japanese Ainus, and numerous American Indians. Unlike Barnum, he did not choose a giant to represent a group (in Barnum's case, the "nation" of China), but he did select a Patagonian because he "illustrated a variety of the Amerind race reputed since the time of Magellan to be gigantic."[15] Reflecting his belief that biological and cultural evolution were intertwined phenomena (see the chapter by Marks), the first category was not mutually exclusive with the second. With respect to the second category, he used the labels "activital or culture types."[16] Examples were African Pygmies selected on the basis of their maternal clan and form of government, Ainus selected for their primitive agriculture, and Patagonians for their use of the bola. He also used the labels "typical representatives" and "ethnic types," which could embrace both categories.

26. Original caption reads: "A comparison between Pygmy, 25 years old, and Patagonian, 16 years old." From the St. Louis Public Library Online Exhibit "Celebrating the Louisiana Purchase."

James Sullivan's terminology was much less precise. He spoke of the "average savage," the "natural all-around ability of the savage in athletic feats," the "marvelous qualities of the Indian as a runner," the poor performance of the Patagonian in contrast with an "ordinary man" (i.e., a typical white American). Even so, he believed in the numerical "records" that he chronicled, stating that "[a] comparison of these records and the other records in the

Almanac will prove particularly interesting," and feeling that the records should be kept for future years in which "the savages" might record better performances. He concluded that "scientific men" would refer to these results for many years to come and challenged them to "substantiate" the alleged feats of the savage, clearly feeling that "records" constituted proof.[17] In sum, like McGee, Sullivan placed his faith in numerical measurements, but he was only interested in "records" and not particularly interested in using statistical measures to delimit the particular groups to which they were attached—he lumped everyone together as "savages." Parezo says that McGee, Woodworth, and Sullivan had planned to conduct special anthropometric and psychometric tests on European and American athletes as they participated in the regular Olympics, but Sullivan lost interest when Anthropology Days convinced him that no further tests were necessary.

Mark Dyreson's chapter explores McGee's use of the phrase "the physical value of races," which reflected his belief that a numerical "value" could be assigned to races based on scientific measurements. This would facilitate establishing their "relative value" along the evolutionary scale that he espoused. McGee clearly believed that "types" could be established through measurements, but as Nancy Parezo's chapter shows, he did not fully grasp the concept of the statistical average. From her discussion, it is possible to see that McGee's concept of representation was not dissimilar from Barnum's, the difference being the addition of a small dose of only partly comprehended mathematics.

As related by Parezo, McGee was concerned that the anthropometric experiments conducted by Robert Woodworth should be measuring "average" representatives of various groups so that the comparisons would be "impeccable" science. Woodworth objected to Anthropology Days because it assumed that Olympic athletes were representative of all Caucasians, and that the small selection of Native athletes could stand for a racial group. McGee countered that each should be considered an "average" representative of his group. Of course, he was wrong, since Olympic athletes had already emerged out of the general population due to their particular skill. Also, putting even that consideration aside, at first no one considered that they should be comparing the first-ever attempts of American champions to these first-ever attempts by the Natives, rather than comparing trained, seasoned competitors with neophytes. Luther Gulick, the head referee, allowed the Natives only one chance to run their races since it would have "violated" the research methodology, that is, the established rules for track meets, in which the white athletes were given only one chance to perform. Anyone who violated the rules was disqualified, with the result that as the trials progressed they had almost no "finalists" for the next day's finals. Parezo observes that "there were no valid measures of 'natural ability' being tested. The games really demonstrated that most Natives were simply not interested in 'Olympic' athletic events (except for the marathon and tug-of-war) or performing for visitors' amusement without compensation." A bit wiser after this first experiment, McGee attempted a second version a month later.

Sullivan never acknowledged the fallacious assumptions of the experiment. McGee did, explaining the poor results by stating that the Natives had been removed from their accustomed environment and had been living indolent lives at the fair, and that they lacked esprit de corps. He concluded that they needed to be coached, engage in practice, and be given financial awards, which he tried to do in the September anthropological meet. His final comment was that "nearly all the primitives were average individuals whose records should be compared not with those of athletic experts or specialists but with those of average whites in order to show useful results."[18] McGee's faith that the scientific establishment of "averages" would solve the problem remained unswerving.

We have no record of Boas's reaction to Anthropology Days, but we can imagine that he would have recognized the flawed science it involved. We do know that Boas's mastery of statistics was as strong as anyone's in 1904.[19] After all, he did have a PhD in physics. In an 1893 article, he had explained that if anthropometric measurements produce a distribution that follows the laws of chance (i.e., the average, mean, and most frequent value are the same), then and only then may the "average" be considered the "type" of the series. If not—and this was more likely the case because heredity does not follow the laws of chance—then the results must be theoretically analyzed. He also criticized the flawed application of anthropometry in physical education.[20]

Entine's Flawed Science

Fast forward to the year 2000, when the publication of Jon Entine's *Taboo: Why Black Athletes Dominate Sports and Why We're Afraid to Talk About It* revealed that century-old conceptions of sport and race were alive and well in slightly modified form. As Barnum had done, the extraordinary and the average are again confused with each other. In his chapter, Jon Marks countered Entine's assertions by reiterating that no research method has been developed to date that can measure group-level endowments with the rigor now required of scientists, because controlled data of sufficient rigor cannot be collected—life histories are not "controlled data," and in any case they cannot be separated from the stereotypes and other social forces that track people into certain sports. And, of course, there is the hundred-year-old problem: one cannot generalize about large populations from their most outstanding members, that is, a black athlete who stands out from other people of similar color of skin for his ability to spin, jump, and dunk cannot be taken as representative of the average of the population of people with like-colored skin.

In short, we are not talking about science here. McGee's desire to use Anthropology Days "to obtain for the first time what may be called interracial athletic records" and Sullivan's faith that records could be used to substantiate the claims of "scientific" men show their own confusion of records with science. Entine's book manifests the fact that racial thinking in some quarters has not progressed much beyond the point reached by McGee and Sullivan a century ago.

The Sports Record as a Cultural Construction

If we are not talking about science, then what are we talking about? The answer to this question lies in an excursion into the meaning of "records." We must recognize that sports records are not science. They are merely numbers that are meaningful within the interpretive frame of "sports." They measure athletic achievements that were attained within a certain framework. Within that frame, the achievements of the athletes of certain races or nations might be meaningful, but since the collection of sports records is not done according to the standards of contemporary science, they cannot be considered to establish population "averages" or "types," or other measures of statistical significance.

Sports records are better conceived as a branch of historical chronicles than as a branch of science. They share common roots, for example, with the kinds of numbers that states collect in order to better govern the populace under their control — population censuses, taxation records, public opinion polls, and election results. These are not "science," either, but they are meaningful within the frameworks that define them, and they give meaning to the institutions that collect them. From the Han to the Sui dynasties in premodern China (ca. 206 BCE to 618 CE), a branch of historical writing flourished that chronicled a category called "anomalies." The category embraced a huge range of phenomena, including "strange" peoples and customs; "marvelous" plants, animals, and things; medical topics; ceremonies, rites, and music; encounters with ghosts; and so on. "Anomalies" were of interest to the imperial court and official historians because these were regarded as portents foretelling the future of the dynasty, since they revealed the presence of the extraordinary within the ordinary, indicating disorder in the cosmic order, which it was the duty of the imperial center to maintain.[21] An official interest in anomalies, including medical anomalies, continued into the Ming (1369–1644) and Qing (1664–1911) dynasties. While we might today admire the meticulous recordkeeping of the Chinese dynastic historians as obviously beneficial to the interests of the state, we might regard the attention to anomalies as a waste of time. But it made sense within the information-gathering framework of the times.

The compilation of anomalies is not so different from the collection of exotic peoples from around the world described in this volume.[22] The impulse behind the compilation of the *Guinness Book of World Records*, as described by Eichberg, is not dissimilar from the premodern impulse. It expresses a modern version of the interest in the extraordinary and the marvelous. Barnum's quest for "extraordinary peculiarities" and the fin-de-siècle freak shows expressed a consumerist version of it. World's fairs took it to new excesses. Modern sports records are a quantified and rationalized version of it.

As Allen Guttmann put it, the quest for records represents the rationalization of the romantic impulse to surpass the limits of possibility.[23] Records attempt to quantify the extraordinary. These are generally "good" performances. As Eichberg reminds us, Sullivan's comment that "[n]ever before in the history of sport in the world were such poor performances recorded for weight throwing" may well be the only case in the history of modern Olympic sport that a "negative record" was recorded.

In *From Ritual to Record* (1978), Guttmann argued that the quantification of sports performances is a manifestation of a modern impulse to rationalize and standardize sports so that performances can be compared across space and time. The quantification of sports took off in Europe in the mid-nineteenth century along with industrialization, capitalism, and the other developments discussed in this book, and the quantification of racial types was certainly another manifestation of the same underlying impulse that led to the pursuit of the sports record.

Henning Eichberg has devoted a great deal of effort to arguing against the "naturalization" of the record, and to showing that records themselves are arbitrary, that is, created under culturally constructed circumstances. His chapter in this book repeats that effort and summarizes his earlier work.

Parezo provides us with two good examples of the arbitrariness of the

27. Basilio, an Igorot, wins the pole climbing event. From J. Sullivan, ed., *Spalding's Official Athletic Almanac for 1905: Special Olympic Number, Containing the Official Report of the Olympic Games of 1904,* 248.

records recognized by James Sullivan himself. As the editor of *Spalding's Athletic Almanac,* the national arbiter of records, he was in a position to decide which performances were recognized as "records" and which were not. Parezo observes that in the Anthropology Days pole climbing, all the Native participants beat the American record by at least ten seconds—and although Sullivan praised their "marvelous performances," in his only instance of praise for the "savages," he never noted that they had broken the record and did not record it in the *Athletic Almanac*. Neither did he note the championship won by the Fort Shaw Indian School girls' basketball team, described by Linda Peavy and Ursula Smith in this volume. By contrast, he did note the "Olympic Basketball Tournament" won by the Buffalo Germans of New York, a team composed of German-speaking Americans with German or Dutch backgrounds.[24] The Fort Shaw team were women, and the Buffalo Germans were men. Obviously, the "records" themselves were as flawed as the "science" that tried to establish them. The process was constructed to produce record-holders of preordained sexes and races.

If records are culturally constructed, then the cultural contexts in which they are constructed demand further analysis.

Olympic Chronicles

Like the Chinese dynasties, the institutions of the Olympic Movement need their own records and chronicles. As a result, the events of the past have sometimes been pigeonholed into the categories that serve the needs of the present. Efforts to categorize the 1904 St. Louis Olympic Games are an example. Writers frequently complain that since no "official" records were ever sanctioned by the International Olympic Committee, we do not know which sports events to call "Olympic." This is necessary in order to generate statistics needed by modern historians of the Olympic Movement, who quantify and compare across time such figures as the number of participating foreign nations, "first" medalists for different countries, female participants, sports records, and so on. Much of Bill Mallon's foundational 1999 effort to establish official results for the 1904 Games involved an anachronistic attempt to impose the national categories that evolved in later times onto the events in St. Louis. One illustrative example is that of the two Boer War performers, Len Tau and Jan Mashiani, who, according to recent research by Floris van der Merwe, were apparently not Zulu and were possibly Tswana, and were classified as representatives of the "nation" of "Zululand" by the contemporaneous observer Charles Lucas.[25] Mallon classifies them as representatives of South Africa, using the official IOC three-letter designation SAF.[26] This practice did not enter into official IOC reports, however, until the 1956 Cortina d'Ampezzo Winter Games.[27] This is not "history," it is "chronicling";" it is recordkeeping in the service of modern bureaucratic rationalism. The present volume is the first book-length effort to place the events of 1904 fully within their own cultural and historical contexts.

Recognition, Misrecognition, and Nonrecognition

Eichberg and Mousel Knott deal with the issues of recognition, misrecognition, and nonrecognition that accompany the question, Who represents whom? I would like to end this afterword with an account that illustrates the complexities of these matters as they played out in the life of William "Lone Star" Dietz after 1904.[28] According to Parezo's compilations, Dietz was listed in the available sources as a Rosebud Sioux who won the shot put (at 33 feet, 10½ inches) and placed second in the baseball throw (260 feet) in Anthropology Days. Sullivan described him as an "Americanized Indian" and also has him placing third in trials for "Indians" in the 440-yard run.[29] Tom Benjey's biography also states that Superintendent McCowan recruited Dietz to play for the world's fair Indian baseball team, which amassed a 42–4 win-loss record.[30]

Dietz apparently fell in love with a Winnebago, Angel DeCora, at the world's fair, and followed her to the Carlisle Indian School when she was hired to start a Native Art program. He attended intermittently from 1908 to 1912, playing football under the legendary "Pop" Warner. He left in 1915 to coach at Washington's Pullman State. When the Cougars beat Brown University in the Rose Bowl in 1916, he was on his way to becoming one of the most successful coaches in the United States. As a publicity stunt, he liked to appear in public in buckskin war regalia with a full feather headdress. In 1932 or 1933 he became the head coach for the Boston Braves, an inactive football franchise that was bought and renamed the Boston Redskins, supposedly in his honor.

Dietz's life came under scrutiny in 1992 when seven American Indians, headed by well-known Cheyenne writer and activist Suzan Shown Harjo, sued the Washington Redskins over the moniker "Redskins," alleging that it violated the Lanham trademark act, which prohibits the registration of names that are "disparaging, scandalous, contemptuous or disreputable." The Redskins argued that the name was not disparaging but "honorific," but the initial judgment favored the plaintiffs. However, the Redskins appealed, this time arguing that the name had been instituted in honor of William "Lone Star" Dietz, their first coach, and the initial judgment was overturned in 1999.

John Ewers, an ethnologist for the Smithsonian, had published a romanticized account of Dietz's life in 1977, which was used as evidence in the court case. In 2002 Linda Waggoner published a new version of his biography, which refuted many of the details in Ewers's biography.[31] The story that she reconstructed bordered on bizarre. Dietz was the son of a German engineer and a woman who might or might not have been part Indian. Whether he was or was not Indian, he "looked" Indian enough that he might have been teased about it. He was raised in Wisconsin as a typical European-American boy. It is not clear what he was doing in St. Louis, but there he met an Oglala Sioux named James One Star, a performer in the Wild West show, who told him about his namesake nephew One Star, who had disappeared in 1894. Dietz perhaps assumed the identity of One Star and took the name of Lone Star—although there is a possibility that he actually was James One Star's nephew. In 1919 he was prosecuted for draft evasion since One Star's Indian status exempted him from the draft. Although his mother testified that when she had given birth to a stillborn baby her husband had substituted a baby whom he had fathered with a local Indian woman, neighbors contradicted the testimony and Dietz was convicted and served jail time. However, he insisted he was Indian for the rest of his life.

This story of athletic prowess, stolen identity, and publicity stunts serves as a fitting end to this volume, which was an excursion through the complexities

411

of the question, "Who represents whom?" For many Native Americans to-day the 1999 Redskins decision stands as an emblem of white infatuation with Indian stereotypes combined with an unwillingness actually to try to understand Indian culture, religious beliefs, and identity.[32] Carol Spidel begins her discussion of American Indian mascots by asking, "[W]hy [are] we non-Indian Americans . . . so attached to fictional Indians who live in an imaginary past and a mythological present, an attachment that tells us very little about Indian people, but a great deal about ourselves"?" In the context of the Olympic Games, we might also ask why non-Greeks are so attached to fictional ancient Greeks. The answer, of course, is that these fictions are part of the great symbolic systems that give meaning to the times in which we live, now as in 1904. They cannot easily be dismantled. We should rather attend carefully to the question of which groups they advantage and which they disadvantage, to the ways in which "science" has been misused in their service. At the same time, we should not forget that these symbolic systems also open up "intercultural spaces" and "contact zones" in the interstices where cultures collide, and that a great deal of creative energy can be released out of the crack between worlds. Indeed, the greater part of the creativity of the twentieth century came from just this collision.

Eichberg hypothesizes, "Maybe the future is no longer what it has been." I hope that this reexamination of the 1904 St. Louis Olympic Games and Anthropology Days will help ensure that it is not.

Notes

1. B. Adams, *E Pluribus Barnum*, 175–80.

2. Bogdan, *Freak Show*, 108.

3. "Yao Ming Measures Up in U.S. and China," *People's Daily*, October 4, 2004, http://english.people.com.cn/200410/12/print20041012_159901.html.

4. S. Hall, *Representation*.

5. MacAloon, *This Great Symbol*, 134.

6. Quoted in B. Adams, *E Pluribus Barnum*, 166.

7. B. Adams, *E Pluribus Barnum*, 181.

8. Cited in B. Adams, *E Pluribus Barnum*, 177.

9. B. Adams, *E Pluribus Barnum*, 158–59.

10. B. Adams, *E Pluribus Barnum*, 183.

11. Bogdan, *Freak Show*, 106–7.

12. Bogdan, *Freak Show*, 274–75, 116.

13. Bogdan, *Freak Show*, 63–64.

14. WJ McGee, "Anthropology at the Louisiana Purchase Exposition," 821.

15. WJ McGee, "Anthropology at the Louisiana Purchase Exposition," 822.

16. WJ McGee, "Anthropology at the Louisiana Purchase Exposition," 823.

17. J. Sullivan, "Anthropology Days at the Stadium," 249, 251, 259.

18. WJ McGee, "Anthropology at the Louisiana Purchase Exposition," 19.

19. Stocking, *A Franz Boas Reader*, 59.

20. Boas, "Remarks on the Theory of Anthropometry."

21. Campany, *Strange Writing*.

22. Campany, *Strange Writing*, 8–17.

23. Guttmann, *From Ritual to Record*, 51–52.

24. Hofmann, "1904 Olympic Basketball Tournament," 3, 19–21.

25. C. Lucas, *Olympic Games 1904*, 17; van der Merwe, "Africa's First Encounter with the Olympic Games."

26. Mallon, *1904 Olympic Games*, 58, 237, 255–56.

27. Mallon and Karlsson, "IOC and OCOG Abbreviations for NOCs," 25.

28. Thanks to Gerald Gems for bringing Dietz's story to my attention.

29. J. Sullivan, "Anthropology Days at the Stadium," 251, 261. His name is spelled "Diedz" in the 440 results.

30. Benjey, *Keep A-goin'*. Benjey states, apparently erroneously, that Dietz did not participate in any of the running races, perhaps because of a bad knee.

31. Waggoner, "Reclaiming James One Star," a special five-part series for *Indian Country Today* (www.indiancountry.com, July 2–August 2, 2004), accessed at http://www.aistm.org/lonestar.htm.

32. Spidel, *Dancing at Halftime*, 287.

References

Archival Collections

Bishop Charles H. Brent Papers, Library of Congress, Washington DC

Carleton S. Coon Papers, National Anthropological Archives, Department of Anthropology, National Museum of Natural History, Smithsonian Institution, Washington DC

Chilocco Indian School Papers, Oklahoma Historical Society, Oklahoma City

Dean C. Worcester Papers, Bentley Library, University of Michigan, Ann Arbor

Department of Anthropology Papers, Field Museum of Natural History, Chicago, Illinois

Fort Shaw Vertical File, Montana Historical Society Library, Helena, Montana

Frederic S. Marquardt Papers, Bentley Library, University of Michigan, Ann Arbor

Frederick Starr Papers, University of Chicago Special Collections, Chicago, Illinois

Louisiana Purchase Exposition Collection, Missouri Historical Society, St. Louis, Missouri

National Anthropological Archives, Suitland, Maryland

National Archives, Denver National Archives, Washington DC

National Baseball Hall of Fame Archives, Philippines file, Cooperstown, New York

Philippines Correspondence Reports, 1911–68, YMCA Archives, University of Minnesota, Minneapolis–St. Paul

Pierre de Coubertin Section, International Olympic Committee Archives, Lausanne, Switzerland

Robert S. Woodworth Personal Papers, Columbia University Archives, New York

William J McGee Papers, Library of Congress, Washington DC

World's Fairs Microfilm Collection, Smithsonian Institution Libraries, Washington DC

Published Sources

Adams, Bluford. 1991. *E Pluribus Barnum: The Great Showman and the Making of U.S. Popular Culture*. Minneapolis: University of Minnesota Press.

Adams, David Wallace. 1995. *Education for Extinction: American Indians and the Boarding School Experience, 1875–1928.* Lawrence: University Press of Kansas.

Alkemeyer, Thomas. 1996. *Körper, Kult, und Politik: Von der "Muskelreligion" Pierre de Coubertins zur Inszenierung von Macht in den Olympischen Spielen von 1936.* Frankfurt am Main: Campus.

Allen, Theodore W., ed. 1998. *The Invention of the White Race: Racial Oppression and Social Control.* London: Verso.

Amador Ramirez, Fernando, Ulises Castro Nunez, and José Miguel Alamo Mendoza, eds. 1997. *Luchas, deportes de combate, y juegos tradicionales.* Madrid: Gymnos.

Anagnostou, Yiorgos. 2004. "Forget the Past, Remember the Ancestors! Modernity, 'Whiteness,' American Hellenism, and the Politics of Memory in Early Greek America." *Modern Greek Studies Journal* 22, no. 1 (May): 25–71.

Anderson, Benedict. 1991. *Imagined Communities: Reflections on the Origin and Spread of Nationalism.* New York: Verso.

Andrews, L. B., and D. Nelkin. 1996. "The Bell Curve: A Statement." *Science* 271:13–14.

Antonides, Theodorus, and Meinart Antonides. 1732. *Olympia, dat is, Olymp-speelen der Grieken* [Olympia and the Olympic Games of the Greeks]. Netherlands: Te Groningen.

Archuleta, Margaret, Brenda Child, and K. Tsianina Lomawaima. 2000. *Away from Home: American Indian Boarding School Experiences, 1879–2000.* Phoenix: Heard Museum.

Arendt, Hannah. 1973. *The Origins of Totalitarianism.* New York: Harcourt Brace Jovanovich. (Orig. pub. 1951.)

Arlott, John, ed. 1975. *The Oxford Companion to Sports and Games.* London: Oxford University Press.

Ashcroft, Bill, Gareth Griffiths, and Helen Tiffin. 2000. *Post-Colonial Studies: The Key Concepts.* London and New York: Routledge.

Auger, Fabrice. 1998. "Une histoire politique du mouvement olympique: L'exemple de l'Entre-deux-guerres." PhD diss., University Paris X-Nanterre.

———. 2003. "Pierre de Coubertin et la paix sociale dans les colonies (1890–1914)." *Les Études Sociales* 137:37–52.

Augustinos, Gerasimos. *Consciousness and History: Nationalist Critics of Greek Society, 1897–1914.* Boulder CO: East European Quarterly, 1977.

Badger, R. Reid. 1979. *The Great American Fair: The World's Columbian Exposition and American Culture.* Chicago: Nelson Hall.

Baker, Lee D. 1998. *From Savage to Negro: Anthropology and the Construction of Race, 1896–1954.* Berkeley: University of California Press.

Bakhtin, Mikhail. 1968. *Rabelais and His World.* Cambridge: MIT.

Baldwin, Dorothy. 1945. "History of Fort Shaw." Fort Shaw Vertical File, Montana Historical Society Library, Helena MT.

Bale, John. 2002a. *Imagined Olympians: Body Culture and Colonial Representation in Rwanda.* Minneapolis: University of Minnesota Press.

———. 2002b. "Lassitude and Latitude: Observations on Sport and Environmental Determinism." *International Review for the Sociology of Sport* 37:147–58.

———. 2004. *Running Cultures: Racing in Time and Space.* London and New York: Routledge.

Bale, John, and Joe Sang. 1996. *Kenyan Running: Geography, Movement Culture, and Global Change.* London: Cass.

Balibar, Etienne. 1990. "Gibt es einen 'Neo-Rassismus'?" In *Rasse, Klasse, Nation: Ambivalente Identitäten,* ed. E. Balibar and I. Wallerstein, 23–38. Hamburg: Argument-Verlag.

Balibar, Etienne, and Immanuel Wallerstein, eds. 1990. *Rasse, Klasse, Nation: Ambivalente Identitäten.* Hamburg: Argument-Verlag.

Bancel, Nicolas, Pascal Blanchard, Gilles Boetsch, Éric Deroo, and Sandrine Lemarie, eds. 2002. *Zoos humains: De la vénus hottentote aux reality shows; 19e et 20e siècles.* Paris: Editions de la Découverte.

Bancel, Nicolas, Pascal Blanchard, and Françoise Vergès. 2002. "Zoos humains: Entre mythe et réalité." In *Zoos humains: De la vénus hottentote aux reality shows; 19e et 20e siècles,* ed. N. Bancel, P. Blanchard, G. Boetsch, E. Deroo, and S. Lemaire, 5–17. Paris: Editions de la Découverte.

Bancel, Nicolas, Pascal Blanchard, and Françoise Vergès. 2003. *La République coloniale.* Paris: Hachette.

Bancel, Nicolas, and Patrick Clastres. 2003. "Pierre de Coubertin et Hubert Lyautey—Deux hommes d'action sociale." *Les Etudes Sociales* 137:53–54.

Bancel, Nicolas, and Jean-Marc Gayman. 2002. *Du guerrier à l'athlète: Eléments d'histoire de pratiques corporelles.* Paris: Presses Universitaires de France.

Banton, Michael. 1987. *Racial Theories.* Cambridge: Cambridge University Press.

Barbujani, G., A. Magagni, E. Minch, and L. L. Cavalli-Sforza. 1997. "An Apportionment of Human DNA Diversity." *Proceedings of the National Academy of Sciences* 94:4516–19.

Barnard, F. M. 1965. *Herder's Social and Political Thought: From Enlightenment to Nationalism.* Oxford: Clarendon Press.

Barnett, C. Robert. 2004. "St. Louis, 1904." In *Encyclopedia of the Modern Olympic Movement,* ed. J. E. Findling and K. D. Pelle, 33–40. Westport CT: Greenwood.

Barney, Robert K. 1991. "A Myth Arrested: Theodore Roosevelt and the 1904 Olympic Games." In *Umbruch and Kontinuität im Sport: Reflexionen im Umfeld der Sportgeschichte*, ed. Andreas Luh and Edger Beckers, 218–29. Bochum: Brockmeyer.

———. 1992. "Born from Dilemma: America Awakens to the Modern Olympic Games, 1901–1903." *Olympika* 1:92–135.

Barney Robert K., and David E. Barney. 2004. "Angst, Argument, and Antiquity: A Centennial View of Aquatics at the 1904 St. Louis Olympics." In *Cultural Relations Old and New: The Transitory Olympic Ethos—Seventh International Symposium for Olympic Research*, ed. Kevin B. Wamsley, Scott G. Martyn, and Robert K. Barney, 77–92. London, Canada: International Centre for Olympic Studies, University of Western Ontario.

Barnum, P. T. 1981. *Struggles and Triumphs: Edited and Abridged with an Introduction by Carl Bode*. New York: Penguin Books. (Orig. pub. 1855, 1869.)

Barreau, Jean-Jacques, and Guy Jaouen, eds. 1998. *Éclipse et renaissance des jeux populaires: Des traditions aux régions de l'Europe de demain*. Karaez: FALSAB.

———, eds. 2001. *Les jeux traditionnels en Europe: Éducation, culture et société au 21e siècle*. Plonéour Ronarc'h: Confédération FALSAB.

Barrett, John. 1898. "The Problem of the Philippines." *North American Review* 167 (September): 259–67.

Bartlett, R. M., and R. J. Best. 1988. "The Biomechanics of Javelin Throwing: A Review." *Journal of Sports Science* 6:1–38.

Baumann, Wolfgang, ed. 1986. *Fundamentals of Sport for All: International Congress*. Frankfurt am Main: DSB.

Baumgartner, Ted A., and Andrew S. Jackson. 1983. *Measurement for Evaluation in Physical Education and Exercise Science*. 3rd ed. Dubuque IA: William C. Brown.

Becht, June W. 2004. "George Poage: Clearing Hurdles at the 1904 Olympics." *Gateway Heritage* 24, no. 4:56–58.

Bederman, Gail. 1995. *Manliness and Civilization: A Cultural History of Gender and Race in the United States, 1880–1917*. Chicago: University of Chicago Press.

Behringer, Wolfgang, and Constance Ott-Koptschalijski. 1991. *Der Traum vom Fliegen: Zwischen Mythos und Technik*. Frankfurt am Main: S. Fischer.

Benedict, Burton. 1983. *The Anthropology of World's Fairs: San Francisco's Panama Pacific International Exposition of 1915*. London and Berkeley: Lowie Museum of Anthropology.

Benjey, Tom. 2006. *Keep A-goin': The Life of Lone Star Dietz*. Carlisle PA: Tuxedo Press.

Bennitt, Mark, and Stockbridge, Frank Parker, eds. 1905. *History of the Louisiana Purchase Exposition*. St. Louis: Universal Exposition Publishing Company. (Repr., New York: Arno Press, 1976.)

Beran, Janice A. 1989. "Americans in the Philippines: Imperialism or Progress through Sports?" *International Journal of the History of Sport* 6 (May): 62–87.

Bernal, Martin. 1987. *Black Athena: The Afroasiatic Roots of Classical Civilization*. Vol. 1 of *The Fabrication of Ancient Greece 1785–1985*. New Brunswick NJ: Rutgers University Press.

Bertels, Ursula. 1993. *Das Fliegerspiel in Mexiko: Historische Entwicklung und gegenwärtige Erscheinungsformen*. Münster: Lit.

Bieder, Robert E. 1989. *Science Encounters the Indian, 1820–1880: The Early Years of American Ethnology*. Norman: University of Oklahoma Press. (Orig. pub. 1986.)

Blain, Neil, Raymond Boyle, and Hugh O'Donnell. 1993. *Sport and National Identity in the European Media*. Leicester: Leicester University Press.

Blanchard, David. 1983. "Entertainment, Dance, and Northern Mohawk Showmanship." *American Indian Quarterly* 7, no. 1:2–26.

Blickle, Peter. 2002. *Heimat: A Critical Theory of the German Idea of Homeland*. Rochester NY: Camden House.

Bloom, John. 2000. *To Show What an Indian Can Do: Sports at Native American Boarding Schools*. Minneapolis: University of Minnesota Press.

Blum, John M., Edmund S. Morgan, Willie Lee Rose, Arthur M. Schlesinger, Jr., Kenneth M. Stampp, and C. Vann Woodward. 1981. *The National Experience: A History of the United States*. New York: Harcourt, Brace, Jovanovich.

Boas, Franz. 1887a. "Museums of Ethnology and Their Classification." *Science* 9:587–89.

———. 1887b. "The Occurence of Similar Inventions in Areas Widely Apart." *Science* 9:485–86.

———. 1893. "Remarks on the Theory of Anthropometry." *Quarterly Publications of the American Statistical Association* 3:569–75.

———. 1904. "The History of Anthropology." *Science* 20:513–24. (Repr. in *A Franz Boas Reader: The Shaping of American Anthropology, 1883–1911*, ed. George W. Stocking, Jr., 23–35. Chicago: University of Chicago Press, 1968.)

Bogdan, Robert. 1988. *Freak Show: Presenting Human Oddities for Amusement and Profit*. Chicago: University of Chicago Press.

Boulongne, Yves-Pierre. 1975. *La vie et l'oeuvre pédagogique de Pierre de Coubertin 1863–1937*. Ottawa: Leméac.

———. 1994a. *The International Olympic Committee—One Hundred Years*. Vol. 1. Lausanne: International Olympic Committee.

———. 1994b. "The Presidencies of Demetrius Vikelas (1894–1896) and Pierre de Coubertin (1896–1925)." In *The International Olympic Committee—One Hundred Years: The Idea—The Presidents—The Achievements*, ed. Raymond Gafner, 1:15–207. Lausanne: International Olympic Committee.

———. 1999. *Pierre de Coubertin, humanisme et pédagogie: Dix leçons sur l'olympisme*. Lausanne: Musée Olympique.

Bowler, Peter J. 1984. *Evolution: The History of an Idea*. Berkeley: University of California Press.

Bradfield, Larry. 1963. "A History of Chilocco Indian School." Master's thesis, University of Oklahoma.

Bradford, Philips Verner, and Harvey Blume. 1992. *Ota Benga: The Pygmy in the Zoo*. New York: St. Martin's Press.

Breitbart, Eric. 1997. *A World on Display: Photographs from the St. Louis World's Fair, 1904*. Albuquerque: University of New Mexico Press.

Brinton, Daniel G. 1895. "Current Notes on Anthropology (11): Racial and Ethnic Traits." *Science* 2:66.

Brodkin, Karen. 1998. *How Jews Became White Folks and What That Says About Race in America*. New Brunswick NJ: Rutgers University Press.

Brohm, Jean-Marie. 1981. *Le mythe olympique*. Paris: Christian Bourgois.

———. 1983. *Jeux Olympiques à Berlin*. Bruxelles: Editions Complexe.

———. 1985. "Pierre de Coubertin et l'avènement du sport bourgeois." In *Les athlètes de la République: Gymnastique, sport, et idéologie républicaine 1870–1914*, ed. Pierre Arnaud, 283–300. Toulouse: Privat.

———. 1995. "Olympisme et national-socialisme: Un exemple de collaboration politique." In *Critique de la modernité sportive*, ed. François Bailette and Jean-Marie Bohm, 223–39. Paris: Editions de la Passion.

Brown, Elwood S. 1912–13. *Annual Report: Oct. 1, 1912–Oct. 1, 1913*. YMCA Archives.

Brown, William Wells. 1998. "On Race and Change." In *Black on White: Black Writers on What It Means to Be White*, ed. David R. Roediger. New York: Schocken Books.

Brownell, Susan. 1995. *Training the Body for China: Sports in the Moral Order of the People's Republic*. Chicago and London: University of Chicago Press.

———. 2004. "Summary of Discussion." International Congress on the 1904 St. Louis Olympic Games and Anthropology Days: A Centennial Retrospective, October 2004.

———. 2005a. "Anthropology." In *Encyclopedia of International Sport Studies*, ed. Roger Bartlett, Chris Gratton, and Christer Rolf. London: Routledge.

———. 2005b. "The View from Greece: Questioning Eurocentrism in the History of the Olympic Games." *Journal of Sport History* 32, no. 2(Summer): 203–16.

———. 2006a. "Athletic Geography: Coubertin's Enduring Legacy." Unpublished manuscript.

———. 2006b. "Figure Skating in St. Louis." *2006 U.S. Figure Skating Championships*, St. Louis (official program), January 7–15, 81–86.

————. 2008. *Beijing's Games: What the Olympics Mean to China*. Lanham MD: Rowman and Littlefield.

Buber, Martin. 1986. *Ich und Du* [I and Thou]. New York: Collier. (Orig. pub. 1923.)

Buck-Morss, Susan. 1991. *The Dialectics of Seeing*. Cambridge: MIT Press.

Buel, J. W., ed. 1904. *Louisiana and the Fair: An Exposition of the World, Its People, and Their Achievements*. Vols. 4 and 5. St. Louis: World's Progress Publishing Co.

Bulosan, Carlos. 1946. *America Is in the Heart: A Personal History*. New York: Harcourt, Brace.

Buschmann, Jürgen, and Stephan Wassong, eds. 2005. *Langlauf durch die olympische Geschichte: Festschrift Karl Lennartz* [Long-distance Run through Olympic History: Festschrift to Karl Lennartz]. Vol. 2 of *Selected Writings on Olympic History*. Cologne: Carl und Liselott Diem Archiv.

Buss, D. M. 1994. *The Evolution of Desire: Strategies of Human Mating*. New York: Basic Books.

Callebat, Louis. 1988. *Pierre de Coubertin*. Paris: Fayard.

Campany, Robert Ford. 1989. *Strange Writing: Anomaly Accounts in Early Medieval China*. New York: State University of New York.

Cannadine, David. 1983. "The Context, Performance, and Meaning of Ritual: The British Monarchy and the 'Invention of tradition,' c. 1820–1977." In *The Invention of Tradition*, ed. Eric Hobsbawm and Terence Ranger. Cambridge: Cambridge University Press.

Carlson, Lew. 1989. "Giant Patagonians and Hairy Ainu: Anthropology Days at the 1904 St. Louis Olympics." *Journal of American Culture* 12 (Fall): 19–26.

Carnes, Mark C., and Clyde Griffen, eds. 1990. *Meanings for Manhood: Construction of Masculinity in Victorian America*. Chicago: University of Chicago Press.

Carter, Marshall, and Arnd Krüger, eds. 1990. *Ritual and Record: Sports Records and Quantification in Pre-Modern Societies*. New York: Greenwood.

Casselman, A. B. 1904. "The Old and Novel Sport of Archery, Appropos of its Inclusion in the Olympic Games at the St. Louis Exposition." *Century Illustrated Magazine* 68 (August): 628–38.

Castle, Terry. 1986. *Masquerade and Civilization: The Carnivalesque in Eighteenth-Century English Culture and Fiction*. Stanford: Stanford University Press.

Cavalli-Sforza, Luca, and Francesco Cavalli-Sforza. 1993. *Chi siamo: La storia de la diversità umana*. Milano: Arnoldo Mondatori.

Cavallo, Dominick. 1981. *Muscles and Morals: Organized Playgrounds and Urban Reform, 1880–1920*. Philadelphia: University of Pennsylvania Press.

Césaire, Aimé. 2004. *Discours sur le colonialisme suivi du Discours sur la Négritude*. Paris: Présence Africaine.

Chagnon, Napoleon A. 1988. "Life Histories, Blood Revenge, and Warfare in a Tribal Population." *Science* 239:985–92.

Chappelet, Jean-Loup. 1991. *Le système olympique.* Grenoble: Presses Universitaires de Grenoble.

Chatwin, Bruce. 1988. *The Songlines.* London: Penguin.

Child, Brenda. 1995. *Boarding School Seasons: American Indian Families, 1900–1940.* Lincoln: University of Nebraska Press.

Cholley, Patrick. 1995. *Pierre de Coubertin: La deuxième croisade.* Lausanne: Comité International Olympique.

"Choreography." *Revue Olympique* (June 1906): 89.

Chrysafes, Ioannes. 1930. *Oi Sygchronoi Diethneis Olympiakoi Agones* [The Modern International Olympic Games]. Athens: Sergiadis.

Claremont, A. D., D. I. Costill, W. Fink, and P. Van Handel. 1976. "Heat Tolerance Following Diuretic Induced Dehydration." *Medicine and Science in Sports* 8:239–43.

Cloke, Paul, and Ron Johnston, eds. 2005. *Spaces of Geographical Thought.* London: Sage.

Coats, A. W. 1961. "American Scholarship Comes of Age: The Louisiana Purchase Exposition 1904." *Journal of the History of Ideas* 22, no. 3(July-Sept.): 404–17.

Cogliano, Francis D. 2004. "Baseball and American Exceptionalism." In *Sport and National Identity in the Post-War World,* ed. Adrian Smith and Dilwyn Porter, 145–67. London and New York: Routledge.

Cole, Douglas. 1985. *Captured Heritage: The Scramble for Northwest Coast Artifacts.* Seattle: University of Washington Press.

Colin, Susi. 1989. "The Wild Man and the Indian in Early Sixteenth-Century Book Illustration." In *Indians of Europe: An Interdisciplinary Collection of Essays,* ed. Christian Feest, 5–36. Lincoln and London: University of Nebraska Press.

Columbian Exposition Album. 1893. Chicago: Rand McNally.

Conn, Steven. 1992. *Museums and American Intellectual Life, 1876–1926.* Chicago: University of Chicago Press.

Coon, C. S. 1960. Letter to C. Putnam, June 17. Carleton S. Coon Papers, National Anthropological Archives.

Cordes, Hiltrud. 1992. *Pencak Silat: Die Kampfkunst der Minangkabau und ihr kulturelles Umfeld.* Frankfurt am Main: Afra.

Correnti, V., and B. Zauli. 1964. *Olimpionici 1960.* Rome: Marves.

Coubertin, Pierre de. 1890. *Universités transatlantiques.* Paris: Hachette.

———. 1891. "L'athlétisme, son rôle et son histoire." *Revue Athlétique* 2, no. 4: 93–207.

———. 1898a. *L'Évolution française sous la Troisième République.* Paris: Hachette.

———. 1898b. *Lettre aux électeurs de l'arrondissement du Havre.* Le Havre: Librairie Havraise.

———. 1898c. "The Present Problems and Politics of France." *American Monthly Review of Reviews* 18, no. 2:187–94.

———. 1899. "L'urgente Réforme." *La Nouvelle Revue* (April 1): 385–401.

———. 1900. "A French View of the German Empire." *American Monthly Review of Reviews* 21, no. 2:178–83.

———. 1901a. "Emile Loubet, President of the Third Republic." *The Century Magazine* 17, no. 5.

———. 1901b. "France on the Wrong Track." *American Monthly Review of Reviews* 23, no. 4:447–50.

———. 1902a. *Chronique de France.* Vol. 2. Auxerre: A. Lanier.

———. 1902b. "Le drame sud-africain." *Revue du pays de Caux* 2:57–70.

———. 1902c. "La fille sauvage." *Revue du Pays de Caux* 1:36–39.

———. 1902d. "Le professeur Virchov [sic]." *Revue du Pays de Caux* 4:135.

———. 1902e. "Que faut-il penser du socialisme?" *Revue du Pays de Caux* 4:136–46.

———. 1902f. *Le Roman d'un Rallié.* Auxerre: A. Lanier.

———. 1903a. "La question nègre." *Le Figaro* 26 (September): 1.

———. 1903b. "La Thèse des Néo-Monarchistes." *Revue du Pays de Caux* 3:116–19.

———. 1904. Letter to Jiři Guth-Jarkovsky, March 13. Lausanne: Archives of the International Olympic Committee.

———. 1905. *L'Education des adolescents au XXesiècle: L'Education Physique; La Gymnastique utilitaire: Sauvetage-Défense—Locomotion.* Paris: Alcan.

———. 1906a. "Art, letters, and sport." *Revue pour les Français* 1 (June): 211–15.

———. 1906b. "Un Collège modèle." *Revue pour les Français* 1 (October): 379–99.

———. 1908. "L'ouverture de la 4e Olympiade." *Revue Olympique* (July): 103–5.

———. 1909a. *Pages d'histoire contemporaine.* Paris: Plon.

———. 1909b. *Une campagne de vingt-et-un ans.* Paris: Librairie de l'Education Physique.

———. 1910a. "Une Olympie moderne: IV—Les qualifiés." *Revue Olympique* (January): 9–13.

———. 1910b. "Une Olympie moderne. VI—Les cérémonies." *Revue Olympique* (March): 41–44.

———. 1911a. "Ce qu'il y a de changé aux Etats-Unis." *Revue des Français* (25 January): 39–46.

———. 1911b. "La géographie sportive." *Revue Olympique* (April): 51–52.

———. 1912a. "Chronique du mois." *Revue Olympique* (May): 76–78.

———. 1912b. "L'Eugénie." *Revue Olympique* 12 (November): 163–66.

———. 1912c. "L'ode au sport." *Revue Olympique* 12 (November): 179–81.

———. 1912d. "Les sports et la colonisation." *Revue Olympique* (January): 7–10.

———. 1914a. "1870–1914." *La Petite Gironde* (8 October 1914), p. 1.

———. 1914b. "Le sport et la société moderne. Discours prononcé en Sorbonne, en présence de Raymond Poincaré, Président de la République, à l'occasion du XX" anniversaire du rétablissement des Jeux Olympiques." *La Revue Hebdomadaire* (June 20): 376–86.

———. 1915a. "Aux jeunes Français, Le Décalogue de 1915." *Excelsior* 6, no. 1551 (January): 3.

———. 1915b. "Chronique pour après: Notre Philosophie." *La Petite Gironde* (January 14): 1.

———. 1917. *Que es el Olimpismo?* Paris: Rirachowski.

———. 1918a. "Ce que nous pouvons maintenant demander au Sport." Conférence faite à l'Association des Hellènes Libéraux de Lausanne, le 24 février 1918. Lausanne: Edition de l'Association des Hellènes Libéraux de Lausanne.

———. 1918b. "La Belgique devant l'histoire." *Tribune de Genève* (August 24): 2.

———. 1918c. "Lettre Olympique VIII." *Gazette de Lausanne* 341(December 14): 2.

———. 1923a. "Discours prononcé par le président du Comité à la séance inaugurale en présence de S.M. le Roi d'Italie, le 7 avril 1923." In *Session de 1923, tenue au Capitole, Rome*, ed. Comité International Olympique. Lausanne: Imprimerie La Concorde.

———. 1923b. *Où va l'Europe?* Paris: Editions G. Grès.

———. 1926–27. *Histoire universelle*. Vols. 1–4. Aix-en-Provence: Société de l'Histoire Universelle.

———. 1929. *Olympie*. Genève: Imprimerie Burgi.

———. 1931. "Colonisation sportive." *Bulletin du Bureau International de Pédagogie Sportive* 5:12–14.

———. 1932. "Mémoires Olympiques VI." *L'Equipe* (January 1): 2.

———. 1936. "Les sources et les limites du progrès sportif." (Manuscript: Archives of the International Olympic Committee, Section P. de Coubertin, no. Inv. 140, n.d. [1936]), 13.)

———. 1967. *The Olympic Idea: Discourses and Essays*. Schorndorf bei Stuttgart: Karl Hofmann.

———. 1975. "Mes mémoires." In *La vie et l'oeuvre pédagogique de Pierre de Coubertin*, ed. Yves Pierre Boulongne, 455–62. (Orig. pub. 1936.)

———. 1979. *Olympic Memoirs* [translation of *Mémoires Olympiques*, 1932, 1996]. Lausanne: International Olympic Committee. (Repr. 1989.)

———. 1986. "Un programme: Le Play." In *Pierre de Coubertin: Textes Choisis; Tome I: Révélation*, ed. Georges Rioux and Norbert Müller, 543–59. Zürich, Hildesheim, New York: Weidmann. (Orig. pub. 1887.)

—. 1996. *Mémoires Olympiques*. Lausanne: Bureau International de Pédagogie Sportive. New ed., Paris: Revue EP.S. (Orig. pub. 1932.)

—. 2000. *Olympism: Selected Writings*, ed. Norbert Müller. Lausanne: International Olympic Committee.

Croft-Cookes, Rupert, and Peter Cotes. 1976. *Circus: A World History*. New York: Mac-Millan.

Croney, John. 1981. *Anthropometry for Designers*. New York: Van Nostrand Reinhold.

Culin, Stewart. 1907. "Games of the North American Indians." In *Twenty Fourth Annual Report of the Bureau of American Ethnology to the Smithsonian Institution, 1902–1903*. W. H. Holmes, chief. Washington: GPO.

Cureton, T. K., Jr. 1951. *Physical Fitness of Champion Athletes*. Urbana: University of Illinois Press.

Curtis, Thomas P. 1931. "High Hurdles and White Gloves." *The Sportsman* 12 (July 1): 60–61.

Daly, M., and M. Wilson. 1988. *Homicide*. New York: Aldine de Gruyter.

Darnell, Regna. 1998. *And Along Came Boas: Continuity and Revolution in American Anthropology*. Amsterdam: John Benjamins.

—. 2002. "WJ McGee." In *Celebrating a Century of the American Anthropological Association: Presidential Portraits*, ed. Regna Darnell and Frederic W. Gleach. Arlington VA: American Anthropological Association; Lincoln: University of Nebraska Press.

Darnell, Regna, and Frederic W. Gleach, eds. 2002. *Celebrating a Century of the American Anthropological Association: Presidential Portraits*. Arlington VA: American Anthropological Association; Lincoln: University of Nebraska Press.

Davenport, Joanna. 1991. "The Tides of Change in Women's Basketball Rules." In *A Century of Women's Basketball: From Frailty to Final Four*, ed. Joan Hult and Marianna Trekell. Reston VA: National Association of Girls and Women in Sport.

Davis, Janet M. 2002. *The Circus Age: Culture and Society under the American Big Top*. Chapel Hill: University of North Carolina Press.

de Garay, Alfonso L., Louis Levine, and J. E. Lindsay Carter. 1974. *Genetic and Anthropological Studies of Olympic Athletes*. New York: Academic Press.

Degler, Carl N. 1991. *In Search of Human Nature: The Decline and Revival of Darwinism in American Social Thought*. New York: Oxford University Press.

Delacampagne, Christian. 1983. *L'invention du racisme: Antiquité et Moyen Age*. Paris: Fayard.

Detjen, David. 1985. *The Germans in Missouri, 1900–1918: Prohibition, Neutrality, and Assimilation* Columbia: University of Missouri Press.

Deville-Danthu, Bernadette. 1996. *Le sport en noir et blanc*. Paris: L'Harmattan.

Dieckert, Jürgen, and Jakob Mehringer. 1991. "Mit 147 kg durch die Savanne: Forschungsbericht zu den Klotzrennen der Canela-Indianer Brasiliens." *Sportwissenschaft* 21:48–61.

Diem, Carl. 1990. *Die Olympische Spiele 1912* [The Olympic Games of 1912], with an introduction by Karl Lennartz. Kassel: Kasseler Sportsverlag.

Dorgan, Ethel. 1934. *Luther Halsey Gulick*. New York: Teachers College, Columbia University.

Dozier, Bill. 1954. "Tribesman Jumped 7' 6"." *Track and Field News* 7, no. 11 (1954): 4.

Dozon, Jean-Pierre. 2003. *Frères et sujets: La France et l'Afrique en perspective*. Paris: Flammarion.

Dufaitre, Anne. 1989. "Traditional Games: Preliminary Observations on the Preparation of a National or Regional Catalogue or Inventory." Paper of the Council of Europe, Strasbourg.

Durry, Jean. 1994. *Le vrai Pierre de Coubertin*. Paris: Comité Français Pierre de Coubertin.

Dyreson, Mark. 1992. "America's Athletic Missionaries: Political Performance, Olympic Spectacle, and the Quest for an American National Culture, 1896–1912." *Olympika* 1:70–91.

———. 1993. "The Playing Fields of Progress: American Athletic Nationalism and the 1904 Olympics." *Gateway Heritage* 14 (Fall): 4–23.

———. 1998. *Making the American Team: Sport, Culture, and the Olympic Experience*. Urbana and Chicago: University of Illinois Press.

———. 2001. "American Ideas About Race and Olympic Races from the 1890s to the 1950s: Shattering Myths or Reinforcing Scientific Racism?" *Journal of Sport History* 28 (2001): 173–215.

———. 2004a. "The Foot Runners Conquer Mexico and Texas: Endurance Racing, Indigenismo, and Nationalism." *Journal of Sport History* 31 (Spring): 1–31.

———. 2004b. "Globalizing American Sporting Culture: The U.S. Government Plan to Conquer the World Sports Market in the 1930s." *Sportwissenschaft* 34, no. 2:145–51.

———. 2006. "'To Construct a Better and More Peaceful World' or 'War Minus the Shooting'?: The Olympic Movement's Second Century." In *Onward to the Olympics: Historical Perspectives on the Olympic Games*, ed. Stephen Wenn, 337–51. Waterloo, Ontario: Wilfrid Laurier University Press.

Easterling, Pat. 1999. "The Early Years of the Cambridge Greek Play: 1882–1912." In *Classics in Nineteenth- and Twentieth-Century Cambridge: Curriculum, Culture, and Community*, ed. Christopher Stray, 27–48. Cambridge: The Cambridge Philosophical Society.

Eberhardt, Jennifer L. 2005. "Imaging Race." *American Psychologist* 60, no. 2:181–90.

Eichberg, Henning. 1978. *Leistung, Spannung, Geschwindigkeit*. Stuttgart: Klett-Cotta.

———. 1990. "Forward Race and the Laughter of Pygmies: On Olympic Sport." In *Fin de Siècle and Its Legacy*, ed. Mikulás Teich and Roy Porter, 115–31. Cambridge: Cambridge University Press.

———. 1998. *Body Cultures: Essays on Sport, Space, and Identity*, ed. John Bale and Chris Philo. London: Routledge.

———. 2003a. "Die Produktion des 'Unproduktiven.'" In *Der "Künstliche Mensch": Eine Sportwissenschaftliche Perspektive?*, ed. Manfred Lämmer and Barbara Ränsch-Trill, 112–40. Sankt Augustin: Academia.

———. 2003b. "Three Dimensions of Playing the Game: About Mouth Pull, Tug-of-War and Sportization." In *The Essence of Sport*, ed. Verner Møller and John Nauright, 51–80. Odense: University Press of Southern Denmark.

———. 2003c. "Three Dimensions of Pull and Tug: Towards a Philosophy of Popular Games." *Studies in Physical Culture and Tourism* 10, no. 1:51–73.

———. 2004. *The People of Democracy: Understanding Self-Determination on the Basis of Body and Movement*. Århus: Klim.

———. 2005. "Racing in the Labyrinth? About Some Inner Contradictions of Running." In *Athletics, Society, and Identity*, 169–92. Athens: Foundation of the Hellenic World.

Encyclopaedia Britannica. 2004. *Ultimate Reference Suite 2004*. Keyword Racism. DVD. Chicago: Encyclopaedia Britannica.

Eriksen, Thomas Hylland, and Finn Sivert Nielsen. 2001. *A History of Anthropology*. London: Pluto Press.

Everett, Marshall. 1904. *The Book of the Fair*. Philadelphia: P. W. Ziegler.

Fabian, Johannes. 2000. *Out of our Minds: Reason and Madness in the Exploration of Central Africa*. Berkley: University of California Press.

Fatès, Youcef. 1994. *Sport et Tiers-Monde*. Paris: PUF.

Feest, Christian F., ed. 1989. *Indians of Europe: An Interdisciplinary Collection of Essays*. Lincoln and London: University of Nebraska Press.

Fernsebner, Susan. 2002. "Material Modernities: China's Participation in World's Fairs and Expositions, 1876–1955." PhD diss., University of California–San Diego.

Filcher, J. A. 1904. "South African Boer War." *World's Fair Bulletin* 5 (November): 47.

Findling, John E. 2004. "Chicago Loses the 1904 Olympics." *Journal of Olympic History* 12, no. 3 (October): 24–29.

Findling, John E., and Kimberly D. Pelle. 1996. *Historical Dictionary of the Modern Olympic Movement*. Westport: Greenwood Press.

Forbes, Jack D. 1990. "The Manipulation of Race, Caste, and Identity: Classifying Afroamericans, Native-Americans, and Red-Black People." *Journal of Ethnic Studies* 17, no. 4 (Winter): 1–51.

Ford, Clellan S. 1941. *Smoke from Their Fires: The Life of a Kwakiutl Chief.* New Haven CT: Yale University Press.

Forsyth, Janice. 2000. "From Assimilation to Self-Determination: The Emergence of J. Wilton Littlechild's NAI Games." Master's thesis, University of Western Ontario.

Fossett, Judith Jackson, and Jeffrey A. Tucker, eds. 1997. *Race Consciousness: African American Studies for the New Century.* New York: New York University Press.

Foucault, Michel. 1966. *Les mots et les choses.* Paris: Gallimard.

Fouillé, Alfred. 1898. *Psychologie du peuple français.* 2nd ed. Paris: Alcan.

Fox, Timothy, and Duane Sneddeker. 1997. *From the Palaces to the Pike: Visions of the 1904 World's Fair.* St. Louis: Missouri Historical Society.

Francis, David R. 1904. "Novel Athletic Contest." *World's Fair Bulletin* 50 (September).

———. 1913. *The Universal Exposition of 1904.* St. Louis: Louisiana Purchase Exposition Co.

Frederickson, George M. 1997. *The Comparative Imagination: On the History of Racism, Nationalism, and Social Movements.* Berkeley: University of California Press.

———. 2002. *Racism: A Short history.* Princeton: Princeton University Press.

Freeman, D. 1983. *Margaret Mead and Samoa.* Cambridge: Harvard University Press.

Garrett, H. H. 1961. "The Equalitarian Dogma." *Mankind Quarterly* 1:253–57.

Gatewood, Willard B., Jr. 1987. *"Smoked Yankees" and the Struggle for Empire: Letters from Negro Soldiers, 1898–1902.* Fayetteville: University of Arkansas Press.

George, W. C. 1962. *The Biology of the Race Problem.* Commission of the Governor of Alabama.

Georgiadis, Konstantinos. 2000. *Die ideengeschichtliche Grundlage der Erneuerung der Olympischen Spiele im 19. Jahrhundert in Griechenland und ihre Umsetzung 1896 in Athen* [The Intellectual-Historical Foundations of the Revival of the Olympic Games in the Nineteenth Century in Greece and Their 1896 Transplantation into Athens]. Kassel: Agon-Sportverlag.

———. 1996. "Olympic Ceremonies in the Athens Games of 1896 and 1906." In *Olympic Ceremonies: Historical Continuity and Cultural Exchange,* ed. Miquel de Moragas, John MacAloon, and Montserrat Llinés, 81–91. Lausanne: International Olympic Committee.

———. 2003. *Olympic Revival: The Revival of the Olympic Games in Modern Times.* Athens: Ekdotike Athenon, S.A.

Gershovich, Moshe. 2004. "Collaboration and 'pacification': French conquest,

Moroccan combatants, and the transformation of the Middle Atlas." *Comparative Studies of South Asia, Africa, and the Middle East* 24, no. 1:139–46.

Geulen, Christian. 2004. *Wahlverwandte: Rassendiskurs und Nationalismus im späten 19. Jahrhundert.* Hamburg: Hamburger Edition.

Gleeck, Lewis E., Jr. 1976. *American Institutions in the Philippines.* Manila: Historical Conservation Society.

Go, Julian. 2004. "Racism and Colonialism: Meanings of Difference and Ruling Practices in America's Pacific Empire." *Qualitative Sociology* 37, no. 1:35–58.

Gobineau, Arthur de. 1853–55. *Essai sur l'inégalité des races humaines.* Vols. 1–6. Paris: Firmin Didot.

Goffman, Erving. 1974. *Frame Analysis: An Essay on the Organization of Experience.* New York: Harper and Row.

Goksøyr (mistaken: Goksyr), Matti. 1990. "'One Certainly Expected a Great Deal More from the Savages': The Anthropology Days in St. Louis, 1904, and Their Aftermath." *International Journal of the History of Sport* 7, no. 2:297–306.

Gossett, Thomas F. 1997. *Race: The History of an Idea in America.* New York: Oxford University Press.

Gould, Stephen Jay. 1977. *Ever Since Darwin.* New York: W. W. Norton.

———. 1982. *The Mismeasure of Man.* New York: W. W. Norton.

Greenberg, Stan. 1983. *The Guinness Book of Olympics: Fact and Feast.* London: Guinness Superlative.

Greenhalgh, Paul. 1988. *Ephemeral Vistas: The Expositions Universelles, Great Expositions, and World's Fairs, 1851–1939.* Manchester: Manchester University Press.

Grundy, Pamela, and Susan Shackelford. 2007. *Shattering the Glass: The Remarkable Story of Women's Basketball.* Chapel Hill: University of North Carolina Press.

Guibert, Joël, and Guy Jaouen, eds. 2005. *Jeux traditionnels: Quels loisirs sportifs pour la société de demain?* Vannes: Institut Culturel de Bretagne.

Guinness Book of World Records 1990. 1989. Enfield: Guinness Superlatives.

Gulick, Luther H. 1898. "Some Psychical Aspects of Muscular Exercise." *Popular Science Monthly* 43:793–805.

———. 1899. "Psychological, Pedagogical, and Religious Aspects of Group Games." *Pedagogical Seminary* 6 (March):135–51.

———. 1919. *Morals and Morale.* New York: Association Press.

Guterl, Matthew Pratt. 2001. *The Color of Race in America, 1900–1940.* Cambridge: Harvard University Press.

Guttmann, Allen. 1978. *From Ritual to Record.* New York: Columbia University Press.

———. 1984. *The Games Must Go On: Avery Brundage and the Olympic Movement.* New York: Columbia University Press.

————. 1992. *The Olympics: A History of the Modern Games.* Urbana: University of Illinois Press.

————. 1994. *Games and Empires: Modern Sports and Cultural Imperialism.* New York: Columbia University Press.

Hache, Françoise. 1992. *Les Jeux Olympiques: La flamme de l'exploit.* Paris: Gallimard.

Hafner, Ute, and Edith Crombach. 1992. *Spiele, Tänze, und Sportarten der Welt, präsentiert beim 1: Internationalen Festival Sportkulturen der Welt.* Frankfurt am Main: DSB.

Hagenbeck, Carl. 1909. *Beasts and Men: Being Carl Hagenbeck's Experiences for Half a Century Among Wild Animals.* New York, Bombay, and Calcutta: Longmans, Green.

Hall, Edith, and Fiona Macintosh. 2005. *Greek Tragedy and the British Theatre 1660–1914.* Oxford: Oxford University Press.

Hall, Stuart, ed. 1997a. *Representation: Cultural Representations and Signifying Practices.* London and Thousand Oaks CA: Sage.

————. 1997b. "The Spectacle of the 'Other.'" In *Representation: Cultural Representations and Signifying Practices,* ed. Stuart Hall, 223–90. London and Thousand Oaks CA: Sage.

Haller, John S. 1975. *Outcasts from Evolution: Scientific Attitudes of Racial Inferiority, 1859–1900.* New York: McGraw-Hill.

Hamer, D., and P. Copeland. 1998. *Living with Our Genes: Why They Matter More Than You Think.* New York: Doubleday.

Hannaford, Ivan. 1996. *Race: The History of an Idea in the West.* Baltimore: Johns Hopkins University Press.

Handelman, Don. 1990. *Models and Mirrors: Towards an Anthropology of Public Events.* Cambridge: Cambridge University Press.

Hanson, John W. 1905. *The Official History of the St. Louis World's Fair.* St. Louis: Louisiana Purchase Exposition Co.

Haraway, Donna. 1988. "Remodeling the Human Way of Life: Sherwood Washburn and the New Physical Anthropology, 1950–1980." In *Bones, Bodies, Behavior: Essays on Biological Anthropology,* vol. 5 of *History of Anthropology,* ed. George Stocking, 206–59. Madison: University of Wisconsin Press.

Hargreaves, John. 2000. *Freedom for Catalonia? Catalan Nationalism, Spanish Identity, and the Barcelona Olympic Games.* Cambridge: Cambridge University Press.

Harper, Kenn. 2000. *Give Me My Father's Body: The Life of Minik, the New York Eskimo.* South Royalton VT: Steerforth Press.

Herrnstein, Richard, and C. Murray. 1995. *The Bell Curve.* New York: Free Press.

Herzfeld, Michael. 1982. *Ours Once More: Folklore, Ideology, and the Making of Modern Greece.* Austin: University of Texas Press.

Higginbotham, Evelyn Brooks. 1992. "African-American Women's History and the Metalanguage of Race." *Signs: Journal of Women in Culture and Society* 17, no. 2:251–74.

Hines, Thomas S. 1979. *Burnham of Chicago: Architect and Planner.* Chicago: University of Chicago Press.

Hinsley, Curtis. 1981. *Savages and Scientists: The Smithsonian Institution and the Development of American Anthropology 1846–1910.* Washington DC: Smithsonian Institution Press.

———. 1990. "The World as Marketplace: Commodification of the Exotic at the World's Columbian Exposition, Chicago, 1893." In *Exhibiting Cultures: The Poetics and Politics of Museum Display,* ed. Ivan Karp and Steven D. Lavine, 344–65. Washington DC: Smithsonian Institution Press.

Hirata, K. 1966. "Physique and Age of Tokyo Olympic Champions." *Journal of Sports Medicine and Physical Fitness* 6:207–22.

Hoare, Quintin, and Geoffrey N. Smith, eds. 1971. *Selections from the Prison Notebooks of Antonio Gramsci.* New York: International Publishers.

Hoberman, John. 1992. *Mortal Engines.* New York: Free Press.

———. 1995. "Towards a Theory of Olympic Internationalism." *Journal of Sport History* 22, no. 1:1–37.

———. 1997. *Darwin's Athletes.* Boston: Houghton Mifflin.

Hobsbawm, Eric. 1992. *Nations and Nationalism Since 1780: Programme, Myth, Reality.* Cambridge: Cambridge University Press.

Hoch, Edmund S. 1903. "The Olympic Games." *World's Fair Bulletin* 4 (March): 10–15.

Hodge, Frederick Webb. 1912. "WJ McGee." *American Anthropologist,* n.s. 14 (October-December): 683–87.

Hoffman, Phil. 1904. "A Study of the Feet of Barefooted Peoples for the Purpose of Comparison with Those of Shoewearers." McGee Papers, Box 16, Library of Congress.

Hofmann, Annette. 2003. "The 1904 Olympic Basketball Tournament in St. Louis." *Journal of Olympic History* 11, no. 3 (September): 19–21.

———. 2004. "The German and German-American Contribution to the 1904 Olympic Games in St. Louis." North American Society for Sport History Conference, May 28–31, Pacific Grove CA.

Holly, R. G., R. J. Barnard, M. Rosenthal, E. Applegate, and N. Pritikin. 1986. "Triathlete Characterization and Response to Prolonged Strenuous Competition." *Medicine and Science in Sports and Exercise* 18:123–27.

Holmes, Geoffrey. 1926. Untitled article, *Ruanda Notes* 14 (1926): 6.

Holmes, W. W. 1907. "Introduction." In *Twenty-Fifth Annual Report of the Bureau of*

American Ethnology to the Secretary of the Smithsonian Institution, 1903–1904. House Documents, 59th Cong., 2d sess., December 3, 1906–March 4, 1907. Vol. 109. Washington DC: Government Printing Office.

Holt, Thomas, Cleveland. 2000. *The Problem of Race in the Twenty-first Century.* Cambridge: Harvard University Press.

Hooton, Ernest A. 1936. "Plain Statements about Race." *Science* 83:511–13.

Horsman, Reginald. 1981. *Race and Manifest Destiny: The Origins of American Racial Anglo-Saxonism.* Cambridge: Harvard University Press.

Hrdlička, Aleš. 1903. *Proposed Plan of a Joint U.S. National Museum and World's Fair Anthropometric Laboratory, St. Louis.* WJ McGee Papers, Item 651, Box 19, Library of Congress.

Hügel, Hans-Otto, ed. 2003. *Handbuch Populäre Kultur: Begriffe, Theorien, und Diskussionen.* Stuttgart/Weimar: J. B. Metzler.

Jackson, J. J., Jr. 2001. "'In Ways Unacademical': The Reception of Carleton S. Coon's *The Origin of Races.*" *Journal of the History of Biology* 34:247–85.

Jackson, John P. 2005. *Science for Segregation.* New York: New York University Press.

Jacobson, Matthew Frye. 1998. *Whiteness of a Different Color: European Immigrants and the Alchemy of Race.* Cambridge: Harvard University Press.

———. 2000. *Barbarian Virtues: The United States Encounters Foreign Peoples at Home and Abroad, 1876–1917.* New York: Hill and Wang.

Jahn, Friedrich Ludwig. 1991. *Deutsches Volkstum.* Berlin: Aufbau Verlag.

Jacquard, Albert. 1978. *Eloge de la différence: La génétique et les hommes.* Paris: Editions du Seuil.

Jarvie, Grant. 1991. *Highland Games: The Making of the Myth.* Edinburgh: Edinburgh University Press.

Jensen, A. 1969. "How Much Can We Boost IQ and Scholastic Achievement?" *Harvard Educational Review* 39:1–123.

Johnson, William Oscar. 1972. *All That Glitters Is Not Gold: The Olympic Game.* New York: G. P. Putnam's Sons.

Jokl, Ernst. 1964. *Medical Sociology and Cultural Anthropology of Sport and Physical Education.* Springfield IL: Charles C. Thomas Publishers.

Jokl, Ernst, M. J. Karvonen, Jaako Kihlberg, Aarni Koskela, and Leo Noro. 1956. *Sport in the Cultural Pattern of the World.* Helsinki: Institute of Occupational Health.

Joyce, Barry Alan. 2001. *The Shaping of American Ethnography: The Wilkes Exploring Expedition, 1838–1842.* Lincoln: University of Nebraska Press.

Kahn, J. 2004. "How a Drug Becomes 'Ethnic': Law, Commerce, and the Production of Racial Categories in Medicine." *Yale Journal of Health Policy, Law, and Politics* 4:1–46.

Kanin, David. 1981. *A Political History of the Olympic Games*. Boulder CO: Westview Press.

Kasson, Joy S. 2000. *Buffalo Bill's Wild West: Celebrity, Memory, and Popular History*. New York: Hill and Wang.

Khosla, T., and V. C. McBroom. 1988. "Age, Height, and Weight of Female Olympic Finalists." *British Journal of Sports Medicine* 19:96–99.

Kidd, Bruce. 1980. *Tom Longboat*. Toronto: Fitzhenry and Whiteside.

Kirkiadou-Nestoros, Alke. 1978. *E Theoria tis Hellenikes Laografias* [The Theory of Greek Folklore Studies]. Athens: Eteria Spoudon.

Kirshenblatt-Gimblett, Barbara. 1991. "Objects of Ethnography." In *Exhibiting Cultures*, ed. Ivan Karp and Steven Levine. Washington DC: Smithsonian Institution Press.

Kitroeff, Alexander. 2004a. "The International Dimension of the Preparations of the Intermediate Olympics." In *Athens: Olympic City, 1896–1906*, ed. Christina Koulouri. Athens: International Olympic Academy.

———. 2004b. *Wrestling with the Ancients: Modern Greek Identity and the Olympics*. New York: Greekworks.

———. 2005. "Greek Images of the Ottomans and Turks (Late Nineteenth and Early Twentieth Centuries)." In *Representations of the "Other/s" in the Mediterranean World and Their Impact on the Region*, ed. Nedret Kuran-Burcoglu and Susan Gilson Miller. Istanbul: Isis Press.

Kitromilides, Paschalis M. 1994. *Enlightenment, Nationalism, Orthodoxy*. Brookfield VT: Ashgate/Variorum.

Koenig, B., S. Lee, and S. Richardson, eds. 2007. *Revisiting Race in a Genomic Age*. Piscataway NJ: Rutgers University Press.

Kohlraush, W. 1929. "Zusammenhange von Körperform und Leistung: Ergebnisse der anthropometrischen Messungen an der Athleten der Amsterdamer Olympiade." *Arbeitphysiologie* 2:187–204.

Kokkinos, Giorgios. 2004. "The Greek Intellectual World and the Olympic Games (1896, 1906)." In *Athens: Olympic City, 1896–1906*, ed. Christina Koulouri, 125–85. Athens: International Olympic Academy.

Koulouri, Christina. 1997a. *Athlitismos kai Opseis tis Astikis Koinokotitas Gymnastika kai Athlitika Somateia 1870–1922* [Sports and Aspects of Bourgeois Sensibility: Gymnastic and Sports Clubs 1870–1922]. Athens: KNE/EIE.

———. 1997b. "Voluntary Associations and New Forms of Sociability: Greek Sports Clubs at the Turn of the Nineteenth Century." In *Greek Society in the Making, 1863–1913: Realities, Symbols, and Visions*, ed. Philip Carabott, 145–60. Brookfield VT: Ashgate/Variorum.

———. 1998. "Athleticism and Antiquity: Symbols and Revivals in Nineteenth-Century Greece." *International Journal of the History of Sport* 15, no. 3:142–44.

Kramer, Paul. 1998. "The Pragmatic Empire: U.S. Anthropology and Colonial Politics in the Occupied Philippines, 1898–1916." PhD diss., Princeton University.

————. 2003. "Reflex Actions: Social Imperialism between the United States and the Philippines, 1898–1929." Paper presented at the American Historical Association 117th Annual Meeting, Chicago, Illinois, January 2–5.

Krist, Stefan. 2004. "Where Going Back Is a Step Forward: The Re-traditionalising of Sport Games in Post-Soviet Buriatiia." *Sibirica: Journal of Siberian Studies* 4, no. 1:104–15.

Kroeber, Karl, and Clifton Kroeber, eds. 2003. *Ishi in Three Centuries.* Lincoln: University of Nebraska Press.

Kuznezova, Zinaida, and Oleg Milstein. 1992. "Traditions of the Tatar Cultural Minority." In *Sport and Cultural Minorities,* ed. Leena Laine, 282–84. Helsinki: Finnish Society for Research in Sport and Physical Education.

Langaney, André. 1988. *Les hommes: Passé, présent, conditionnel.* Paris: Armand Colin.

Larsen, Niels, and Lisbet Gormsen. 1985. *Body Culture: A Monograph of the Body Culture among the Sukuma in Tanzania.* Vejle: DDGU.

Larson, Erik. 2003. *The Devil in the White City: Murder, Magic, and Madness at the Fair That Changed America.* New York: Crown Publishers.

Laska, Peter. "Revisioning the Millennium: Counter-Ideological Reflections on Modernity, Anthropology and Utopia." http://www. leftcurve.org/LC24WebPages/ millennium.html (accessed August 28, 2004).

Leach, Jerry W. 1976. *Trobriand Cricket: An Ingenious Response to Colonialism.* Film. Berkeley: University of California.

————. 1988. "Structure and Message in Trobriand Cricket." In *Anthropological Filmmaking,* ed. Jack R. Rollwagen, 237–51. Chur, Switzerland, and New York: Harwood.

Lefkoma ton en Athinais B' Diethnon Olympiakon Agonon [Album of the Second International Olympic Games in Athens]. 1907. Athens.

Lennartz, Karl. 1983. *Die Beteiligung Deutschlands an den Olympischen Spielen 1900 in Paris und 1904 in St. Louis.* Bonn: Carl Diem Institut.

————. 2003. "The Parade of Nations: A Symbol of Political Legitimation." In *Sport et idéologie: Session spéciale olympique* [Sport and ideology: Special olympic session], ed. Paul Dietschy, Vivier Christian, Loudcher Jean-François, and Jean-Nicolas Renaud. Actes du VIIème Congrès International du Comité Européen de l'Histoire du Sport (CESH). Besançon: Imprimerie BURS, 99–111. (Repr. in Jürgen Buschmann and Stephan Wassong, eds. 2005. *Langlauf durch die olympische Geschichte,* 550–77.)

————. 2004. *Die Spiele der III. Olympiade 1904 in St. Louis.* Kassel: Agon.

————. 2005a. "The Munich October Festival—Roots of Modern Olympism." In *Langlauf durch die olympische Geschichte: Festschrift Karl Lennartz* [Long-distance run through Olympic History: Festschrift to Karl Lennartz], ed. Jürgen Buschmann and Stephan Wassong, 264–87. Vol 2 of *Selected Writings on Olympic History.* Cologne: Carl und Liselott Diem Archiv.

————. 2005b. "The Second International Olympic Games in Athens 1896." In *Langlauf durch die olympische Geschichte: Festschrift Karl Lennartz,* ed. Jürgen Buschmann and Stephan Wassong, 288–348. Vol. 2 of *Selected Writings on Olympic History.* Cologne: Carl und Liselott Diem Archiv.

Lennartz, Karl, et al. 2000. *III Olympiad, St. Louis 1904, Athens 1906.* Vol. 4 of *The Olympic Century: The Official 1st Century History of the Modern Olympic Movement.* Los Angeles: World Sport Research and Publications.

Lennartz, Karl, and Walter Teutenberg. 1992. *Die Olympischen Spiele 1906 in Athen.* Kassel: Kasseler Sport Verlag.

Lewontin, R. C. 1970. "Race and Intelligence." *Bulletin of the Atomic Scientists* 26:2–8.

————. 1972. "The Apportionment of Human Diversity." *Evolutionary Biology* 6: 381–98.

Lidchi, Henrietta. 1997. "The Poetics and the Politics of Exhibiting Other Cultures." In *Representation: Cultural Representations and Signifying Practices,* ed. Stuart Hall, 151–223. London and Thousand Oaks CA: Sage.

Liponski, Wojciech. 2003. *World Sports Encyclopedia.* St. Paul MN: MBI.

Liponski, Wojciech, and Guy Jaouen, eds. 2003. *Ethnology of Sport.* Special issue of *Studies in Physical Culture and Tourism* 10:1.

Liu, Qilu. 1996: "Dragon Boat Racing: A Folk Custom Turned Competitive." In *Spiele der Welt im Spannungsfeld von Tradition und Moderne* [Games of the World in the Tension between Tradition and Modernity], ed. Gertrud Pfister, Toni Niewerth, and Gerd Steins, 1:315–19. Sankt Augustin: Academia.

Llewellyn Smith, Michael. 2005. *Days of 1896: Athens and the Invention of the Modern Olympic Games.* New York: Greekworks.com.

Llinés, Montserrat. 1996. "The History of Olympic Ceremonies: From Athens (1896) to Los Angeles (1984); An Overview." In *Olympic Ceremonies: Historical Continuity and Cultural Exchange,* ed. Miguel de Moragas, John MacAloon, and Montserrat Llinés, 65. Lausanne: International Olympic Committee.

Loland, Sigmund. 1994. "Pierre de Coubertin's Ideology of Olympism from the Perspective of the History of Ideas." In *Critical Reflections on Olympic Ideology,* ed. Robert K. Barney and Klaus V. Meier, 26–45. Second International Symposium for Olympic Research. London, Ontario: University of Western Ontario.

Lomawaima, K. Tsianina. 1994. *They Called It Prairie Light: The Story of Chilocco Indian School*. Lincoln: University of Nebraska Press.

Loomba, Ania. 2004. *Colonialism/Postcolonialism*. London and New York: Routledge.

Louisiana Purchase Exposition Corporation—Departmental Reports, Publicity, and Catalogues. 1904. *Physical Culture: Division of Exhibits*. St. Louis: Louisiana Purchase Exposition Co.

Louisiana Purchase Exposition Corporation—Official Daily Program. 1904. "Field Day for Primitive Peoples." *Official Daily Program*, August 11.

Louisiana Purchase Exposition Corporation. 1904. *The Greatest of Expositions*. St Louis: Louisiana Purchase Exposition Corporation.

———. 1904. *Official Catalogues of Exhibitors, Universal Exposition, St. Louis, USA, 1904*. St. Louis: Louisiana Purchase Exposition Company for the Official Catalogue Company.

Louisiana Purchase Exposition Corporation—World's Fair Bulletin. "A Novel Athletic Contest." *World's Fair Bulletin* 5 (September): 50.

———. 1904a. "A Thanksgiving Feast Given at the Model Playground." *World's Fair Bulletin* 5 (September): 22.

———. 1904b. "Children of All Nations at the Model Playground." *World's Fair Bulletin* 5 (September): 1.

———. 1904c. "Of Surpassing Interest: Athletic Event to Take Place, August 16, at World's Fair." *World's Fair Bulletin* 5 (August): 56.

———. 1904d. "The Model Playground." *World's Fair Bulletin* 5 (September): 12–13.

Loveman, Mara. 1999. "Is 'Race' Essential? A Comment on Bonilla-Silva." *American Sociological Review* 64:891–98.

Lucas, Charles P. 1905. *The Olympic Games 1904*. St. Louis: Woodward and Tiernan Printing Co.

Lucas, John A. 1977. "Early Olympic Antagonists, Pierre de Coubertin and James E. Sullivan." *Stadion* 3, no. 2:258–72.

———. 1980. *The Modern Olympic Games*. South Brunswick NJ: A. S. Barnes.

———. 1981. "American Involvement in the Athens Olympic Games of 1906: Bridge between Failure and Success." *Stadion* 6:217–28.

———. 2004. "The Great Gathering of Sport Scientists: The 1904 St. Louis Olympic Games Exposition Fair Physical Education Lectures." *Journal of Olympic History* 12 (January): 6–12.

Lynch, Arthur. 1904. "The Greek Olympic Games as Compared with Modern Athletics." *Outing* 44 (September): 714–25.

MacAloon, John. 1981. *This Great Symbol: Pierre de Coubertin and the Origins of the Modern Olympic Games*. Chicago: University of Chicago Press.

―――. 1984a. "Olympic Games and the Theory of Spectacle in Modern Societies." In *Rite, Drama, Festival, Spectacle: Rehearsals toward a Theory of Cultural Performance*, ed. John MacAloon, 241–80. Philadelphia: Institute for the Study of Human Issues.

―――, ed. 1984b. *Rite, Drama, Festival, Spectacle: Rehearsals toward a Theory of Cultural Performance*. Philadelphia: Institute for the Study of Human Issues.

―――. 1995. "Humanism as Political Necessity? Reflections on the Pathos of Anthropological Science in Pluricultural Contexts." In *The Conditions of Reciprocal Understanding*, ed. J. Fernandez and M. Singer, 206–35. Chicago: International House.

―――. 1996. "Olympic Ceremonies as a Setting for Intercultural Exchange." In *Olympic Ceremonies: Historical Continuity and Cultural Exchange*, ed. Miguel de Moragas, John MacAloon, and Montserrat Llinés, 29–43. Lausanne: International Olympic Committee.

―――. 1999. "Anthropology at the Olympic Games: An Overview." In *Olympic Games as Performance and Public Event*, ed. Arne Martin Klausen, 9–27. New York: Berghahn Books.

MacCanell, Dean. 1973. "Staged Authenticity: Arrangements of Social Space in Tourist Settings." *American Journal of Sociology* 79, no. 3:589–603.

Macintosh, Donald, Tom Bedecki, and C. E. S. Franks. 1987. *Sport In Canada: Federal Government Involvement Since 1961*. Montréal: McGill University Press.

MacMaster, Neil. 2001. *Racism in Europe 1870–2000*. Hampshire and New York: Palgrave.

MacMechen, Thomas. 1904a. "A Ten Million Dollar Pike and Its Attractions." *The Piker* 1 (May): 5–36.

―――. 1904b. "The Ten Million Dollar Pike." *The Piker* 1 (June): 2–32.

Madsen, Brigham D. 1979. *The Lemhi: Sacajawea's People*. Caldwell ID: Caxton Printers.

Maffesoli, Michel 1988: *Les temps des tribus: Le déclin de l'individualisme dans les sociétés postmodernes*. Paris: La Table Ronde. (Repr. in English as *The Time of the Tribes*. London: Sage, 1996.)

Malina, Robert M. 1994. "Anthropometry, Strength, and Motor Fitness." In *Anthropometry: The Individual and the Population*, ed. S. J. Ulijaszek and C. G. N. Mascie-Taylor, 160–77. Cambridge: Cambridge University Press.

Mallon, Bill. 1999a. *The 1904 Olympic Games: Results for All Competitors in All Events, with Commentary*. London: McFarland.

―――. 1999b. *The 1906 Olympic Games: Results for All Competitors in All Events, with Commentary*. Jefferson NC: McFarland.

―――. 2004. "Athens 1906." In *Encyclopedia of the Modern Olympic Movement*, ed. John E. Findling and Kimberly D. Pelle. Westport CT: Greenwood Press.

Mallon, Bill, and Ove Karlsson. 2004. "IOC and OCOG Abbreviations for NOCs." *Journal of Olympic History* 12 (May): 25.

Manceron, Gilles. 2002. "Les 'sauvages' et les droit de l'homme: un paradoxe républicain." In *Zoos humains: De la vénus hottentote aux reality shows; 19e et 20e siècles*, ed. N. Bancel, P. Blanchard, G. Boetsch, E. Deroo, and S. Lemaire, 399–405. Paris: Editions de la Découverte.

Mandell, Richard D. 1976. *The First Modern Olympics*. Berkeley: University of California Press.

Markovits, Andrei S., and Steven L. Hellerman. 2003. *Offside: Soccer and American Exceptionalism*. Princeton and Oxford: Princeton University Press.

Marks, Jonathan. 1995. *Human Biodiversity: Genes, Race, and History*. New York: Aldine de Gruyter.

———. 2000. "Human Biodiversity as a Central Theme of Biological Anthropology: Then and Now." *Kroeber Anthropological Society Papers* 84:1–10.

Marten, Heinz-Georg. 1999. "Racism, Social Darwinism, Anti-Semitism, and Aryan Supremacy." In *Shaping the Superman: Fascist Body as Political Icon; Aryan Fascism*, ed. James Anthony Mangan, 23–41. Portland: Frank Cass.

Mason, Otis T. 1883. "The Scope and Value of Anthropological Studies." *Science* 2:358–65.

———. 1887. "The Occurrence of Similar Inventions in Areas Widely Apart." *Science* 9:534–35.

Matthew, H. C. G. 1988. "The Liberal Age." In *Oxford History of Britain*, ed. Kenneth O. Morgan, 519–81. Oxford and New York: Oxford University Press.

Matthews, George, and Sandra Marshall. 2003. *St. Louis Olympics 1904*. Chicago: Arcadia.

Maurras, Charles. 2004. *Lettres des Jeux Olympiques*. Presented by Axel Tisseerand. Paris: Flammarion. (Orig. pub. 1901.)

Maxwell, Anne. 1999. *Colonial Photography and Exhibitions*. London: Leicester University Press.

McGee, Emma. 1905. *Life of WJ McGee*. Farley IA: Privately printed.

McGee, WJ. "Anthropology." *The Division of Exhibits*. No date. In World's Fairs microfilm collection, 45, Smithsonian Institution Libraries, Washington DC.

———. 1899. "The Trend of Human Progress." *American Anthropologist*, n.s. 1 (July): 401–47.

———. 1901. "Current Questions in Anthropology." *Science* 14:996–97.

———. 1904a. "Anthropology." *World's Fair Bulletin* 5 (February): 4–8.

———. 1904b. "Department N—Anthropology." *Official Exhibit Catalogue*. St. Louis: Louisiana Purchase Exposition Co.

———. 1904c. Fiscal records. Department of Anthropology, Louisiana Purchase Exposition files, Missouri Historical Society.

———. 1904d. "Introduction." In *Louisiana and the Fair: An Exposition of the World, Its People, and Their Achievements*, ed. J. W. Buel. Vol. 5. St. Louis: World's Progress Publishing Co.

———. 1904e. "Opportunities in Anthropology at the World's Fair." *Science* 20 (503): 253–54.

———. 1904f. Letter to George Dorsey, August 20. McGee Papers, Box 19, Library of Congress.

———. 1904g. Letter to Samuel M. McCowan, June 13. McGee Papers, Box 19, Library of Congress.

———. 1904h. Letter to James Sullivan, June 13; August 18. McGee Papers, Box 19, Library of Congress.

———. 1904i. Letter to William P. Wilson, June 13; June 28. McGee Papers, Box 19, Library of Congress.

———. 1904j. "Strange Races of Men." *The World's Work* 5 (August): 5185–88.

———. 1905a. "Anthropology at the Louisiana Purchase Exposition." *Science* 22 (573): 811–26.

———. 1905b. "Report of the Department of Anthropology to Frederick J. V. Skiff, director, Universal Exposition of 1904." Division of Exhibits, May 10. LPE files, file series 3, subseries 11, Missouri Historical Society.

McWhirter, Norris. 1964. "Unusual Facts and Fallacies." In *Modern Athletics*, ed. H. A. Mayer. London: Oxford University Press.

Mecklenburg, Duke of. 1912. *In the Heart of Africa*. London: Cassell.

"The Memorial of the Indians to the Queen." 1860. *Christian Guardian* 5 (September): 142.

Merwin, Henry Childs. 1896. "The Irish in American Life." *Atlantic Monthly* (March): 289, 294–95, 298.

Mez , Ferenc. 1956. *The Modern Olympic Games*. Budapest: Pannonia Press.

Miller, Don, and Stan Cohen. 1978. *Military and Trading Posts of Montana*. Missoula MT: Pictorial Histories Publishing Co.

Møller, Jørn. 1997. *Gamle idraetslege i Danmark*. New ed. Vols. 1–4. Gerlev: Idraetshistorisk Vaerksted.

———, ed. 2004. *Folk: Om et grundbegreb i demokrati og kultur*. Århus: Klim.

"The Model Playground." 1904. *World's Fair Bulletin* 5 (September): 12–13.

Mommsen, Wolfgang J. 1987. *Imperialismustheorien: Ein Überblick über die neueren Imperialismusinterpretationen*. 3rd augmented ed. Göttingen: Vandenhoeck and Ruprecht.

Montague, M. F. Ashley. 1960. *A Handbook of Anthropometry*. Springfield: Charles C. Thomas.

Moore, Charles, ed. 1909. *Plan of Chicago*. Chicago: Chicago Commercial Club.

Moragas, Miguel de, John MacAloon, and Montserrat Llinés, eds. 1996. *Olympic Ceremonies: Historical Continuity and Cultural Exchange*. Lausanne: International Olympic Committee.

Morgan, Lewis Henry. 1985. *Ancient Society; Or, Researches in the Lines of Human Progress from Savagery to Barbarism to Civilization*. Tucson: University of Arizona Press Classics of Anthropology Series. (Orig. pub. 1877.)

Morley, David, and Kevin Robbins. 1995. *Spaces of Identity*. London: Routledge.

Morris, Andrew. 2004. *Marrow of the Nation: A History of Sport and Physical Culture in Republican China*. Berkeley: University of California Press.

Morrow, Don, and Kevin B. Wamsley. 2005. *Sport in Canada: A History*. Don Mills, Canada: Oxford University Press.

Moses, L. G. 1996. *Wild West Shows and the Images of American Indians, 1883–1933*. Albuquerque: University of New Mexico Press.

Mosse, George L. 1975. *The Nationalization of the Masses*. Ithaca: Cornell University Press.

———. 1985. *Towards the Final Solution: A History of European Racism*. 2nd ed. New York: Howard Fertig.

Mrozek, Donald J. 1983. *Sport and American Mentality, 1880–1910*. Knoxville: University of Tennessee Press.

Muller, Kal. 1970. "Land Diving with the Pentecost Islanders." *National Geographic Magazine* 138, no. 6:799–817.

Müller, Norbert, and Otto Schantz. 1991. *Bibliographie des oeuvres de Pierre de Coubertin*. Lausanne: Comité International de Pierre de Coubertin.

Nabokov, Peter. 1981. *Indian Running: Native American History and Tradition*. Santa Barbara: Capra. (Repr., Santa Fe: Ancient City, 1987.)

Naismith, James. 1892. "Basket Ball." (YMCA) *Triangle* (January): 144–47.

Nash, Stephen E., and Gary M. Feinman, eds. 2003. *Curators, Collections, and Contexts: Anthropology at the Field Museum, 1893–2002*. Fieldiana Anthropology, n. s., no. 36. Chicago: Field Museum of Natural History.

"Native Dwellings at the St. Louis Exposition." 1904. *Scientific American* 91 (September 24): 217–18.

Nelles, H. V. 1999. *The Art of Nation Building: Pageantry and Spectacle at Quebec's Tercentenary*. Toronto: University of Toronto Press.

Nendel, Jim. 2004. "New Hawaiian Monarchy: The Media Representations of Duke Kahanamoku, 1911–1912." *Journal of Sport History* 31 (Spring): 32–52.

Neufeld, Maurice F. 1935. "The Contribution of the World's Columbian Exposition of 1893 to the Idea of a Planned Society in the United States." PhD diss., University of Wisconsin.

Norgan, N. G. 1994. "Anthropometry and Physical Performance." In *Anthropometry: The Individual and the Population*, ed. S. J. Ulijaszek and C. G. N. Mascie-Taylor, 141–59. Cambridge: Cambridge University Press.

Norton, Kevin, and Tim Olds. 1996. *Anthropometrica*. Sydney: University of New South Wales Press.

Novak, Helmut. 1989. *Schottische "Highland Games": Traditioneller Volkssport einer ethnischen Minderheit im Wandel der Zeit*. Düsseldorf: Institut für Sportwissenschaft der Universität.

"The Olympic Games." 1908. *The Outlook* 89 (July 25): 636.

Olympic Games Programme. 1904. Special Circular no. 1. St. Louis: Department of Physical Culture, Louisiana Purchase Exposition.

Osterhammel, Jürgen. 2005. "'The Great Work of Uplifting Mankind': Zivilisierungsmission und Moderne." In *Zivilisierungsmissionen: Imperiale Weltverbesserung seit dem 18. Jahrhundert*, ed. Boris Barth and Jürgen Osterhammel, 363–425. Konstanz: UVK Verlagsgesellschaft.

Oxendine, Joseph B. 1995. *American Indian Sports Heritage*. Lincoln: University of Nebraska Press. (Orig. pub. 1988.)

Parezo, Nancy J. 2004. "The Exposition within the Exposition: The Philippine Reservation." *Gateway Heritage* 24, no. 4:30–39.

Parezo, Nancy J., and Don Fowler. 2007. *Anthropology Goes to the Fair: The 1904 Louisiana Purchase Exposition*. Lincoln: University of Nebraska Press.

Parezo, Nancy J., and John W. Troutman. 2001. "The 'Shy' Cocopa Go to the Fair." In *Selling the Indian: Commercializing and Appropriating American Indian Cultures*, ed. Carter Jones Meyer and Diana Royer, 3–43. Tucson: University of Arizona Press.

Park, Roberta J. 1980. "The *Research Quarterly* and Its Antecedents." *Research Quarterly of Exercise and Sport Science* 51 (March):1–22.

Parnell, R. W. 1958. *Behavior and Physique*. London: Arnold.

Patterson, Thomas C. 2001. *A Social History of Anthropology in the United States*. Oxford: Berg.

Peavy, Linda, and Ursula Smith. 2001. "World's Champions: The 1904 Girl's Basketball Team from Fort Shaw Indian Boarding School." *Montana: The Magazine of Western History* 51, no. 4:2–25.

———. 2005. "World Champions: The 1904 Girls' Basketball Team from Fort Shaw Indian Boarding School." In *Native American Athletes in Sport and Society: A Reader*, ed. C. Richard King, 40–78. Lincoln: University of Nebraska Press.

———. 2008. *Full-Court Quest: The Girls from Fort Shaw Indian School, Basketball Champions of the World*. Norman: University of Oklahoma Press.

Peron, François. 1807. *Voyage de Découvertes aux Terres Australes*. Vol. 1. Paris: Imprimerie Impérial.

Pfister, Gertrud, ed. 1997. *Traditional Games*. Special issue of *Journal of Comparative Physical Education and Sport* 19:2.

———, ed. 2004. *Games of the Past, Sports for the Future? Globalisation, Diversification, Transformation*. Sankt Augustin: Academia.

Pfister, Gertrud, Toni Niewerth, and Gerd Steins, eds. 1996. *Spiele der Welt im Spannungsfeld von Tradition und Moderne* [Games of the World in the Tension between Tradition and Modernity]. Vol. 1. Sankt Augustin: Academia.

Picard, Alfred. 1902–3. *Exposition Universelle de 1900 à Paris*. Paris: Imprimerie Nationale.

Pinker, S. 2002. *The Blank Slate: The Modern Denial of Human Nature*. New York: Viking Penguin.

Poignant, Roslyn. 2004. *Professional Savages: Captive Lives and Western Spectacle*. New Haven CT: Yale University Press.

Politis, Nicolaos G., et. al. 1896. *The Olympic Games, B.C. 776–A.D. 1896*. Athens: C. Beck; New York: American Olympic Committee.

Powell, John Wesley. 1899. "Esthetology; Or the Science of Activities Designed to Give Pleasure." *American Anthropologist*, n.s., 1 (January): 1–40.

Pratt, Mary Louise. 1992. *Imperial Eyes: Travel Writing and Transculturation*. London: Routledge.

Primm, James. 1998. *Lion of the Valley: St. Louis, Missouri, 1764–1980*. Boulder CO: Pruett.

Procter, John R. 1898. "Isolationism or Imperialism." *Forum* 26 (September): 14–26.

Provine, W. B. 1973. "Geneticists and the Biology of Race Crossing." *Science* 182:790–96.

Prucha, Francis Paul, ed. 2000. *Documents of United States Indian Policy*. 3rd ed. Lincoln: University of Nebraska Press.

Putnam, Carl. 1961. *Race and Reason* (Washington DC: Public Affairs Press.

———. 1967. *Race and Reality*. Washington DC: Public Affairs Press.

Quel Corps? 1980. "Coubertin, l'Olympisme, et Berlin '36." *Quel Corps?* 16:32–43.

"The Racial Exhibit at the St. Louis Fair." 1904. *Scientific American* 91 (December 10): 412–14.

Radforth, Ian. 2003. "Performance, Politics, and Representation: Aboriginal People and the 1860 Royal Tour of Canada." *Canadian Historical Review* 84, no. 1 (March): 1–32.

Rafael, Vincente L. 1995. "White Women and United States Rule in the Philippines." *American Literature* 67, no. 4 (December): 639–66.

————. 2004. *Royal Spectacle: The 1860 Visit of the Prince of Wales to Canada and the United States*. Toronto: University of Toronto Press.

Raibmon, Paige. 2000. "Theatres of Contact: The Kwakwaka'wakw Meet Colonialism in British Columbia and at the World's Fair." *Canadian Historical Review* 81, no. 2:157–90.

————. 2005. *Authentic Indians: Episodes of Encounters from the Late-Nineteenth-Century Northwest Coast*. Durham: Duke University Press.

"Realistic Exhibits of Race, Life, and Movement for the World's Fair." 1901. *World's Fair Bulletin* 2, no. 12:5.

Reaves, Joseph A. 2002. *Taking In a Game: A History of Baseball in Asia*. Lincoln: University of Nebraska Press.

"Recent Progress in American Anthropology: A Review of the Activities of Institutions and Individuals from 1902 to 1906." *American Anthropologist* 8, no. 3:466–67.

Reedy, William. 1904. "The End of the Fair." *The Mirror* (December).

Reel, Estelle. 1901. *Uniform Course of Study for the Indian Schools of the United States*. Washington DC: Government Printing Office.

Register of Pupils. 1892–1908. Records of Fort Shaw Indian School, Field Office Records of Non-Reservation Schools, Record Group 75, National Archives, Denver CO, entry 1358.

Renan, Ernest. 1998. "Qu'est-ce qu'une nation?" In *Les nationalismes en Europe: Quête d'identité ou tentation de repli?* ed. Eric Nguyen, 26–28. Paris: Le Monde. (Orig. pub. 1882.)

Renson, Roland, and Herman Smulders. 1981. "Research Methods and Development of the Flemish Folk Games File." *International Review of Sport Sociology* 16, no. 1:97–107.

Renson, Roland, Pascal Delheye, and T. Ameye. 2005. "Olympism and Colonialism: The 1904 St. Louis Olympics and the 1905 Brussels Olympic Congress." Paper presented at the European Congress of Sport Sciences, Belgrade, Serbia, July 14.

Rétat, Laudyce. 2003. "Renan et la symbolique des races." In *L'idée de "race"*, ed. Sarga Moussa, 321–26. Paris: L'Harmattan.

Reynaud Paligot, Carole. 2006. *La République raciale: 1860–1930*. Paris: Presses Universitaires Françaises.

Roche, Maurice. 2000. *Mega-Events and Modernity: Olympics and Expos in the Growth of Global Culture*. London: Routledge.

Roediger, David, ed. 1999. *The Wages of Whiteness: Race and the Making of the American Working Class*. London: Verso.

Roosevelt, Theodore. 1903. Letter to Pierre de Coubertin, June 15. Lausanne: Archives of the International Olympic Committee.

———. 1925. "The Strenuous Life." In *The Works of Theodore Roosevelt*, ed. Herman Hagedorn, 267–81. Memorial ed. Vol. 15. New York: Scriber's Sons. (Orig. pub. 1899.)

Rose, H., and S. Rose. 2000. *Alas, Poor Darwin: Arguments Against Evolutionary Psychology*. London: Jonathan Cape.

Rosenberg, N. A., J. K. Pritchard, J. L. Weber, H. M. Cann, K. K. Kidd, L. A. Zhivotovsky, and M. W. Feldman. 2002. "Genetic Structure of Human Populations," *Science* 298:2181–85.

Ruffié, Jacques. 1976. *De la biologie à la culture*. Paris: Flammarion.

Rushton, J. P. 2000. *Race, Evolution, and Behavior: A Life-History Approach*. Special abridged ed. Port Huron MI: Charles Darwin Research Institute.

Rushton, J. P., and A. Jensen. 2005. "Thirty Years of Research on Race Differences in Cognitive Ability." *Psychology, Public Policy, and Law* 11:235–94.

Rydell, Robert. 1984. *All the World's a Fair: Visions of Empire at American International Exhibitions*. Chicago: University of Chicago Press.

———. 1989. "The Culture of Imperial Abundance." In *Consuming Visions*, ed. Simon J. Bronner, 191 216. New York: Norton.

———. 1993. *World of Fairs: The Century-of-Progress Expositions*. Chicago: University of Chicago Press.

Rydell, Robert, and Nancy E. Gwinn, eds. 1994. *Fair Representations: World's Fairs and the Modern World*. Amsterdam: VU University Press.

Said, Edward. 1978. *Orientalism*. Harmondsworth: Penguin.

———. 1993. *Culture and Imperialism*. New York: Vintage.

Saloutos, Theodore. 1964. *The Greeks in the United States*. Cambridge: Harvard University Press.

Sammons, Jeffrey T. 1994. "'Race' and Sport: A Critical, Historical Examination." *Journal of Sport History* 21, no. 3:203–78.

Samuel, Raphael, ed. 1981. *People's History and Socialist Theory*. London: Routledge and Kegan Paul.

Sarich, V., and F. Miele. 2004. *Race: The Reality of Human Differences*. New York: Westview.

Sawka, M. N., M. M. Toner, R. P. Francesconi, and K. B. Pandolf. 1983. "Hypohydration and Exercise: Effects of Heat Acclimation, Genera and Environment." *Journal of Applied Physiology* 55:1147–53.

Schantz, Otto. 1995–96. "Französische Festkultur als Wegbereiter der Modernen Olympischen Spiele" [French Festival Culture as Precursor of the Modern Olympic Games]. *Stadion* 21–22:64–65. Special issue on *Studien zur Geschichte der Olympischen Spiele*.

———. 1998. "Le 'Gymnase de la Cité': Le droit au sport pour les citadins selon Pierre de Coubertin." In *Le Sport dans la ville*, ed. Christian Vivier and François Loudcher, 15–27. Paris: L'Harmattan.

———. 1999. "L'oeuvre pédagogique de Pierre de Coubertin." In *L'éducation physique au XXe siècle: Approches historique et culturelle*, ed. J. Gleyse et al., 101–17. Paris: Vigot.

———. 2001. "Sport und Leibesübungen als Erziehungsmittel bei Pierre de Coubertin." *Stadion* 27:111–24.

Schantz, Otto, and Norbert Müller. 1986. "Préface." In *Pierre de Coubertin: Textes choisis, tome III; Pratique sportive*, ed. Norbert Müller and Otto Schantz, 1–22. Zürich, Hildesheim, and New York: Weidmann.

Secretary of the Committee on Ceremonies. 1904. *Military Camp and Special Days and Events, Louisiana Purchase Exposition, World's Fair, St. Louis, 1904*. Compiled by the Secretary of the Committee on Ceremonies St. Louis: Woodward and Tiernan.

Senn, Alfred E. 1999. *Power, Politics, and the Olympic Games*. Champaign IL: Human Kinetics.

Seymour, Harold. 1990. *Baseball: The People's Game*. New York: Oxford University Press.

Shipman, Pat. 1994. *The Evolution of Racism: Human Differences and the Use and Abuse of Science*. New York: Simon and Schuster.

Shute, D. K. 1896. "Racial Anatomical Peculiarities." *American Anthropologist* 9:123–32.

Simms, Stephen C. 1904a. Letters to to George Dorsey, August 11; August 15; August 18. Field Museum of Natural History, Department of Anthropology.

———. 1904b. Letters to WJ McGee, August 14; August 16; August 17. McGee Papers, Box 16, Library of Congress.

Skiadas, Eleftherios. 1996. *100 Chronia Neotere Hellenike Olympiake Historia* [100 Years of Modern Greek Olympic History]. Athens: Ta Nea.

Skopetea, Elli. 1988. *To 'Protypo Vasilio' kai e Megali Idea: Opseis tou Ethnikou Provlimatos stin Ellada (1830–1880)* [The "Model Kingdom" and the Great Idea: Aspects of the National Problem in Greece (1830–1880)]. Athens: Polytypo.

Sie, Swanpo. 1978. "Sports and Politics: The Case of the Asian Games and the GANEFO." In *Sport and International Relations*, ed. Benjamin Lowe et al., 279–96. Champaign IL: Stipes.

Sloterdijk, Peter. 1998. *Sphären: Plurale Sphärologie*. Vols. 1–3. Frankfurt am Main: Suhrkamp.

Smith, Michael Llewellyn. 2005. *Days of 1896: Athens and the Invention of the Modern Olympic Games*. New York: Greekworks.Com.

Sowell, Thomas. 1994. *Race and Culture: A World View*. New York: Basic Books.

Spalding, A. G. 1902. Executive Committee Minutes addressed to J. F. W. Skiff, October 9. Louisiana Purchase Exposition Committee Minutes, Louisiana Purchase

Exposition Corporation Collection, series 11, subseries 3, folder 10 (typescript), Missouri Historical Society.

Spears, Betty. 1991. "Senda Berenson Abbott: New Woman, New Sport." In *A Century of Women's Basketball: From Frailty to Final Four*, ed. Joan Hult and Marianna Trekell. Reston VA: National Association of Girls and Women in Sport.

Spidel, Carol. 2000. *Dancing at Halftime: Sports and the Controversy over American Indian Mascots*. New York: New York University Press.

St. Louis, Brett. 2003. "Sport, Genetics, and the 'Natural Athlete': The Resurgence of Racial Science." *Body and Society* 9.

Stanaland, Peggy. 1981. "Pre-Olympic 'Anthropology Days,' 1904: An Aborted Effort to Bridge Some Cultural Gaps." In *Play as Context: 1979 Proceedings of the Association for the Study of Play*, ed. Alyce Taylor Cheska, 101–6. West Point NY: Leisure Press.

Stanley, Peter W. 1974. *A Nation in the Making: The Philippines and the United States, 1899–1921*. Cambridge: Harvard University Press.

Starn, Orin. 2004. *Ishi's Brain: In Search of America's Last "Wild" Indian*. New York: Norton.

Stocking, George W., Jr. 1960. "Franz Boas and the Founding of the American Anthropological Association." *American Anthropologist* 62:1–17.

———. ed. 1974. *A Franz Boas Reader: The Shaping of American Anthropology, 1883–1911*. Chicago: University of Chicago Press.

———. *Victorian Anthropology*. 1987. New York: Free Press.

———, ed. 1989. *Romantic Motives: Essays on Anthropological Sensibility*. Madison: University of Wisconsin Press.

Stoddart, Helen. 2000. *Rings of Desire: Circus History and Representation*. Manchester: Manchester University Press.

Sullivan, James E. 1901. "Athletics in the Stadium." *Cosmopolitan* 31 (September): 501–8.

———. 1904a. "Division of Exhibits: Physical Culture." *World's Fair Bulletin* 5 (April): 57–59.

———. 1904b. Letters to WJ McGee, June 10; August 20. McGee Papers, Box 19, Library of Congress.

———. 1905a. "Universal Exposition, Saint Louis, 1904." *Spalding's Official Athletic Almanac for 1904*, ed. J. Sullivan, 183–92. New York: American Sports Publishing.

———. 1905b. "Physical Training Programme." *Spalding's Official Athletic Almanac for 1904*, ed. J. Sullivan, 185–86. New York: American Sports Publishing.

———. 1905c. "Report of the Department of Physical Culture to Frederick J. V. Skiff, director, Universal Exposition of 1904." Division of Exhibits, May 1905. LPE files, series 3, subseries 11, Missouri Historical Society.

————, ed., 1905d. *Spalding's Official Athletic Almanac for 1904.* New York: American Sports Publishing.

————. 1905e. "Anthropology Days at the Stadium." In *Spalding's Official Athletic Almanac for 1905,* ed. J. Sullivan, 249–66. New York: American Sports Publishing.

————. 1905f. "Review of the Olympic Games of 1904." In *Spalding's Official Athletic Almanac for 1905,* ed. J. Sullivan. New York: American Sports Publishing.

————, ed. 1905g. *Spalding's Official Athletic Almanac for 1905: Special Olympic Number, Containing the Official Report of the Olympic Games of 1904.* New York: American Sports Publishing Co.

————, ed. 1906. "The Olympic Games of 1906 at Athens." *Spalding's Official Athletic Almanac 23,* no. 273. New York: American Sports Publishing.

Sullivan, Robert, ed. 2004. *The Olympics: From Athens to Athens.* New York: Life Books.

Taine, Hippolyte. 1903. *Histoire de la littérature anglaise.* 5 vols. 11thed. Paris: Hachette.

Tanner, J. M. 1964. *The Physique of the Olympic Athlete.* London: George Allen and Unwin.

Taylor, Charles. 1992. "The Politics of Recognition." In *Multiculturalism: Examining the Politics of Recognition,* ed. Amy Gutmann, 25–73. Princeton: Princeton University Press.

Teich, Mikulas, and Roy Porter, eds. 1990. *Fin de Siècle and Its Legacy.* Cambridge: Cambridge University Press.

Thode-Arora, Hilke. 1989. *Für fünfzig Pfennig um die Welt: Die Hagenbeckschen Völkerschauen.* Frankfurt and New York: Campus.

Tittel, L. 1965. "Zur Biotypologie und funktionellen Anatomie des Leistungssportlers." *Nova Acta Leopoldina* 30:172.

Toohey, Kristine, and A. J. Veal. 2000. *The Olympic Games: A Social Science Perspective.* New York: CABI Publishing.

Topinard, Paul. 1878. *Anthropology.* Philadelphia: J. B. Lippincott.

Toqueville, Alexis de. 1981. *De la Démocratie en Amérique.* Vol. 2. Paris: Flammarion. (Orig. pub. 1840.)

Trennert, Robert. 1987. "Selling Indian Education at World's Fairs and Expositions, 1893–1904." *American Indian Quarterly* 11:203–22.

Troutman, John W., and Parezo, Nancy. 1998. "'The Overlord of the Savage World': Anthropology and the Press at the 1904 Louisiana Purchase Exposition." *Museum Anthropology* 22(2): 17–34.

Tucker, William H. 1994. *The Science and Politics of Racial Research.* Urbana: University of Illinois Press.

Tuckerman, Charles K. 1873. *The Greeks of Today.* New York: Putnam.

Ulijaszek, S. J., and Mascie-Taylor, C. G. N., eds. 1994. *Anthropometry: The Individual and the Population.* Cambridge: Cambridge University Press.

United States Census Bureau. 1900. *Twelfth Census of the United States, 1900.* Vol. 1. Population: *Population of States and Territories,* xviii. Available at http://www.census.gov.

United States Congress. 1911. 61st Cong., 3rd sess., Senate Document #747, Abstracts of the Reports of the Immigration Commission, II, Washington.

United States Olympic Committee. 1993. *Athens to Atlanta: One Hundred Years of Glory.* Colorado Springs: United States Olympic Committee.

van der Merwe, F. J. G. 1999. "Africa's First Encounter with the Olympic Games in . . . 1904." *Journal of Olympic History* 7, no. 5:29–34.

Vergès, Françoise. 2005. "'Le nègre n'est pas. Pas plus que le blanc.' Frantz Fanon, esclavage, race et racisme." In "Le racisme après les races," edited by Etienne Balibar for *Actuel Marx* 38:45–64.

Vettenniemi, Erkki. 2002. "Kato neekeri hiihtää! Kiista modernin urheilun leviämisesta" [with English summary, "Negroes on skis! The controversy over the diffusion of modern sport starting (sic)"]. *Suomen Urheiluhistorialallisen Seuren Vuosikirja* [Yearbook of Finnish Society of Sport History].

Walker, John Brisbeen. 1904. "The Pike: Chapter 13 of the World's Fair." *The Cosmopolitan* 37(5):615–20.

Wamsley, Kevin B. 1997. "Nineteenth Century Sport Tours, State Formation, and Canadian Foreign Policy." *Sporting Traditions: Journal of the Australian Society for Sport History* 13, no. 2 (May): 73–89.

Wamsley, Kevin B., and Greg Gillespie. 2003. "The Prince of Wales Tour and the Construction of British Sporting Masculinity in Nineteenth-Century Canada." Paper presented at the North American Society for Sport History, Ohio State University.

Webster, F. A. M. 1937. *Why? The Science of Athletics.* London: Shaw.

Welch, Richard E., Jr. 1972. *Imperialists vs. Anti-Imperialists: The Debate Over Expansionism in the 1890s.* Itasca IL: F. E. Peacock Press.

Weiner, J. S. 1957. "Physical Anthropology: An Appraisal." *American Scientist* 45:79–87.

Wheeler, Robert W. 1979. *Jim Thorpe: World's Greatest Athlete.* Norman: University of Oklahoma Press.

Wiggins, David. 1989. "'Great Speed but Little Stamina': The Historical Debate over Black Athletic Superiority." *Journal of Sport History* 16:158–85.

Winter, T. 2004. 'Luther Halsey Gulick.' *The Encyclopedia of Informal Education,* http://www.infed.org/thinkers/gulick.htm.

Wolff, Leon. 2006. *Little Brown Brother: How the United States Purchased and Pacified the Philippine Islands at the Century's Turn.* New York: History Book Club. (Orig. pub. 1960.)

Wood, Leonard. 1910. Letter to Bishop Brent, March 24. Bishop Charles H. Brent Papers, Box 9, Library of Congress.

Woodhouse, C. M. 1969. *The Philhellenes*. Rutherford NJ: Fairleigh Dickenson University Press.

Woodworth, Robert S. 1904a. Field notes. Woodworth Personal Papers, Columbia University Archives.

———. 1904b. Monthly Reports to McGee, McGee Papers, Box 16, Library of Congress.

———. 1910. "Racial Differences in Mental Traits." *Science*, n.s., 31, no. 788:171–86.

———. 1932. "A History of Psychology in Autobiography." In *The International University Series in Psychology*, ed. Carl Murchison, 2:359–80. Worcester MA: Clark University Press.

Wooley, Monroe. 1913. "'Batter Up' in the Philippines." *Outdoor World and Recreation* (May): 313–14.

Worcester, Dean C. 1913. "The Non-Christian Peoples of the Philippine Islands." *National Geographic* 24, no. 11 (November): 1157–1256.

———. 1914. *The Philippines: Past and Present*. Vol. 2. New York: Macmillan.

"World's Fair Indian Exhibit." 1930. *Chilocco Farmer and Stockgrower* 4, no. 2 (December).

Worster, Donald. 2002. *A River Running West: The Life of John Wesley Powell*. New York: Oxford University Press.

Wrangham, R., and D. Peterson. 1996. *Demonic Males: Apes and the Origins of Human Violence*. Boston: Houghton Mifflin.

Yang, Ssu-Ch'ang. 1943. "The Dragon Boat Race in Wu-Ling, Hunan." Trans. Chao Wei-pang. *Folklore Studies* 2:1–18. (Orig. pub. 1647.)

Young, David C. 1996. *The Modern Olympics: A Struggle for Revival*. Baltimore: Johns Hopkins University Press.

Ziff, Larzer. 1966. *The American 1890s: Life and Times of a Lost Generation*. New York: Viking.

Zurcher, Louis A., and Arnold Meadow. 1967. "On Bullfights and Baseball: An Example of Interaction of Social Institutions." Reprinted in *The Cross-Cultural Analysis of Sport and Games*, ed. Günther Lüschen, 109–31. Champaign IL: Stipes, 1970.

Zweig, Eric. 1996. "Meet Me in St. Louis." *Beaver* (June/July): 25–28.

Contributors

John Bale holds degrees from the University of London and has taught at the Open University, Keele University, and the University of Aarhus. His main academic interest has been geographical dimensions of sport. He has authored many articles and books including *Sport, Space, and the City* (1993), *Landscapes of Modern Sport* (1994), *Kenyan Running: Movement Culture, Geography and Global Change* (with Joe Sang, 1996), and *Imagined Olympians: Body Culture and Colonial Representation in Rwanda* (2002). He has been a visiting professor at the University of Jyvaskyla, the University of Western Ontario, and the University of Queensland. Currently he is an emeritus professor at Keele University and an honorary professor at Queensland and De Montfort Universities. His current research is focused on antisport sentiments in literature.

Susan Brownell is professor and chair of anthropology at the University of Missouri–St. Louis. A former nationally ranked track- and-field athlete in the United States, she was the heptathlon champion in the 1986 Chinese National College Games during a year of language study in Beijing. This experience formed the basis for her book *Training the Body for China: Sports in the Moral Order of the People's Republic* (1995). She is also co-editor (with Jeffrey Wasserstrom) of *Chinese Femininities/Chinese Masculinities: A Reader* (2002). From 2000–2007 she was a member of the Research Council of the Olympic Studies Center of the International Olympic Committee. *Beijing's Games: What the Olympics Mean to China* (2008) examines the scope for multiculturalism amidst the symbolism of Western civilization that predominates at the Olympic Games.

Mark Dyreson is an associate professor of kinesiology and history at Pennsylvania State University. He specializes in American cultural history, particularly in the role of sport in American society. He earned a doctorate in history from the University of Arizona in 1989. He currently serves as the president of the North American Society for Sport History, as an associate editor for the *International Journal of the History of Sport*, and on the editorial boards of the *Journal of Sport History* and *Olympika: The International Journal of Olympic Studies*. He has written extensively on sport and nationalism, and on sport and the social construction of racial and ethnic identities. He is particularly interested in the intersection of race, sport, and science in modern cultures. He is the author of *Making the American Team: Sport, Culture, and the Olympic Experience* (1998), *Crafting Patriotism for Global Dominance: America at the Olympics* (2008), and the editor, with J. A. Mangan, of *Sport in American Society: Insularity, Exceptionalism, and "Imperialism"* (2007). He has published more than a dozen chapters in books and more than two dozen articles in refereed journals.

Henning Eichberg, D.Phil. with habilitation, is a cultural sociologist and historian. He is a professor at the University of Southern Denmark and researches at the Centre for Sports, Health, and Civil Society in Gerlev, Denmark. Formerly professor in Osnabrück/Vechta, Odense, and Copenhagen, Eichberg has also lectured at Austrian, English, Finnish, French, Japanese, Polish, Scottish, and Swedish universities. He has been a member of the editorial boards of *Stadion*, *International Journal of the History of Sport*, *International Review for the Sociology of Sport*, *International Journal of Eastern Sports and Physical Education* (Suwon, Korea), and *Ido-Movement for Culture* (Rzeszów, Poland). Eichberg has cofounded the Institut International d'Anthropologie Corporelle (Rennes, France, 1987), Centre for the Study of Body Culture (Tsukuba, Japan, 2002), and International Network for the Marxist Study of Sport (2005). His research has dealt with the history, sociology, and psychology of body culture and sport; the anthropology of movement culture; the history of technology; and democracy, movement, and identity. His present main fields of research are international comparative studies of body cultures, Sport for All, and sports policies. He has published more than thirty books, including *Leistung, Spannung, Geschwindigkeit* (1978), *Body Cultures* (1998), and *The People of Democracy* (2004).

Gerald R. Gems received his PhD in physical education from the University of Maryland in 1989. He is the author of *Sports in North America: A Documentary History* (1995); *Windy City Wars: Labor, Leisure, and Sport in the Making of Chicago* (1997); *For Pride, Profit, and Patriarchy: Football and the Incorporation of American Cultural Values* (2000); *The Athletic Crusade* (2006); and numerous articles on sport history. He served as president of the North American Society for Sport History (2003–5), and is a member of the Executive Council for the International Society for the History of Physical Education and Sport.

Alexander Kitroeff is an associate professor of history at Haverford College and specializes in the study of identity in Modern Greece and its diaspora. He was born in Athens and studied in Britain, where he received his D.Phil. from Oxford University in 1984. He is the recipient of several awards including an Onassis Foundation graduate studies scholarship, a senior fellowship from the Social Science Research Council, and an innovative teaching award from Haverford College; he is also a member of the editorial board of the *Journal of the Hellenic Diaspora*. His publications include *The Greeks in Egypt, 1919–1937* (1989); *Griegos en América, 1492–1992* (1992); and *Wrestling with the Ancients: Modern Greek Identity and the Olympics* (2004).

Jonathan Marks is a professor of biological anthropology at the University of North Carolina at Charlotte. He earned master's degrees in genetics and anthropology and a doctorate in anthropology from the University of Arizona. His research has been published in *Nature, Journal of Human Evolution, History and Philosophy of the Life Sciences*, and other journals. He is the coauthor of *Evolutionary Anthropology* (1993) and author of *Human Biodiversity* (1995) and *What It Means to Be 98 Percent Chimpanzee* (2002), which was awarded the W. W. Howells prize in Biological Anthropology from the American Anthropological Association (AAA). He received the 1999 AAA/Mayfield Award for Excellence in Undergraduate Teaching, and served as president of the General Anthropology Division of the AAA from 2000–2002. In 2006 he was elected a Fellow of the American Association for the Advancement of Science.

Suzuko Mousel Knott is a PhD candidate in the Department of Germanic Languages and Literatures at Washington University in St. Louis. Her dissertation is on intermediality in Yoko Tawada's works. She has published on twentieth-century and contemporary German literature, including Rolf Dieter Brinkmann and Yoko Tawada.

Christine M. O'Bonsawin received her PhD in sport history from the University of Western Ontario in Canada, in 2006, for a dissertation on "Spectacles, Policy, and Social Memory: Images of Canadian Indians at World's Fairs and Olympic Games." She is an assistant professor and director of the Indigenous Studies Minor Program at the University of Victoria, British Columbia. She is interested in aboriginal sport, sport policy and questions of national identity, and Canadian sport history, with particular interest in the modern Olympic movement. She worked for the Sports Department of the Canadian Broadcasting Corporation at the 2000 and 2002 Olympics and the 2001 World Track and Field Championships.

Nancy J. Parezo is a professor of American Indian studies and anthropology at the University of Arizona. She teaches courses on cultural preservation, contemporary issues, ethnohistory, art, methodology and theory. Her current book, *Anthropology Goes to the Fair: The 1904 Louisiana Purchase Exposition*, coauthored with Don D. Fowler and published by the University of Nebraska Press, documents how almost three thousand indigenous men and women

454

were brought to St. Louis to "show one half of the world how the other half lived" using an evolutionary interpretive paradigm. She is currently working on a new book, *The Indian Fashion Show, 1942–1972*.

Linda Peavy, an independent scholar residing in Vermont, holds an M.A. in English from the University of North Carolina, Chapel Hill, and an M.F.A. in creative writing from Washington University in St. Louis. She and her co-author, Ursula Smith, have published widely in the field of women's history and biography. Their titles include *Women Who Changed Things* (1984), *Women in Waiting in the Westward Movement* (1994), *Pioneer Women* (1998), and *Frontier House* (2002). The two have given more than six hundred presentations and workshops at venues across the United States and Canada. After ten years of research and writing, they look forward to the forthcoming publication of *Full-Court Quest: The Girls from Fort Shaw Indian School, Basketball Champions of the World*.

Otto J. Schantz was associate professor in the Department of Sport Sciences at the University of Franche-Comté in Besançon, France, from 1991 to 1993 and associate professor at the University Marc Bloch in Strasbourg, France, from 1993 to 2004. Since 2004 he has been professor of social sciences in the Institute of Sports Sciences at the University of Koblenz-Landau, Germany, and is currently the dean of the institute. He is an editorial board member of different journals and co-editor of the book series Sport, Culture, and Society. His main research interests are the ideology of the Olympic and Paralympic Movement, Pierre de Coubertin, sport as culture, the extraordinary body, and the epistemology and sociology of sciences. He co-edited and wrote the commentary for volume 3 of *Textes choisis de Pierre de Coubertin* (1986) and is coauthor of *The International Olympic Committee — One Hundred Years* (1995).

Ursula Smith, independent scholar from Middletown Springs, Vermont, earned a degree in history at the University of San Francisco, followed by a year of graduate work at San Francisco State University. Her scholarly work has focused on the lives of women and children. She has co-authored nine books with Linda Peavy, including *Dreams into Deeds* (1985), *The Gold Rush Widows of Little Falls* (1990), and *Frontier Children* (1999). They have also published articles in popular magazines and juried journals, including *Montana: The Magazine of Western History*, where their first article on the girls' basketball team from Fort Shaw Indian School appeared in the winter 2001 issue.

Index

457